RYUKO

VOL. 2

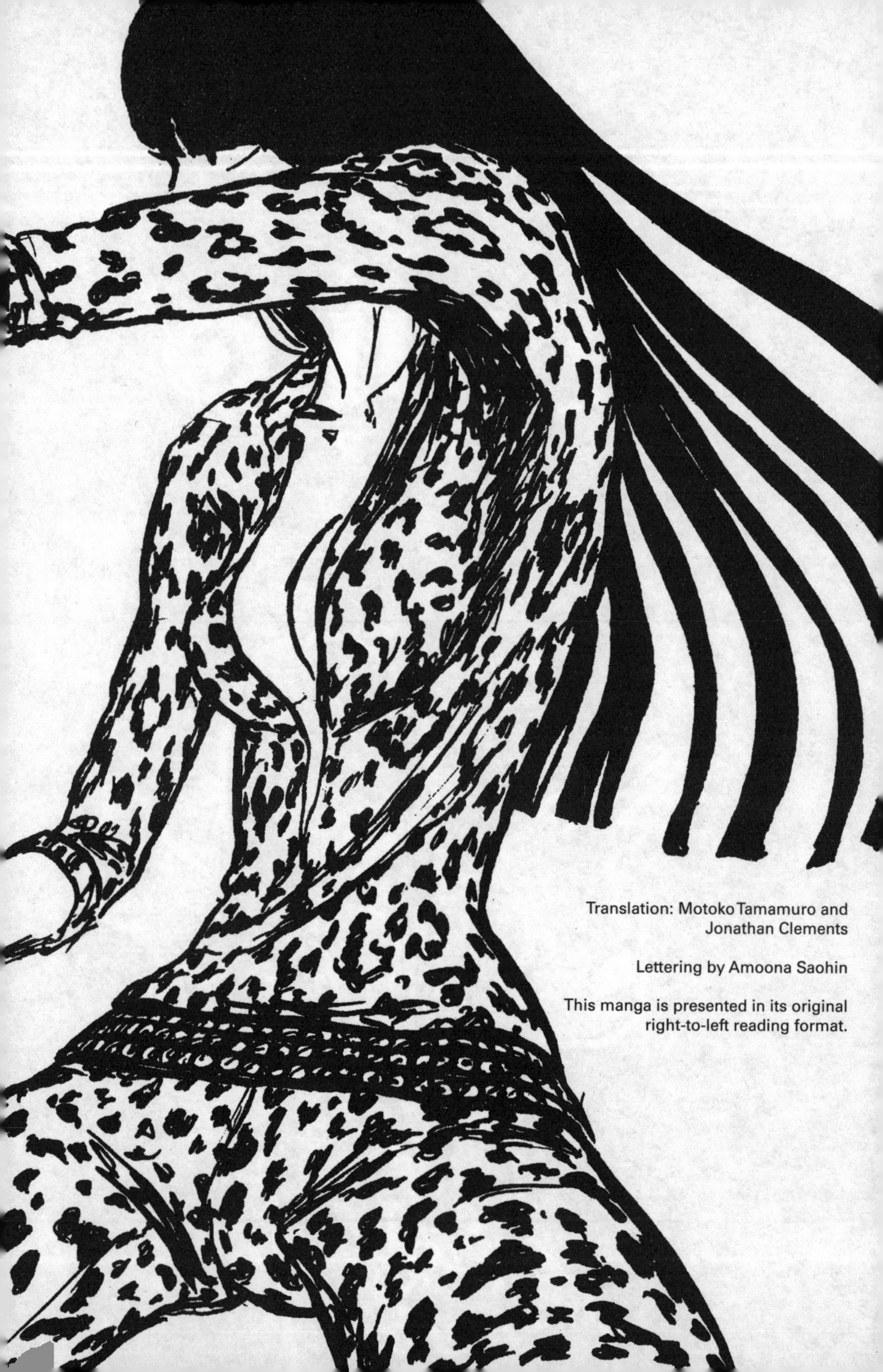

Translation: Motoko Tamamuro and Jonathan Clements

Lettering by Amoona Saohin

This manga is presented in its original right-to-left reading format.

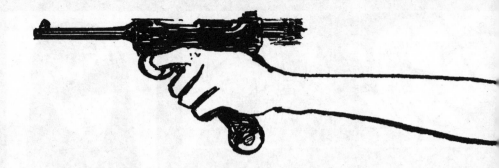

RYUKO

VOL. 2

BY ELDO YOSHIMIZU

TITAN COMICS

Managing Editor
Martin Eden

Consulting Editor
Charles Ardai

Designer Donna Askem

Production Controller
Peter James

Senior Production Controller
Jackie Flook

Art Director Oz Browne

Sales & Circulation Manager
Steve Tothill

Publicist Imogen Harris

Publishing Director
Darryl Tothill

Operations Director
Leigh Baulch

Executive Director
Vivian Cheung

Publisher Nick Landau

Ryuko Volume Two.

Published by Titan Comics, a division of Titan
Publishing Group, Ltd, 144 Southwark Street, London
SE1 0UP, UK.
Titan Comics is a registered trademark of Titan
Publishing Group Ltd.

The name *Hard Case Crime* and the Hard Case Crime logo
are trademarks of Winterfall LCC. Hard Case Crime Comics
are produced with editorial guidance from Charles Ardai.

10 9 8 7 6 5 4 3 2 1

First printed in India in October 2019
ISBN: 9781787732551

A CIP catalogue record for this title is available
from the British Library.

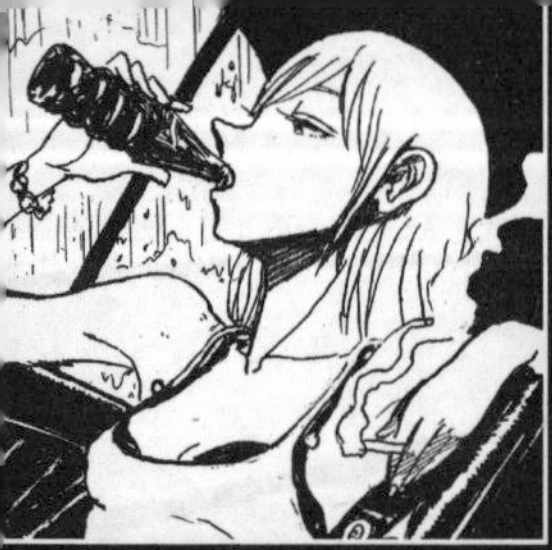

SASORI
Everything Sasori knows, she learned from Ryuko. She struggles between her own independence and trying to impress her commander.

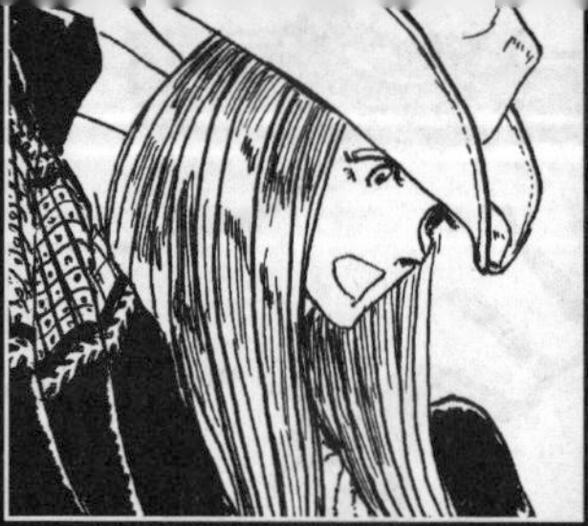

VALER
Valer was taken in by Ryuko as a baby to protect her from Rashid. She has discovered that she is the daughter of the Arab King Jibril.

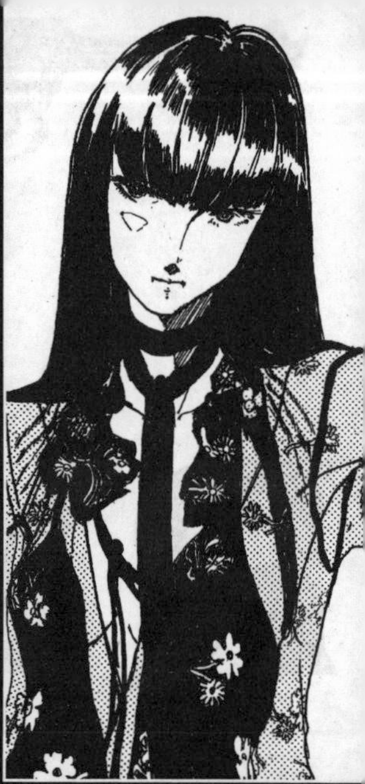

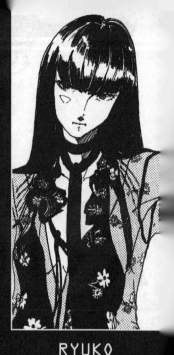

RYUKO
Ryuko is the headstrong leader of the Yakuza based in the Middle East. Having killed her father 18 years ago, she is tormented by her sins and seeks to atone with the firm but just rule of her clan. As she is about to find out, her destiny is to be more than just a killer...

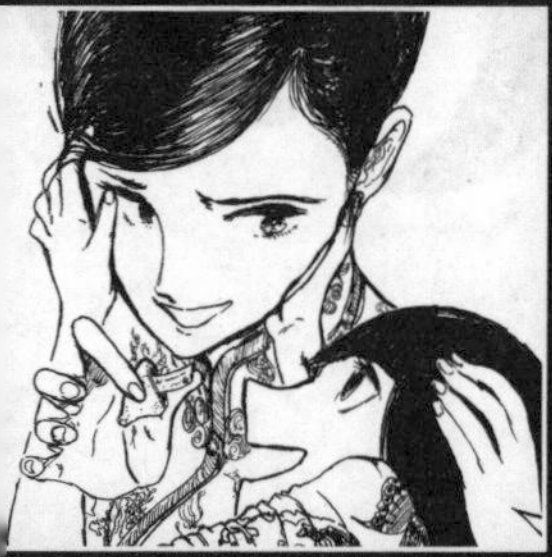

SHORYUHI
Ryuko's mother, kidnapped by Ikeuchi, Garyu's scheming underling, when Ryuko was a small child. She is now a captive of the Sheqing-Ban gang.

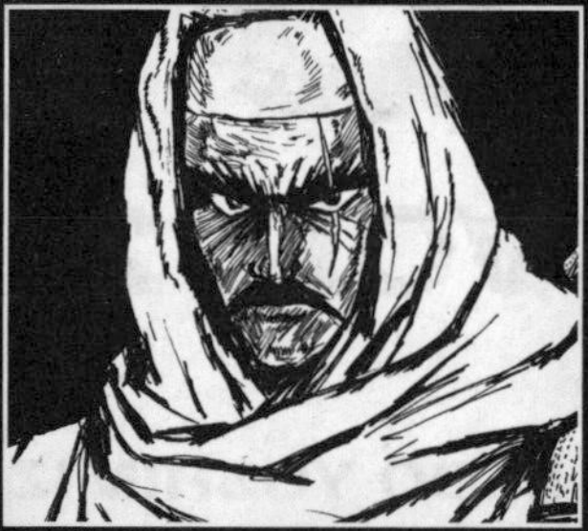

GARYU
Ryuko's father, former leader of the Black Dragon group until his death. He made questionable alliances in order to keep his wife alive.

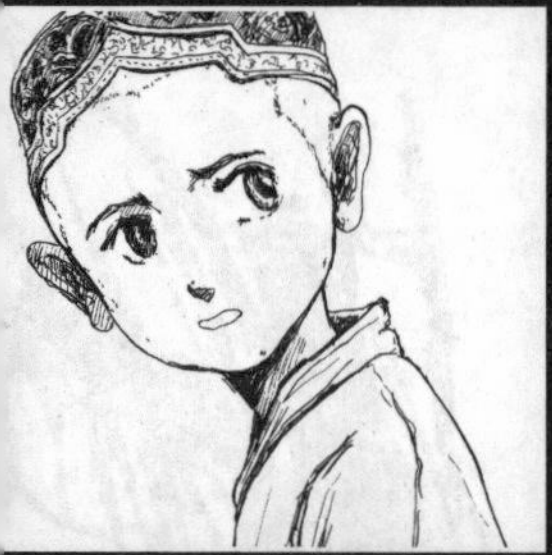

HARIM
As a boy in Afghanistan, Harim saw the good in Nikolai, and also stood up to the soldiers who tried to kill Ryuko, leaving him scarred.

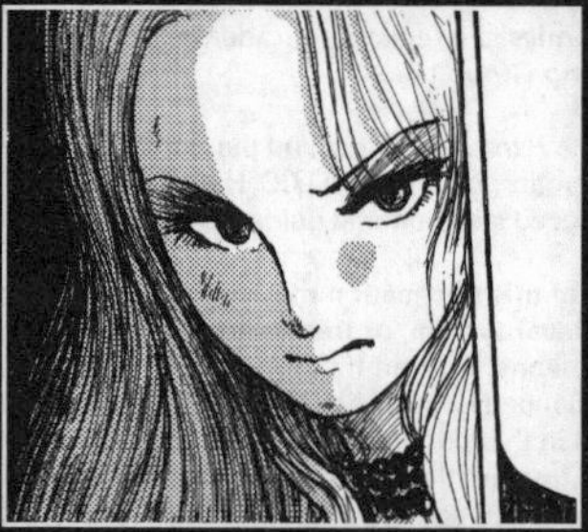

TATIANA
The daughter of Major Pavlov. She has sought out Nikolai in order to get closure on her father's supposedly dishonorable death.

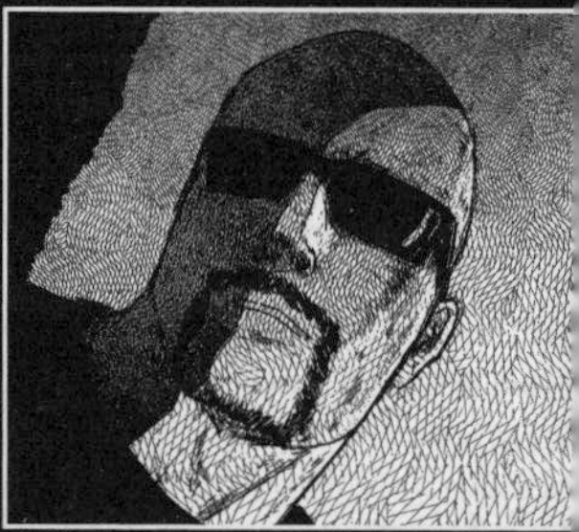

NIKOLAI
The former Soviet soldier who befriended Harim, Nikolai works as Ryuko's bodyguard. He lives with the guilt of watching Major Pavlov die for nothing.

PREVIOUSLY...

28 YEARS AGO...

Ryuko's father, Garyu, is banished from Japan following the kidnapping and apparent death of Ryuko's mother. While in Afghanistan, Ryuko saves a boy named Harim from the occupying Soviets. Ryuko's father recruits Nikolai, a defector who had protected the boy.

TEN YEARS LATER...

Garyu is in command of the Yakuza – the Japanese Mafia – in Forossyah, a small kingdom in the Middle East. After learning that he has been dealing in drugs and corruption with General Rashid, the insurgent who incited a revolt against King Jibril, Ryuko kills her father and takes his place.

PRESENT DAY...

After Ryuko's subordinates, Valer and Sasori, rebelliously steal a fortune from General Rashid, Ryuko is forced to kill him, but not before learning that her mother is still alive. He gives her a mysterious pendant that belonged to her mother... Ryuko travels to Japan, only to find her mother has been taken by the Chinese gang Sheqing-Ban. Before she can investigate further, however, an unknown terrorist group kidnaps Sasori, Nikolai, and a dancer named Tatiana...

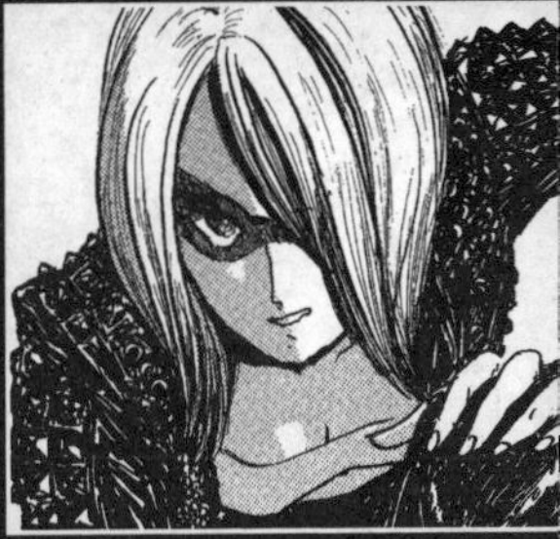

SITU ZI

The granddaughter of Situ Lon
She is a skilled fighter, huntin
Ryuko for something known a
the Dragon Head.

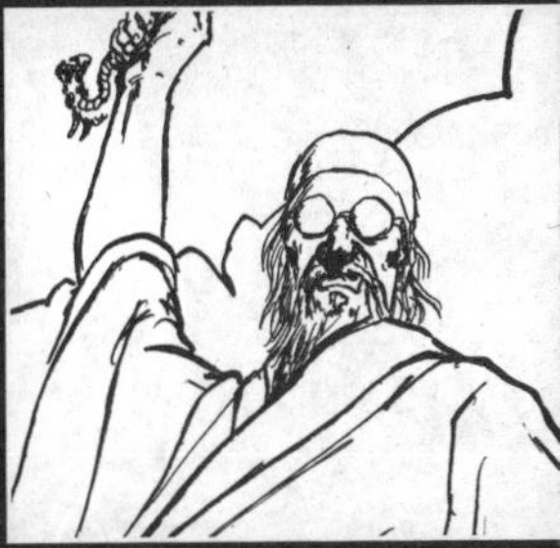

SITU LONG

The leader of the Sheqing-Ban, the Chinese gang that is increasing its influence and power in Japan.

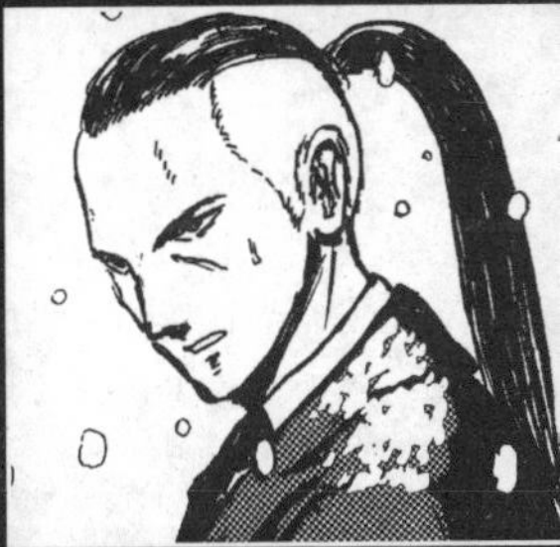

KANDORI

Former operative of Garyu – now loyal to Ryuko.

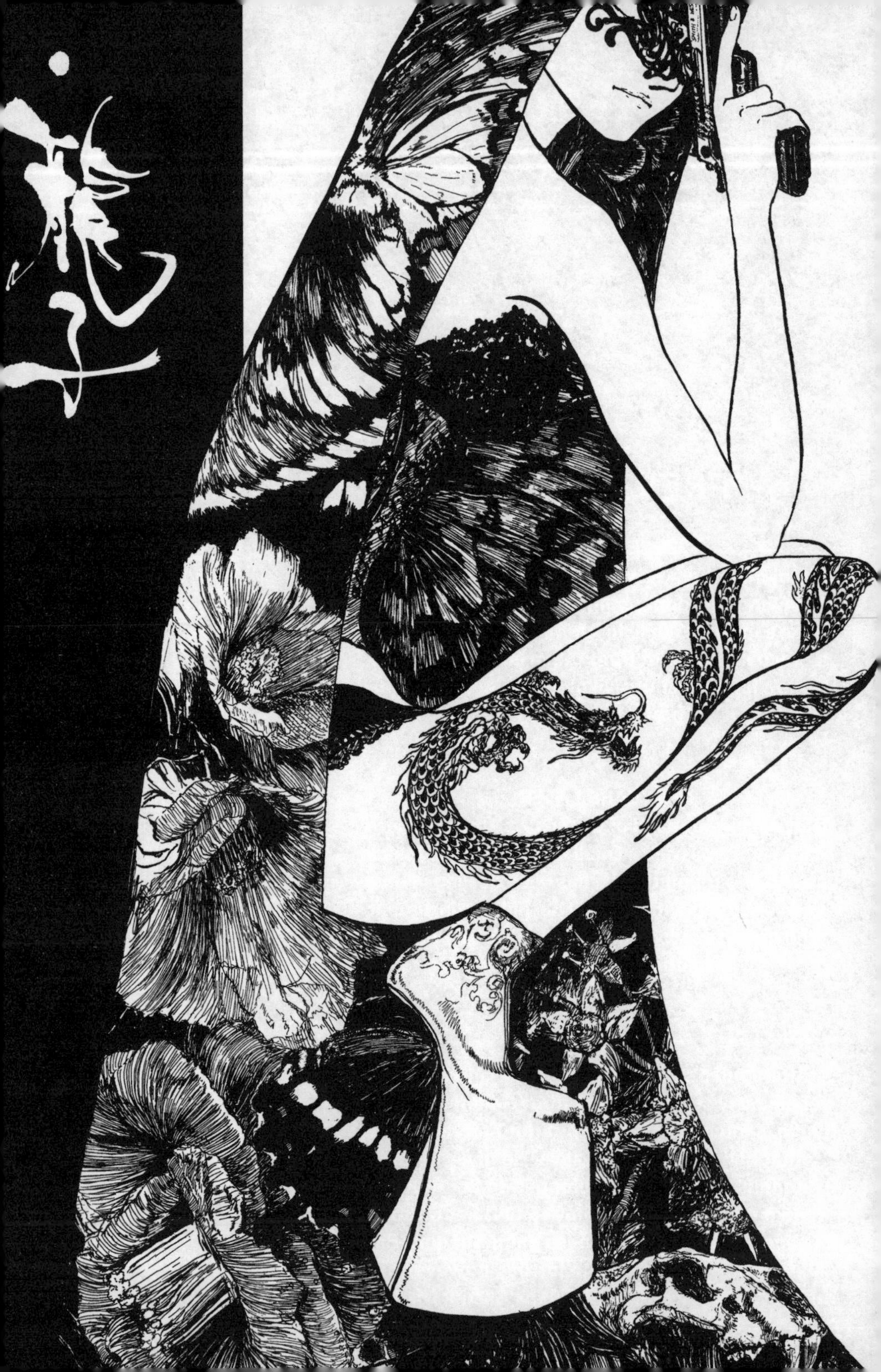
龍子

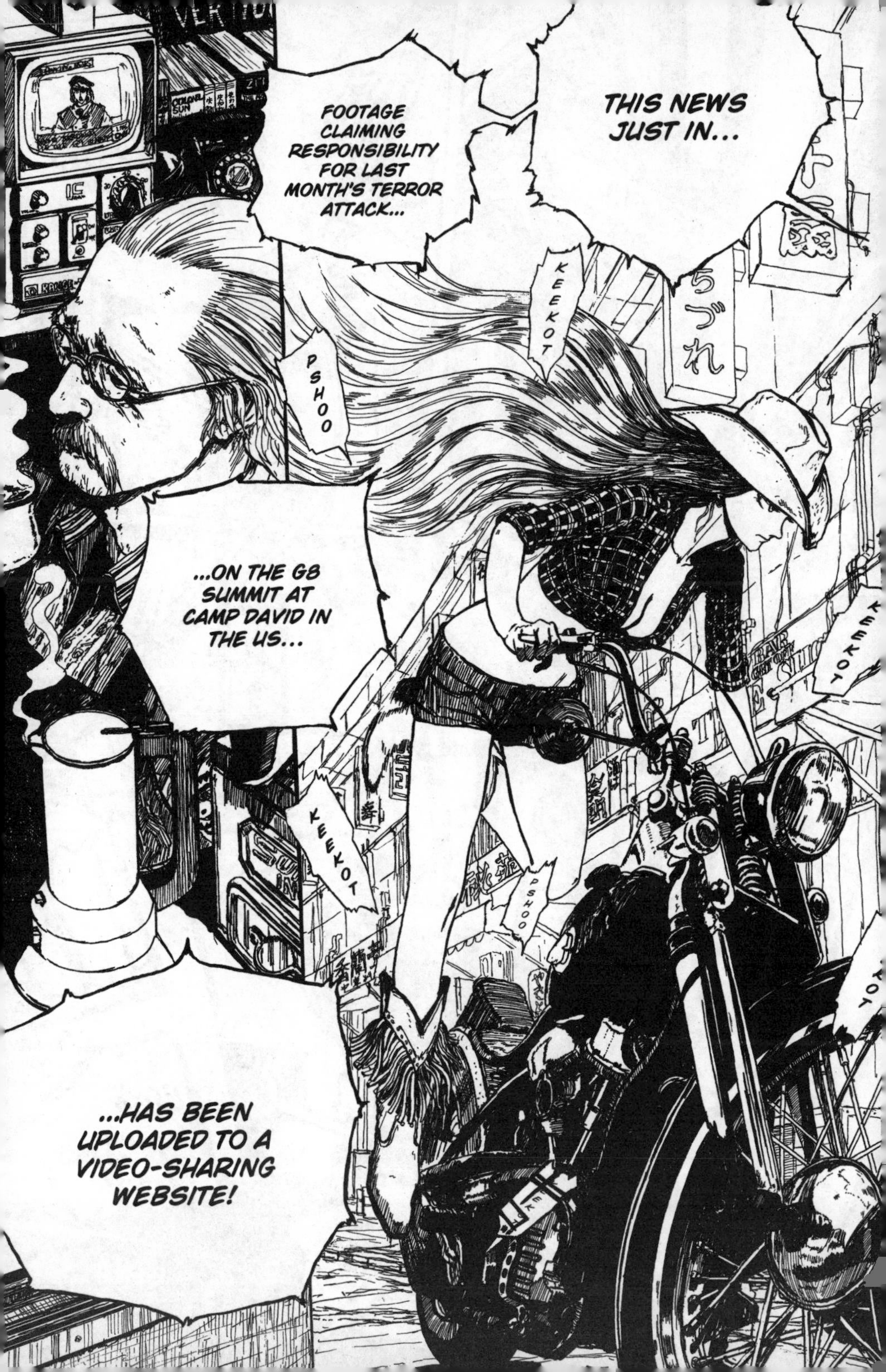
THIS NEWS JUST IN...
FOOTAGE CLAIMING RESPONSIBILITY FOR LAST MONTH'S TERROR ATTACK...
KEEKOT
PSHOO
...ON THE G8 SUMMIT AT CAMP DAVID IN THE US...
KEEKOT
KEEKOT
PSHOO
...HAS BEEN UPLOADED TO A VIDEO-SHARING WEBSITE!

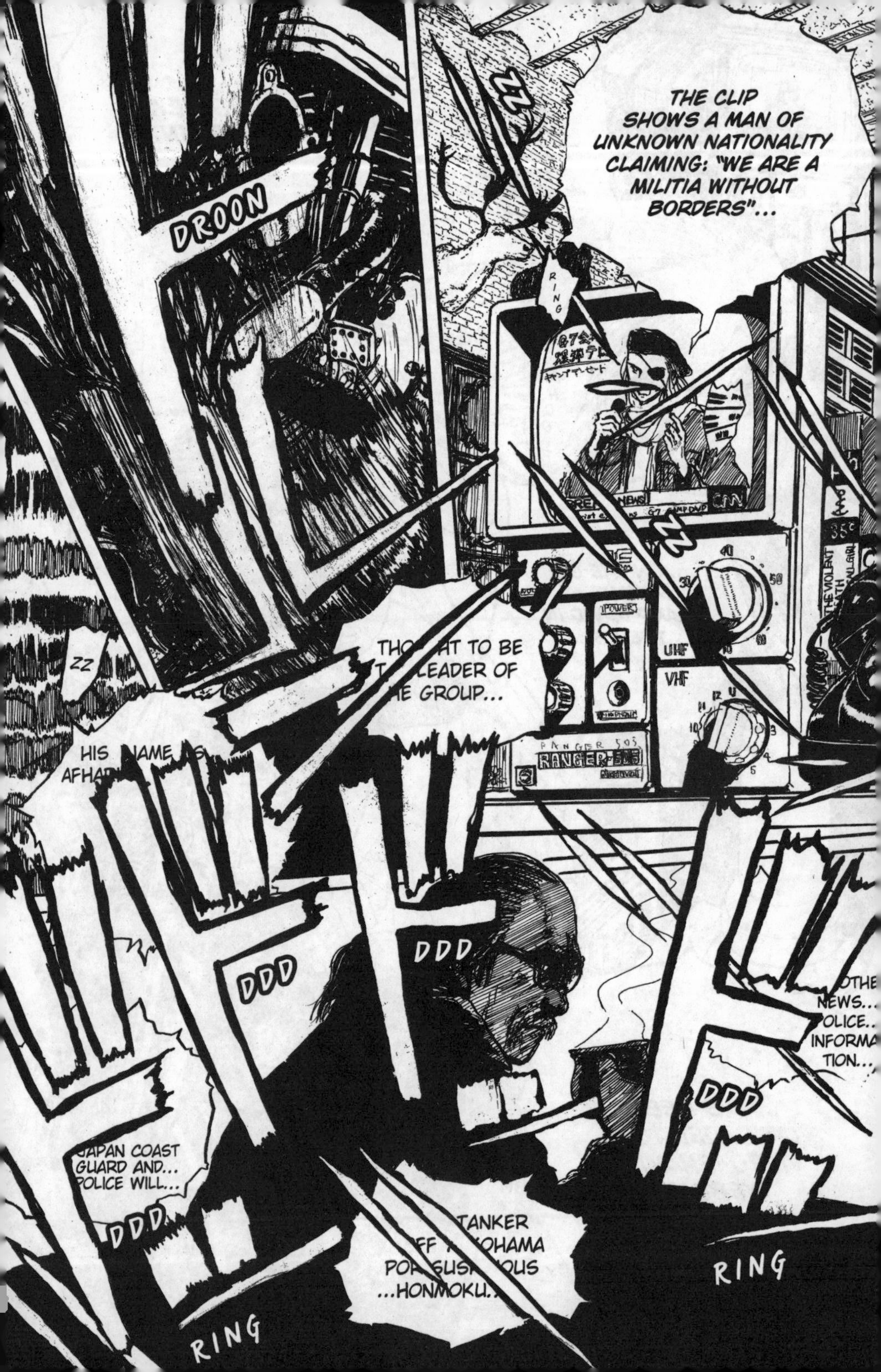

THE CLIP SHOWS A MAN OF UNKNOWN NATIONALITY CLAIMING: "WE ARE A MILITIA WITHOUT BORDERS"...
ZZ
RING
DROON
THO HT TO BE T LEADER OF HE GROUP...
ZZ
HIS NAME AFHA
ZZ
OTHE NEWS... OLICE... INFORMA TION...
DDD
DDD
DDD
JAPAN COAST GUARD AND... POLICE WILL...
DDD
TANKER FF OHAMA POR SUS IOUS ...HONMOKU...
RING
RING

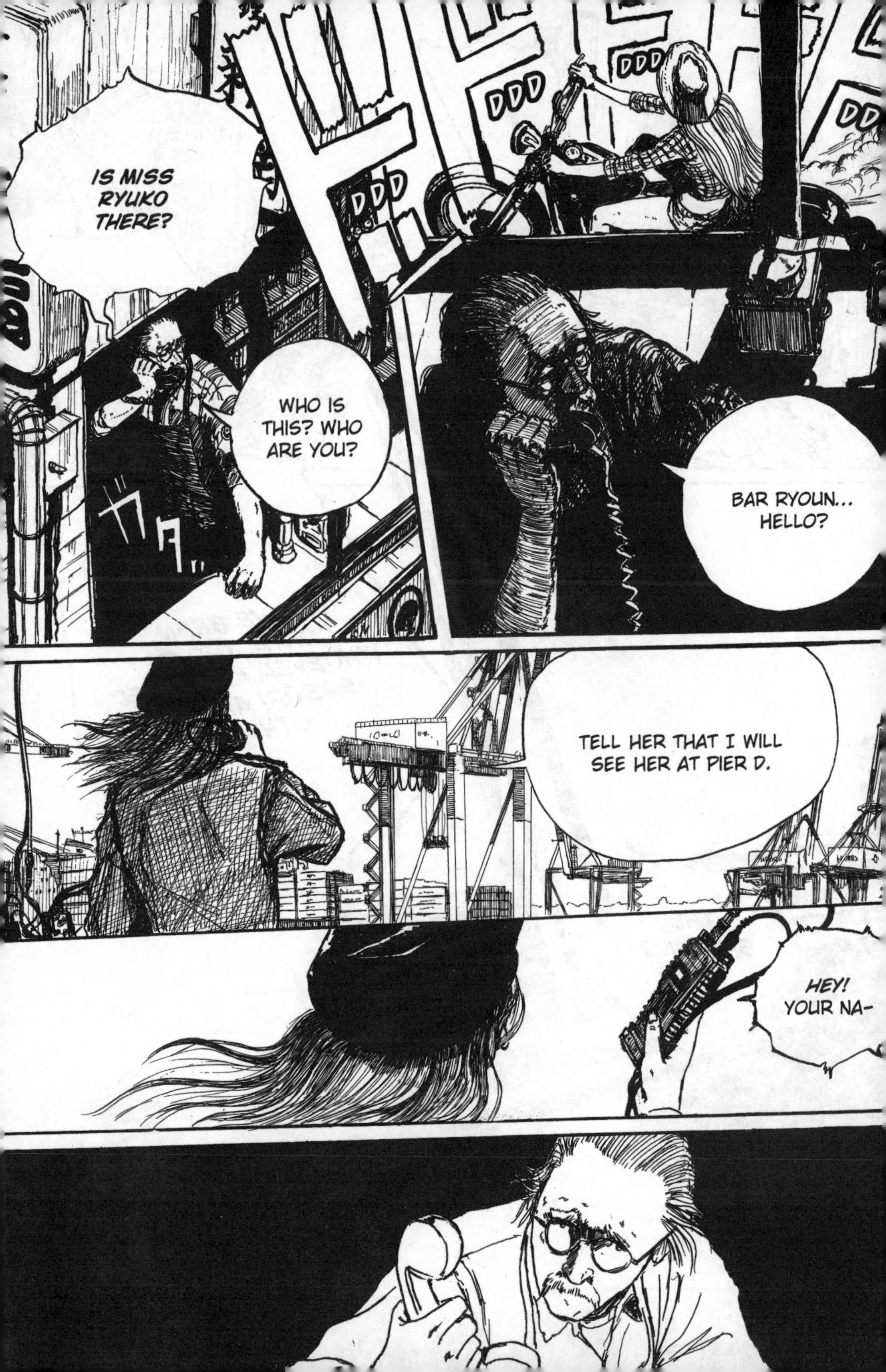
BAR RYOUN... HELLO?
IS MISS RYUKO THERE?
WHO IS THIS? WHO ARE YOU?
TELL HER THAT I WILL SEE HER AT PIER D.
HEY! YOUR NA-

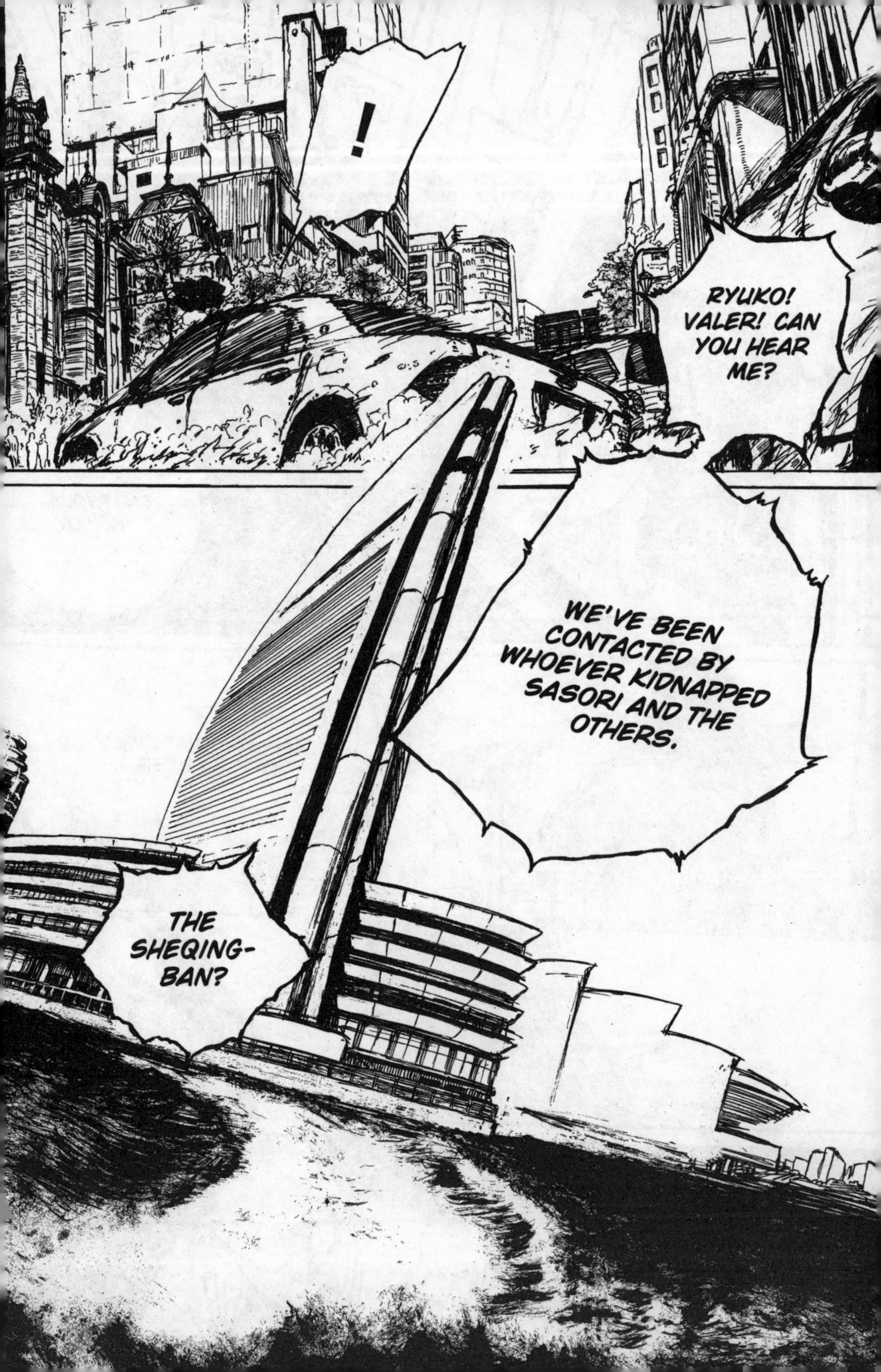
!
RYUKO! VALER! CAN YOU HEAR ME?
WE'VE BEEN CONTACTED BY WHOEVER KIDNAPPED SASORI AND THE OTHERS.
THE SHEQING-BAN?

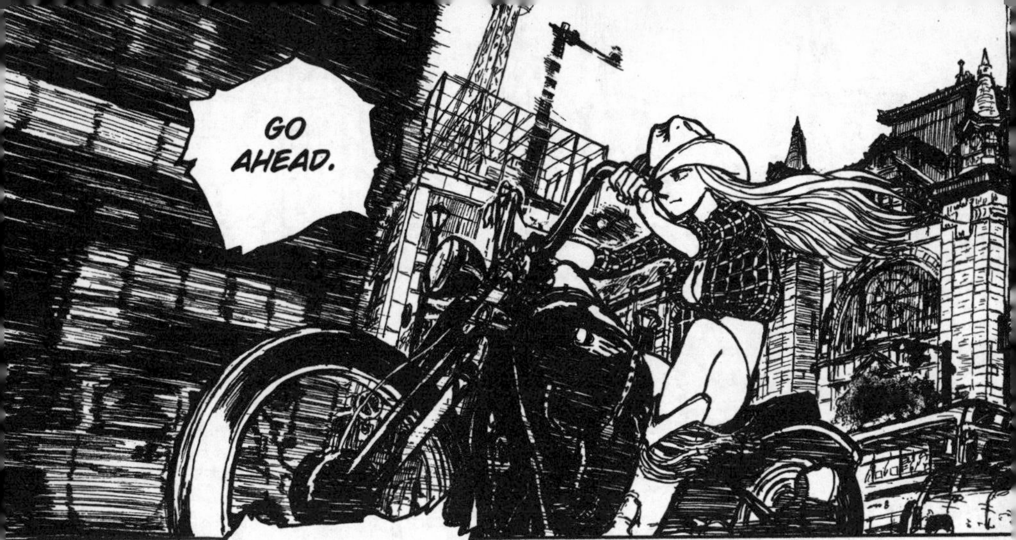
GO AHEAD.
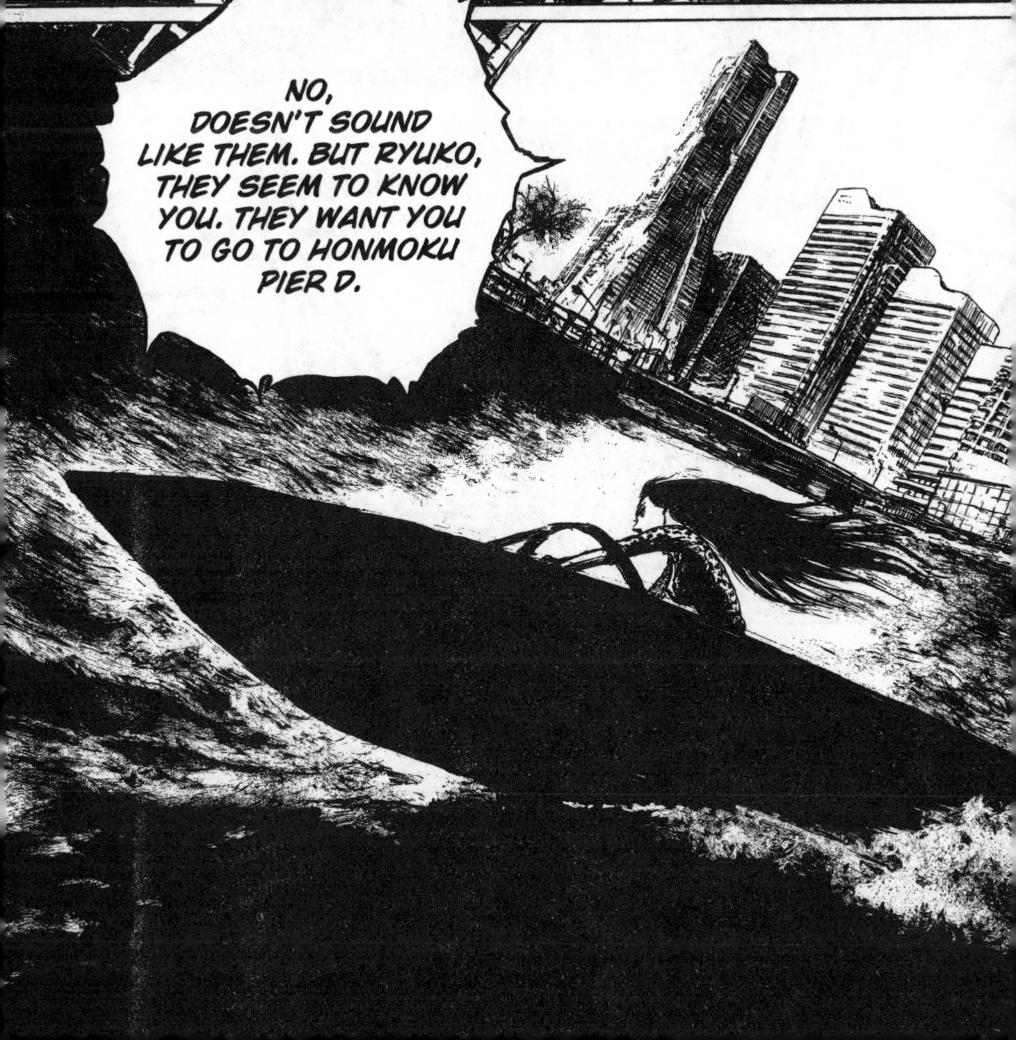
NO, DOESN'T SOUND LIKE THEM. BUT RYUKO, THEY SEEM TO KNOW YOU. THEY WANT YOU TO GO TO HONMOKU PIER D.

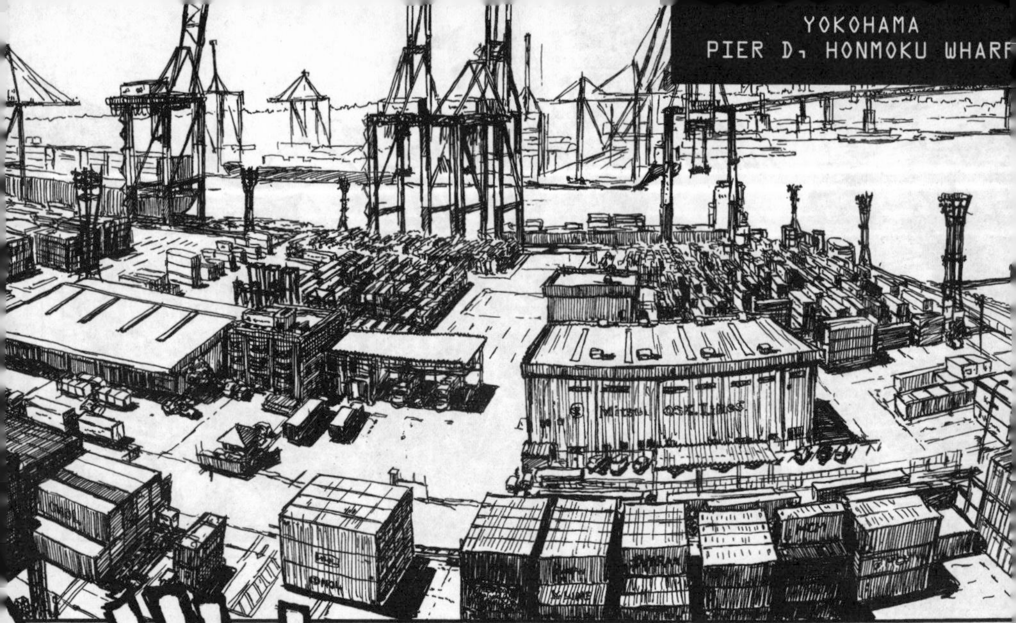
YOKOHAMA
PIER D, HONMOKU WHARF
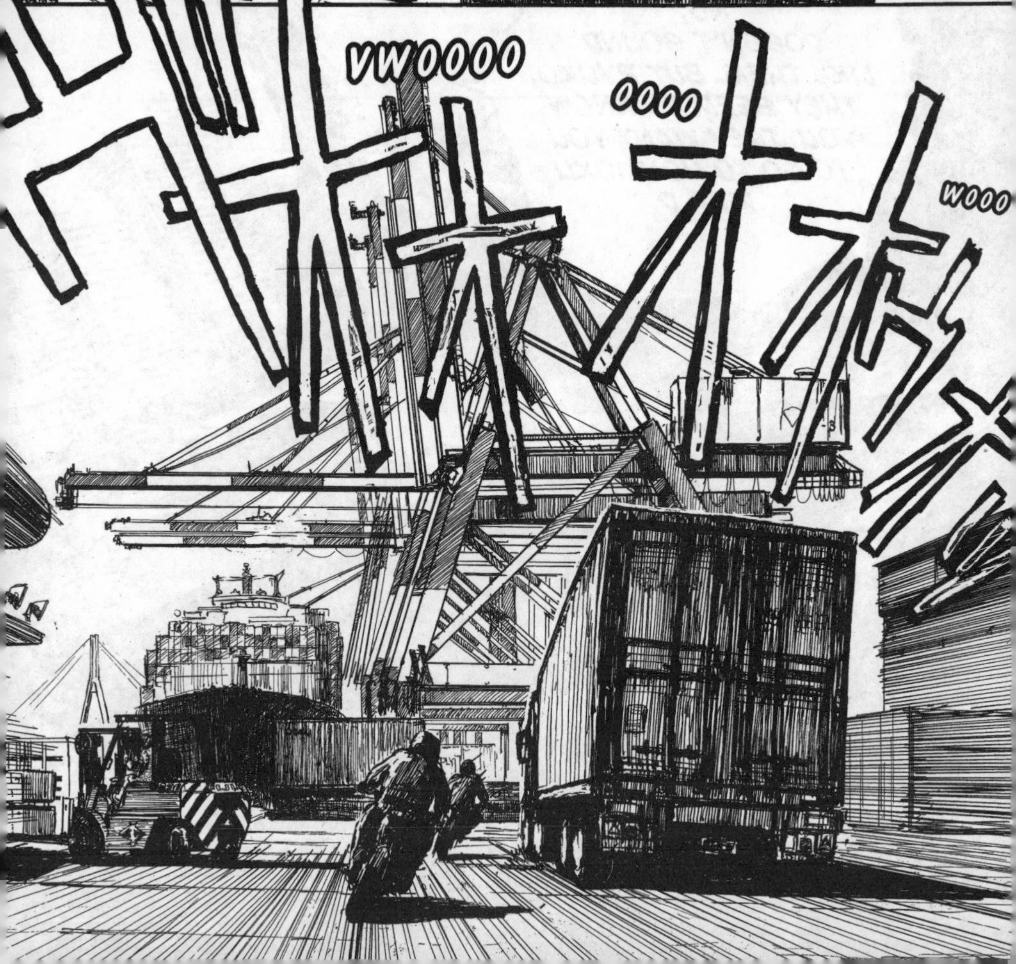
VWOOOO
OOOO
WOOO

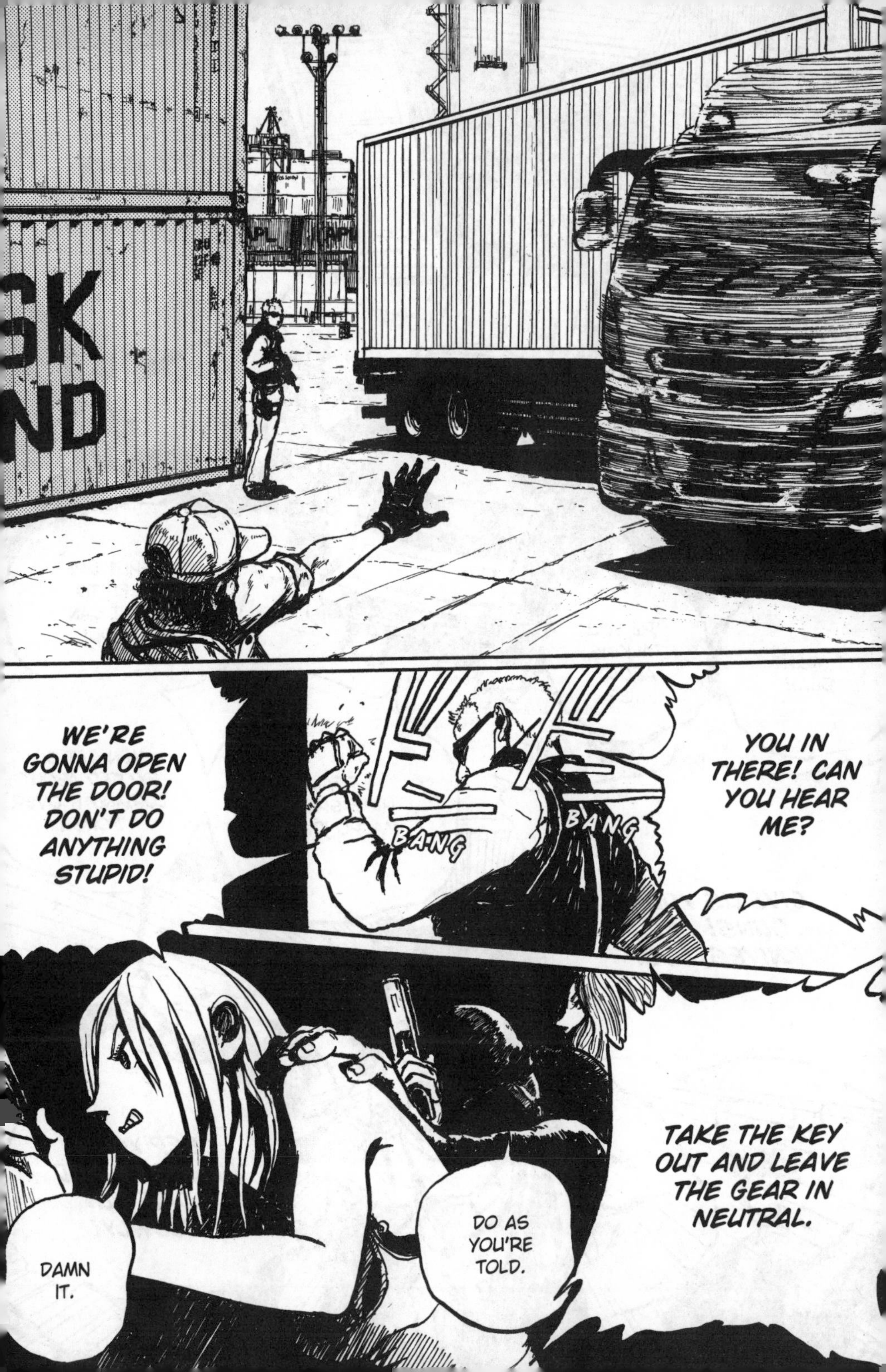
YOU IN THERE! CAN YOU HEAR ME?
BANG
BANG
WE'RE GONNA OPEN THE DOOR! DON'T DO ANYTHING STUPID!
TAKE THE KEY OUT AND LEAVE THE GEAR IN NEUTRAL.
DO AS YOU'RE TOLD.
DAMN IT.

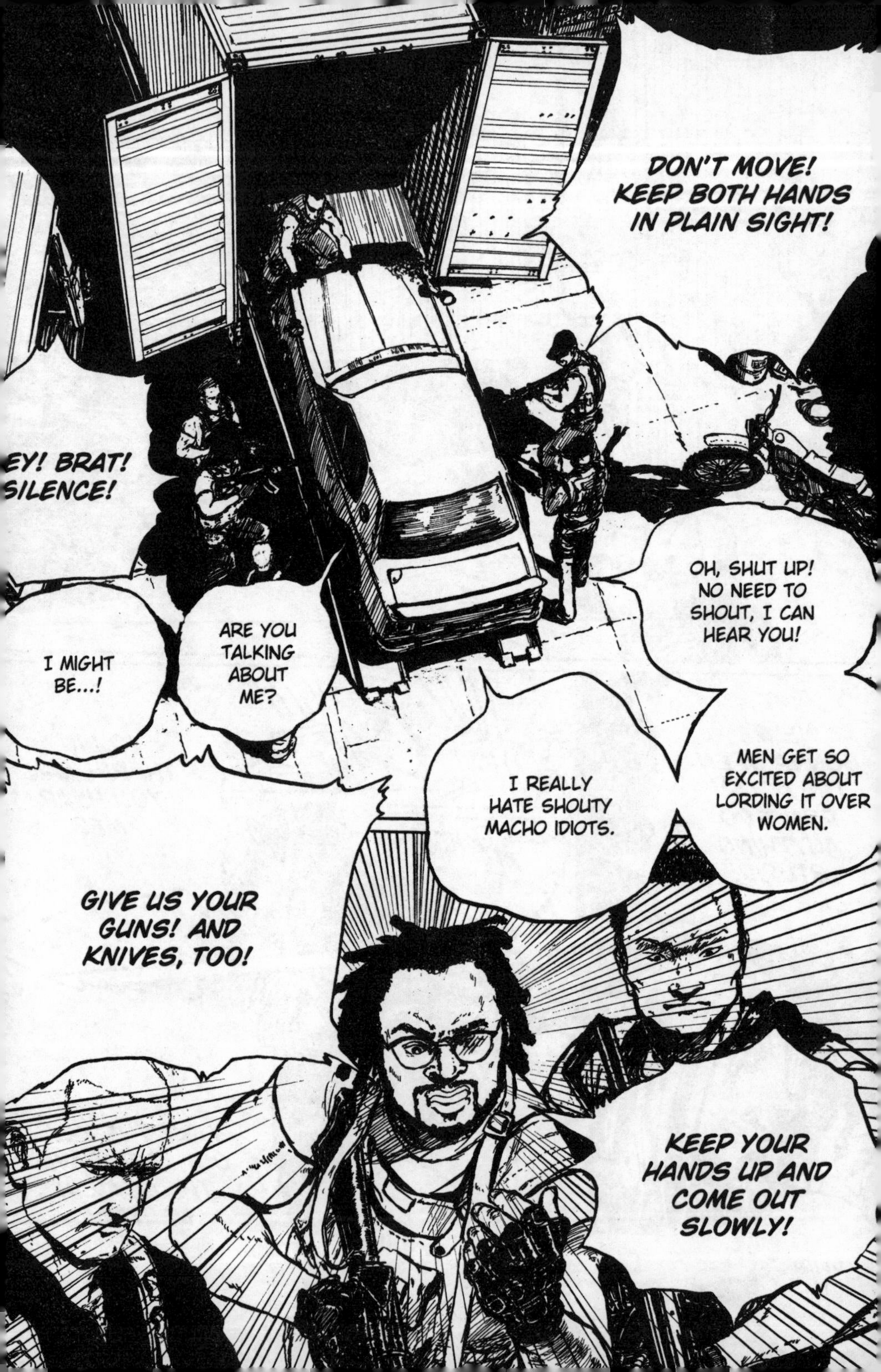
DON'T MOVE! KEEP BOTH HANDS IN PLAIN SIGHT!
EY! BRAT! SILENCE!
OH, SHUT UP! NO NEED TO SHOUT, I CAN HEAR YOU!
ARE YOU TALKING ABOUT ME?
I MIGHT BE...!
MEN GET SO EXCITED ABOUT LORDING IT OVER WOMEN.
I REALLY HATE SHOUTY MACHO IDIOTS.
KEEP YOUR HANDS UP AND COME OUT SLOWLY!
GIVE US YOUR GUNS! AND KNIVES, TOO!

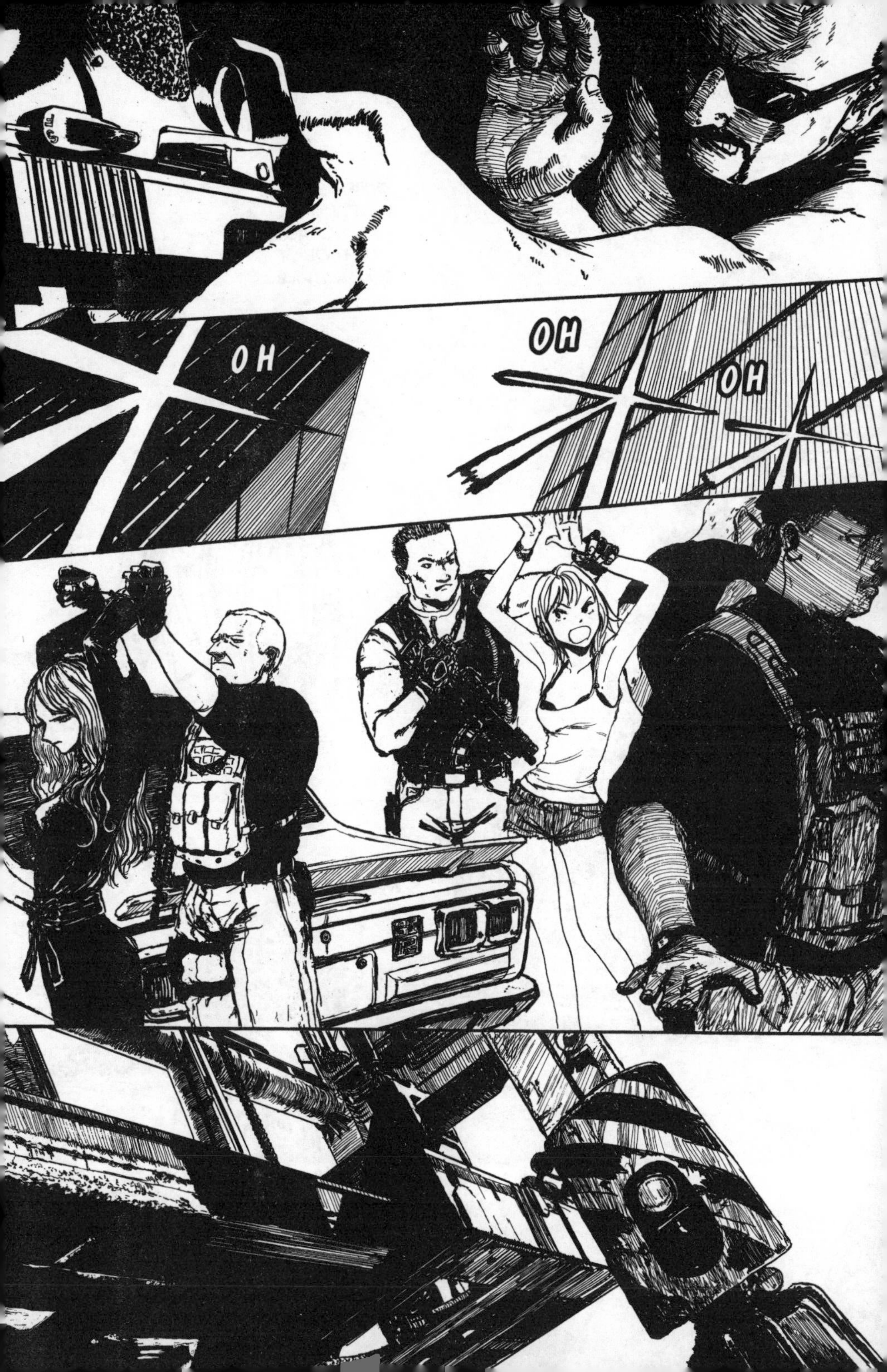
OH
OH
OH

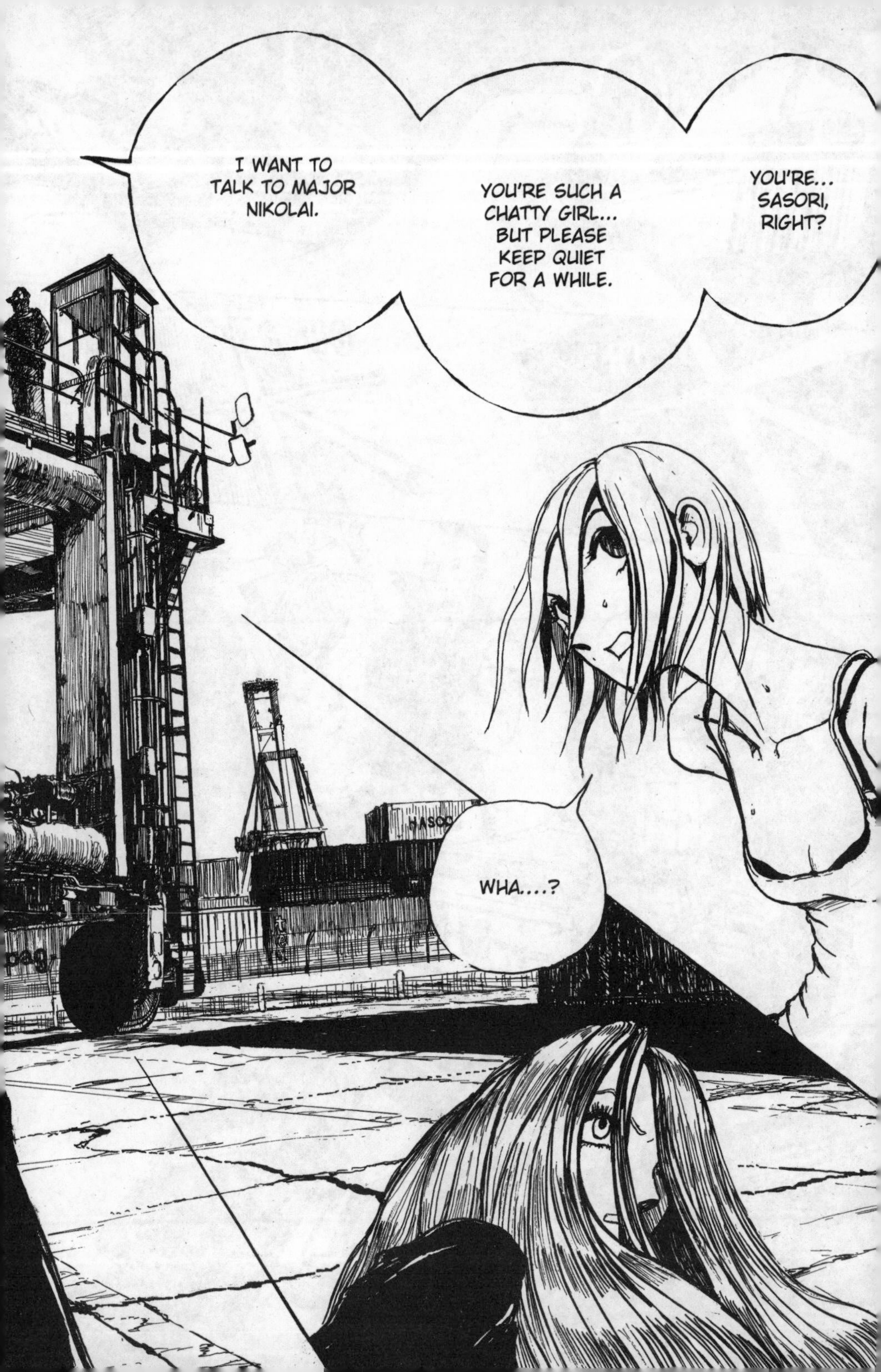
YOU'RE... SASORI, RIGHT?
YOU'RE SUCH A CHATTY GIRL... BUT PLEASE KEEP QUIET FOR A WHILE.
I WANT TO TALK TO MAJOR NIKOLAI.
WHA...?

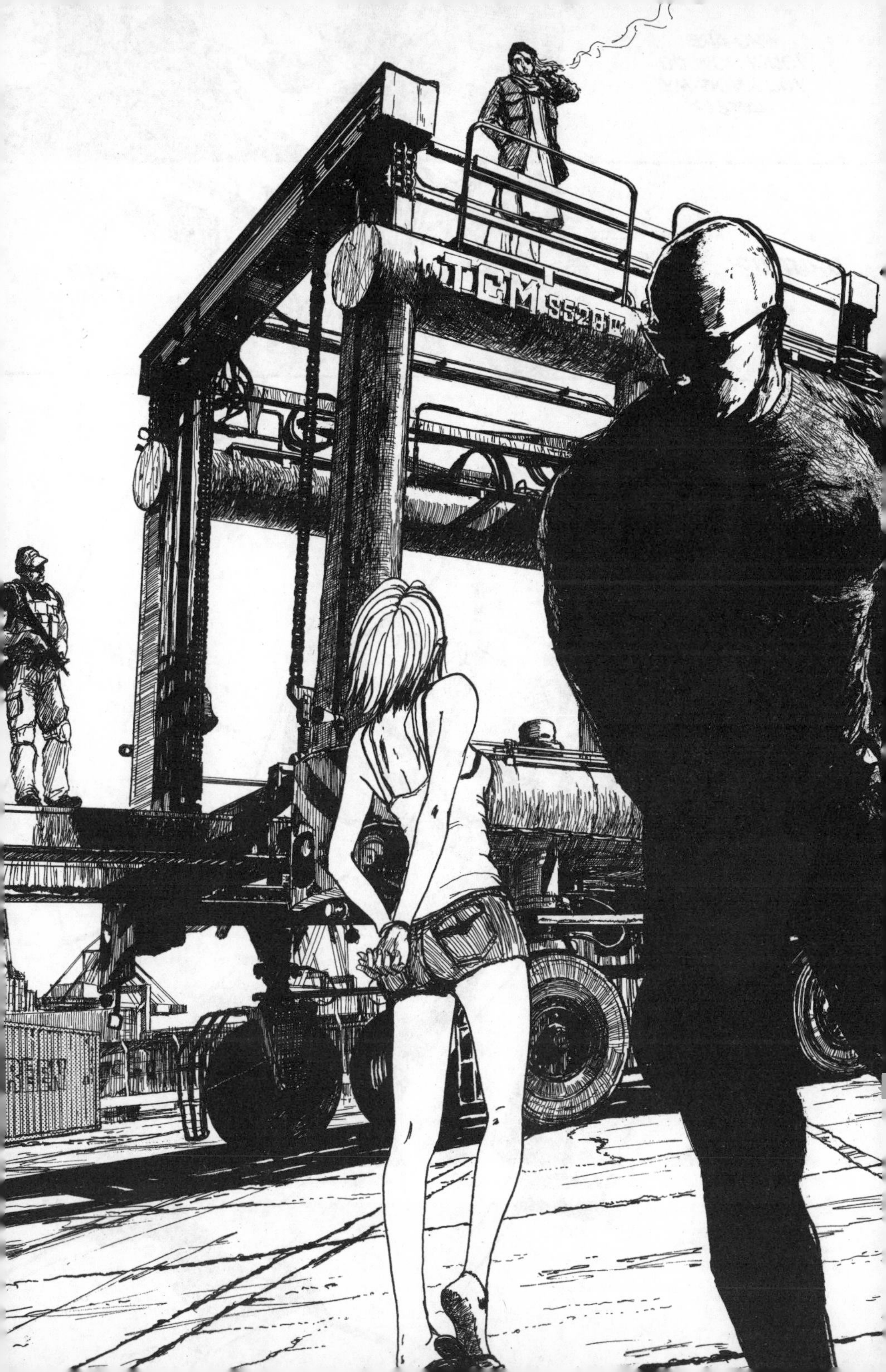
TCM

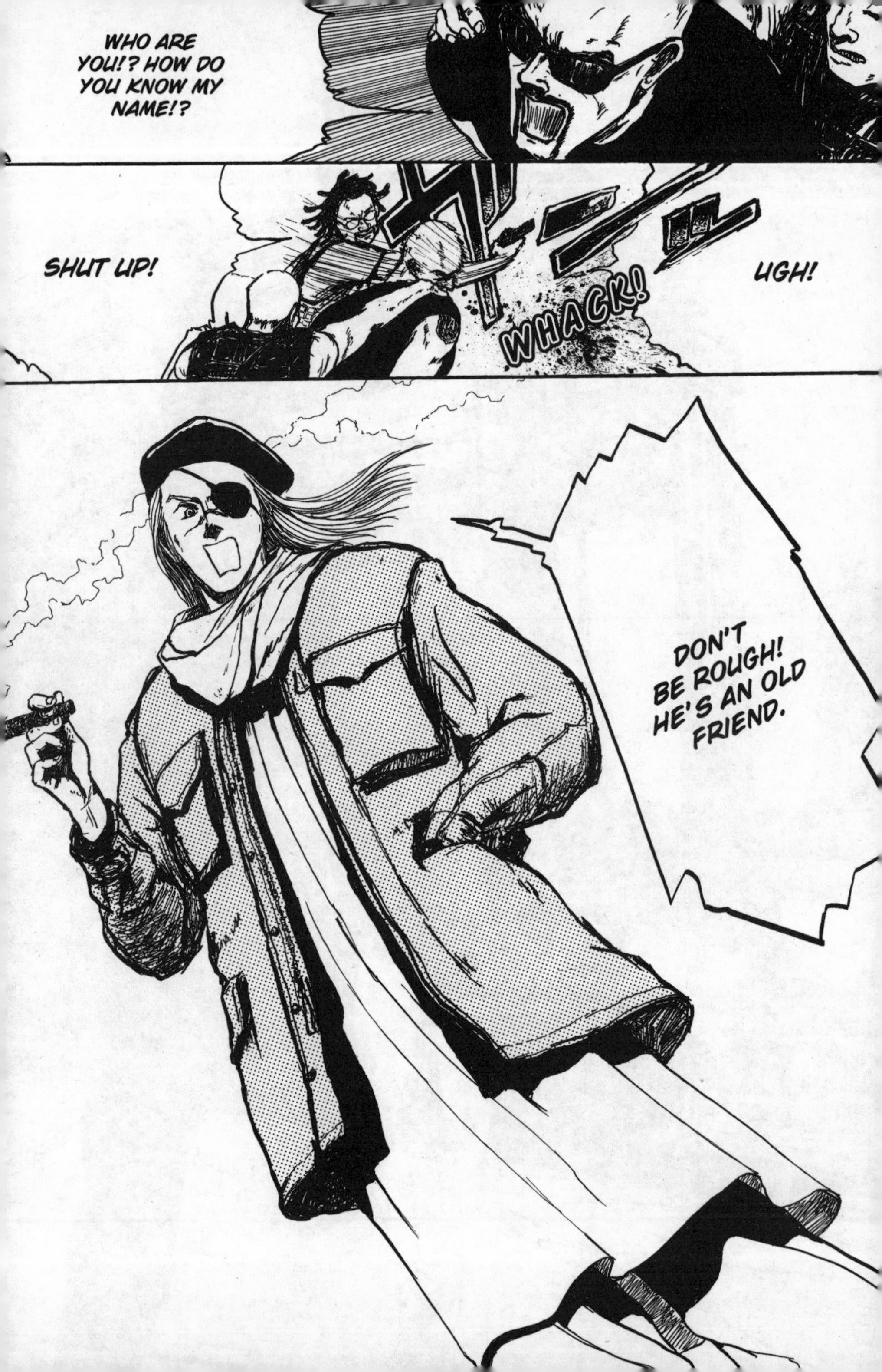
WHO ARE YOU!? HOW DO YOU KNOW MY NAME!?
UGH!
WHACK!
SHUT UP!
DON'T BE ROUGH! HE'S AN OLD FRIEND.

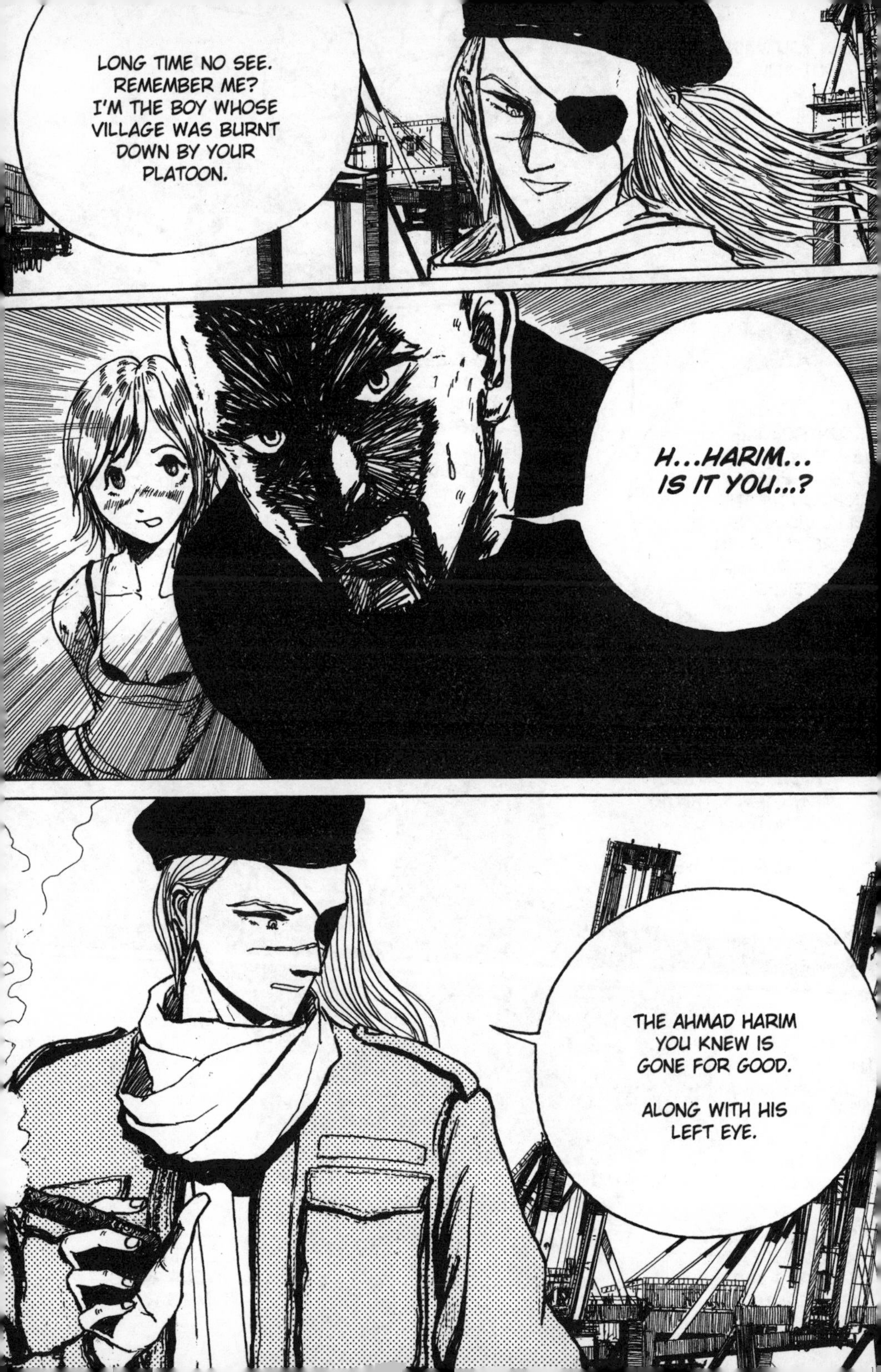
LONG TIME NO SEE. REMEMBER ME? I'M THE BOY WHOSE VILLAGE WAS BURNT DOWN BY YOUR PLATOON.
H...HARIM... IS IT YOU...?
THE AHMAD HARIM YOU KNEW IS GONE FOR GOOD.
ALONG WITH HIS LEFT EYE.

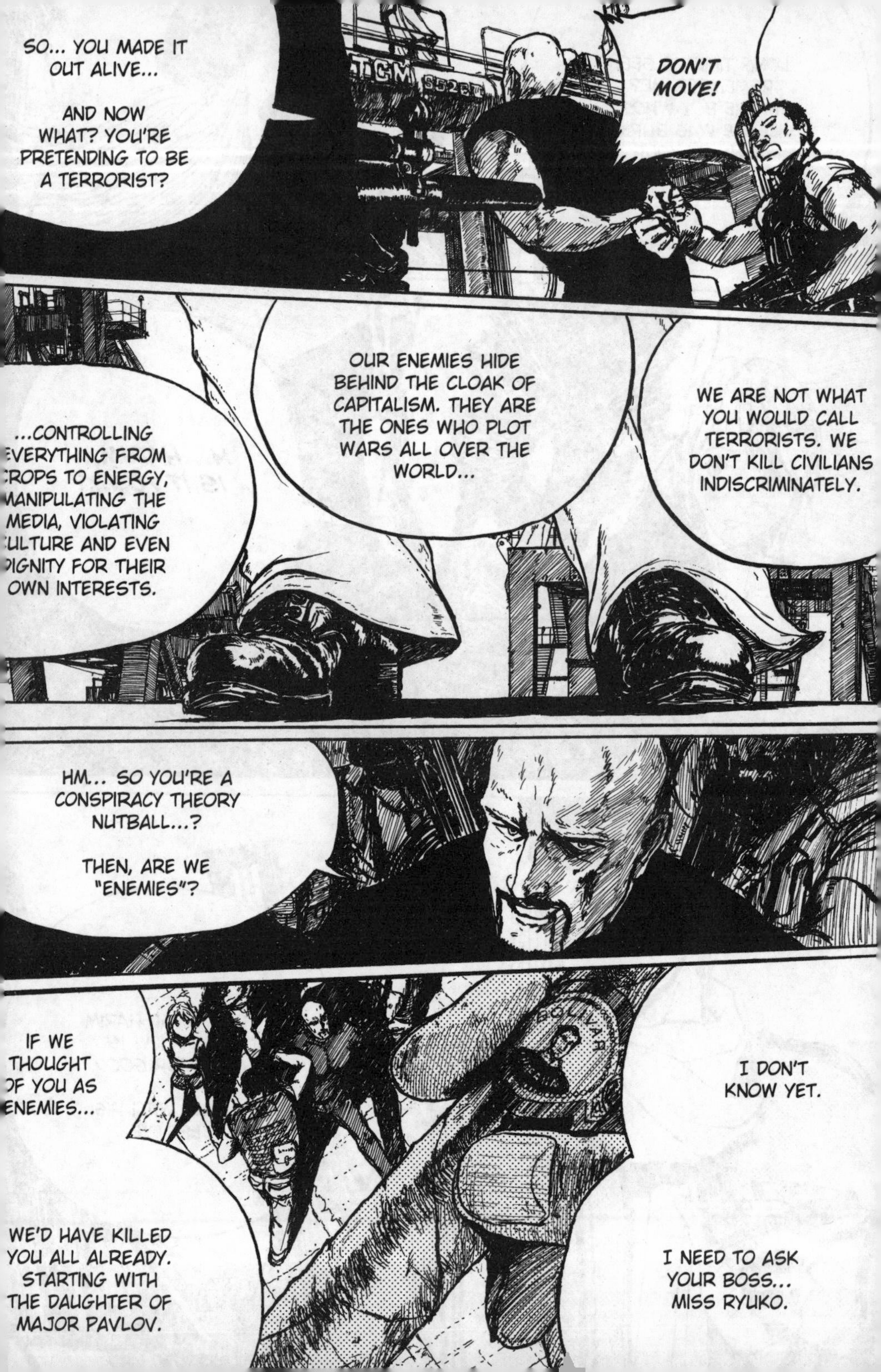
DON'T MOVE!
SO... YOU MADE IT OUT ALIVE... AND NOW WHAT? YOU'RE PRETENDING TO BE A TERRORIST?
WE ARE NOT WHAT YOU WOULD CALL TERRORISTS. WE DON'T KILL CIVILIANS INDISCRIMINATELY.
OUR ENEMIES HIDE BEHIND THE CLOAK OF CAPITALISM. THEY ARE THE ONES WHO PLOT WARS ALL OVER THE WORLD...
...CONTROLLING EVERYTHING FROM CROPS TO ENERGY, MANIPULATING THE MEDIA, VIOLATING CULTURE AND EVEN DIGNITY FOR THEIR OWN INTERESTS.
HM... SO YOU'RE A CONSPIRACY THEORY NUTBALL...? THEN, ARE WE "ENEMIES"?
I DON'T KNOW YET.
I NEED TO ASK YOUR BOSS... MISS RYUKO.
IF WE THOUGHT OF YOU AS ENEMIES...
WE'D HAVE KILLED YOU ALL ALREADY. STARTING WITH THE DAUGHTER OF MAJOR PAVLOV.

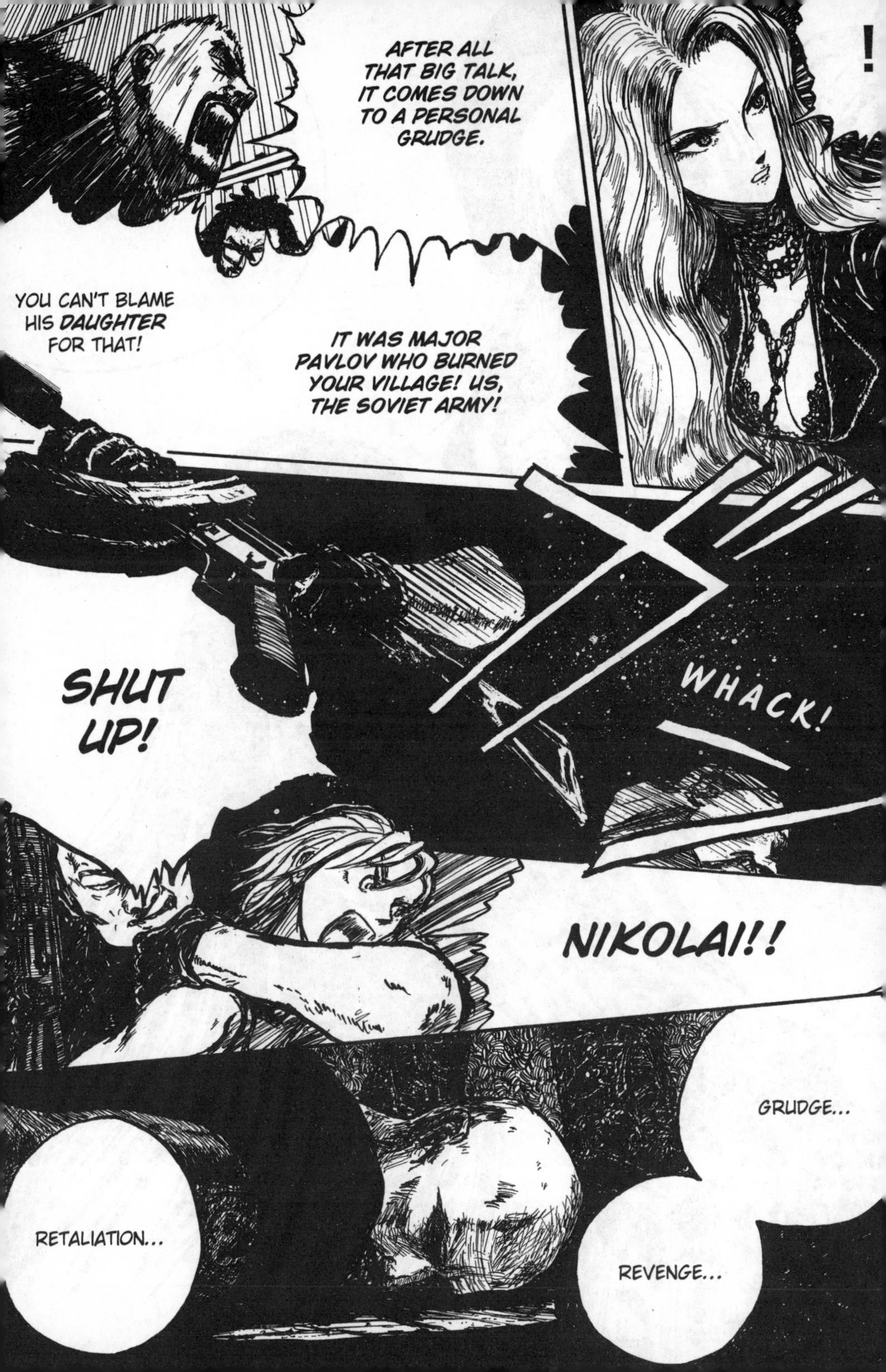

!
AFTER ALL THAT BIG TALK, IT COMES DOWN TO A PERSONAL GRUDGE.
IT WAS MAJOR PAVLOV WHO BURNED YOUR VILLAGE! US, THE SOVIET ARMY!
YOU CAN'T BLAME HIS DAUGHTER FOR THAT!
WHACK!
SHUT UP!
NIKOLAI!!
GRUDGE...
REVENGE...
RETALIATION...

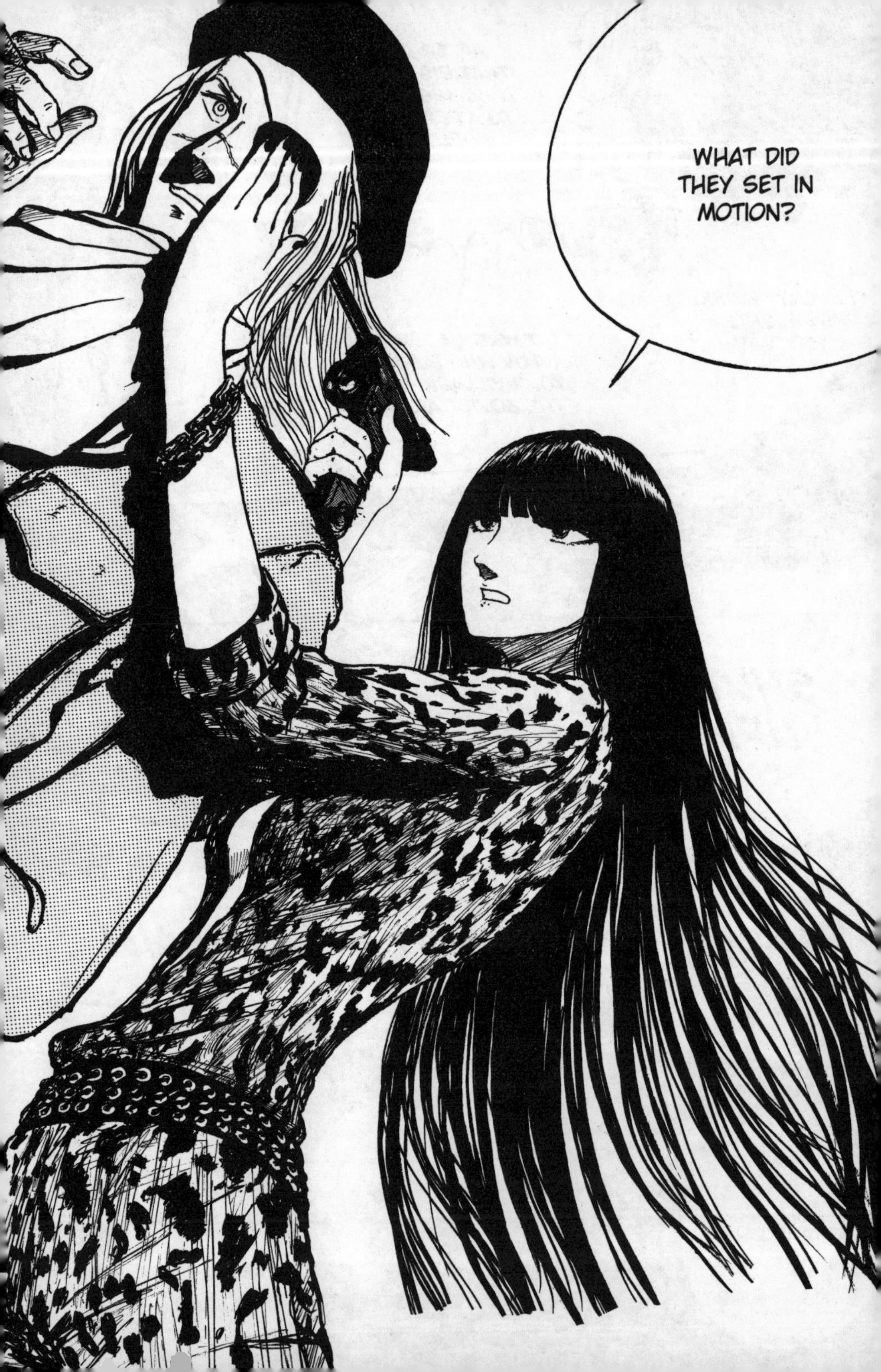
WHAT DID THEY SET IN MOTION?

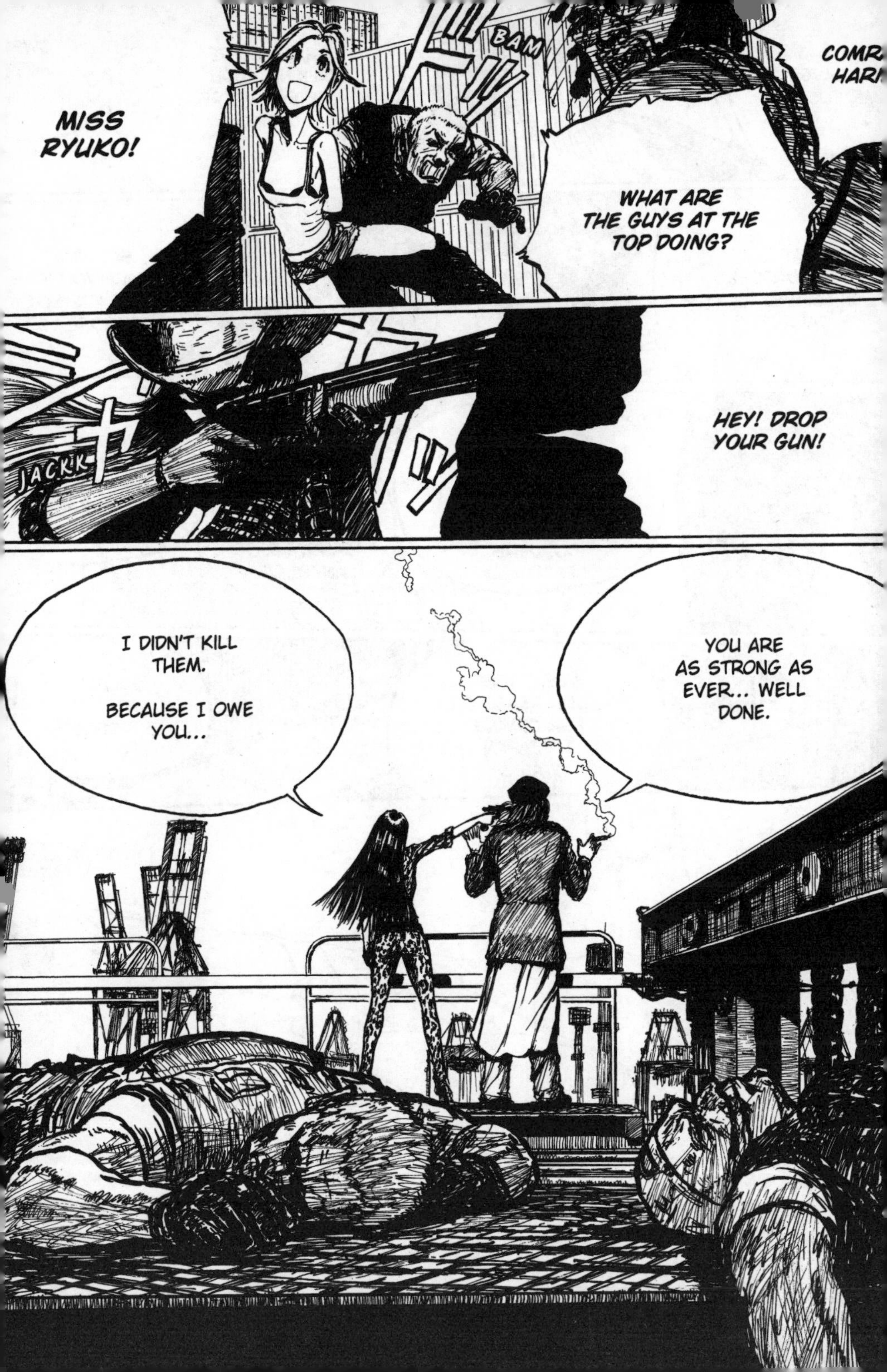
WHAT ARE THE GUYS AT THE TOP DOING?
BAM
MISS RYUKO!
HEY! DROP YOUR GUN!
JACKK
YOU ARE AS STRONG AS EVER... WELL DONE.
I DIDN'T KILL THEM.
BECAUSE I OWE YOU...

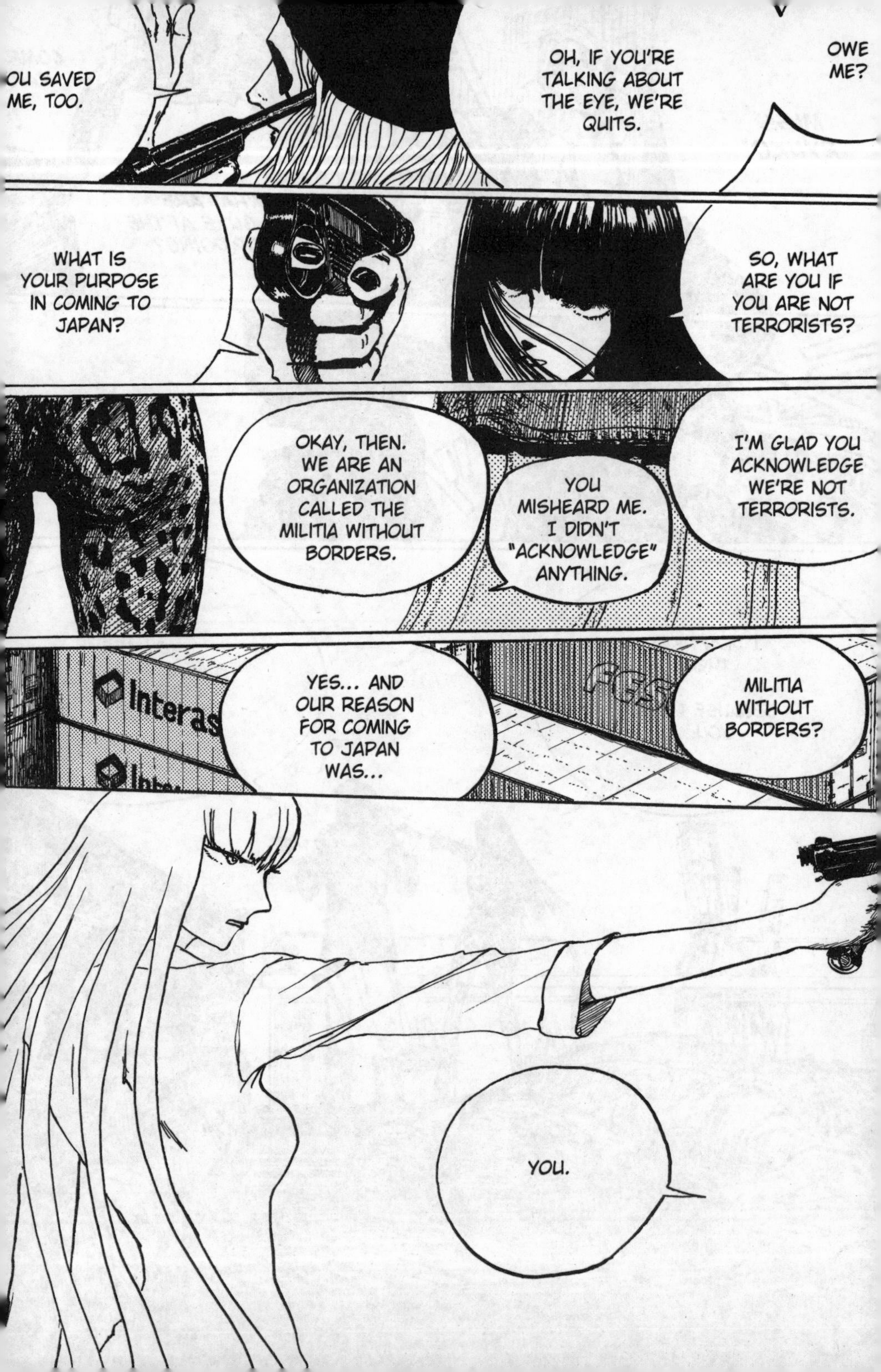
OWE ME?
OH, IF YOU'RE TALKING ABOUT THE EYE, WE'RE QUITS.
OU SAVED ME, TOO.
SO, WHAT ARE YOU IF YOU ARE NOT TERRORISTS?
WHAT IS YOUR PURPOSE IN COMING TO JAPAN?
I'M GLAD YOU ACKNOWLEDGE WE'RE NOT TERRORISTS.
YOU MISHEARD ME. I DIDN'T "ACKNOWLEDGE" ANYTHING.
OKAY, THEN. WE ARE AN ORGANIZATION CALLED THE MILITIA WITHOUT BORDERS.
MILITIA WITHOUT BORDERS?
YES... AND OUR REASON FOR COMING TO JAPAN WAS...
YOU.

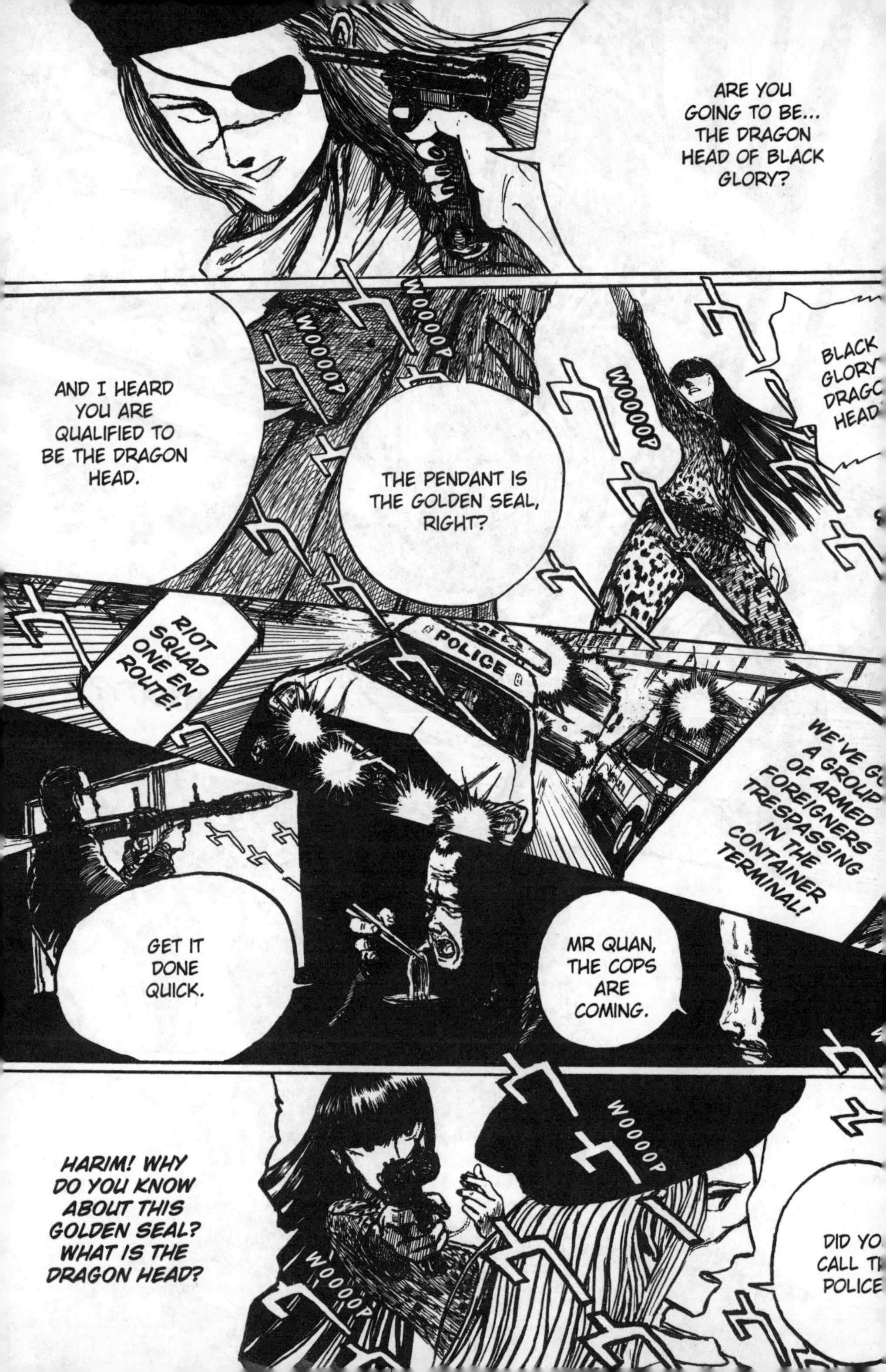

ARE YOU GOING TO BE... THE DRAGON HEAD OF BLACK GLORY?
BLACK GLORY DRAG HEAD
WOOOOP
WOOOOP
WOOOOP
THE PENDANT IS THE GOLDEN SEAL, RIGHT?
AND I HEARD YOU ARE QUALIFIED TO BE THE DRAGON HEAD.
WE'VE G A GROUP OF ARMED FOREIGNERS TRESPASSING IN THE CONTAINER TERMINAL!
POLICE
RIOT SQUAD ONE EN ROUTE!
MR QUAN, THE COPS ARE COMING.
GET IT DONE QUICK.
DID YO CALL T POLICE
WOOOOP
WOOOOP
HARIM! WHY DO YOU KNOW ABOUT THIS GOLDEN SEAL? WHAT IS THE DRAGON HEAD?

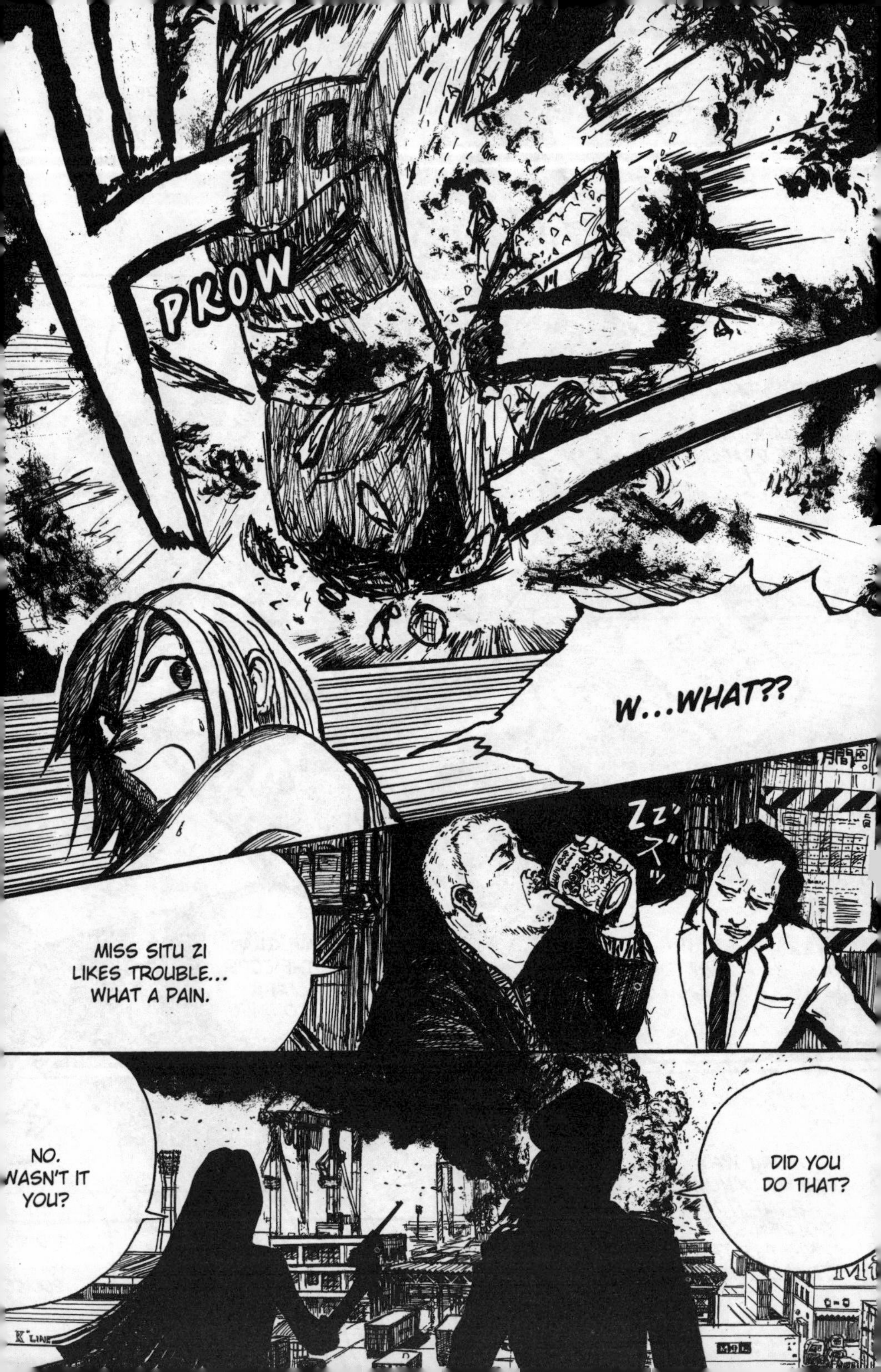
PROW
W...WHAT??
ZZ ズズッ
MISS SITU ZI LIKES TROUBLE... WHAT A PAIN.
DID YOU DO THAT?
NO. WASN'T IT YOU?

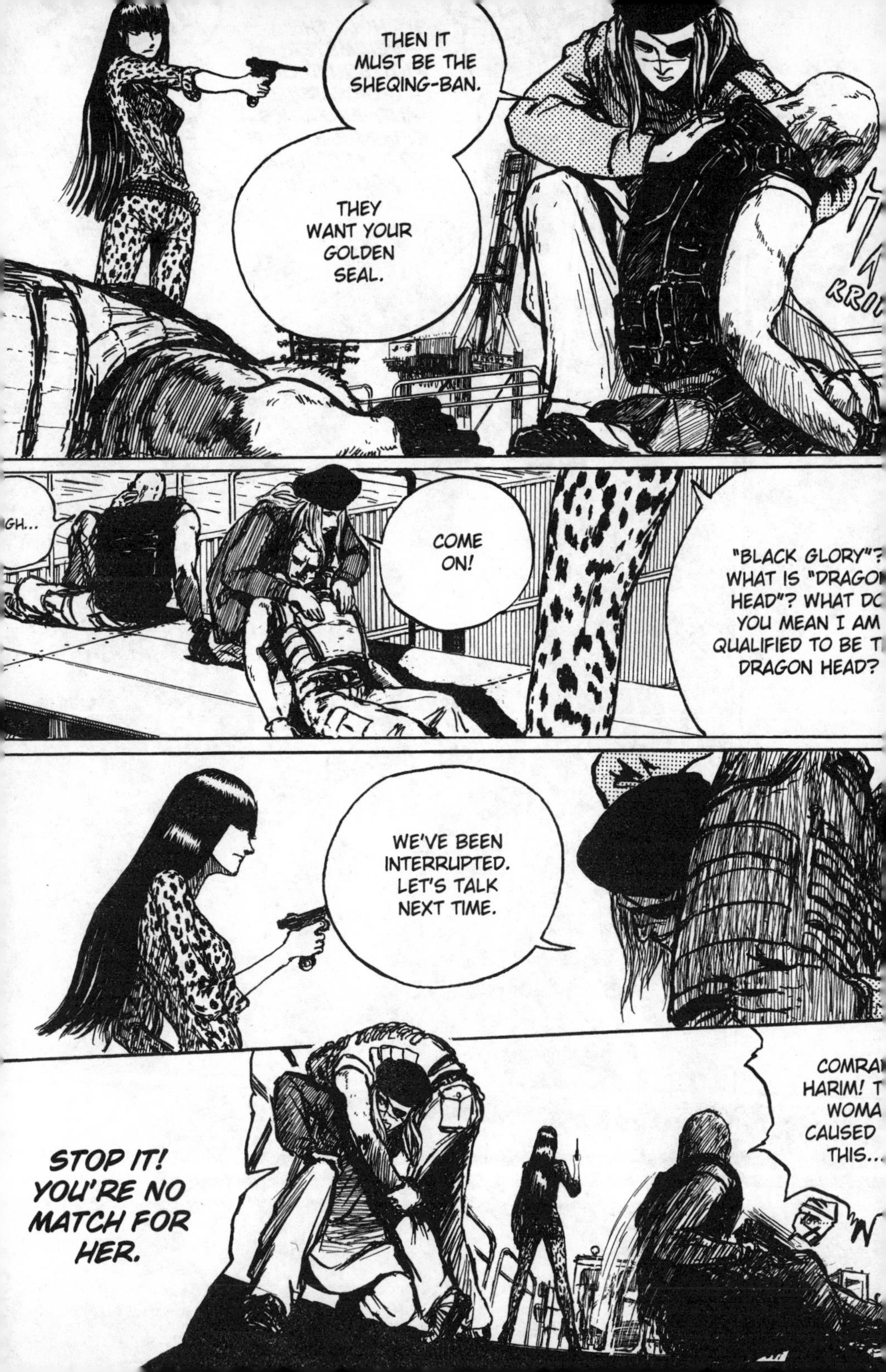
THEN IT MUST BE THE SHEQING-BAN.
THEY WANT YOUR GOLDEN SEAL.
"BLACK GLORY"? WHAT IS "DRAGO HEAD"? WHAT DO YOU MEAN I AM QUALIFIED TO BE T DRAGON HEAD?
COME ON!
GH...
WE'VE BEEN INTERRUPTED. LET'S TALK NEXT TIME.
COMRA HARIM! T WOMA CAUSED THIS...
STOP IT! YOU'RE NO MATCH FOR HER.

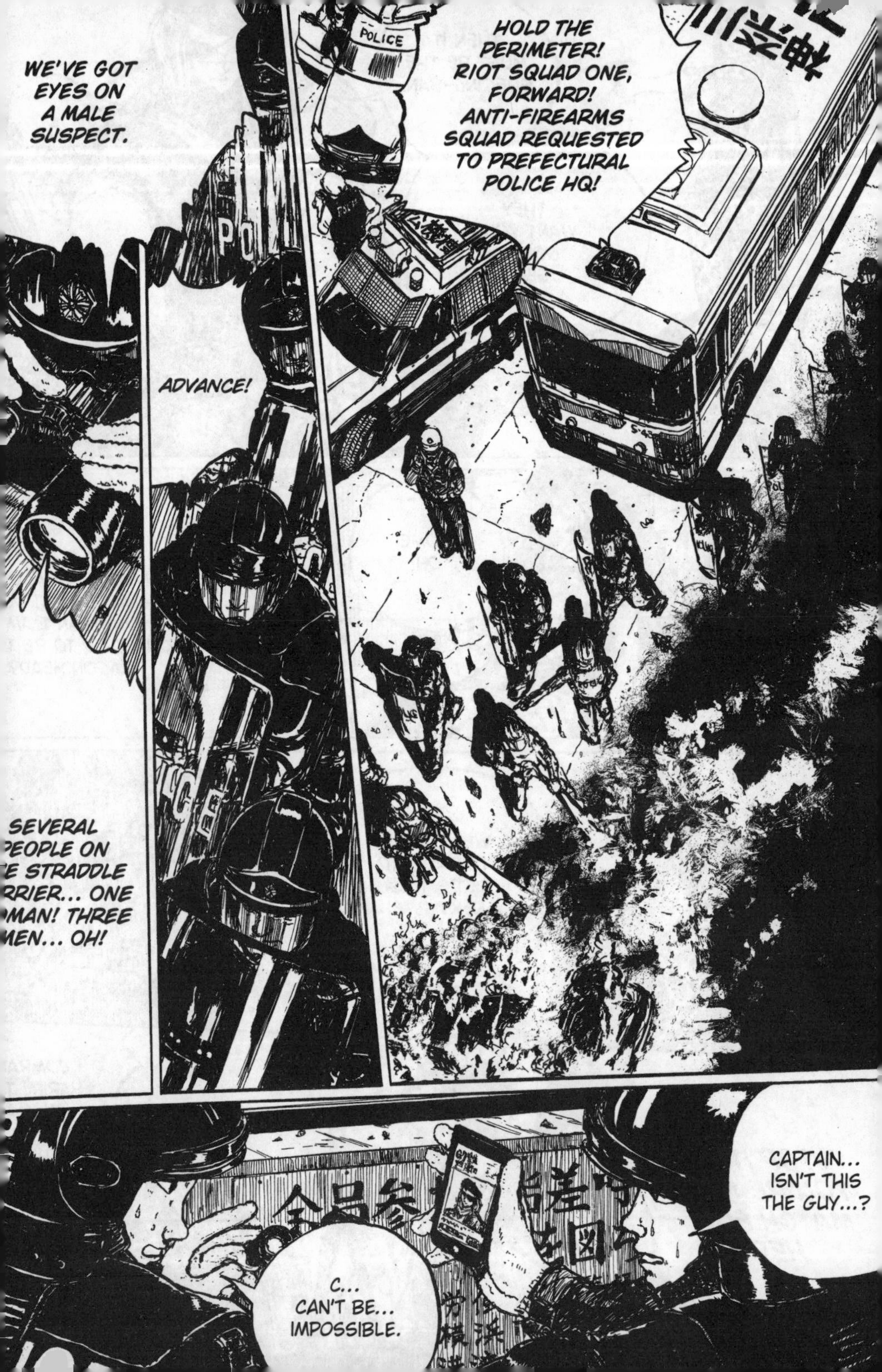
HOLD THE PERIMETER! RIOT SQUAD ONE, FORWARD! ANTI-FIREARMS SQUAD REQUESTED TO PREFECTURAL POLICE HQ!
ADVANCE!
WE'VE GOT EYES ON A MALE SUSPECT.
SEVERAL PEOPLE ON E STRADDLE RRIER... ONE OMAN! THREE MEN... OH!
CAPTAIN... ISN'T THIS THE GUY...?
C... CAN'T BE... IMPOSSIBLE.

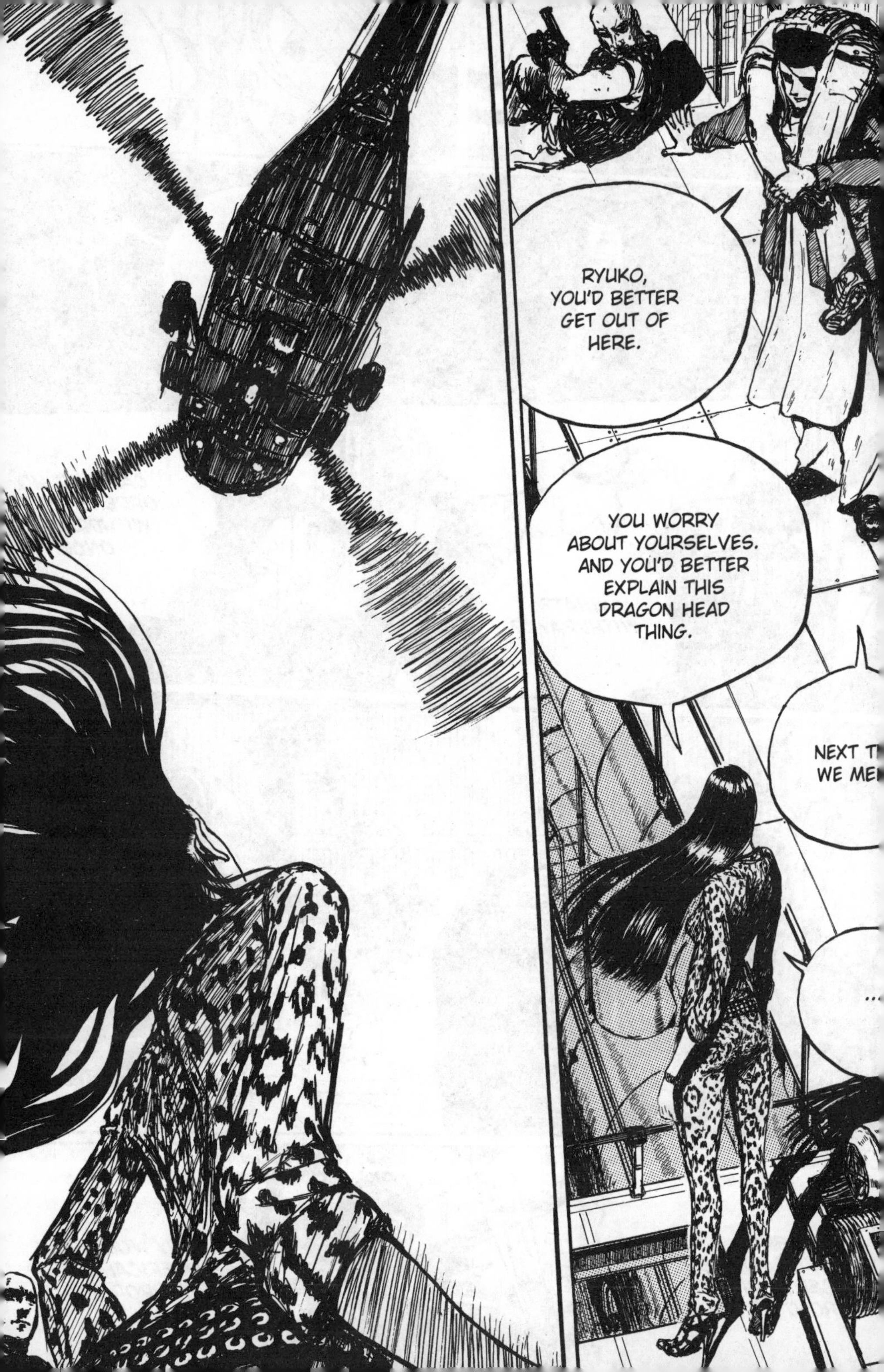
RYUKO, YOU'D BETTER GET OUT OF HERE.
YOU WORRY ABOUT YOURSELVES. AND YOU'D BETTER EXPLAIN THIS DRAGON HEAD THING.
NEXT T
WE ME

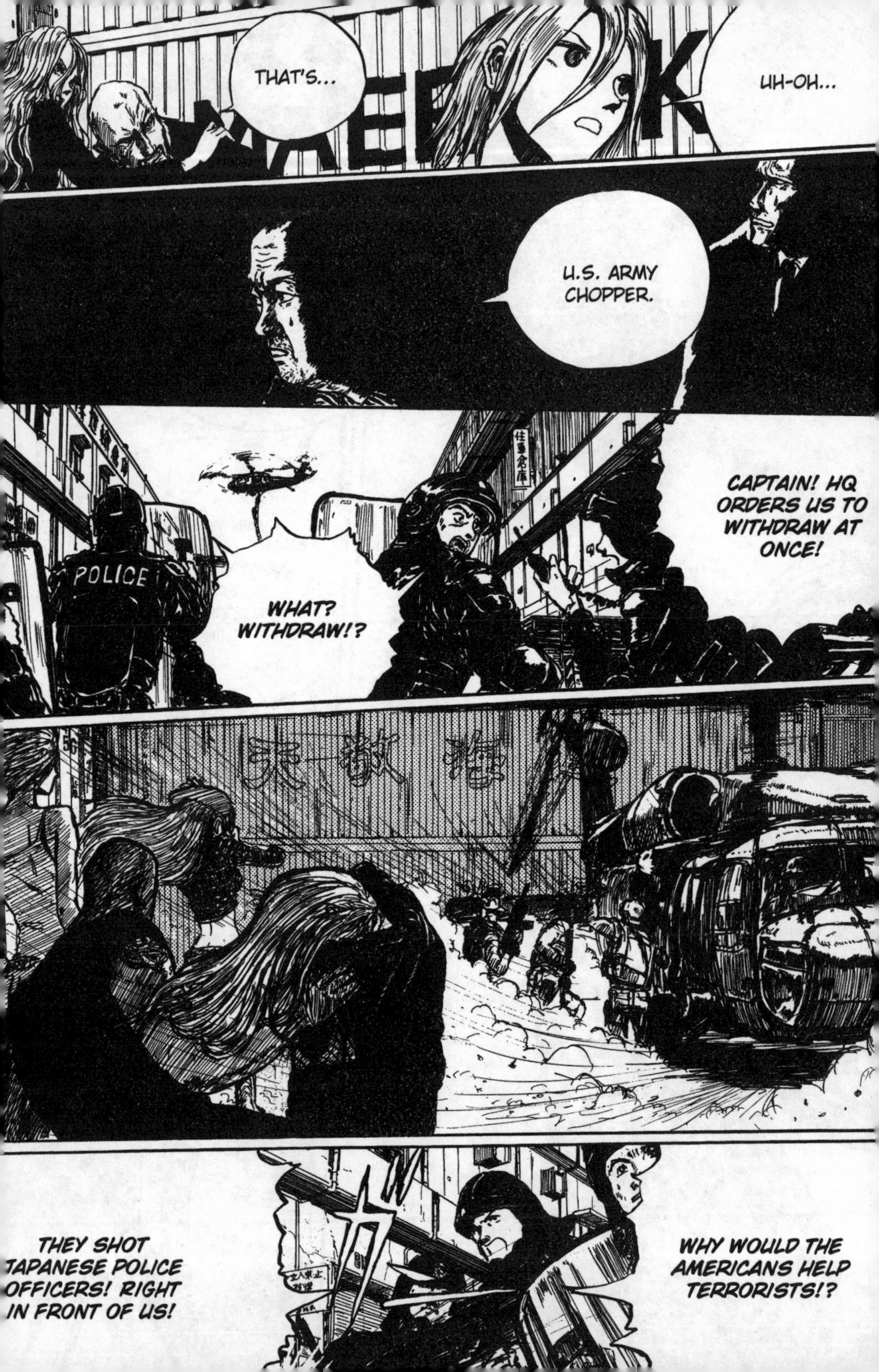
UH-OH...
THAT'S...
U.S. ARMY CHOPPER.
CAPTAIN! HQ ORDERS US TO WITHDRAW AT ONCE!
WHAT? WITHDRAW!?
POLICE
WHY WOULD THE AMERICANS HELP TERRORISTS!?
THEY SHOT JAPANESE POLICE OFFICERS! RIGHT IN FRONT OF US!

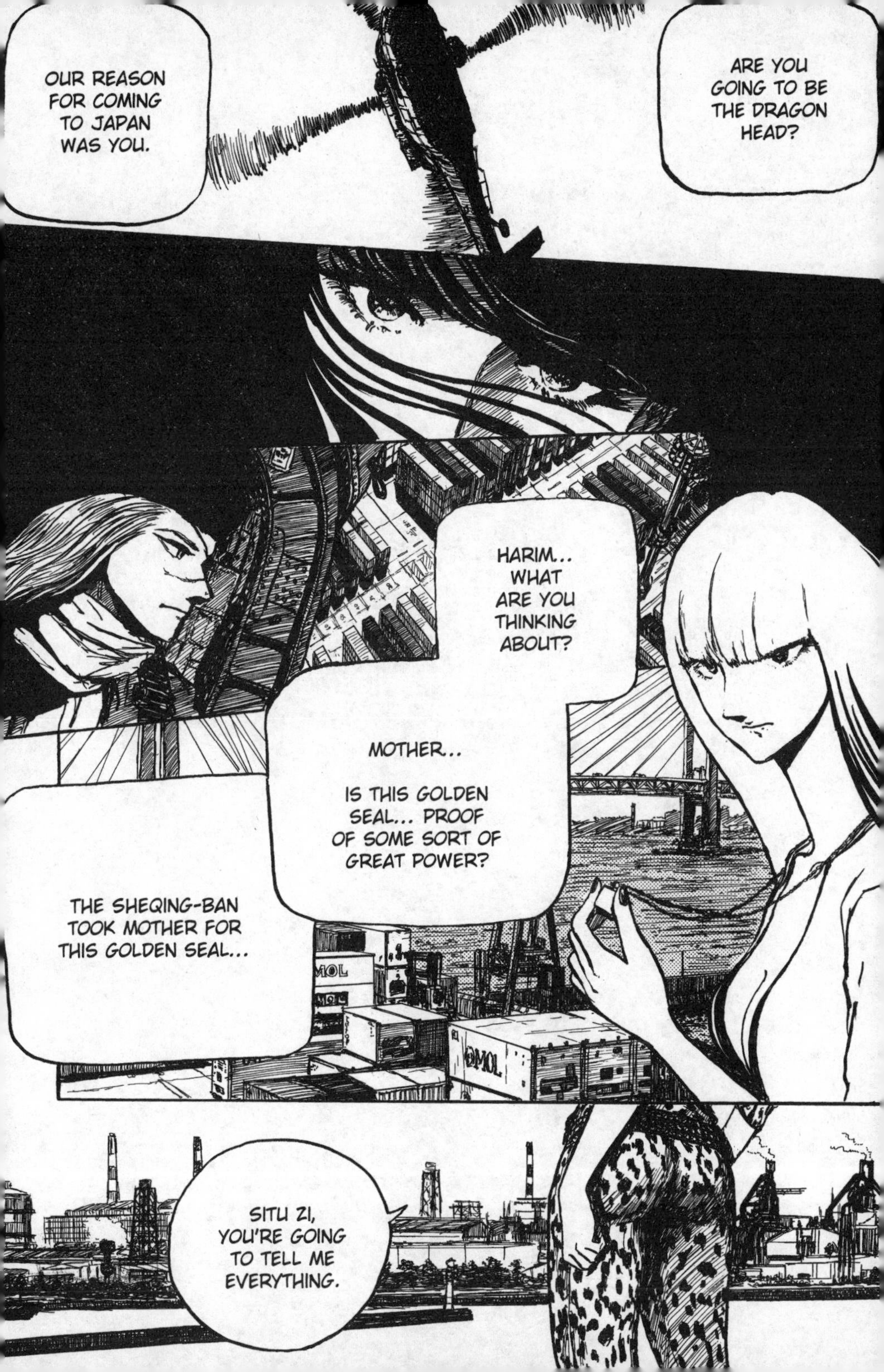
ARE YOU GOING TO BE THE DRAGON HEAD?
OUR REASON FOR COMING TO JAPAN WAS YOU.
HARIM... WHAT ARE YOU THINKING ABOUT?
MOTHER...
IS THIS GOLDEN SEAL... PROOF OF SOME SORT OF GREAT POWER?
THE SHEQING-BAN TOOK MOTHER FOR THIS GOLDEN SEAL...
SITU ZI, YOU'RE GOING TO TELL ME EVERYTHING.

CHAPTER 7:
THE OTHER FATHER/
DAUGHTER

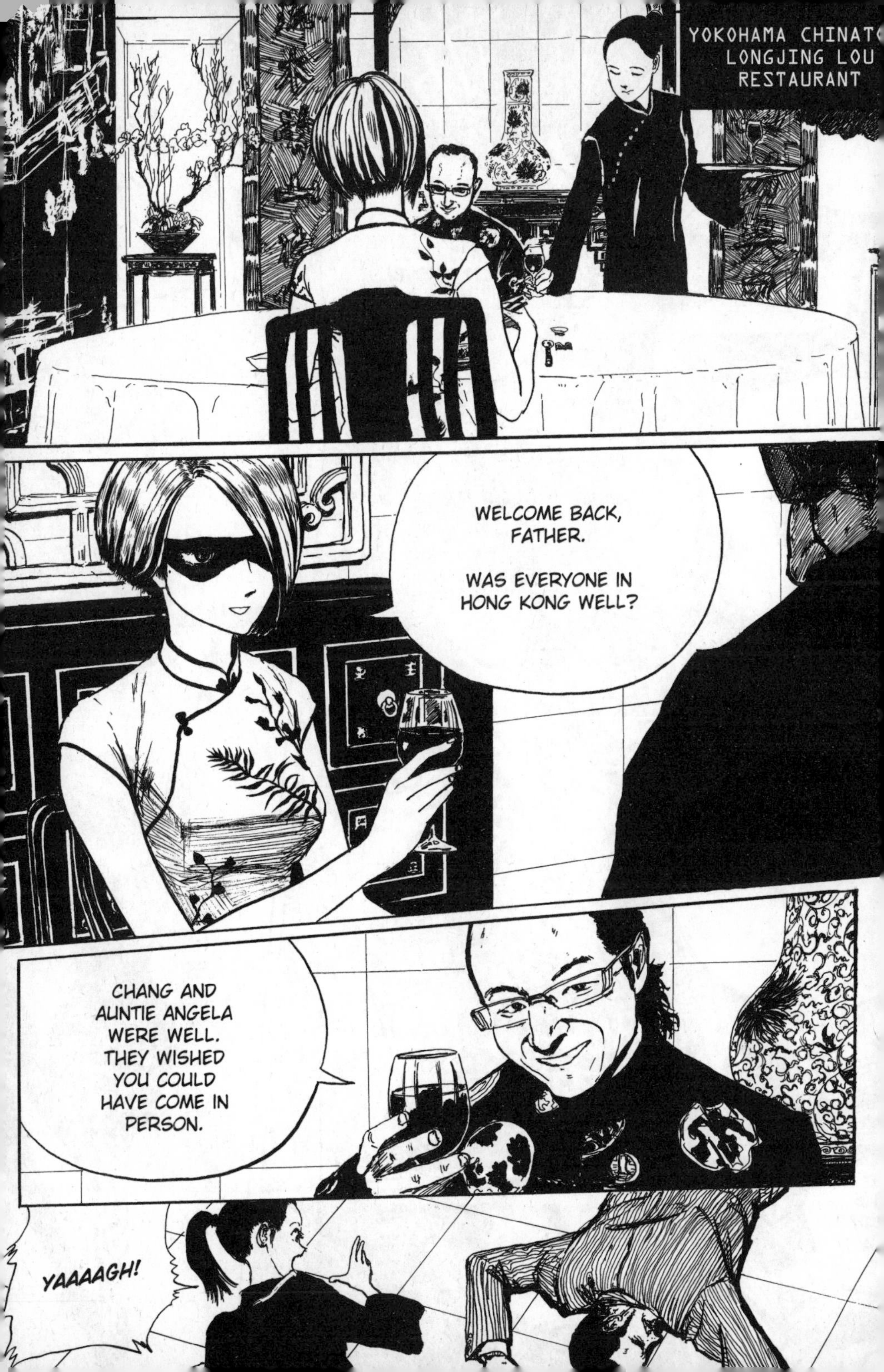
YOKOHAMA CHINATO LONGJING LOU RESTAURANT
WELCOME BACK, FATHER. WAS EVERYONE IN HONG KONG WELL?
CHANG AND AUNTIE ANGELA WERE WELL. THEY WISHED YOU COULD HAVE COME IN PERSON.
YAAAAGH!

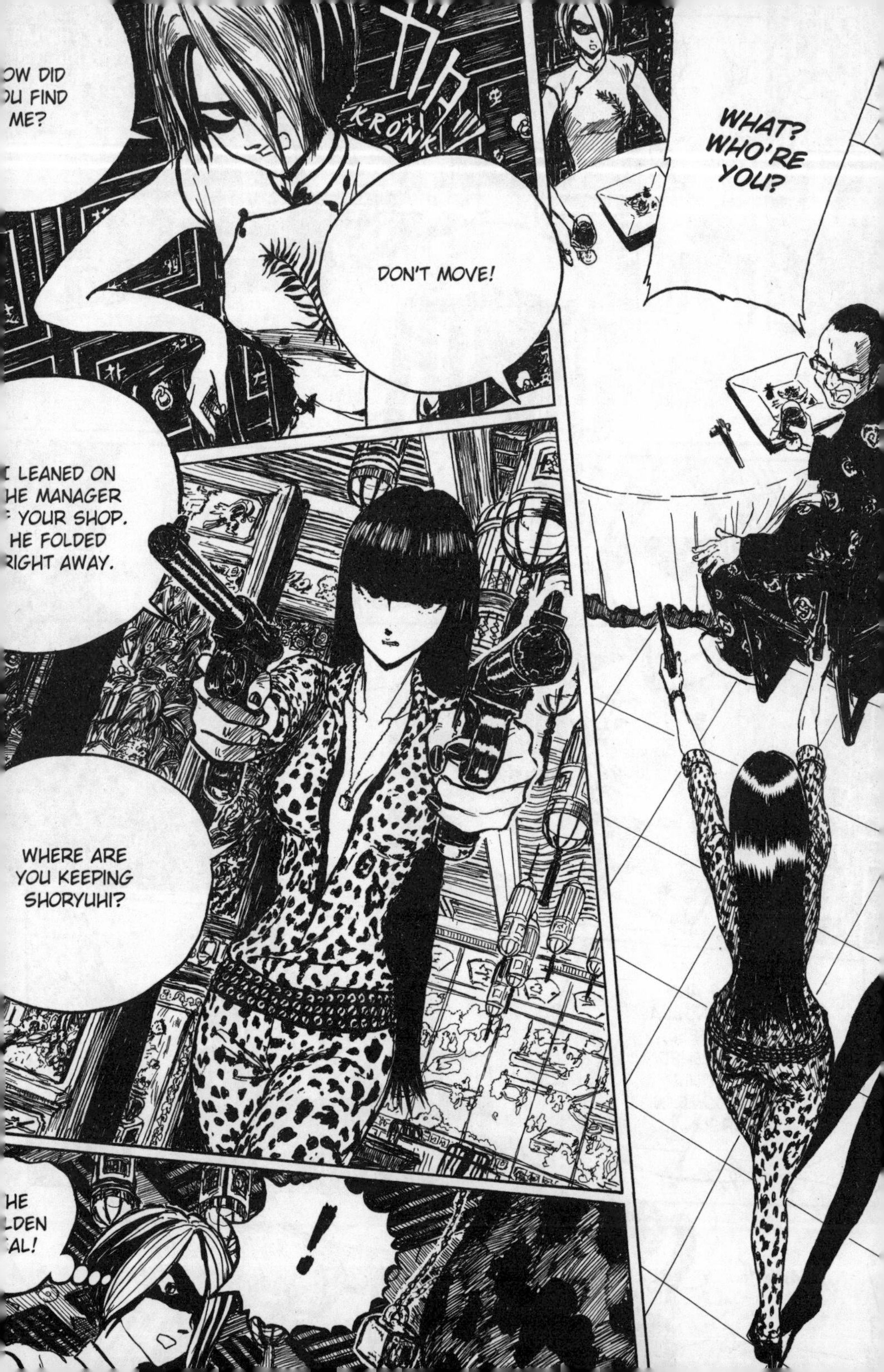
KRONK
DON'T MOVE!
WHAT? WHO'RE YOU?
OW DID OU FIND ME?
I LEANED ON HE MANAGER F YOUR SHOP. HE FOLDED RIGHT AWAY.
WHERE ARE YOU KEEPING SHORYUHI?
HE LDEN AL!
...
!

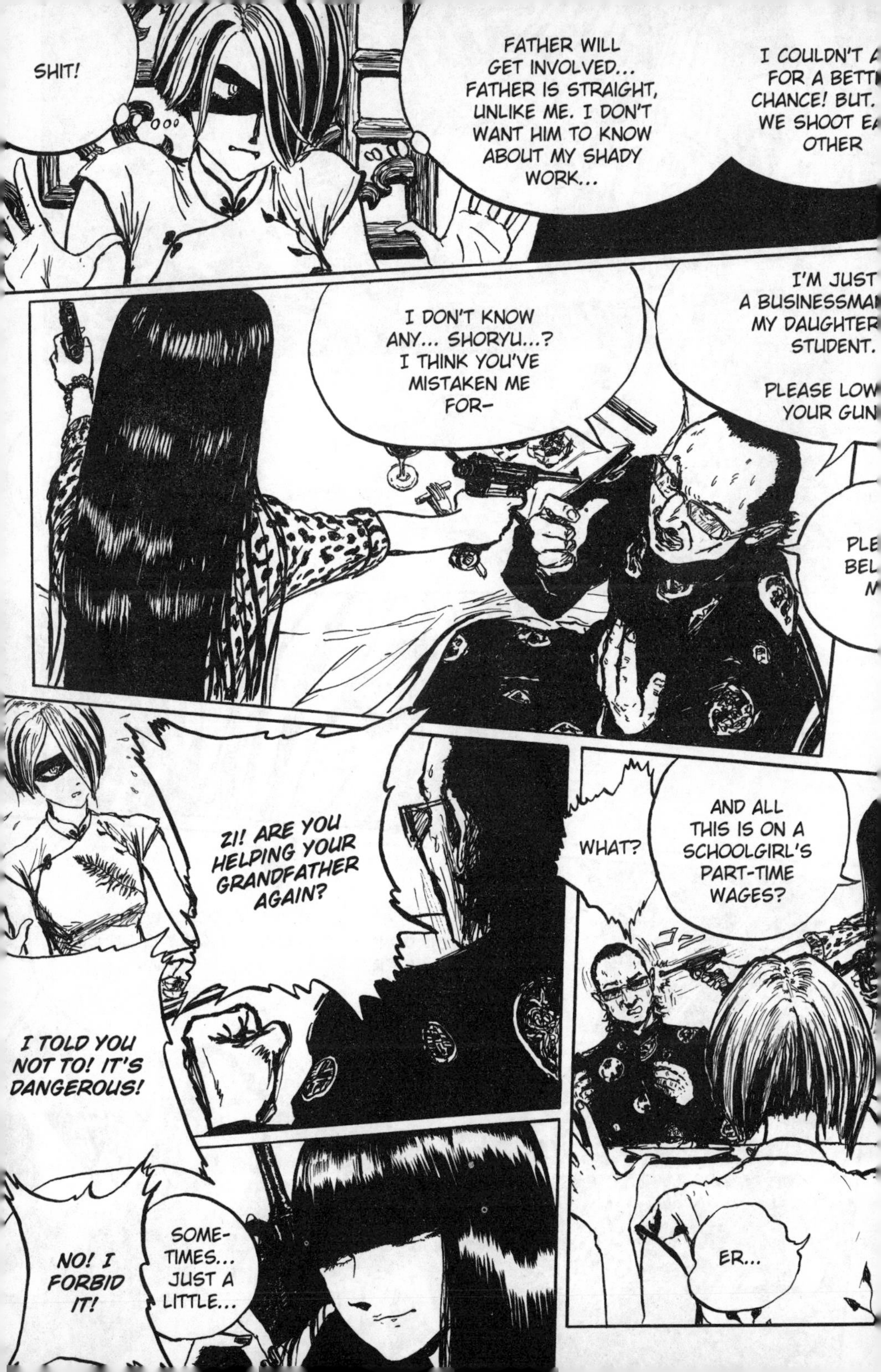
I COULDN'T A FOR A BETT CHANCE! BUT. WE SHOOT EA OTHER
FATHER WILL GET INVOLVED... FATHER IS STRAIGHT, UNLIKE ME. I DON'T WANT HIM TO KNOW ABOUT MY SHADY WORK...
SHIT!
I DON'T KNOW ANY... SHORYU...? I THINK YOU'VE MISTAKEN ME FOR-
I'M JUST A BUSINESSMA MY DAUGHTER STUDENT.
PLEASE LOW YOUR GUN
PLE BEL M
AND ALL THIS IS ON A SCHOOLGIRL'S PART-TIME WAGES?
WHAT?
ER...
ZI! ARE YOU HELPING YOUR GRANDFATHER AGAIN?
I TOLD YOU NOT TO! IT'S DANGEROUS!
SOME-TIMES... JUST A LITTLE...
NO! I FORBID IT!

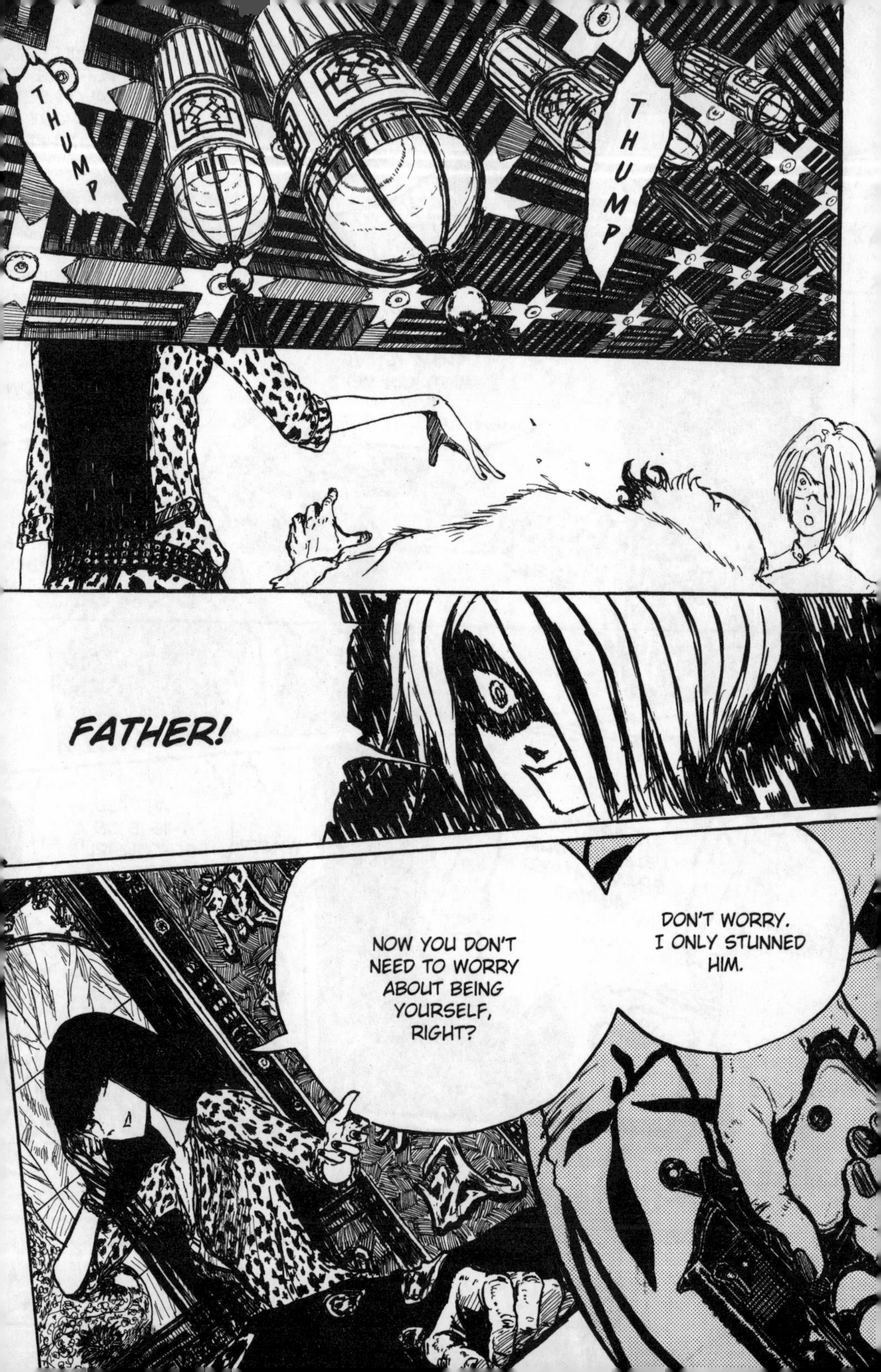
THUMP
THUMP
FATHER!
DON'T WORRY. I ONLY STUNNED HIM.
NOW YOU DON'T NEED TO WORRY ABOUT BEING YOURSELF, RIGHT?

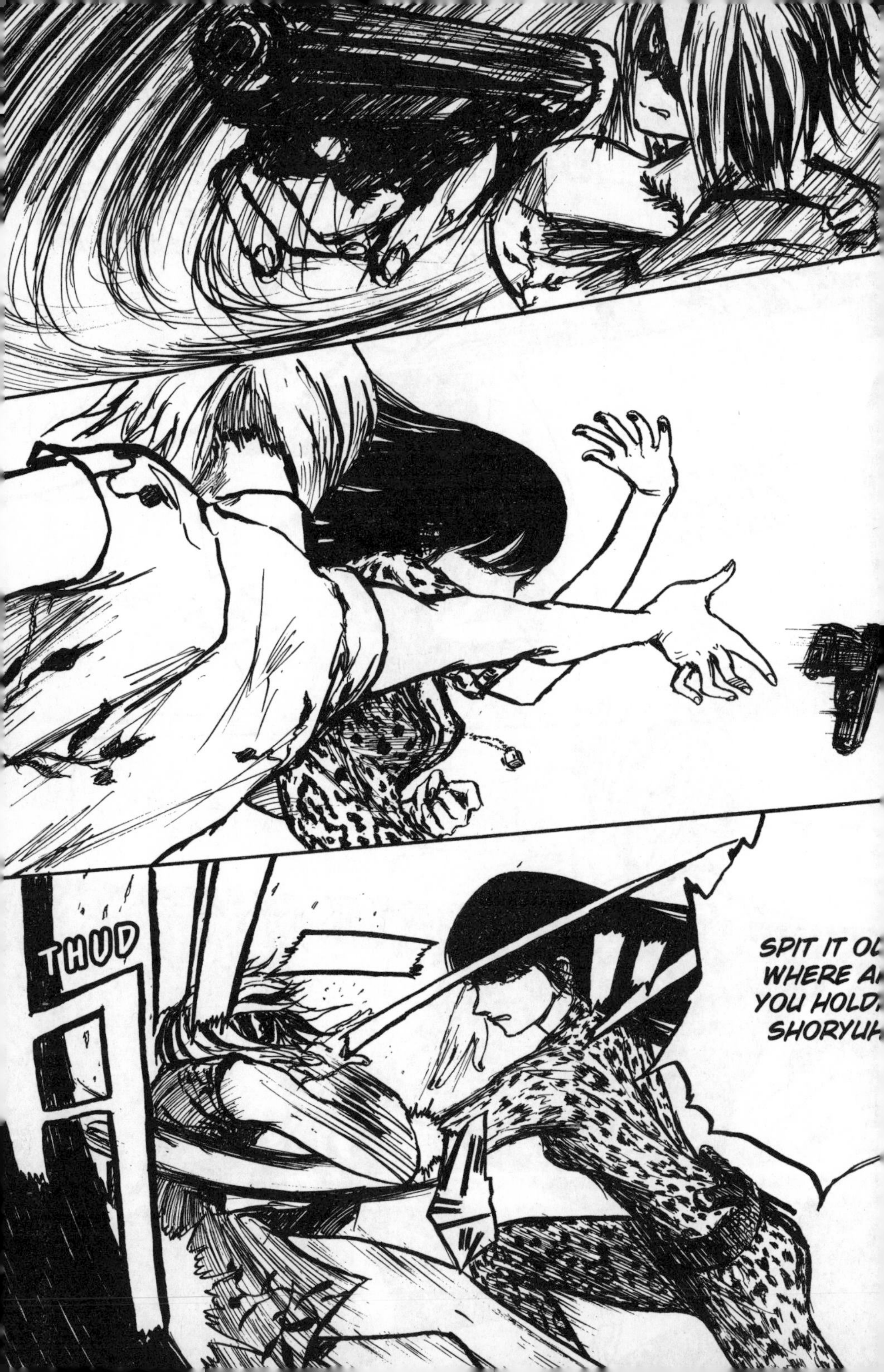
SPIT IT OU
WHERE A
YOU HOLD
SHORYUK
THUD

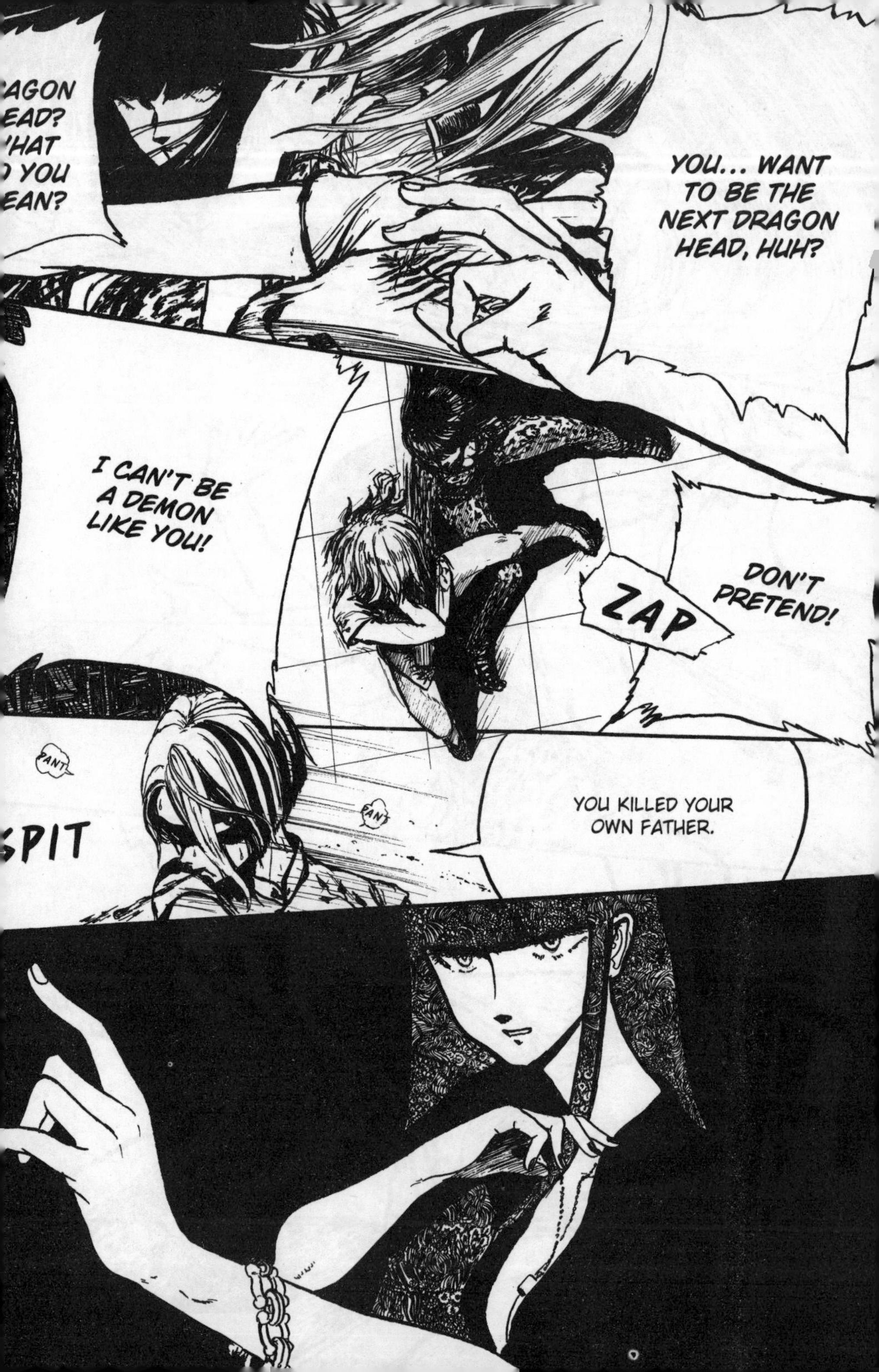
YOU... WANT TO BE THE NEXT DRAGON HEAD, HUH?
AGON EAD? 'HAT YOU EAN?
DON'T PRETEND!
ZAP
I CAN'T BE A DEMON LIKE YOU!
YOU KILLED YOUR OWN FATHER.
PANT
PANT
SPIT

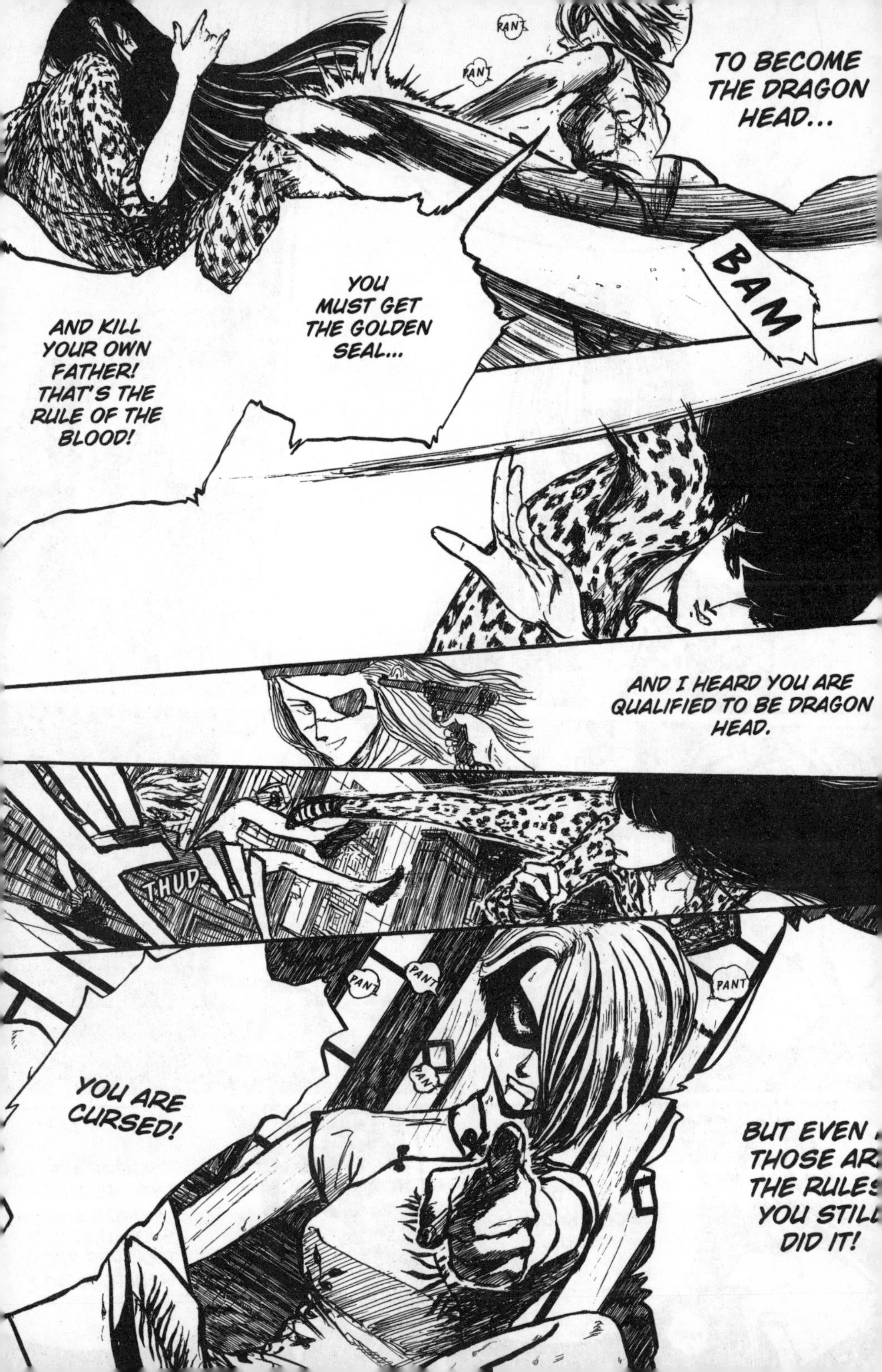
PANT
PANT
TO BECOME THE DRAGON HEAD...
YOU MUST GET THE GOLDEN SEAL...
AND KILL YOUR OWN FATHER! THAT'S THE RULE OF THE BLOOD!
BAM
AND I HEARD YOU ARE QUALIFIED TO BE DRAGON HEAD.
THUD
PANT
PANT
PANT
PANT
BUT EVEN THOSE AR THE RULE YOU STILL DID IT!
YOU ARE CURSED!

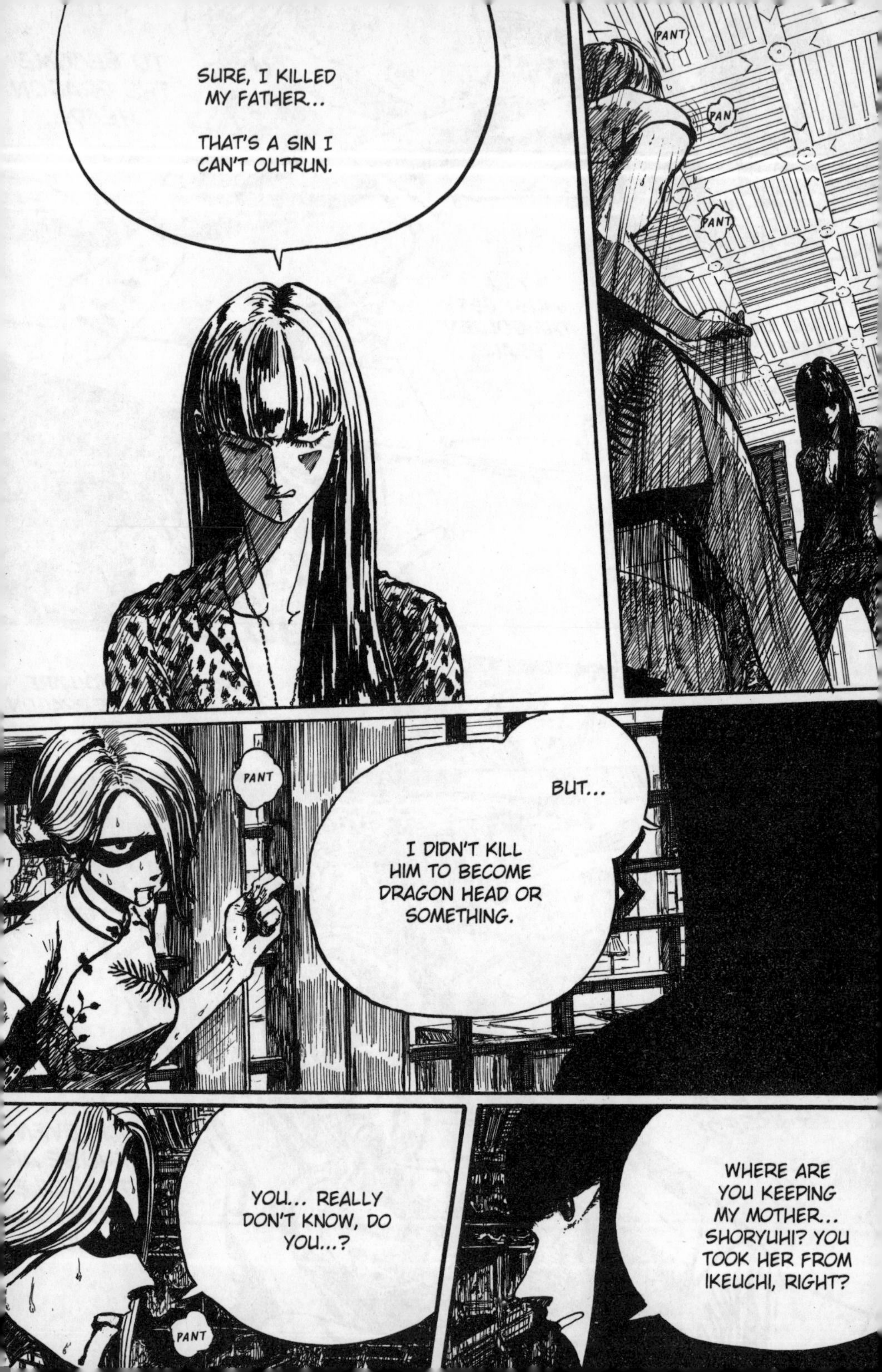
PANT
PANT
PANT
SURE, I KILLED MY FATHER...
THAT'S A SIN I CAN'T OUTRUN.
PANT
BUT...
I DIDN'T KILL HIM TO BECOME DRAGON HEAD OR SOMETHING.
WHERE ARE YOU KEEPING MY MOTHER... SHORYUHI? YOU TOOK HER FROM IKEUCHI, RIGHT?
YOU... REALLY DON'T KNOW, DO YOU...?
PANT

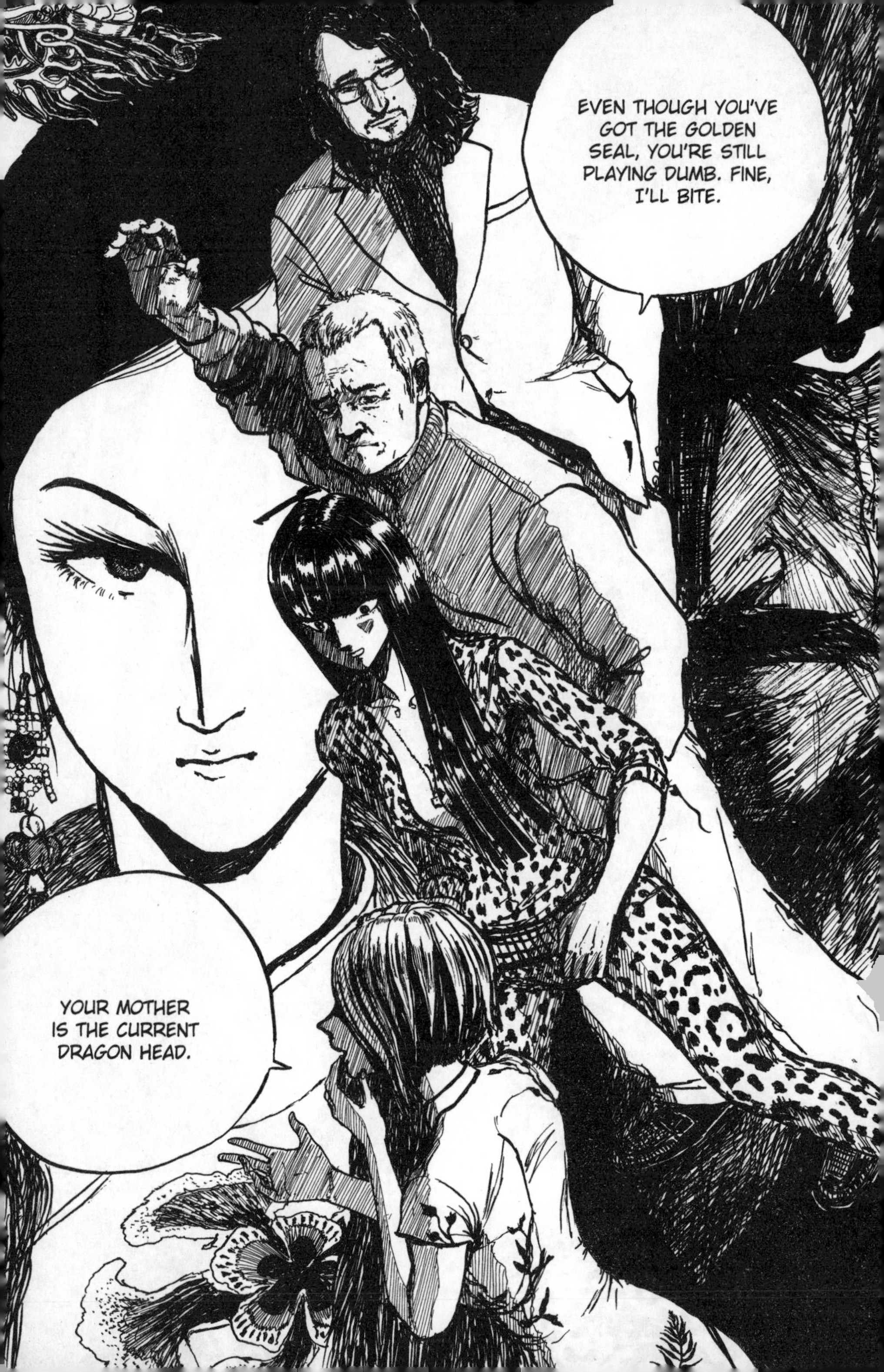
EVEN THOUGH YOU'VE GOT THE GOLDEN SEAL, YOU'RE STILL PLAYING DUMB. FINE, I'LL BITE.
YOUR MOTHER IS THE CURRENT DRAGON HEAD.

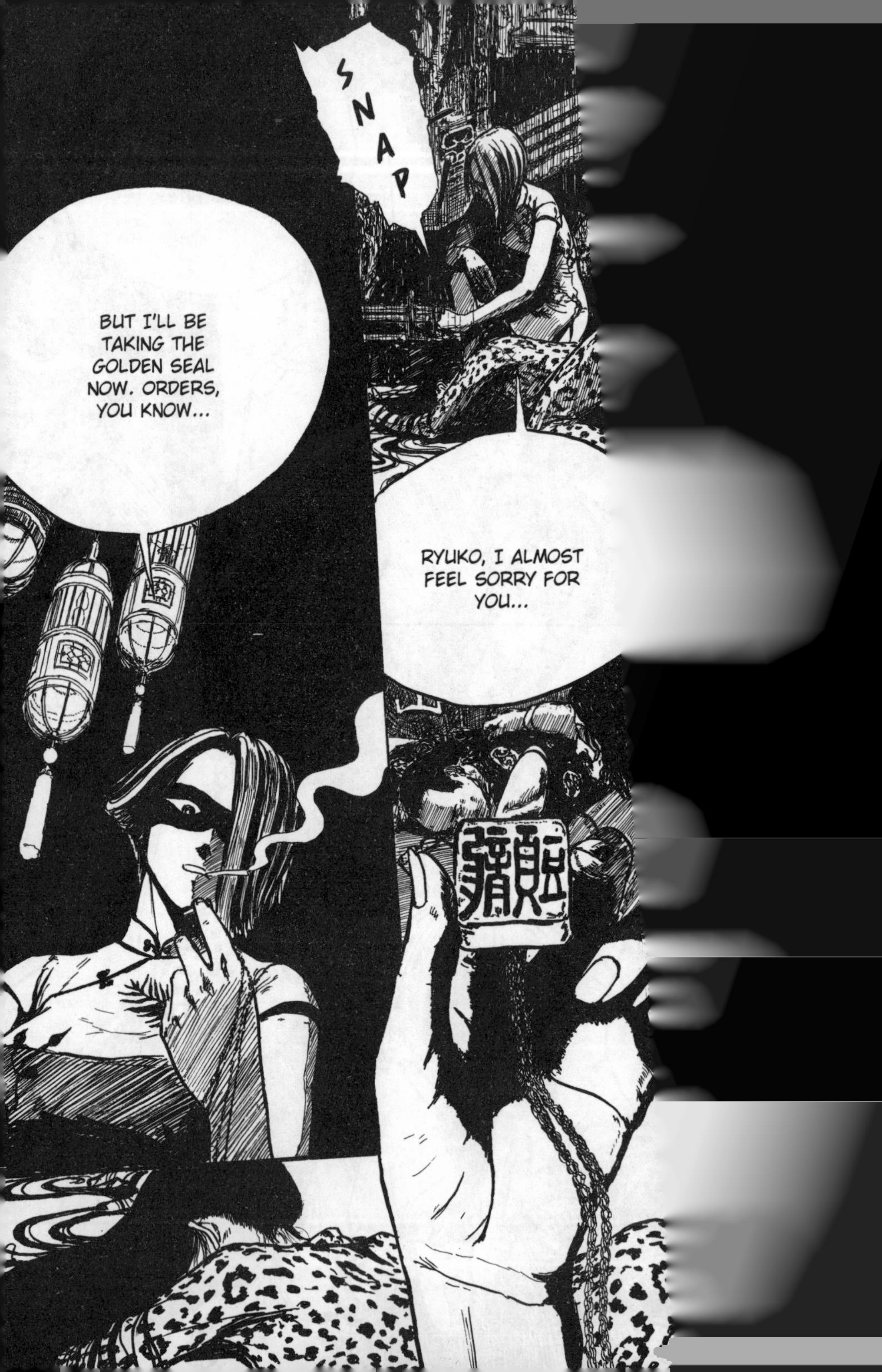
SNAP
RYUKO, I ALMOST FEEL SORRY FOR YOU...
BUT I'LL BE TAKING THE GOLDEN SEAL NOW. ORDERS, YOU KNOW...

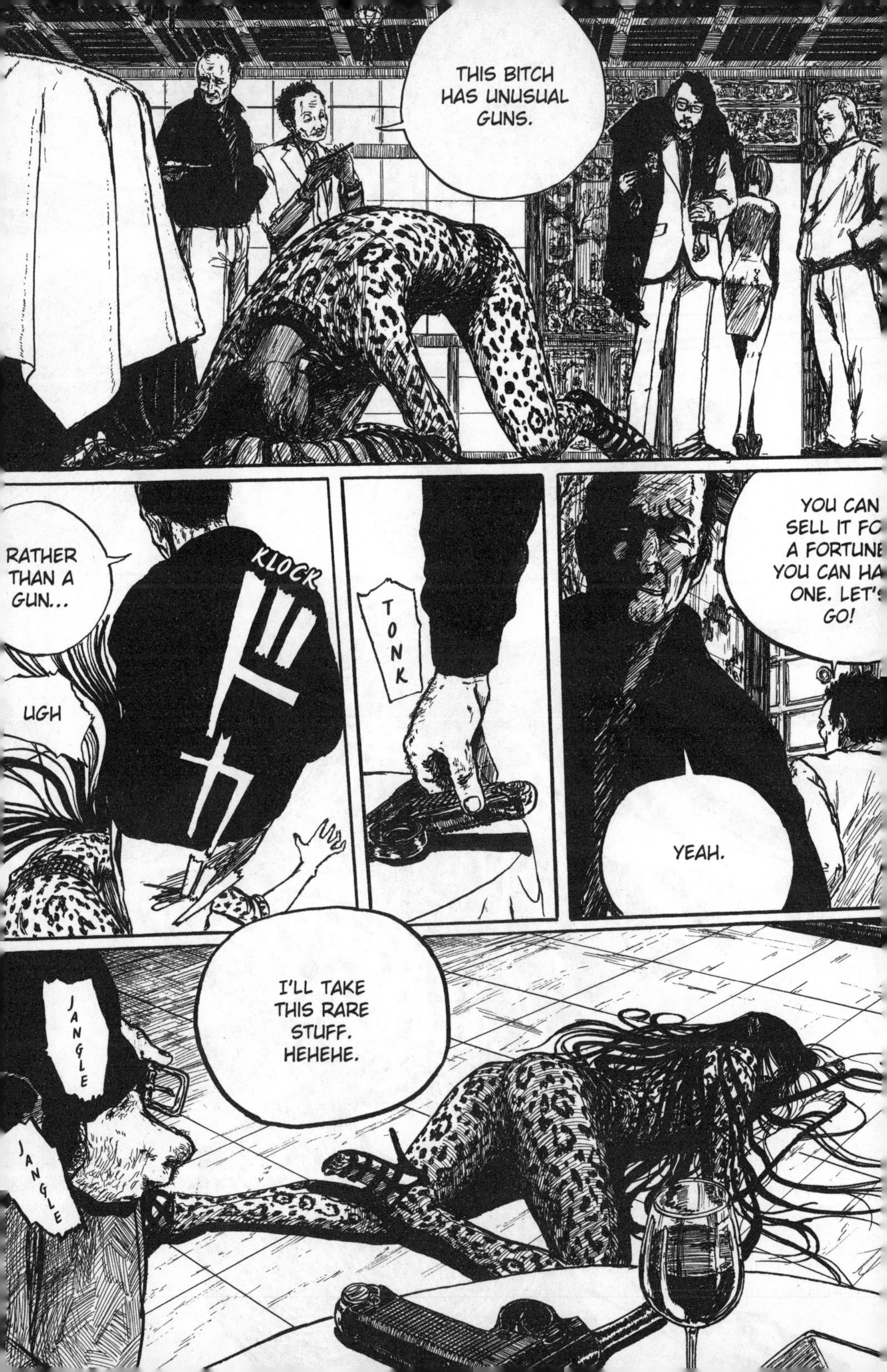
THIS BITCH HAS UNUSUAL GUNS.
YOU CAN SELL IT FO A FORTUNE YOU CAN HA ONE. LET'S GO!
YEAH.
TONK
RATHER THAN A GUN...
KLOCK
UGH
I'LL TAKE THIS RARE STUFF. HEHEHE.
JANGLE
JANGLE

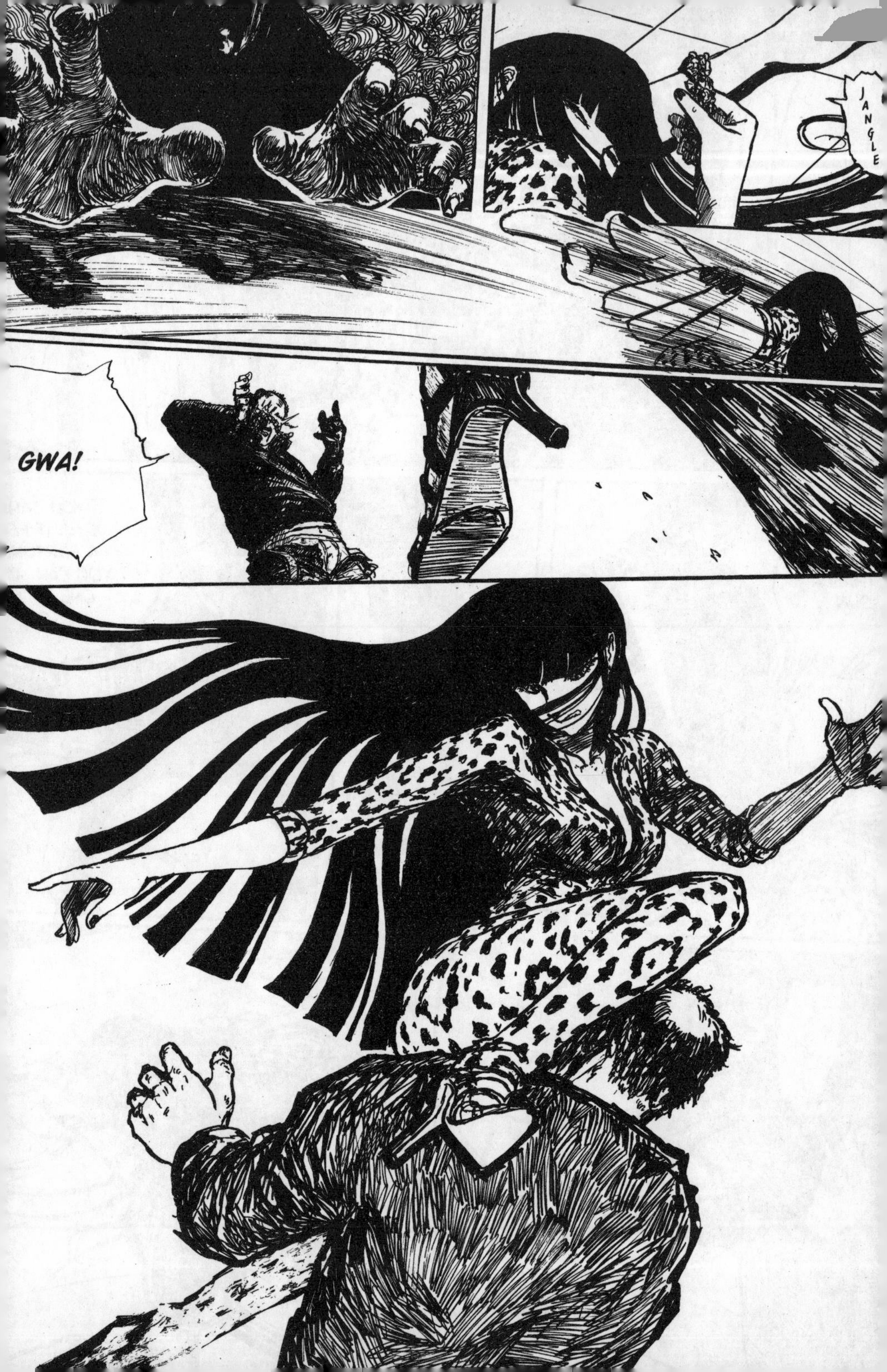
JANGLE
GWA!

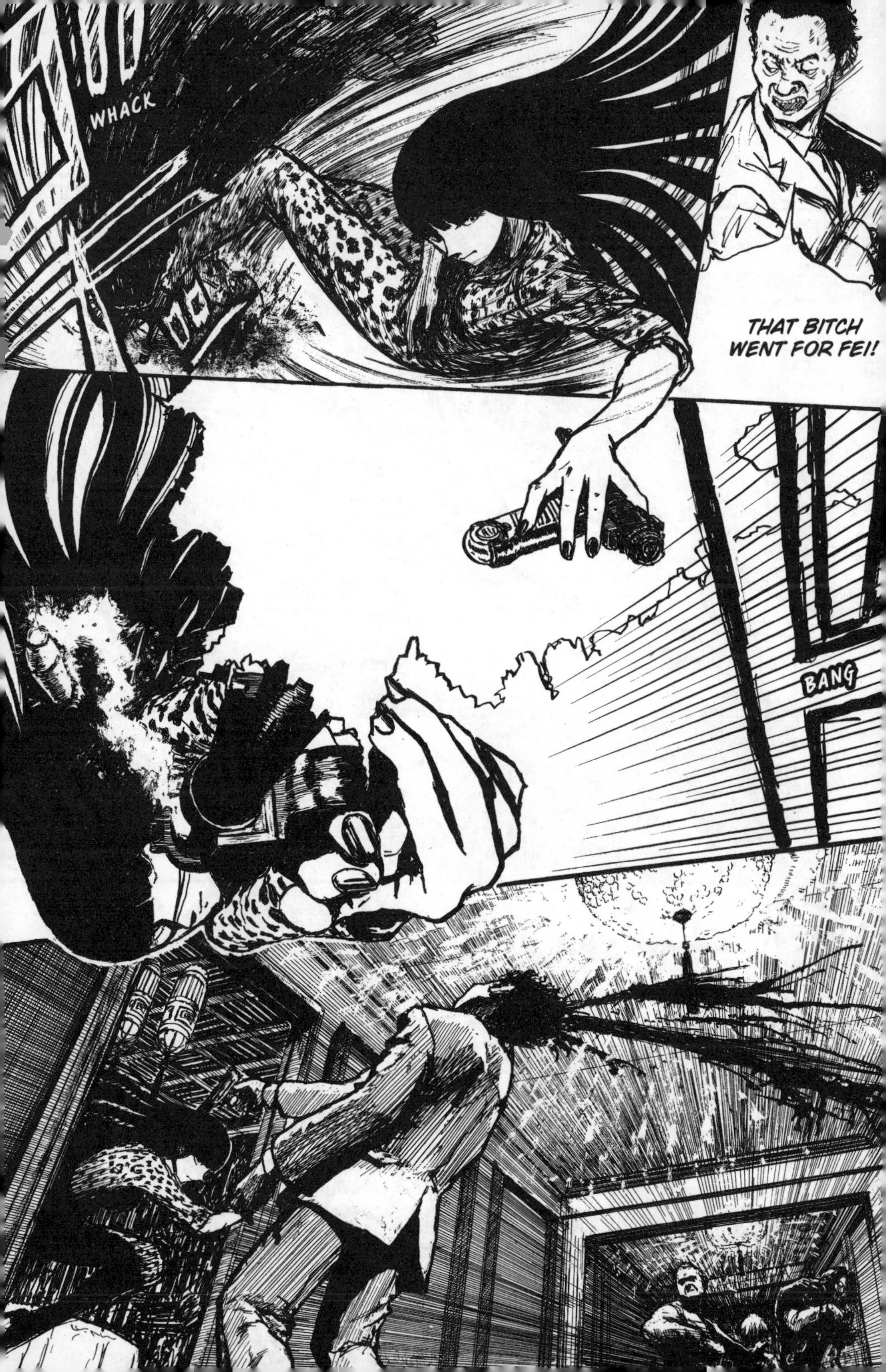
THAT BITCH WENT FOR FEI!
WHACK
BANG

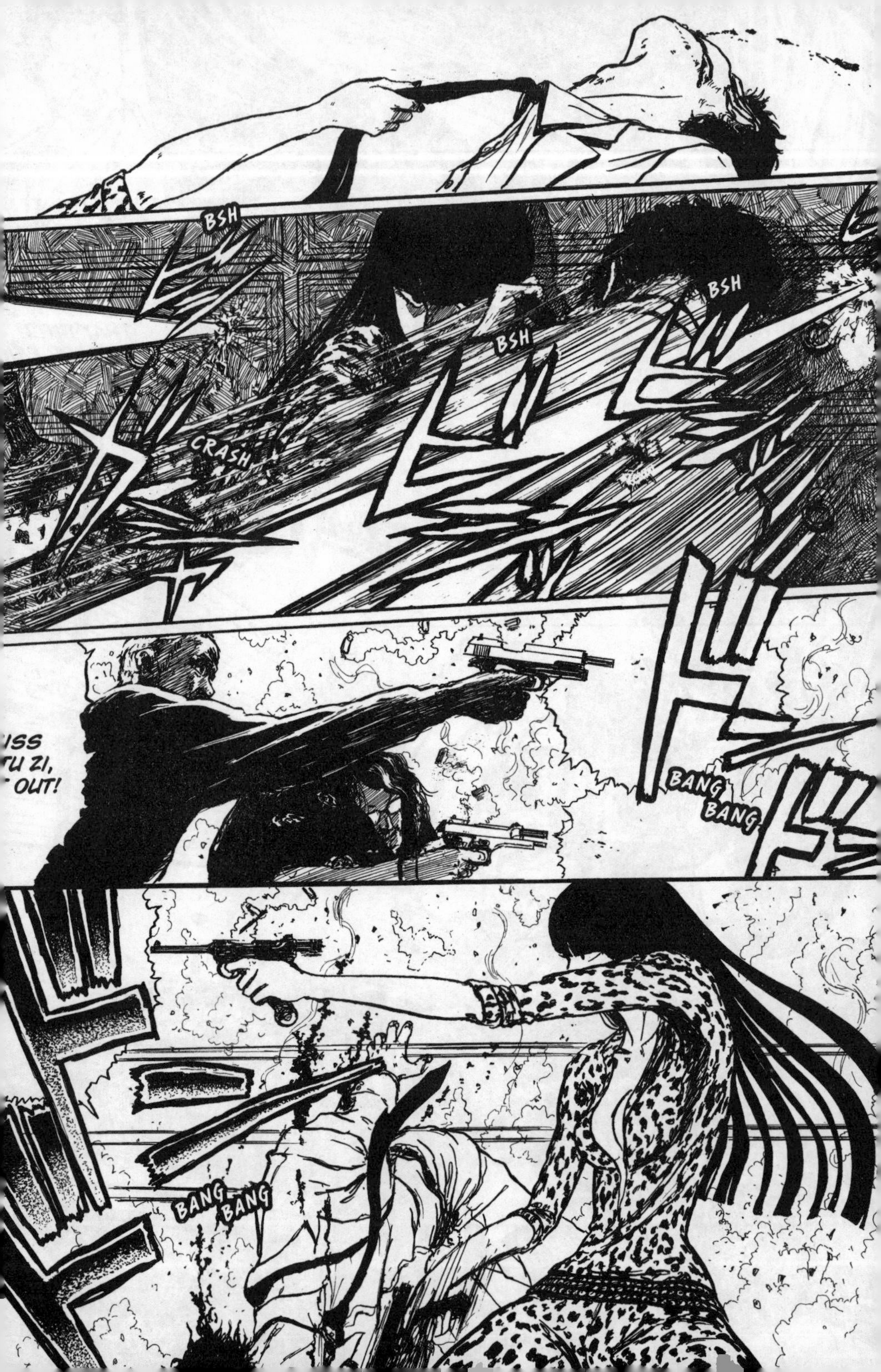
BSH
BSH
BSH
CRASH
BANG BANG
ISS
TU ZI,
OUT!
BANG BANG

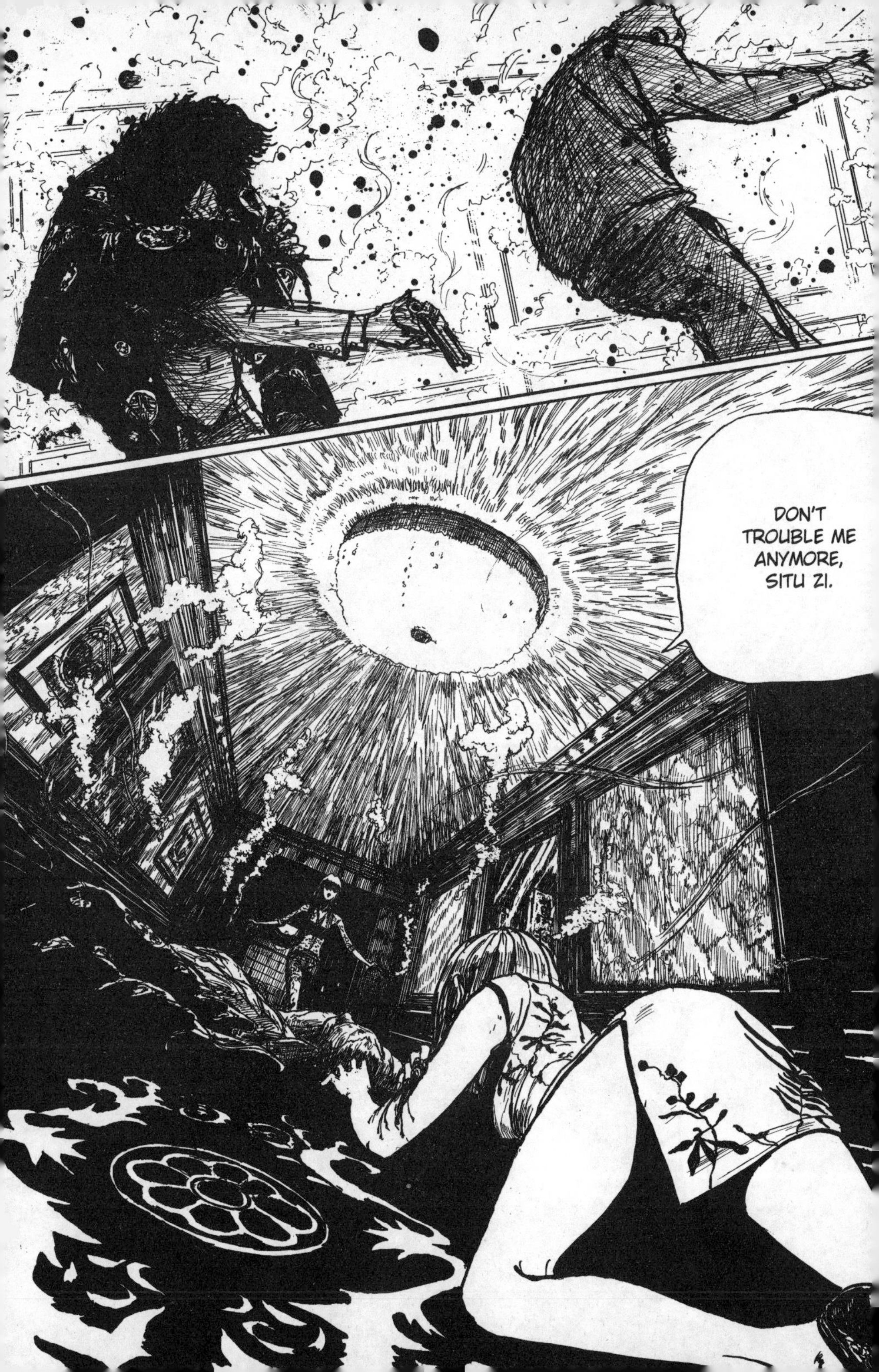
DON'T TROUBLE ME ANYMORE, SITU ZI.

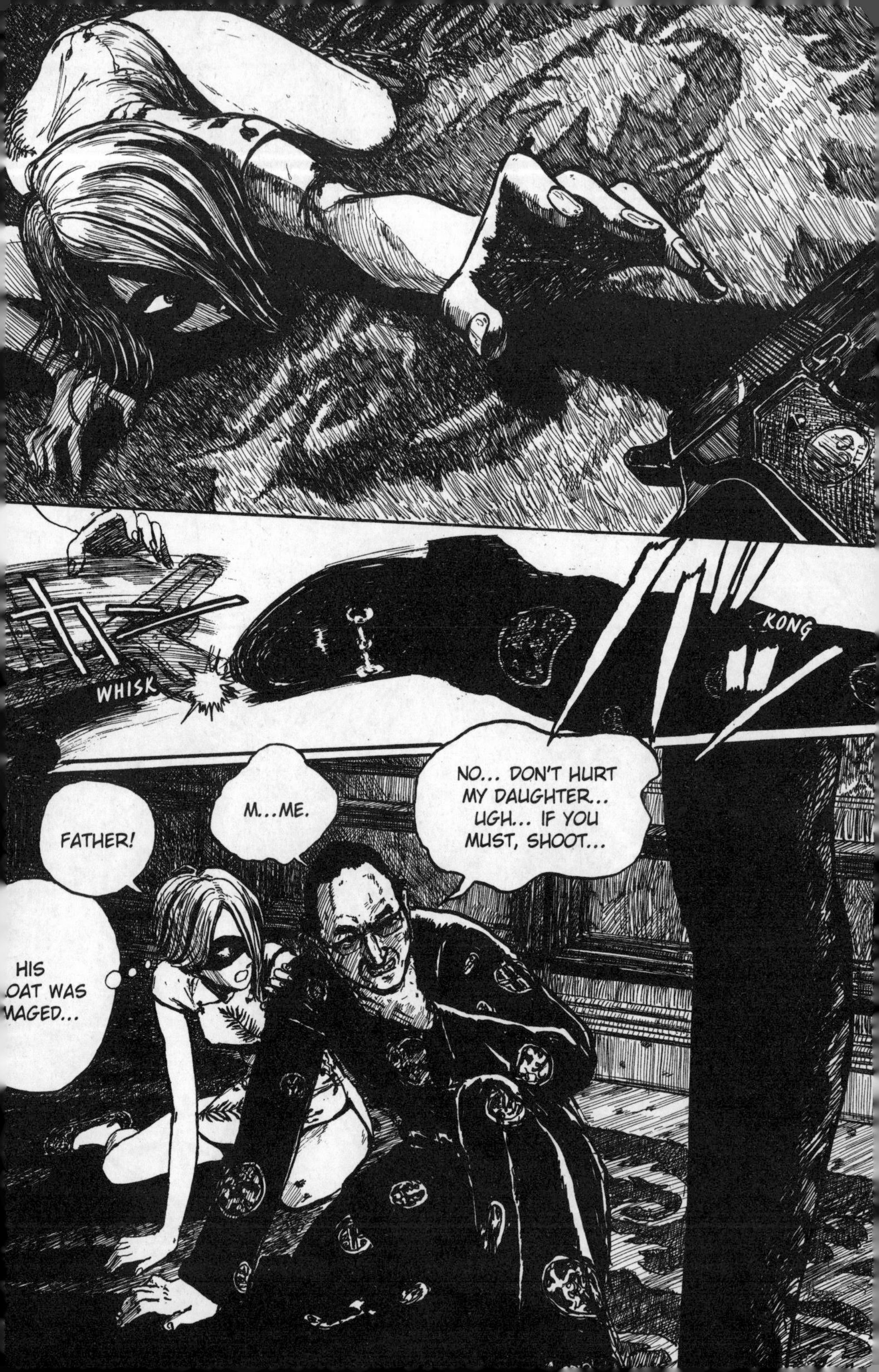
KONG
WHISK
NO... DON'T HURT MY DAUGHTER... UGH... IF YOU MUST, SHOOT...
M...ME.
FATHER!
HIS OAT WAS MAGED...

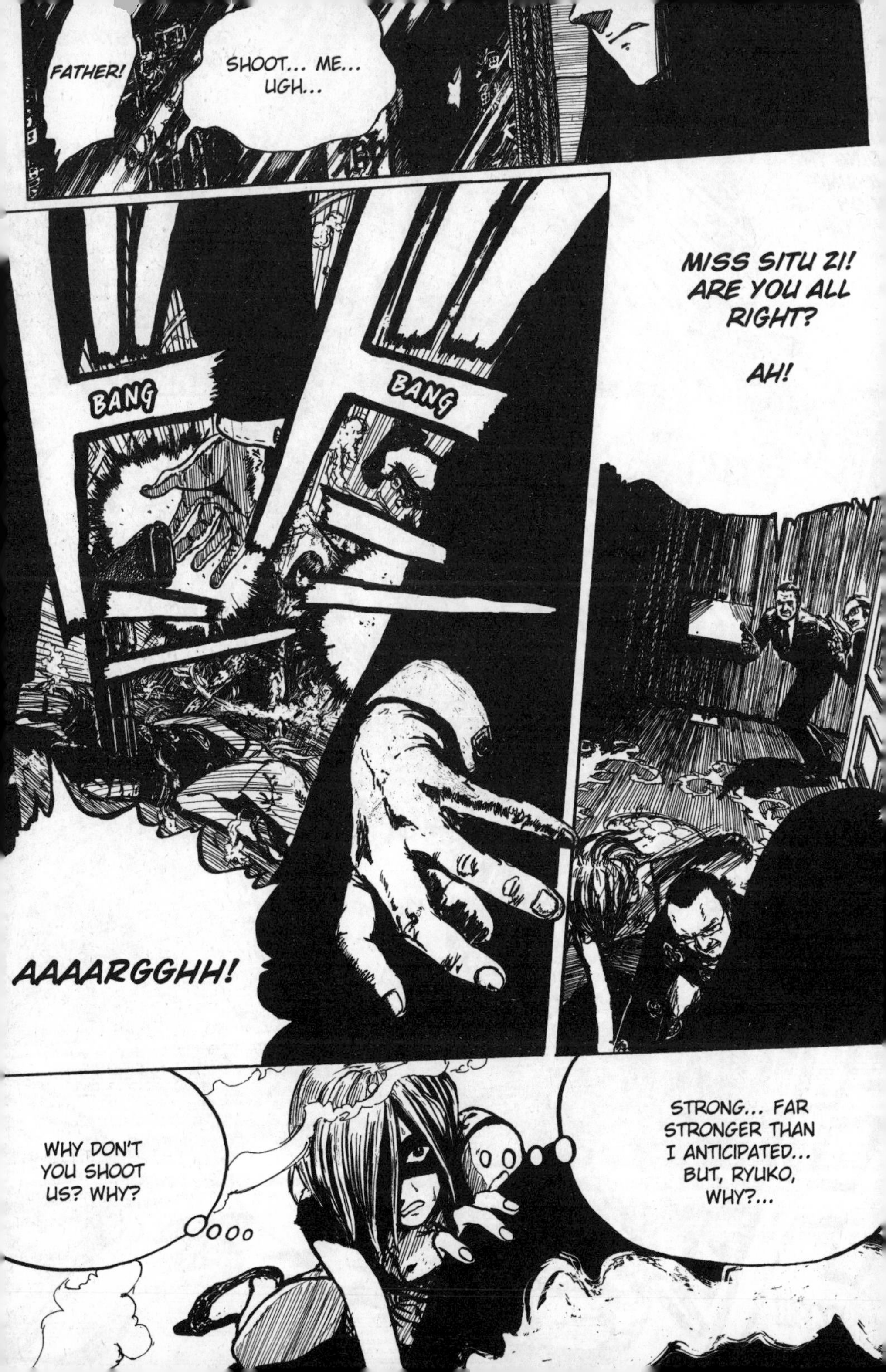
SHOOT... ME... UGH...
FATHER!
MISS SITU ZI! ARE YOU ALL RIGHT?
AH!
BANG
BANG
AAAARGGHH!
STRONG... FAR STRONGER THAN I ANTICIPATED... BUT, RYUKO, WHY?...
WHY DON'T YOU SHOOT US? WHY?

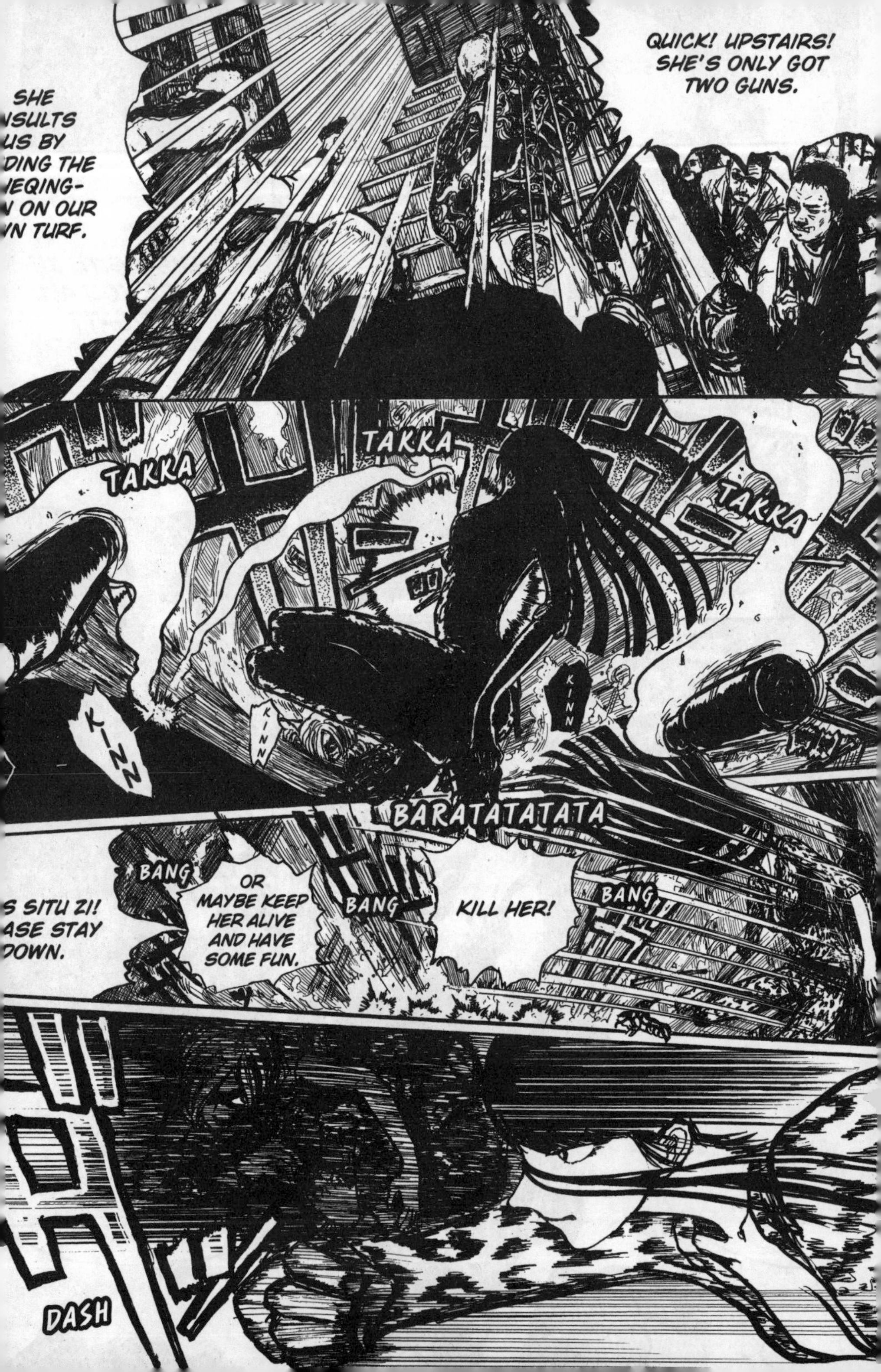
QUICK! UPSTAIRS! SHE'S ONLY GOT TWO GUNS.
SHE NSULTS US BY DING THE IEQING- N ON OUR VN TURF.
TAKKA
TAKKA
TAKKA
KINN
KINN
KINN
BARATATATATA
BANG
KILL HER!
BANG
OR MAYBE KEEP HER ALIVE AND HAVE SOME FUN.
BANG
S SITU ZI! ASE STAY DOWN.
DASH

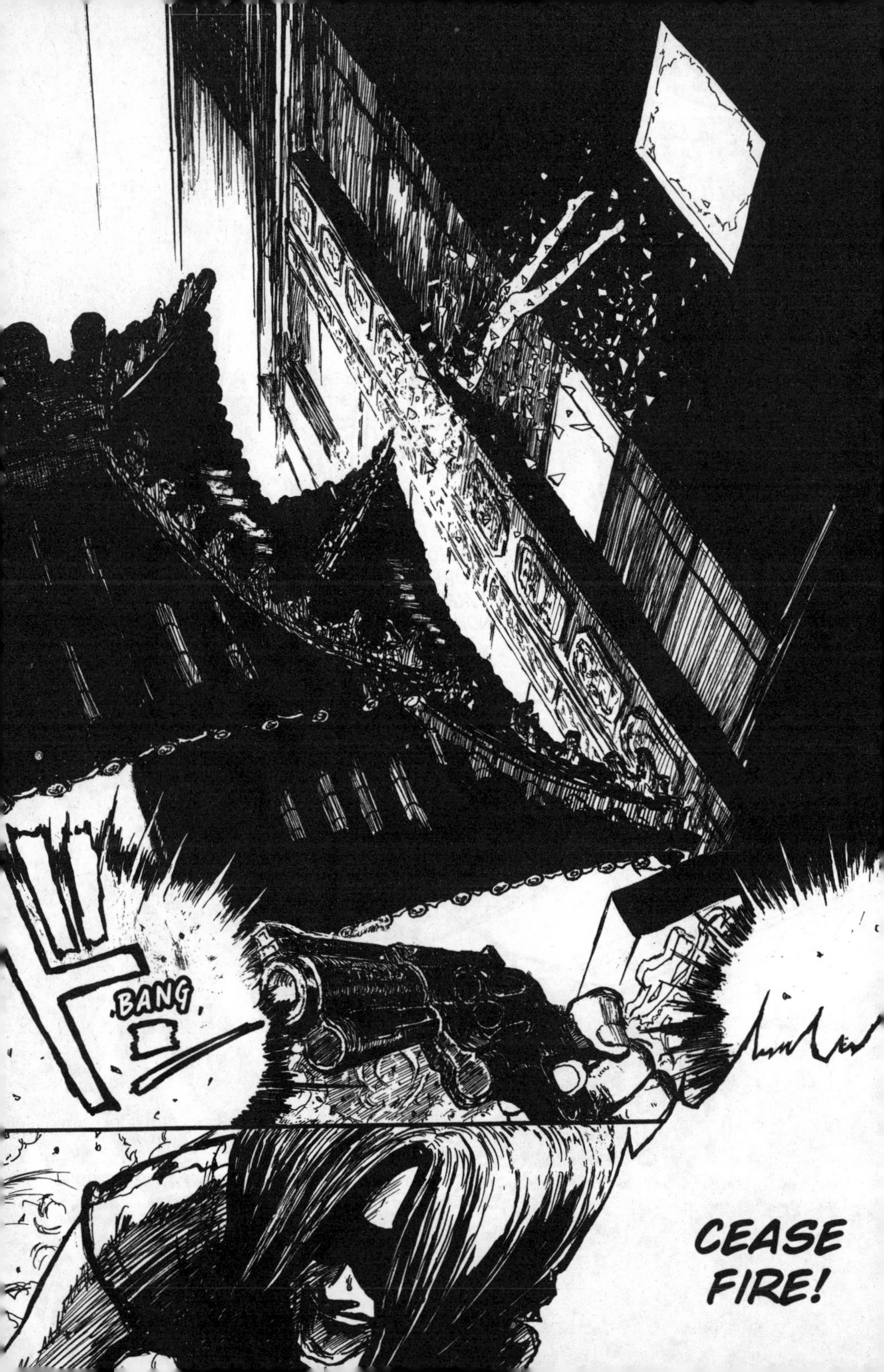
BANG
CEASE FIRE!

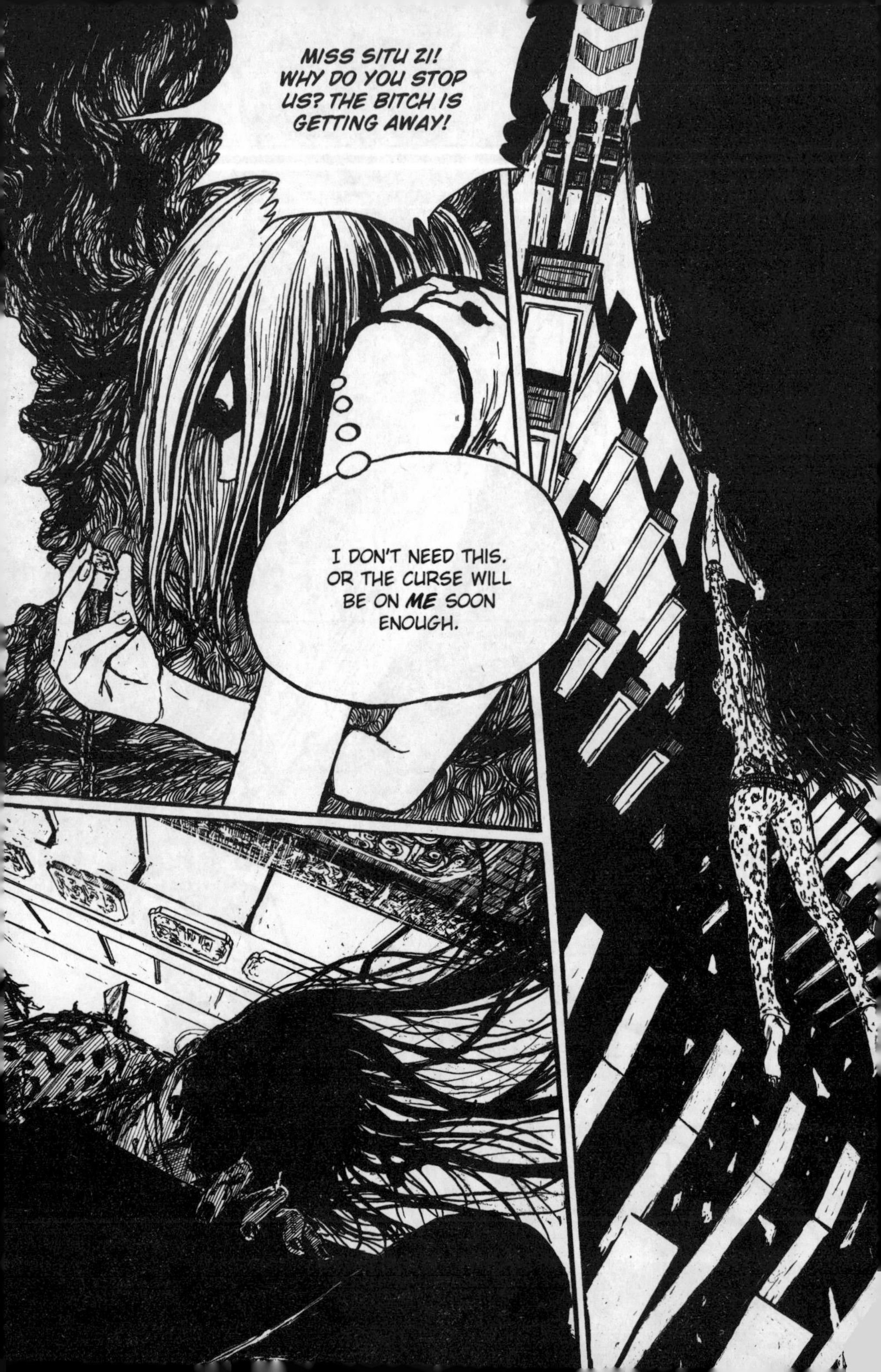
MISS SITU ZI! WHY DO YOU STOP US? THE BITCH IS GETTING AWAY!
I DON'T NEED THIS. OR THE CURSE WILL BE ON *ME* SOON ENOUGH.

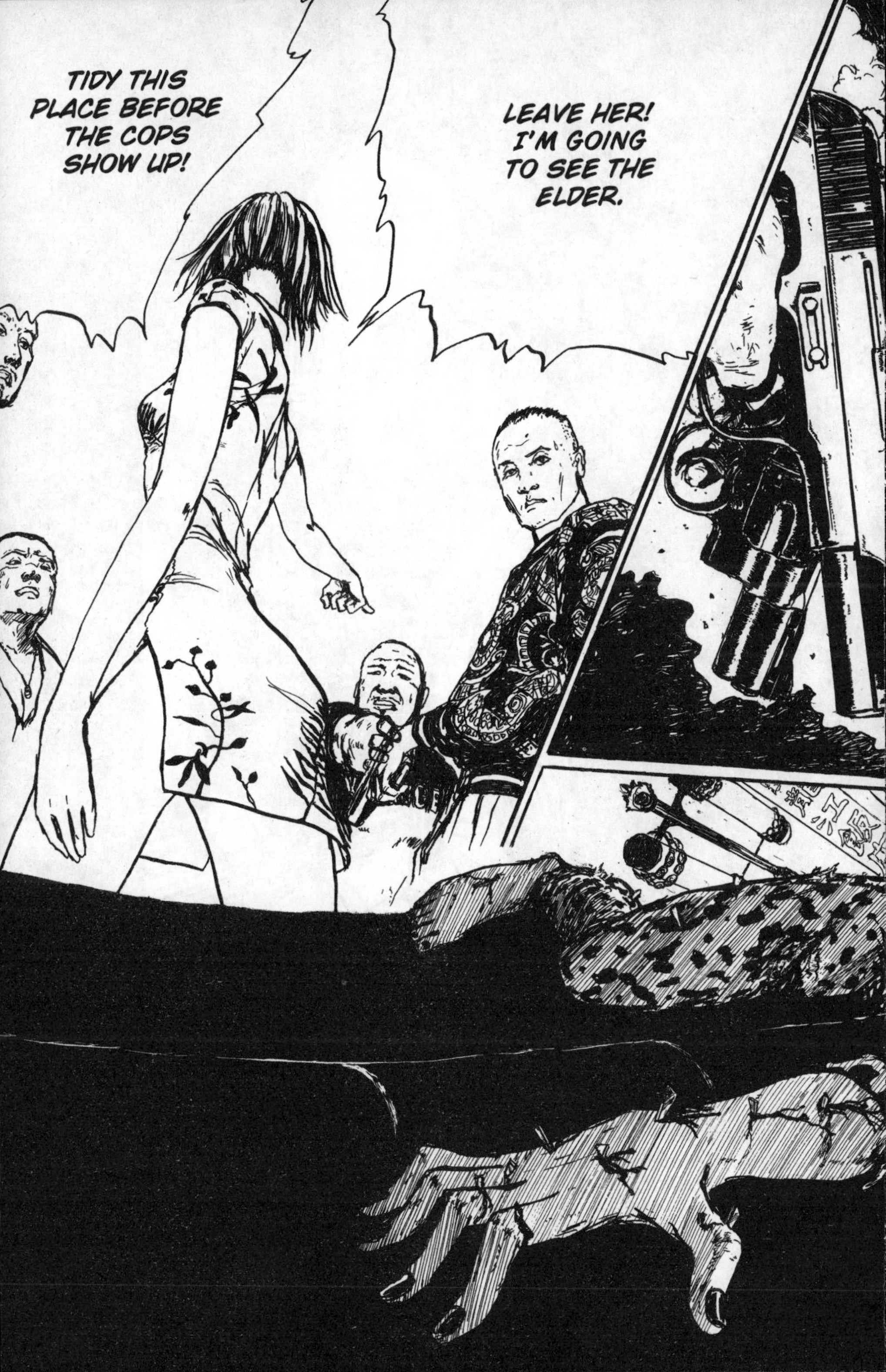
LEAVE HER! I'M GOING TO SEE THE ELDER.
TIDY THIS PLACE BEFORE THE COPS SHOW UP!

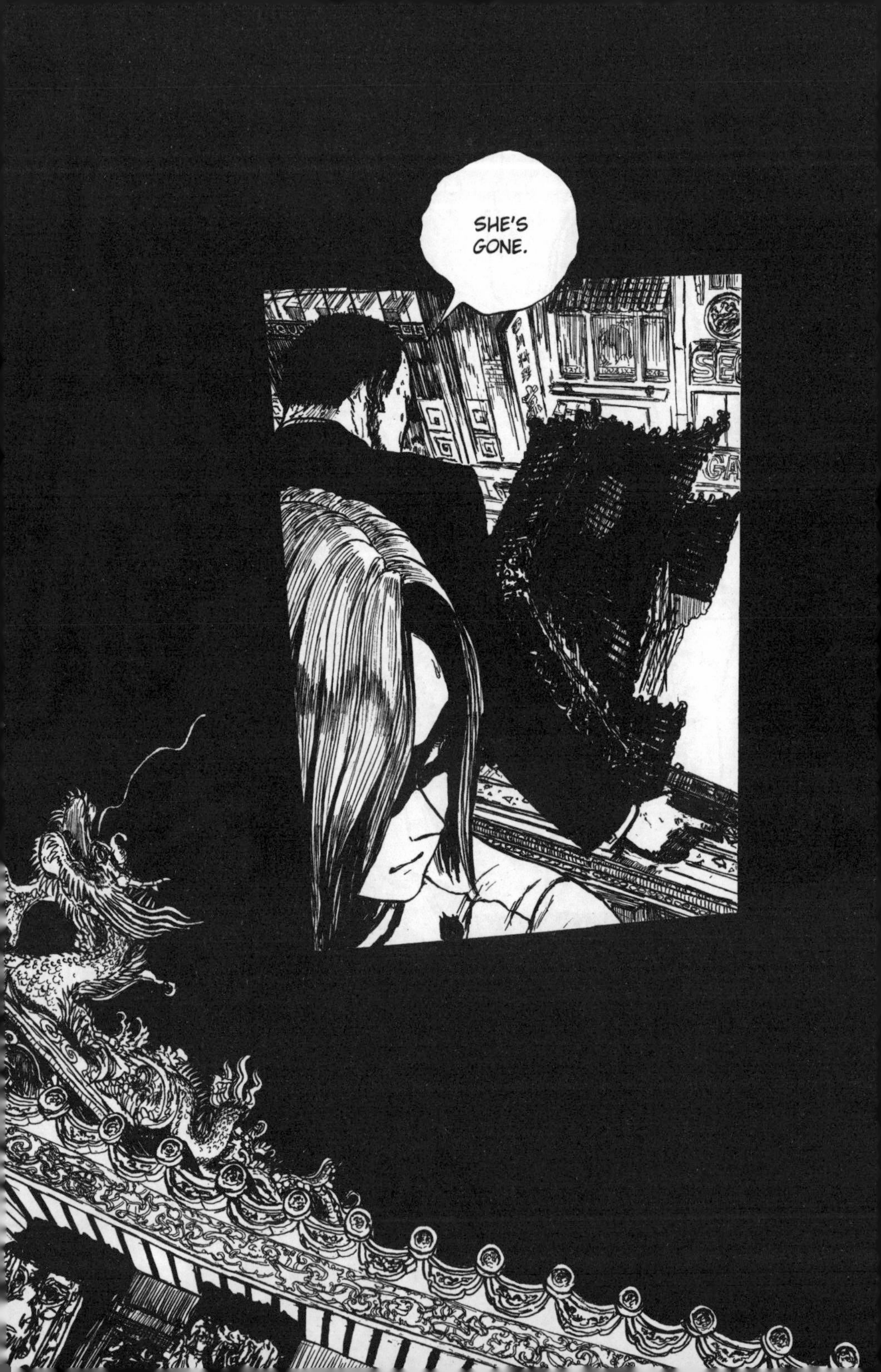
SHE'S GONE.

CHAPTER 8:
FATE AND FORTUNE

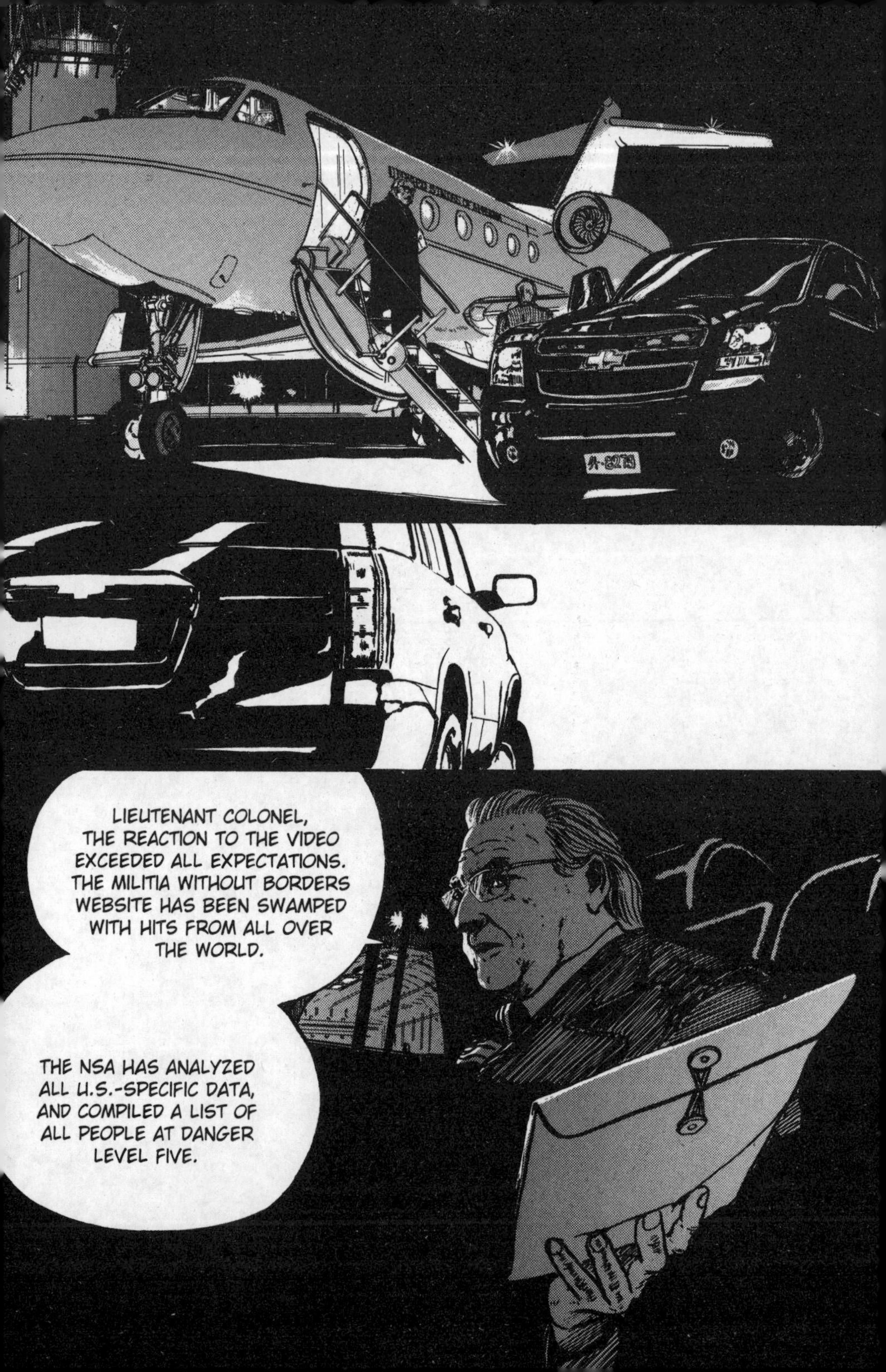
LIEUTENANT COLONEL, THE REACTION TO THE VIDEO EXCEEDED ALL EXPECTATIONS. THE MILITIA WITHOUT BORDERS WEBSITE HAS BEEN SWAMPED WITH HITS FROM ALL OVER THE WORLD.
THE NSA HAS ANALYZED ALL U.S.-SPECIFIC DATA, AND COMPILED A LIST OF ALL PEOPLE AT DANGER LEVEL FIVE.

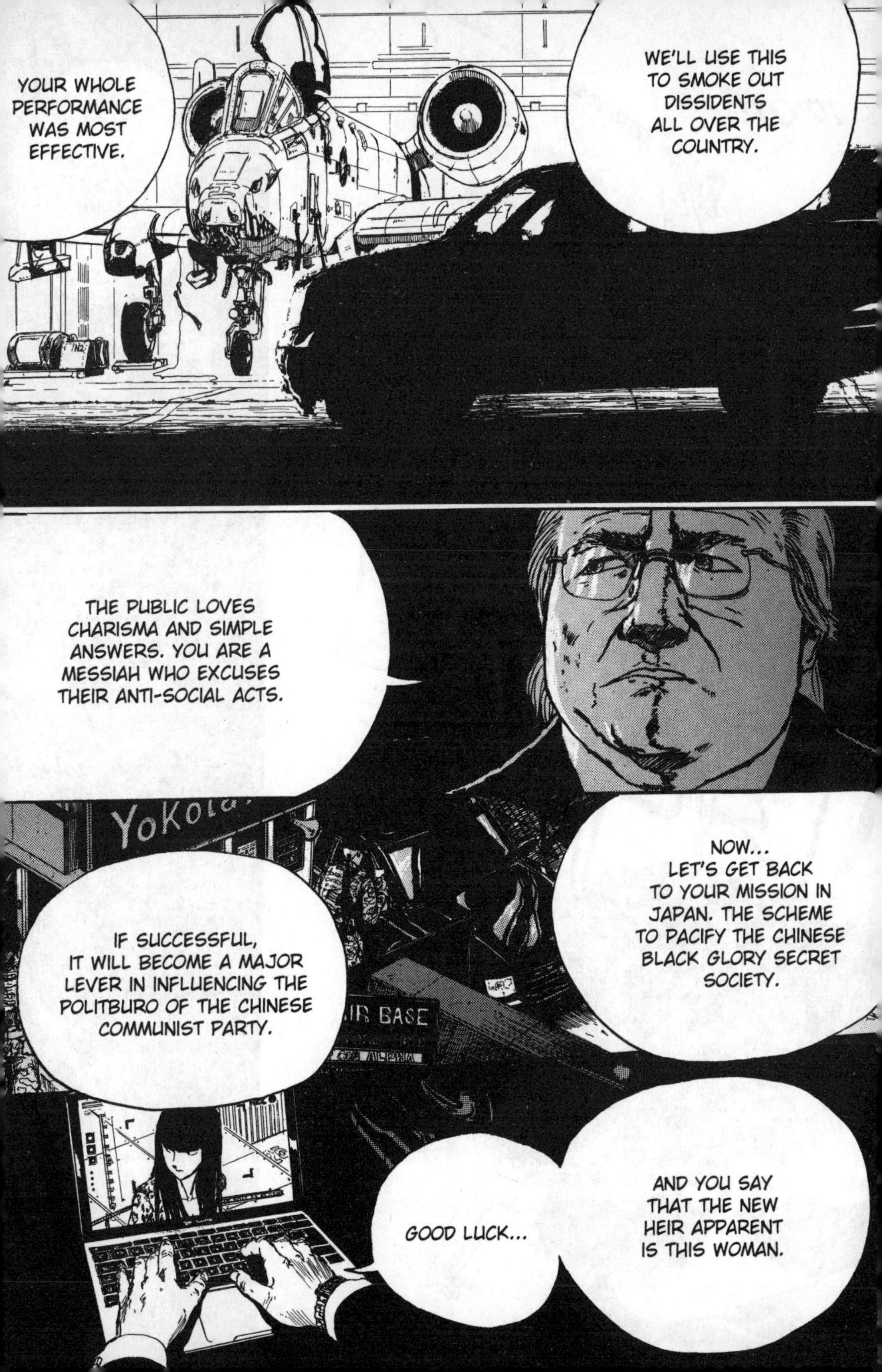
WE'LL USE THIS TO SMOKE OUT DISSIDENTS ALL OVER THE COUNTRY.
YOUR WHOLE PERFORMANCE WAS MOST EFFECTIVE.
THE PUBLIC LOVES CHARISMA AND SIMPLE ANSWERS. YOU ARE A MESSIAH WHO EXCUSES THEIR ANTI-SOCIAL ACTS.
NOW... LET'S GET BACK TO YOUR MISSION IN JAPAN. THE SCHEME TO PACIFY THE CHINESE BLACK GLORY SECRET SOCIETY.
IF SUCCESSFUL, IT WILL BECOME A MAJOR LEVER IN INFLUENCING THE POLITBURO OF THE CHINESE COMMUNIST PARTY.
AND YOU SAY THAT THE NEW HEIR APPARENT IS THIS WOMAN.
GOOD LUCK...

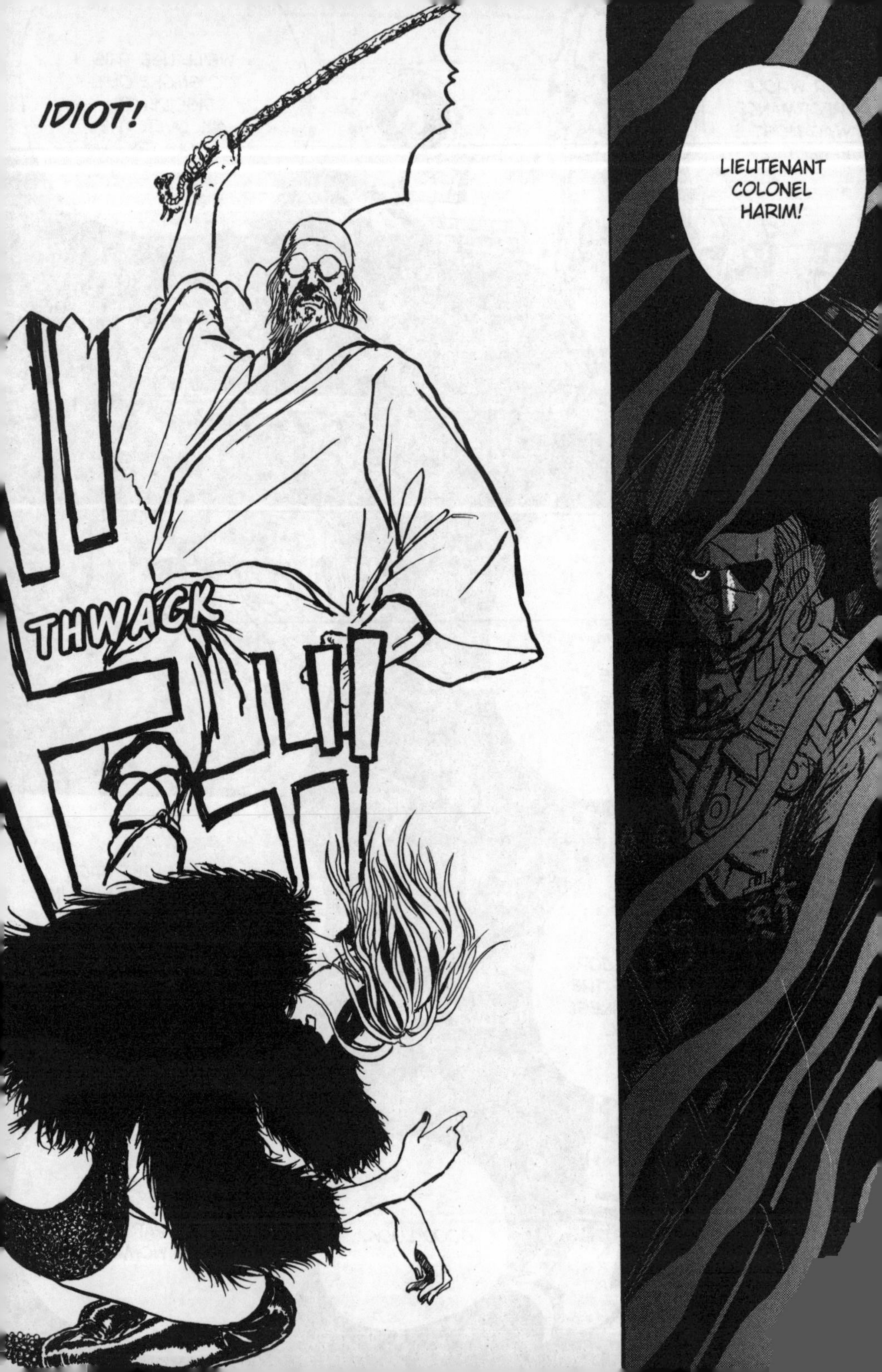
LIEUTENANT COLONEL HARIM!
IDIOT!
THWACK

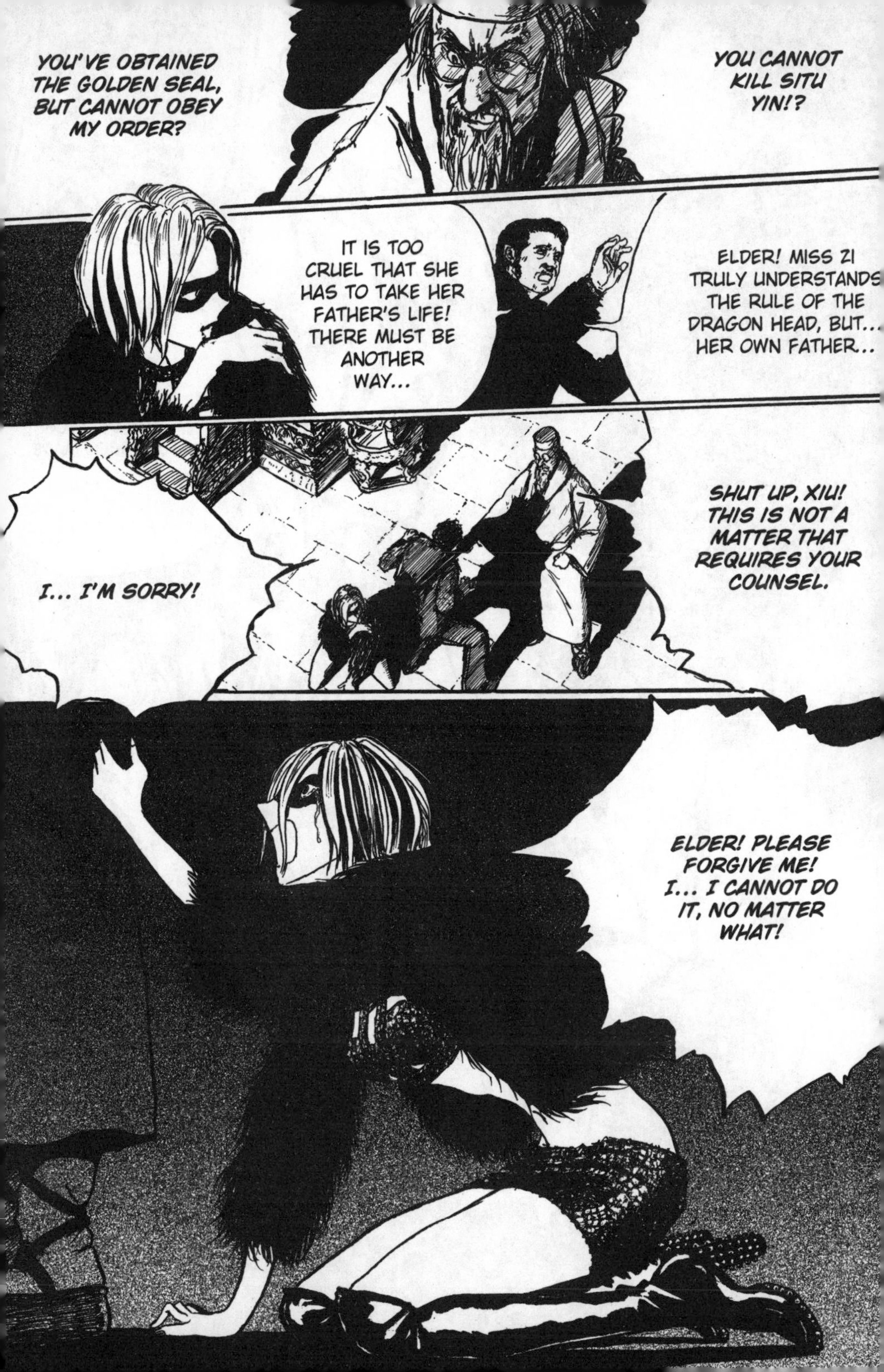
YOU CANNOT KILL SITU YIN!?
YOU'VE OBTAINED THE GOLDEN SEAL, BUT CANNOT OBEY MY ORDER?
ELDER! MISS ZI TRULY UNDERSTANDS THE RULE OF THE DRAGON HEAD, BUT... HER OWN FATHER...
IT IS TOO CRUEL THAT SHE HAS TO TAKE HER FATHER'S LIFE! THERE MUST BE ANOTHER WAY...
SHUT UP, XIU! THIS IS NOT A MATTER THAT REQUIRES YOUR COUNSEL.
I... I'M SORRY!
ELDER! PLEASE FORGIVE ME! I... I CANNOT DO IT, NO MATTER WHAT!

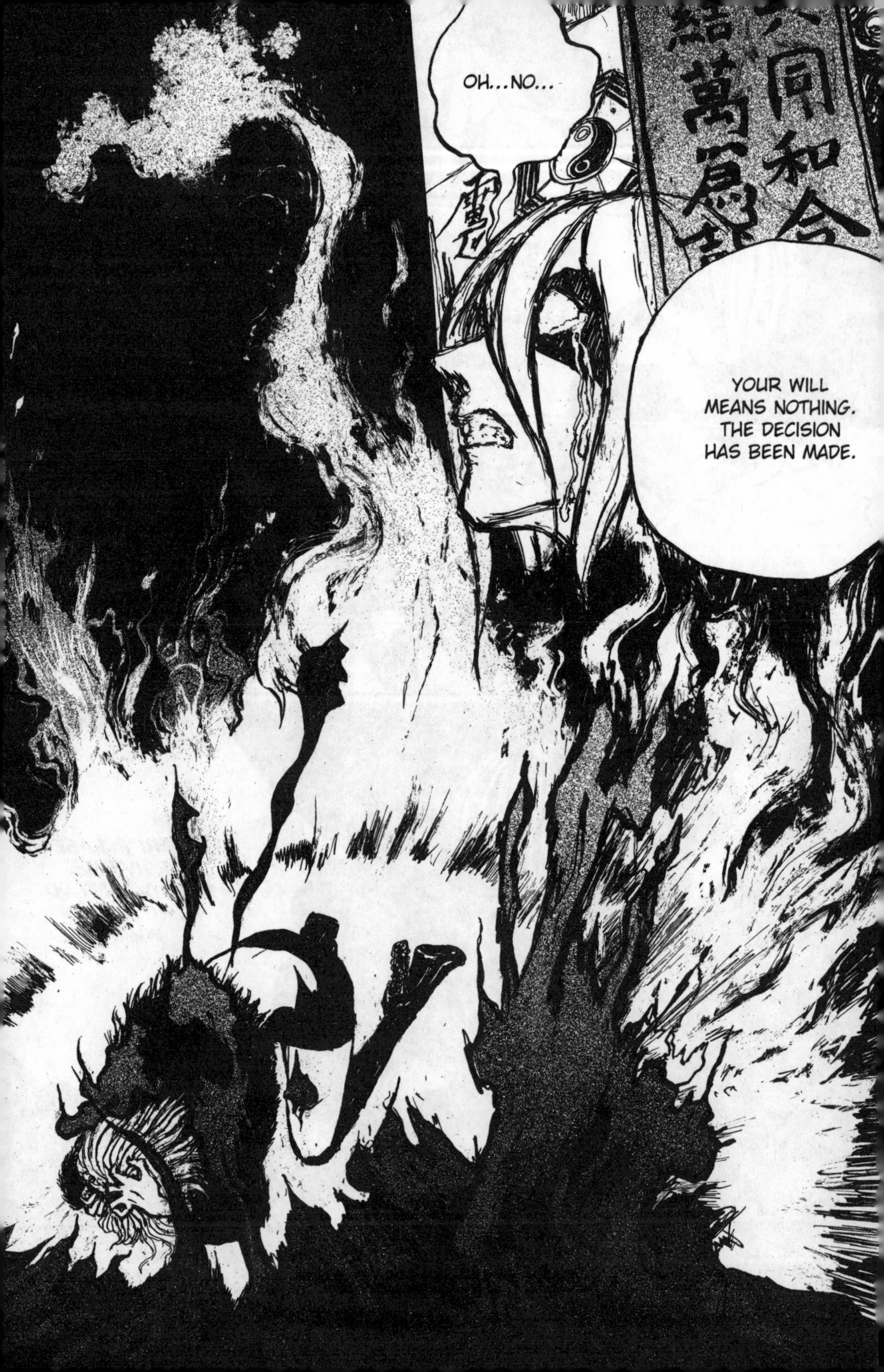
OH...NO...
YOUR WILL MEANS NOTHING. THE DECISION HAS BEEN MADE.

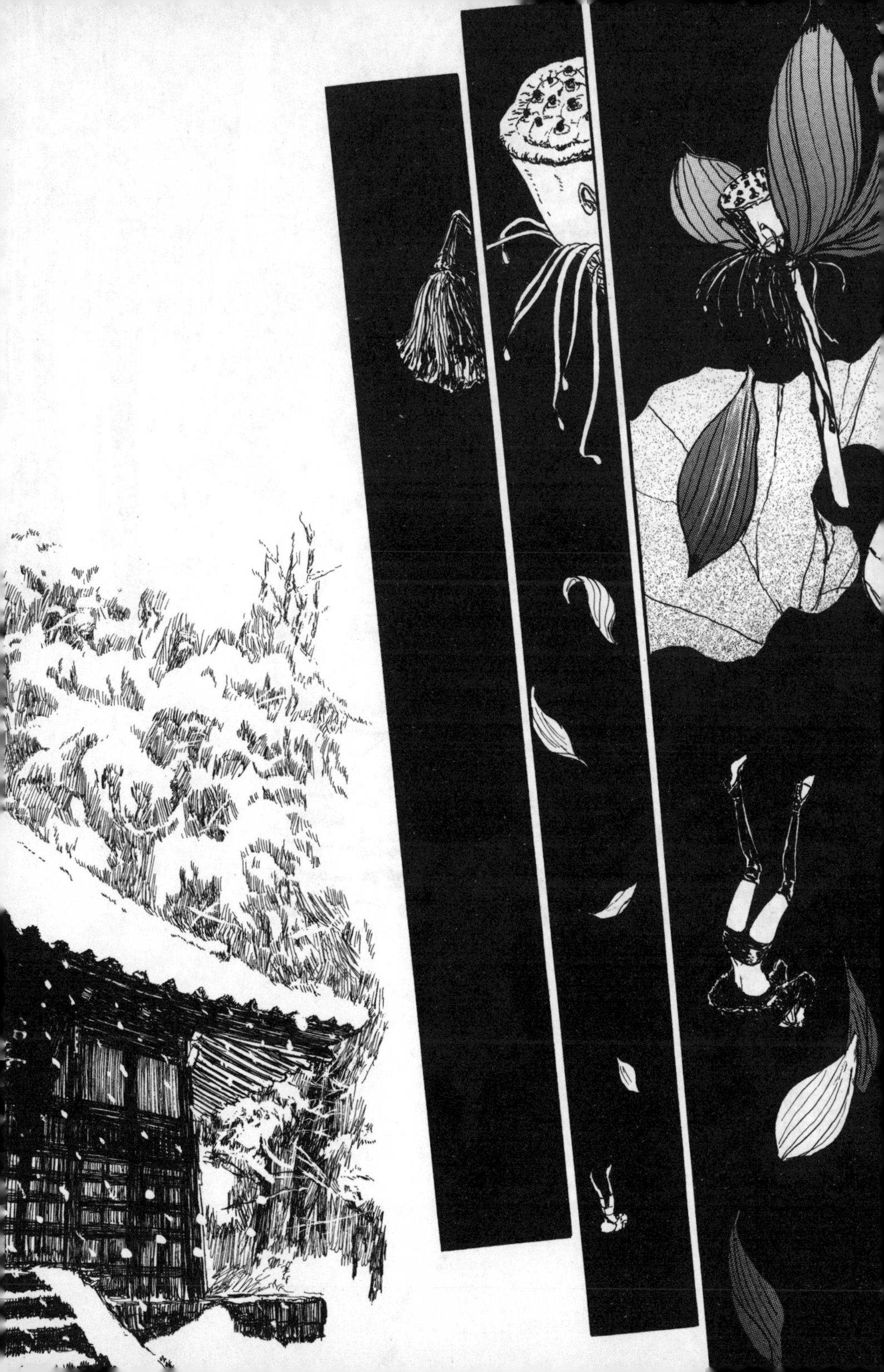

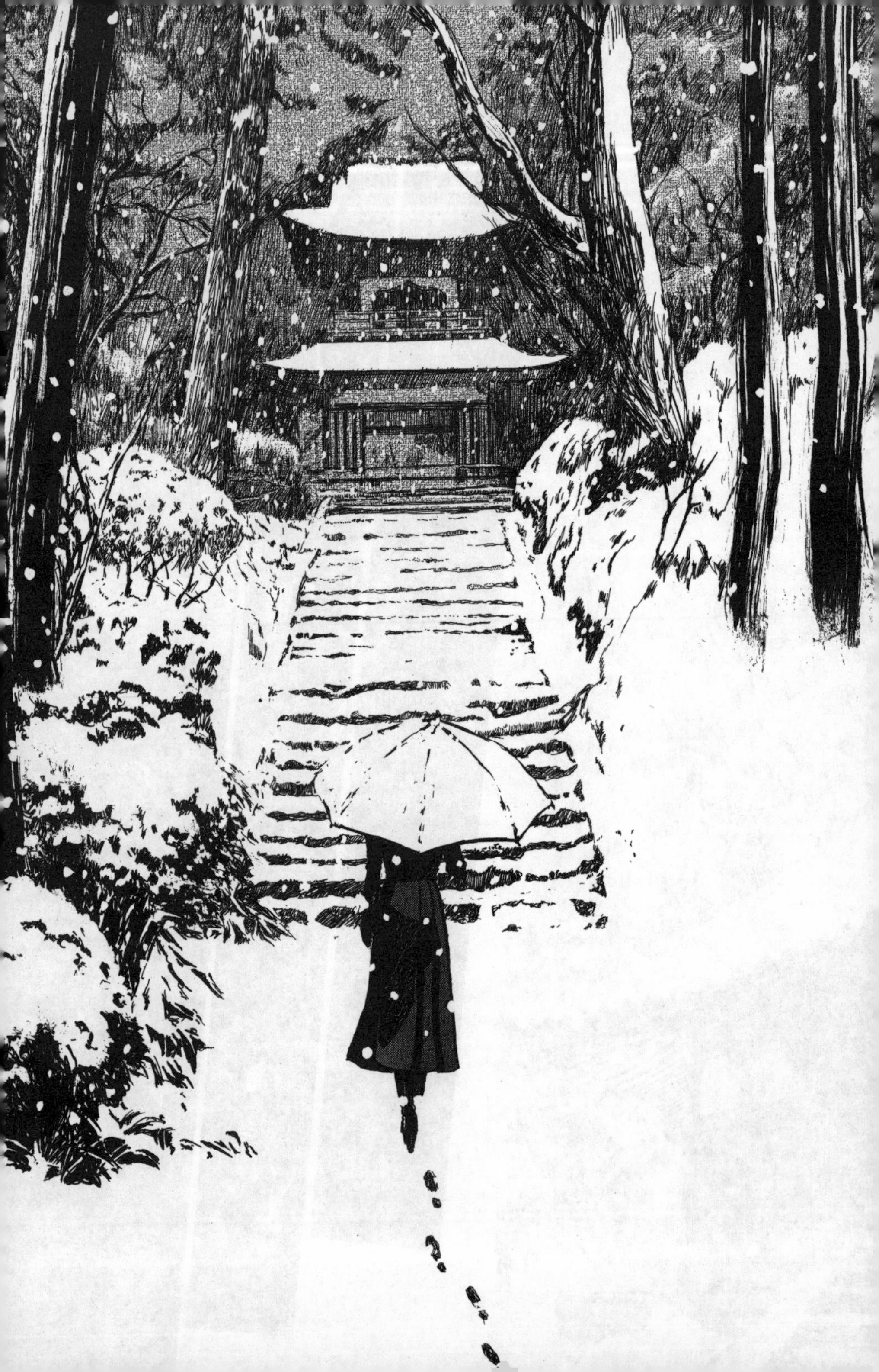

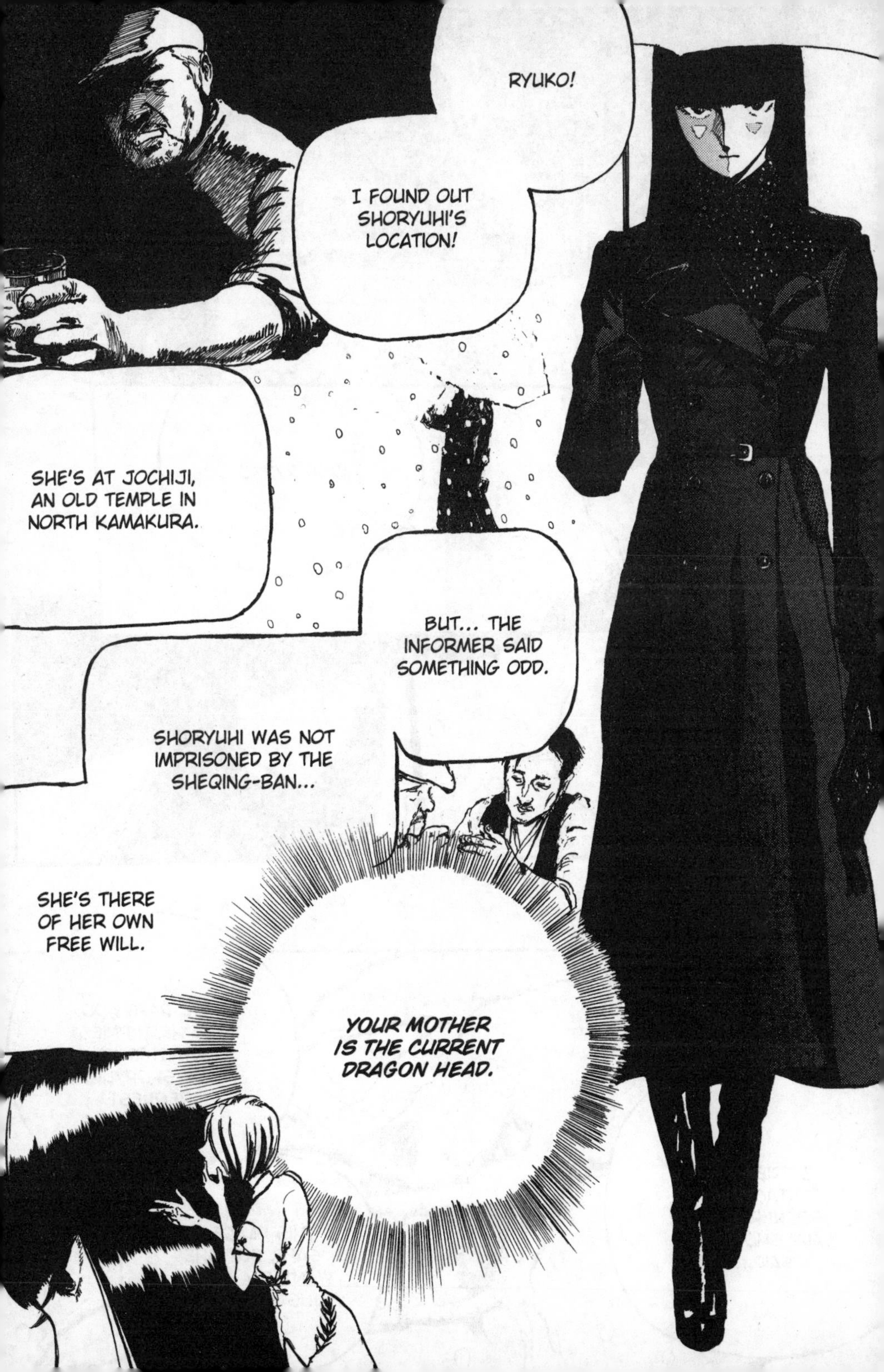
RYUKO!
I FOUND OUT SHORYUHI'S LOCATION!
SHE'S AT JOCHIJI, AN OLD TEMPLE IN NORTH KAMAKURA.
BUT... THE INFORMER SAID SOMETHING ODD.
SHORYUHI WAS NOT IMPRISONED BY THE SHEQING-BAN...
SHE'S THERE OF HER OWN FREE WILL.
YOUR MOTHER IS THE CURRENT DRAGON HEAD.

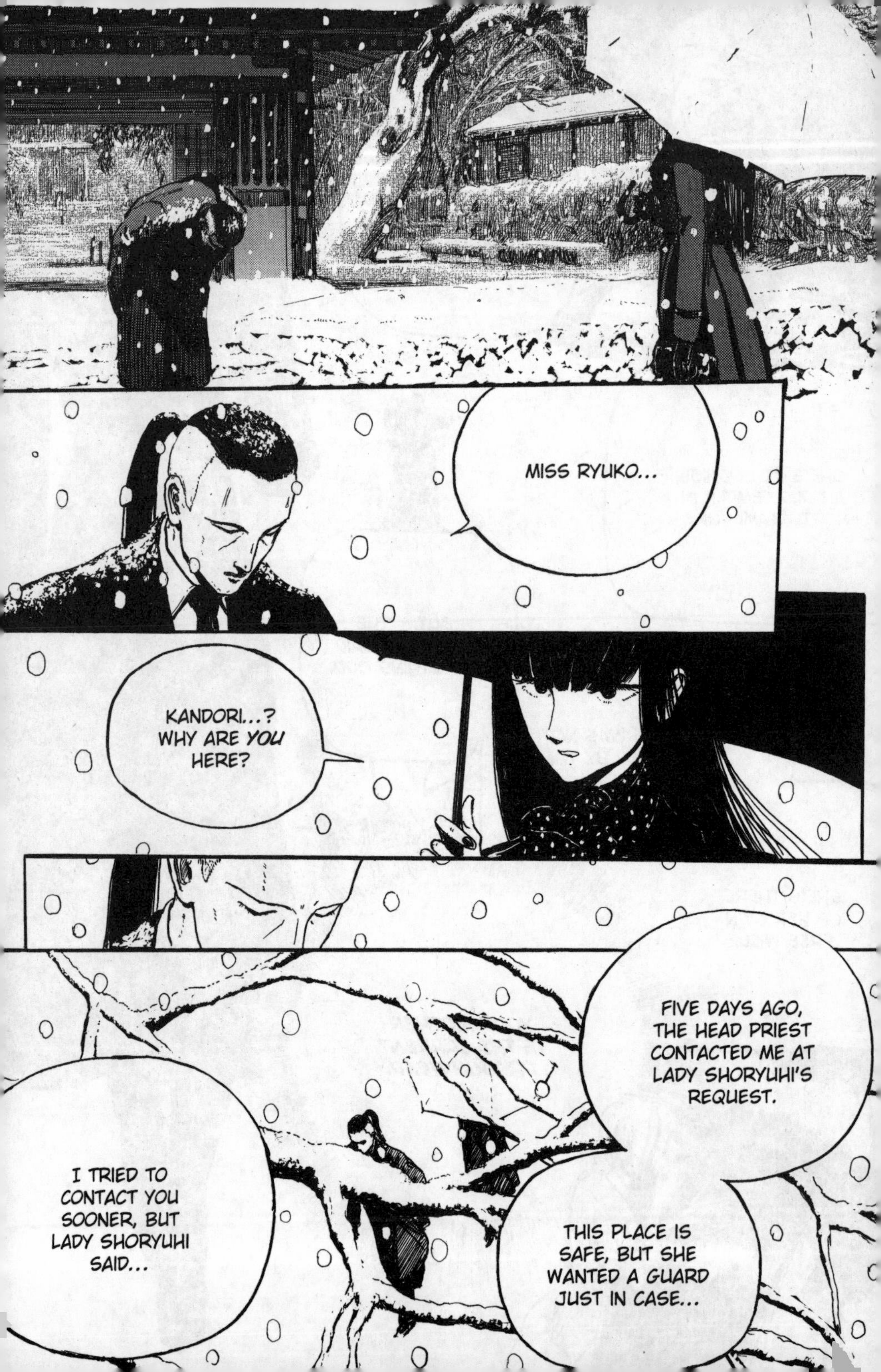
MISS RYUKO...
KANDORI...? WHY ARE *YOU* HERE?
FIVE DAYS AGO, THE HEAD PRIEST CONTACTED ME AT LADY SHORYUHI'S REQUEST.
THIS PLACE IS SAFE, BUT SHE WANTED A GUARD JUST IN CASE...
I TRIED TO CONTACT YOU SOONER, BUT LADY SHORYUHI SAID...

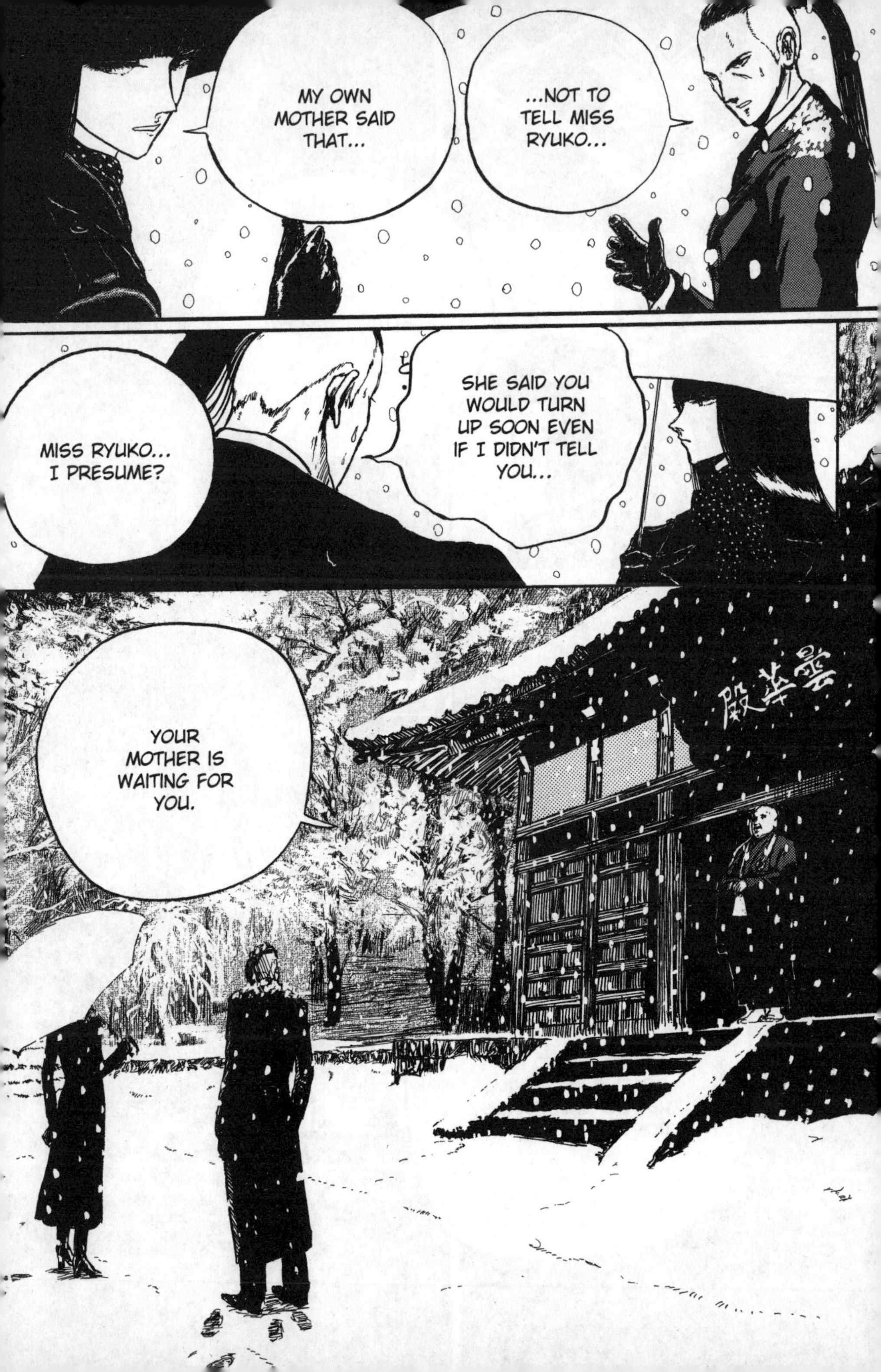
MY OWN MOTHER SAID THAT...
...NOT TO TELL MISS RYUKO...
MISS RYUKO... I PRESUME?
SHE SAID YOU WOULD TURN UP SOON EVEN IF I DIDN'T TELL YOU...
YOUR MOTHER IS WAITING FOR YOU.
曇華殿

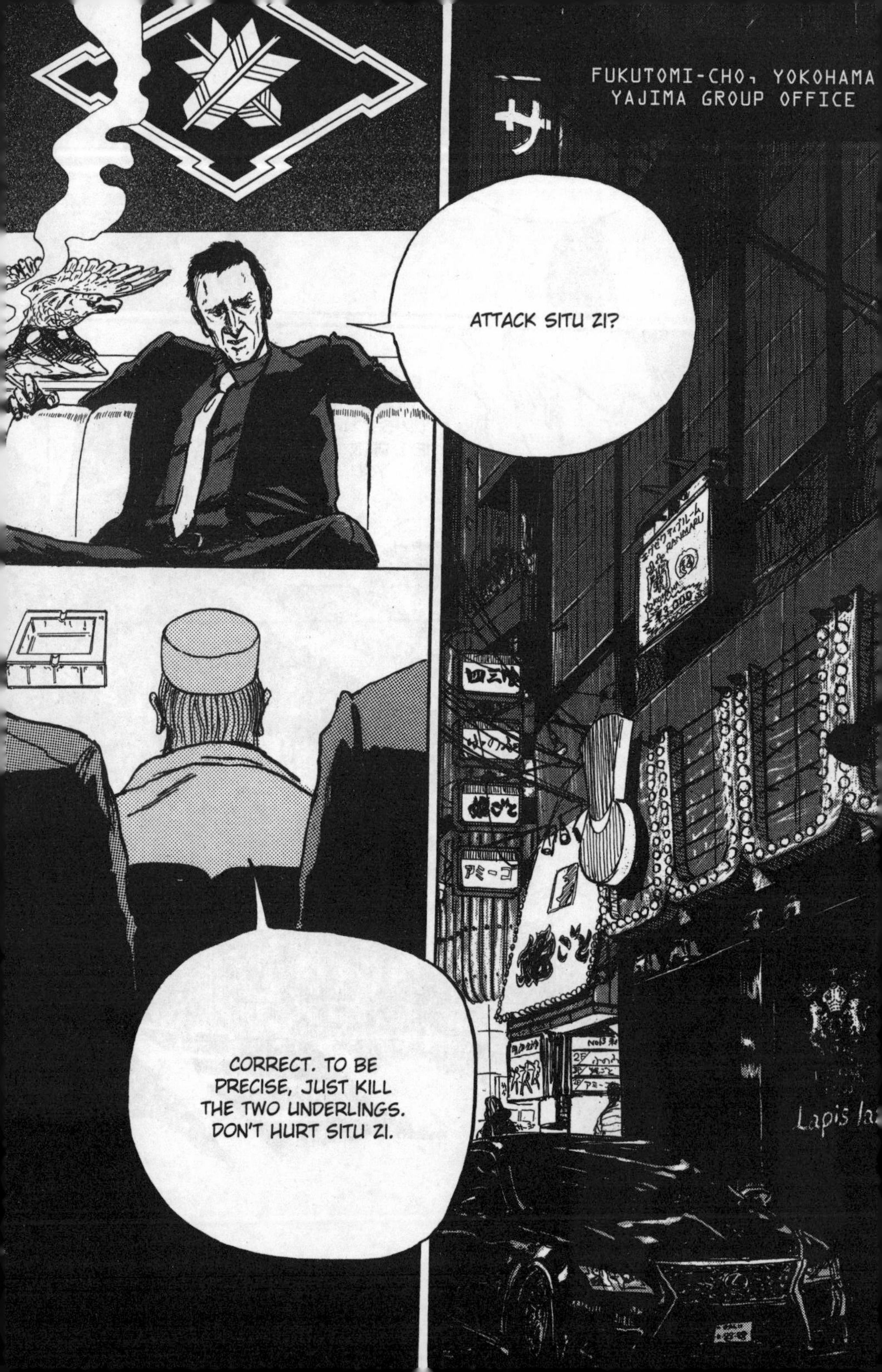
FUKUTOMI-CHO, YOKOHAMA
YAJIMA GROUP OFFICE
ATTACK SITU ZI?
CORRECT. TO BE PRECISE, JUST KILL THE TWO UNDERLINGS. DON'T HURT SITU ZI.

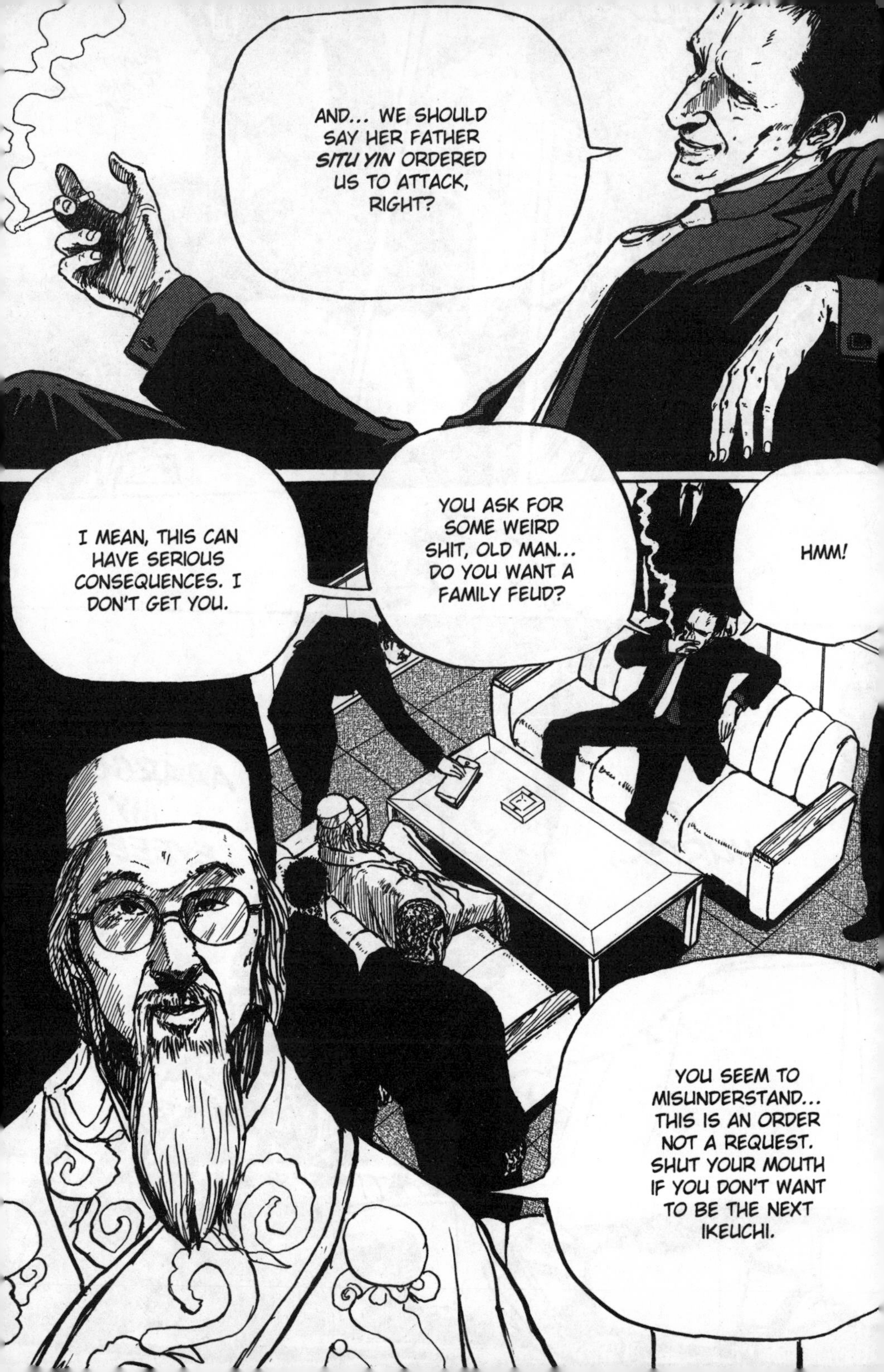
AND... WE SHOULD SAY HER FATHER *SITU YIN* ORDERED US TO ATTACK, RIGHT?
HMM!
YOU ASK FOR SOME WEIRD SHIT, OLD MAN... DO YOU WANT A FAMILY FEUD?
I MEAN, THIS CAN HAVE SERIOUS CONSEQUENCES. I DON'T GET YOU.
YOU SEEM TO MISUNDERSTAND... THIS IS AN ORDER NOT A REQUEST. SHUT YOUR MOUTH IF YOU DON'T WANT TO BE THE NEXT IKEUCHI.

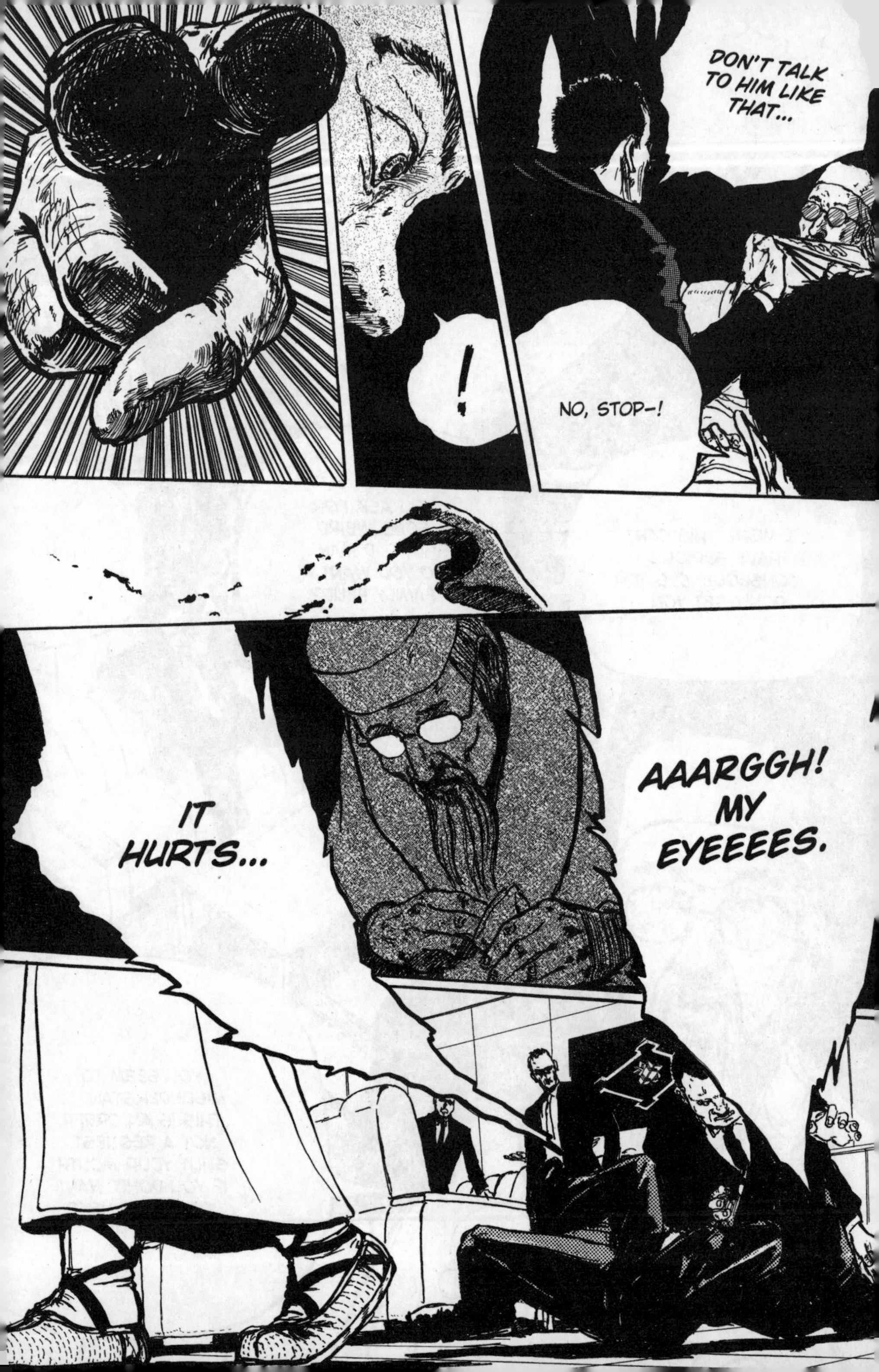
DON'T TALK TO HIM LIKE THAT...
NO, STOP-!
!
AAARGGH! MY EYEEEES.
IT HURTS...

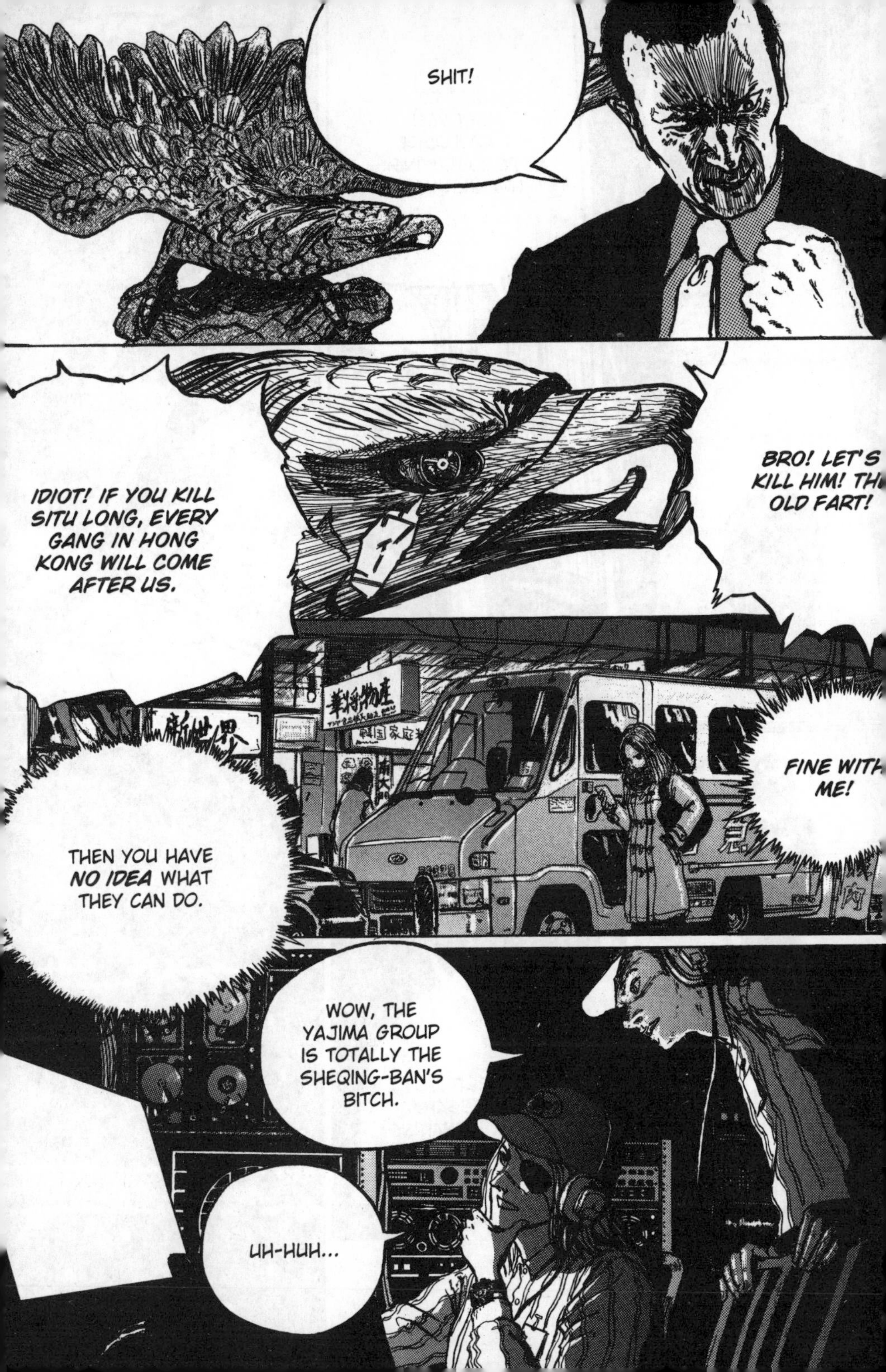
SHIT!
BRO! LET'S KILL HIM! TH OLD FART!
IDIOT! IF YOU KILL SITU LONG, EVERY GANG IN HONG KONG WILL COME AFTER US.
FINE WITH ME!
THEN YOU HAVE *NO IDEA* WHAT THEY CAN DO.
WOW, THE YAJIMA GROUP IS TOTALLY THE SHEQING-BAN'S BITCH.
UH-HUH...

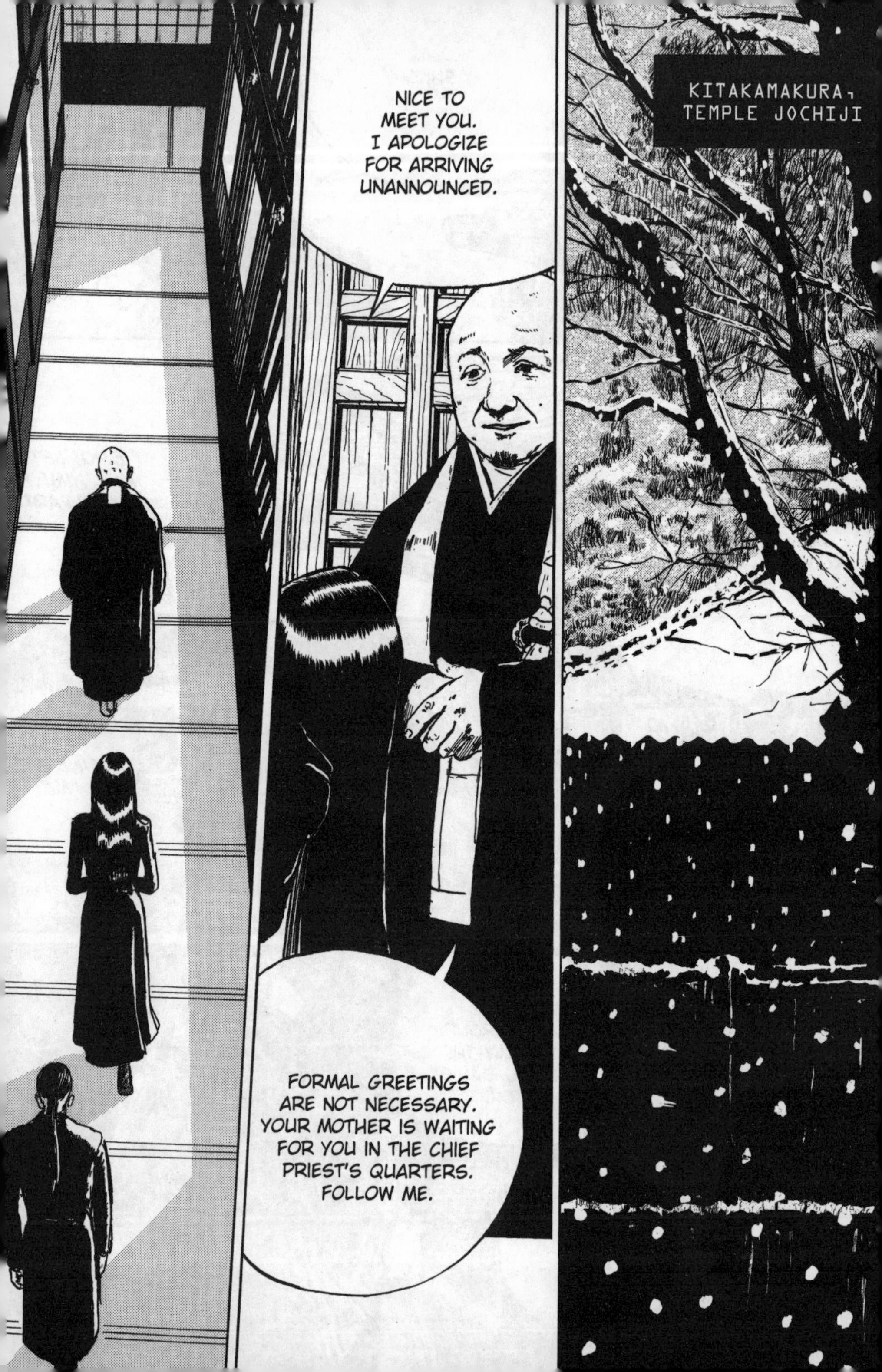
KITAKAMAKURA, TEMPLE JOCHIJI
NICE TO MEET YOU. I APOLOGIZE FOR ARRIVING UNANNOUNCED.
FORMAL GREETINGS ARE NOT NECESSARY. YOUR MOTHER IS WAITING FOR YOU IN THE CHIEF PRIEST'S QUARTERS. FOLLOW ME.

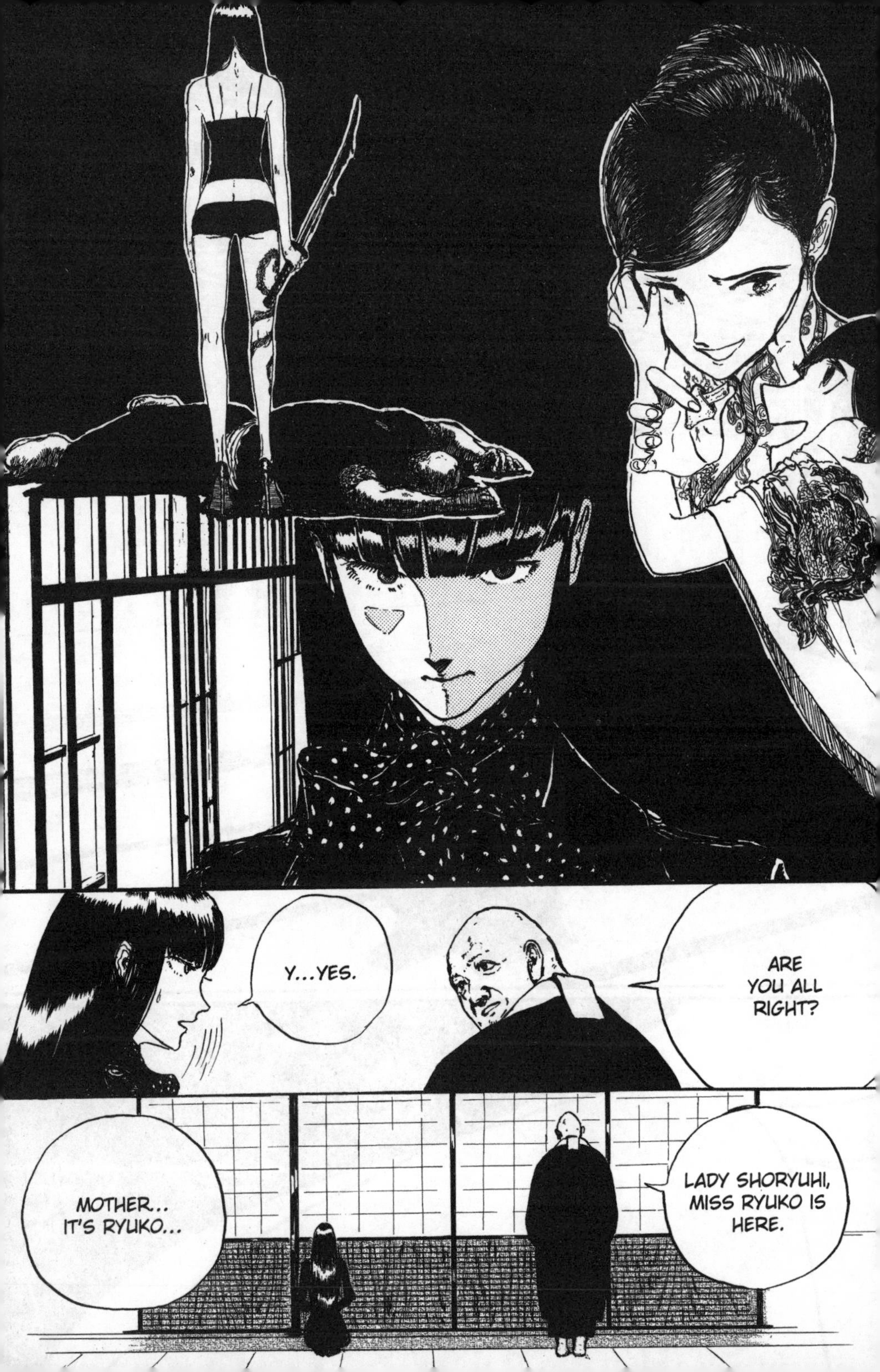
ARE YOU ALL RIGHT?
Y...YES.
LADY SHORYUHI, MISS RYUKO IS HERE.
MOTHER... IT'S RYUKO...

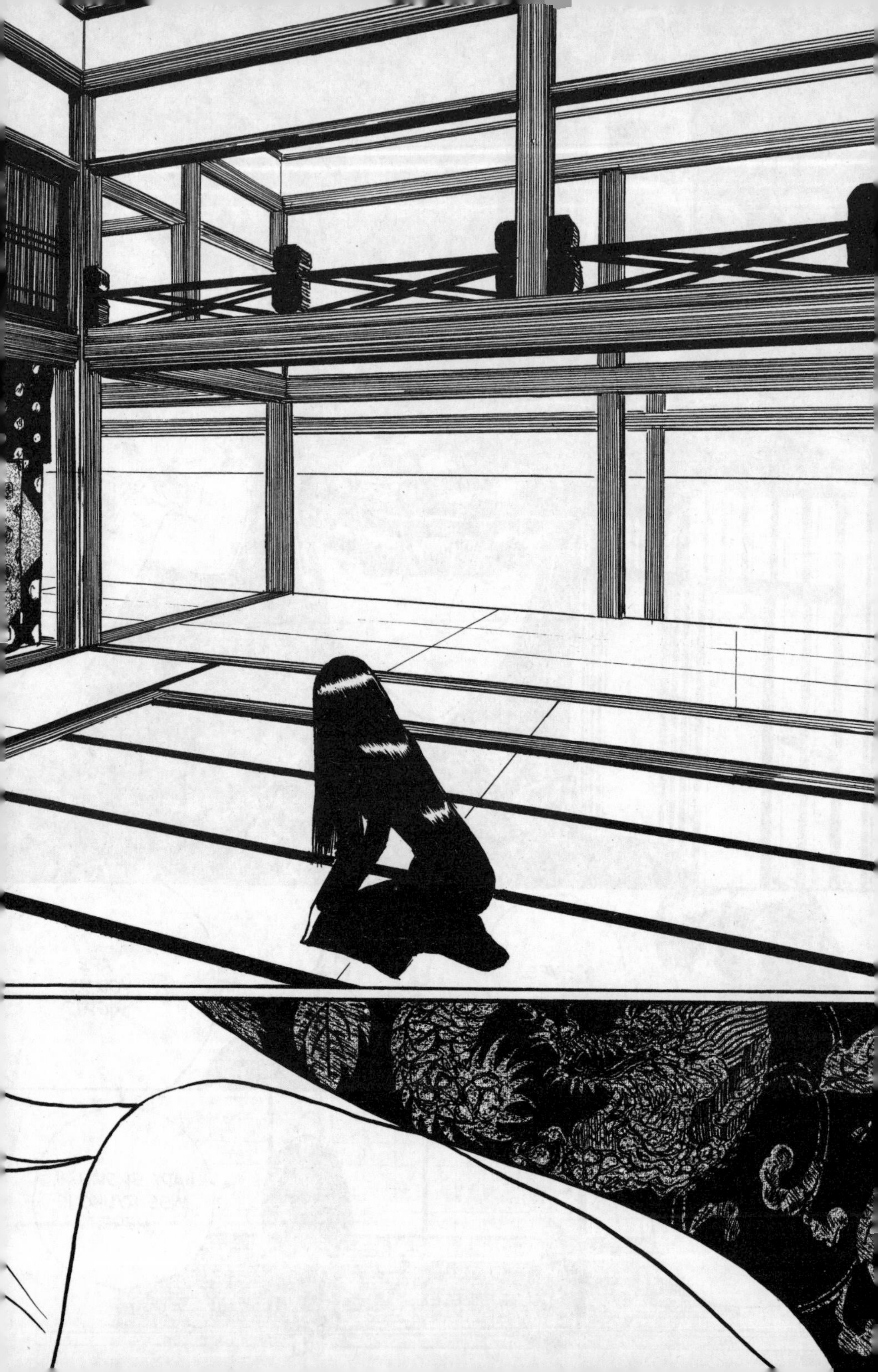

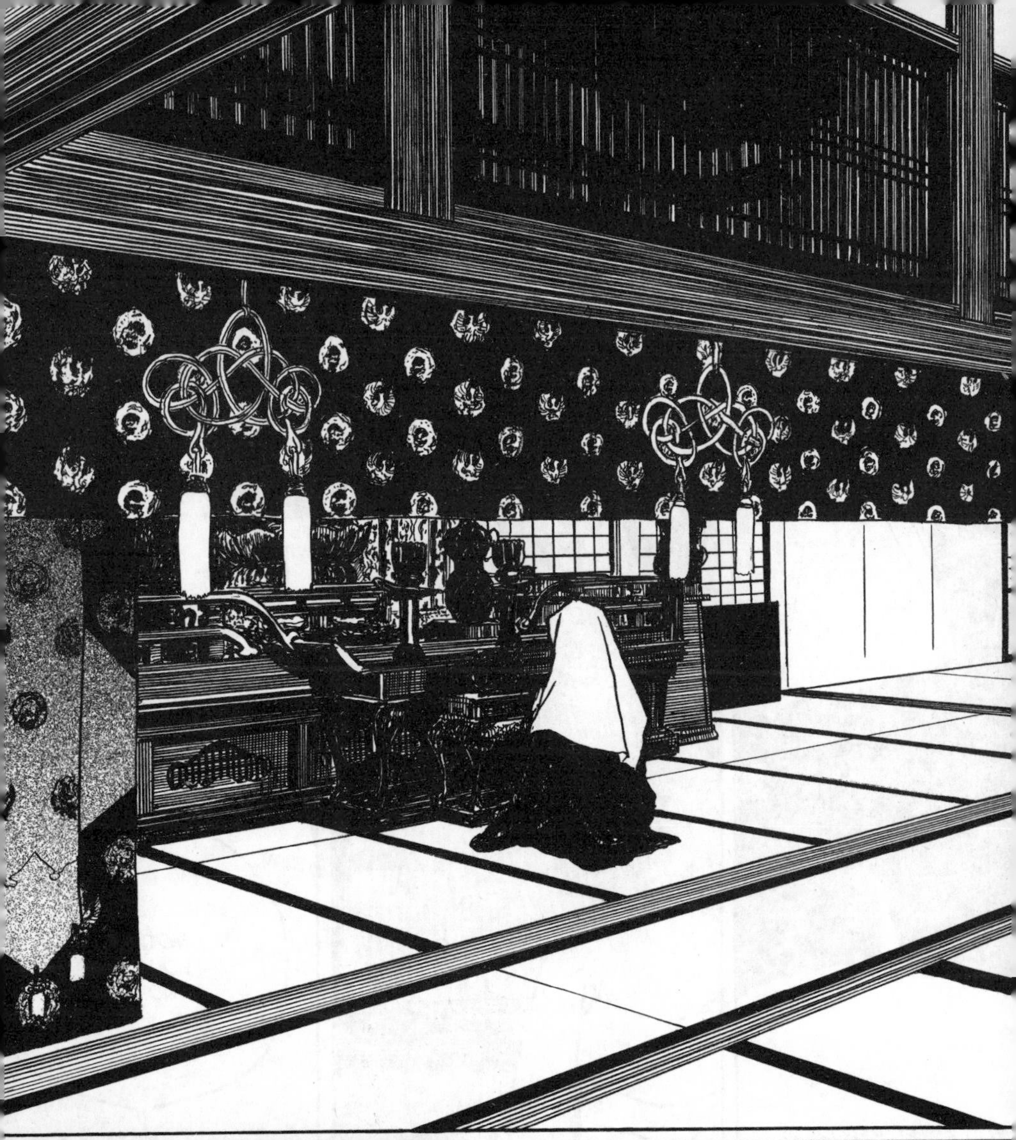
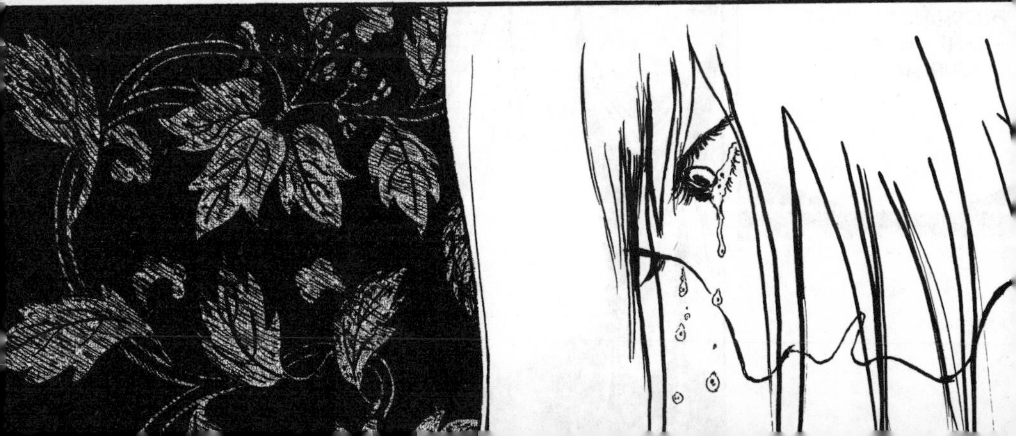

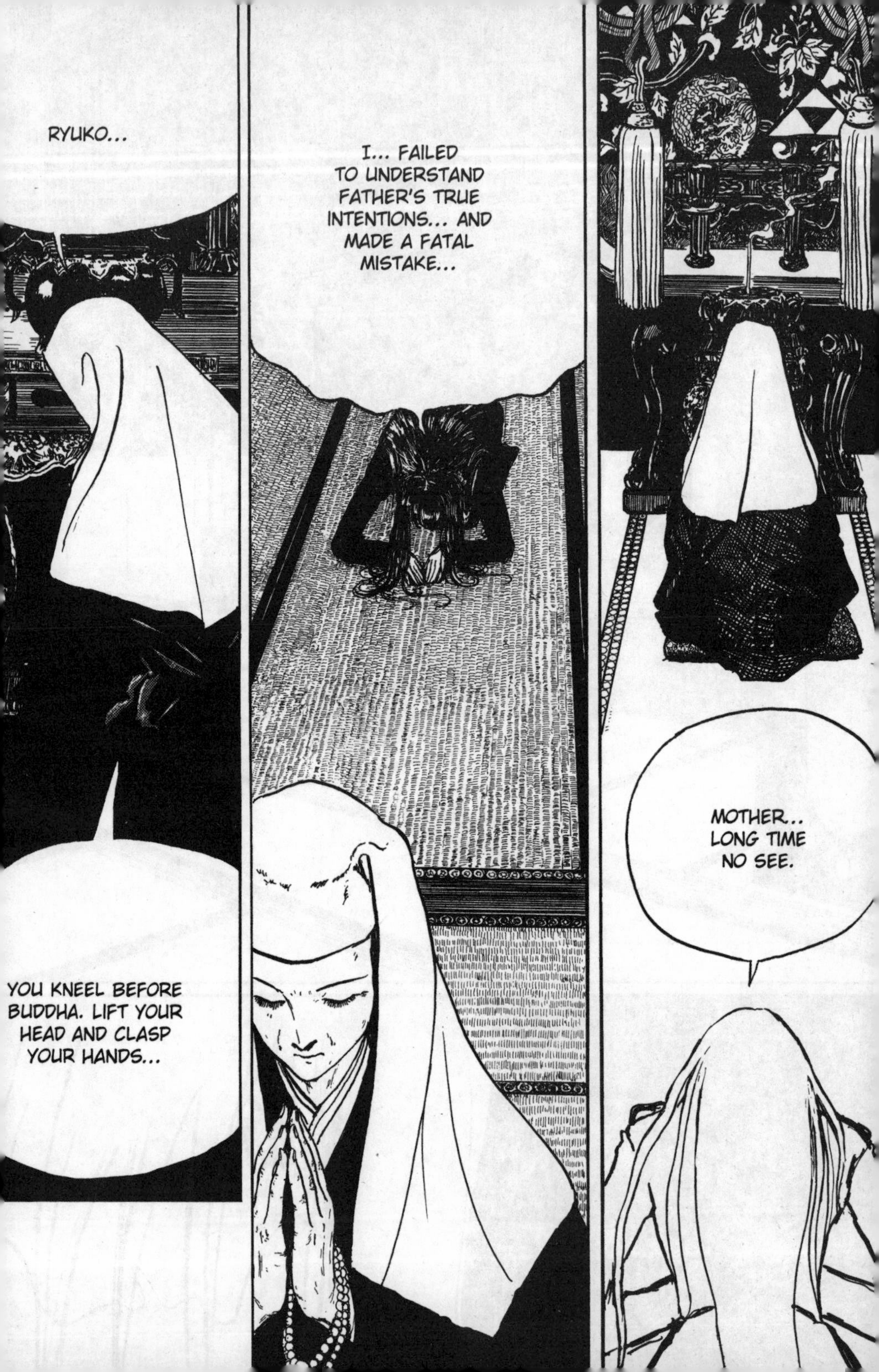
MOTHER.. LONG TIME NO SEE.
I... FAILED TO UNDERSTAND FATHER'S TRUE INTENTIONS... AND MADE A FATAL MISTAKE...
RYUKO...
YOU KNEEL BEFORE BUDDHA. LIFT YOUR HEAD AND CLASP YOUR HANDS...

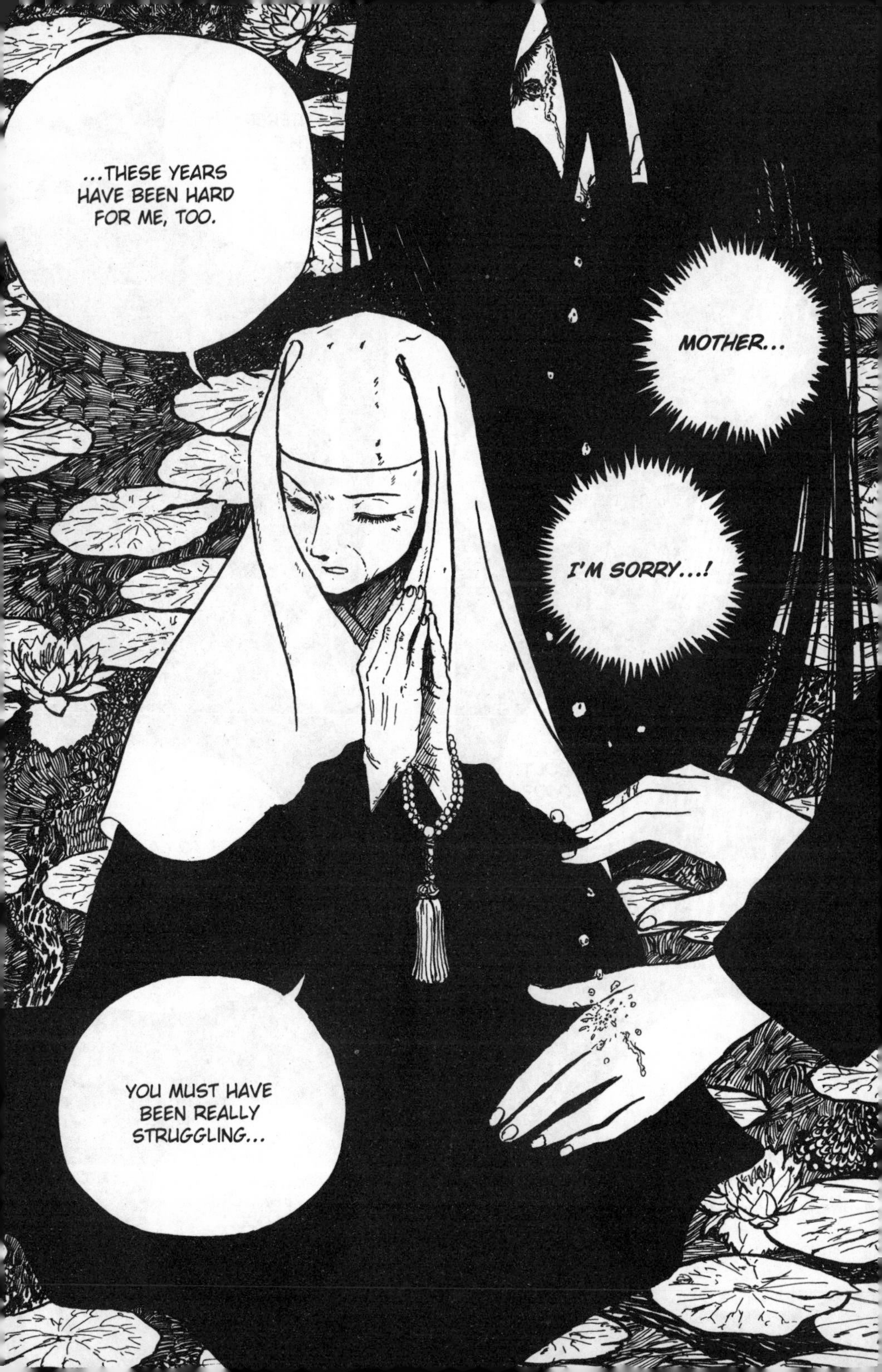
MOTHER...
I'M SORRY...!
YOU MUST HAVE BEEN REALLY STRUGGLING...
...THESE YEARS HAVE BEEN HARD FOR ME, TOO.

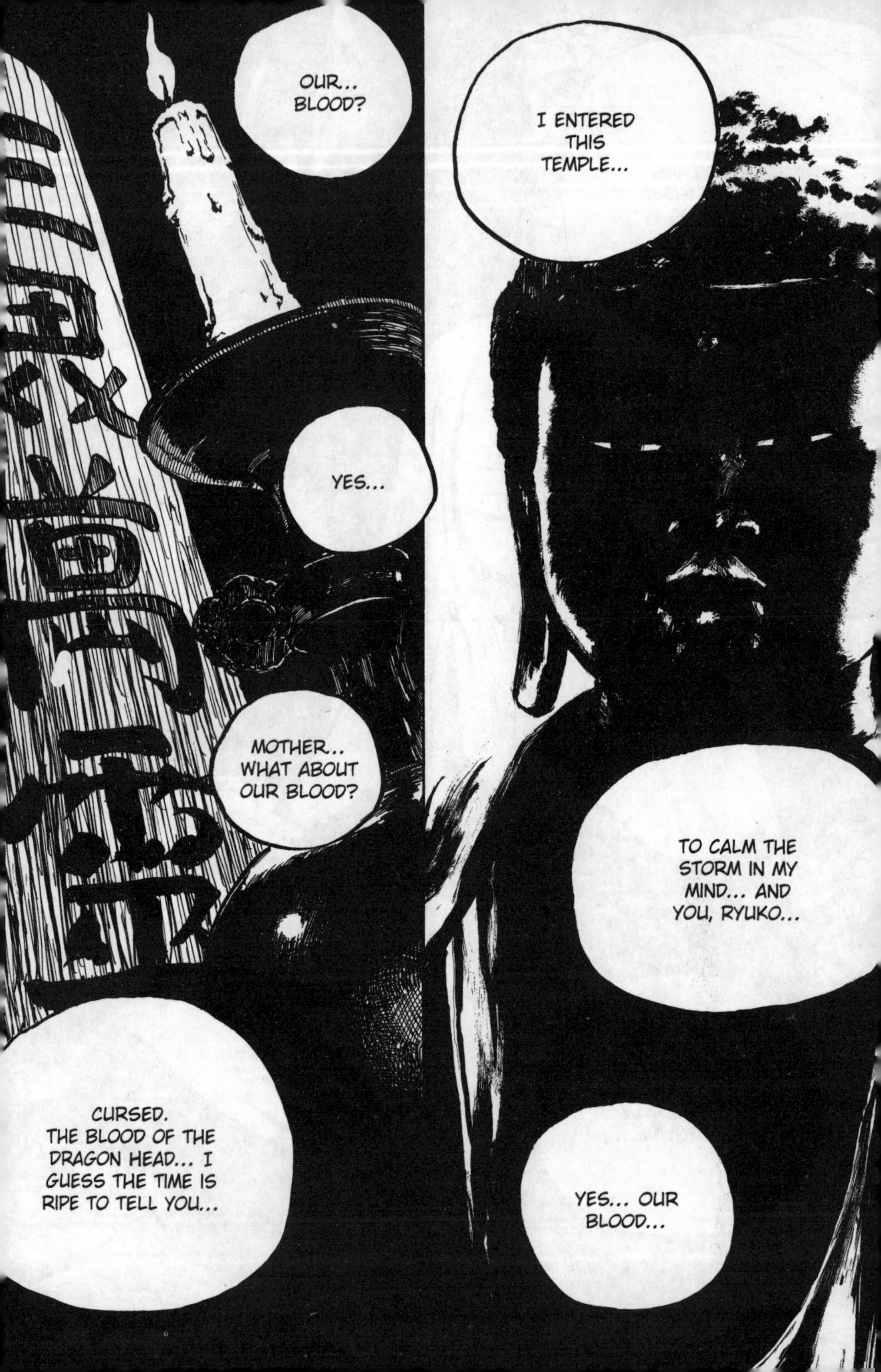
I ENTERED THIS TEMPLE...
TO CALM THE STORM IN MY MIND... AND YOU, RYUKO...
YES... OUR BLOOD...
OUR... BLOOD?
YES...
MOTHER... WHAT ABOUT OUR BLOOD?
CURSED. THE BLOOD OF THE DRAGON HEAD... I GUESS THE TIME IS RIPE TO TELL YOU...

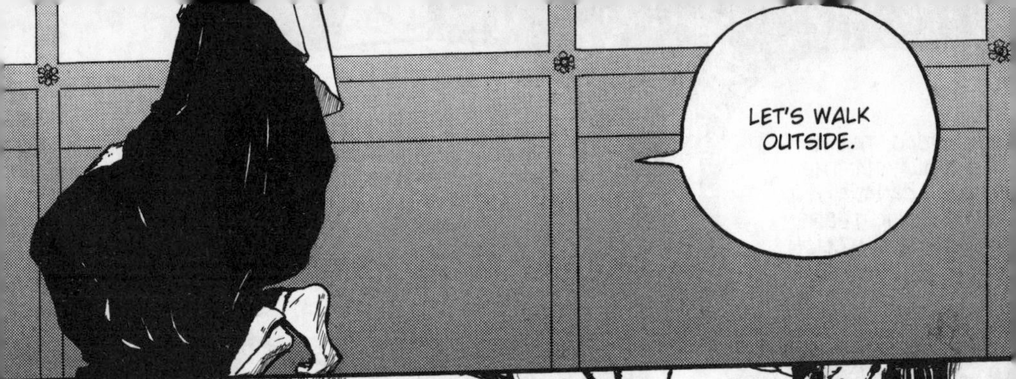
LET'S WALK OUTSIDE.
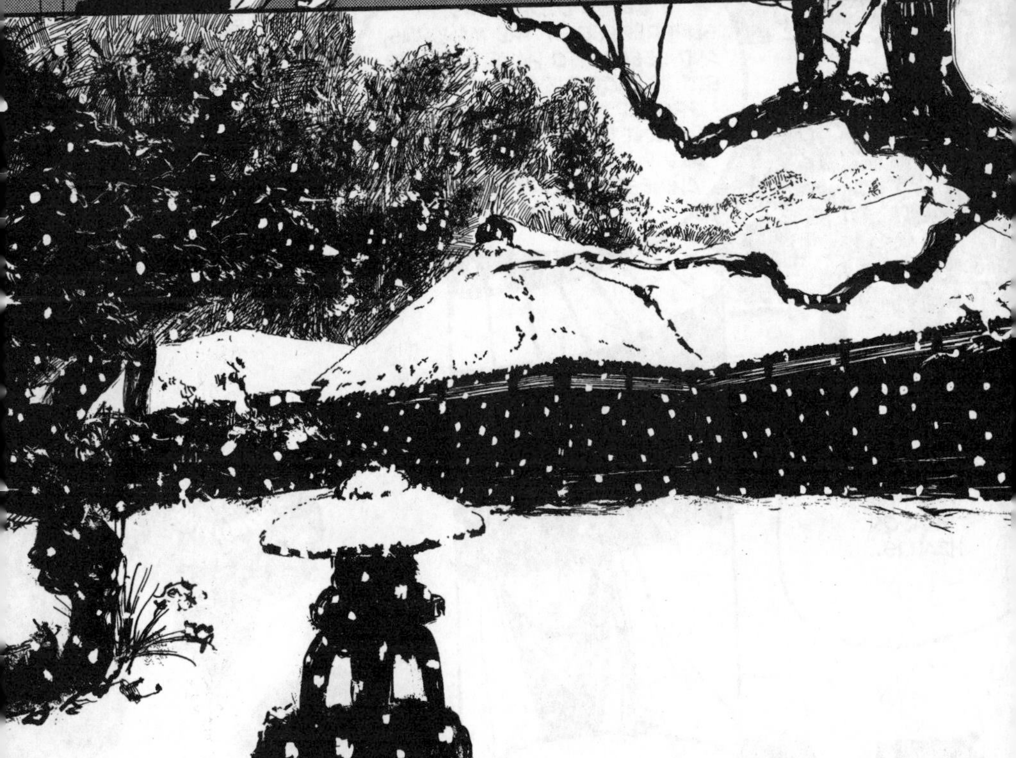

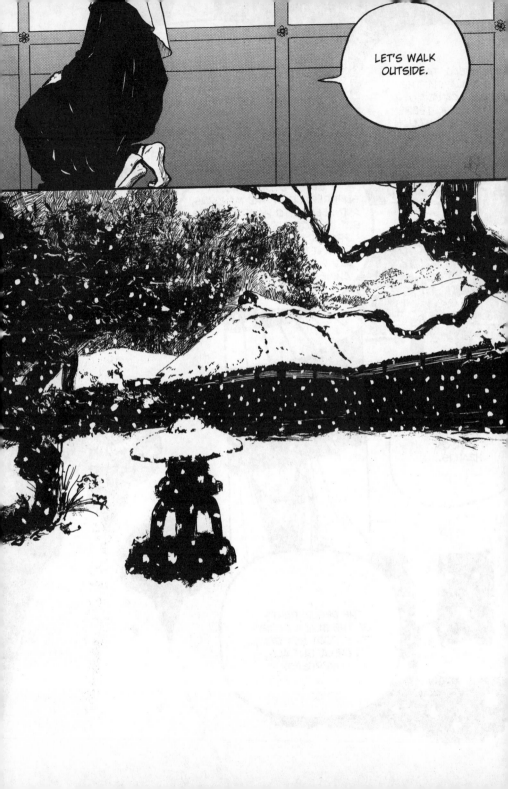

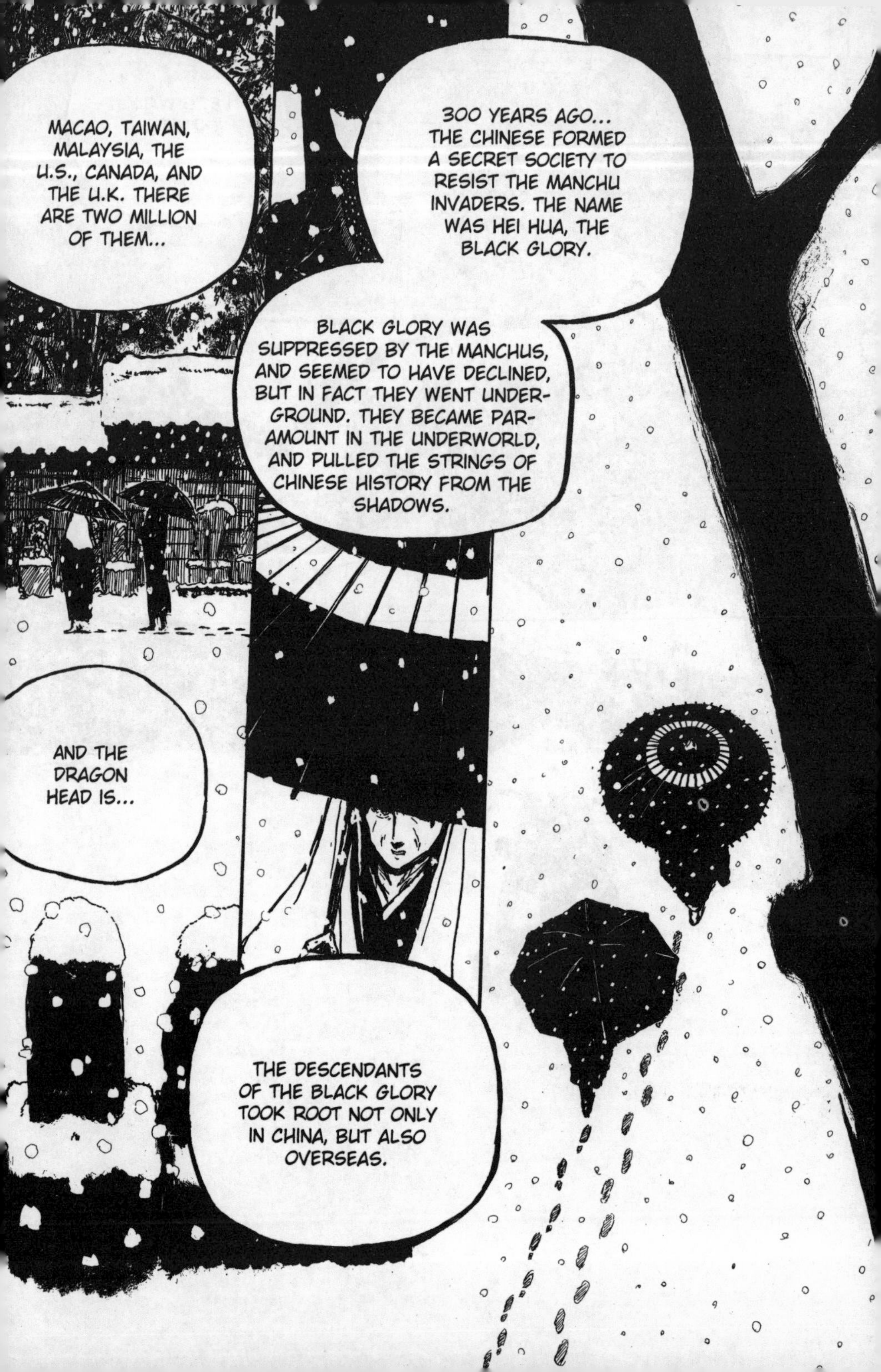
300 YEARS AGO... THE CHINESE FORMED A SECRET SOCIETY TO RESIST THE MANCHU INVADERS. THE NAME WAS HEI HUA, THE BLACK GLORY.
BLACK GLORY WAS SUPPRESSED BY THE MANCHUS, AND SEEMED TO HAVE DECLINED, BUT IN FACT THEY WENT UNDER-GROUND. THEY BECAME PAR-AMOUNT IN THE UNDERWORLD, AND PULLED THE STRINGS OF CHINESE HISTORY FROM THE SHADOWS.
THE DESCENDANTS OF THE BLACK GLORY TOOK ROOT NOT ONLY IN CHINA, BUT ALSO OVERSEAS.
MACAO, TAIWAN, MALAYSIA, THE U.S., CANADA, AND THE U.K. THERE ARE TWO MILLION OF THEM...
AND THE DRAGON HEAD IS...

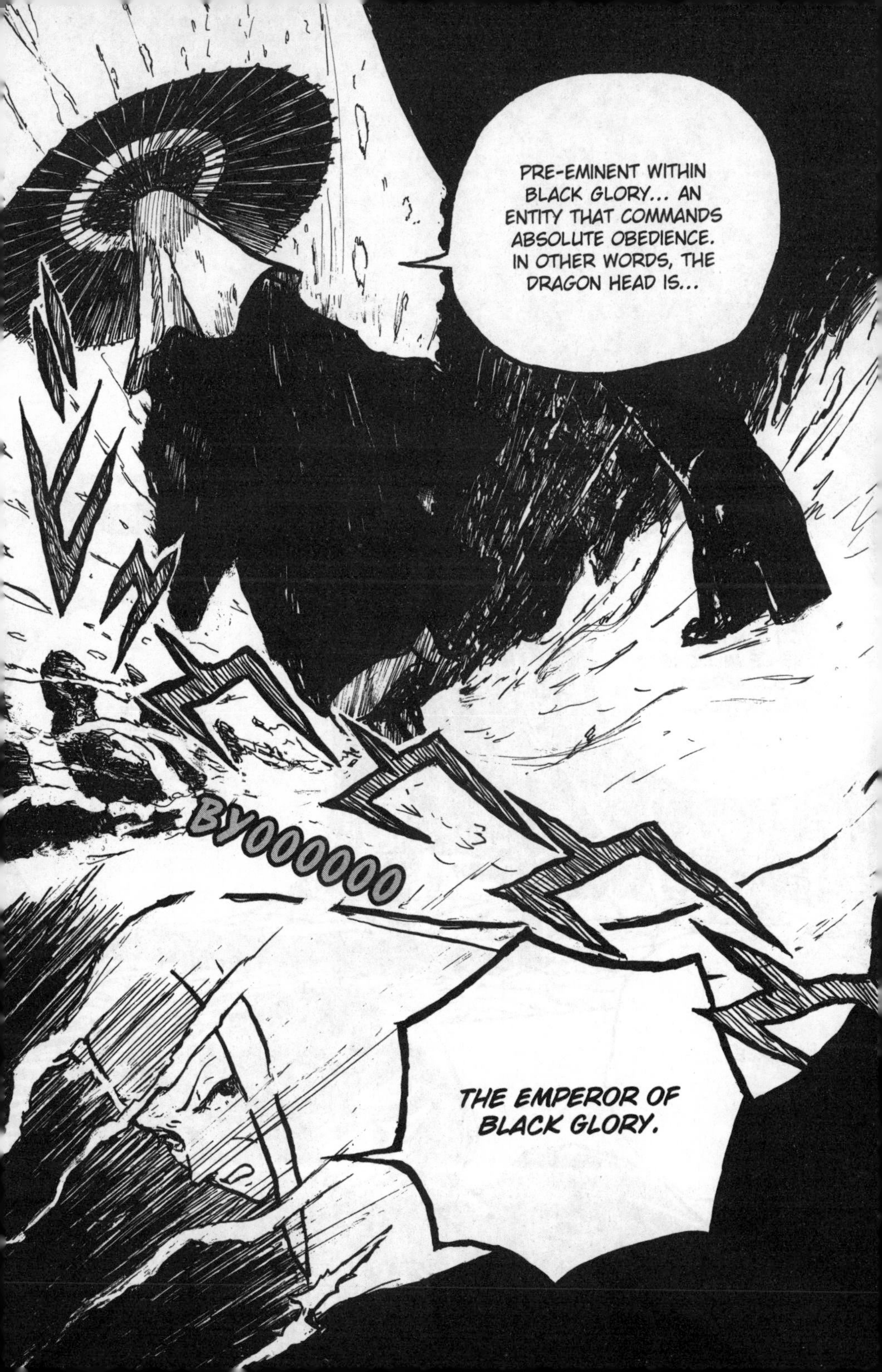
PRE-EMINENT WITHIN BLACK GLORY... AN ENTITY THAT COMMANDS ABSOLUTE OBEDIENCE. IN OTHER WORDS, THE DRAGON HEAD IS...
BYOOOOOO
THE EMPEROR OF BLACK GLORY.

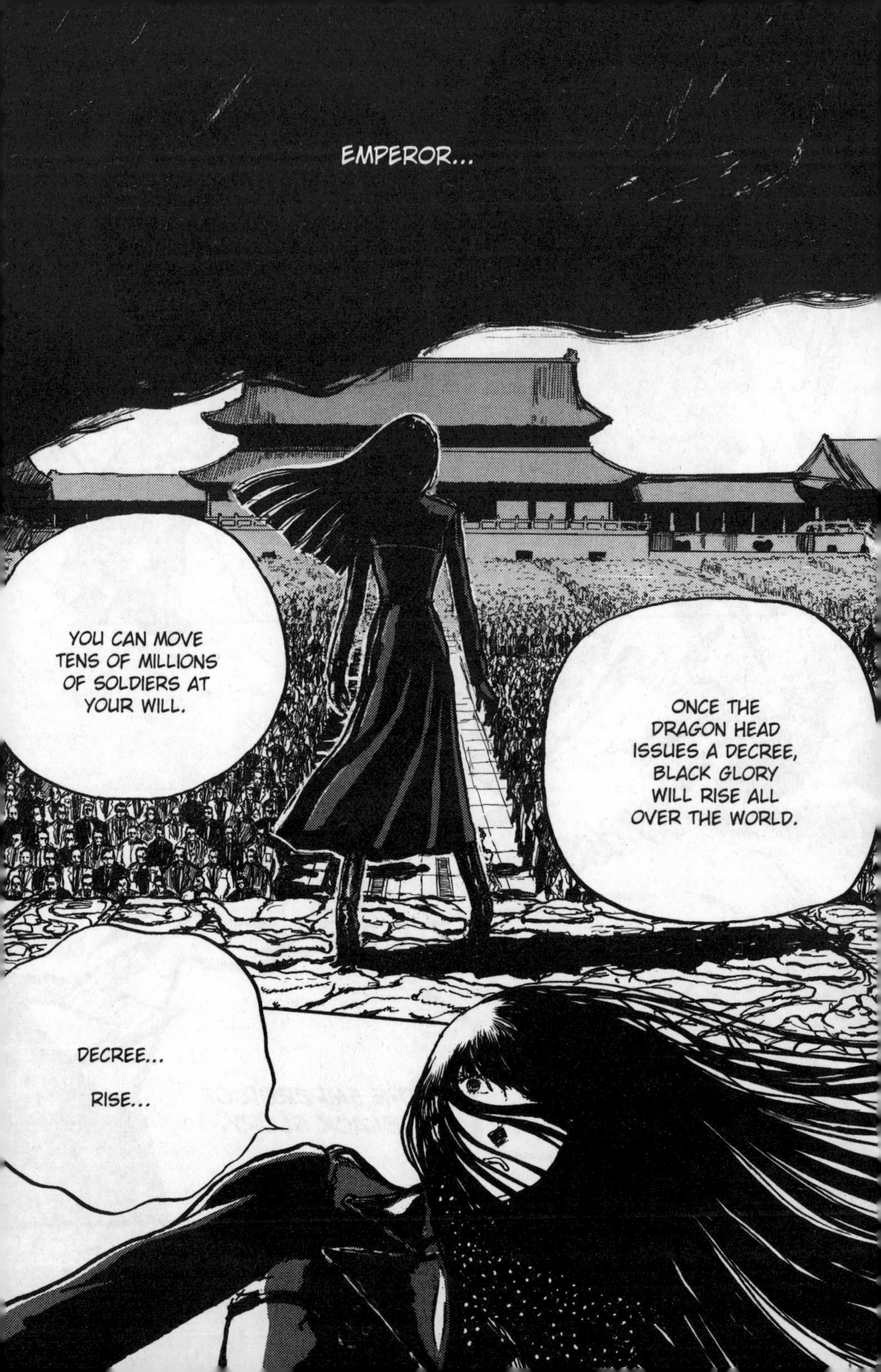
EMPEROR...
ONCE THE DRAGON HEAD ISSUES A DECREE, BLACK GLORY WILL RISE ALL OVER THE WORLD.
YOU CAN MOVE TENS OF MILLIONS OF SOLDIERS AT YOUR WILL.
DECREE... RISE...

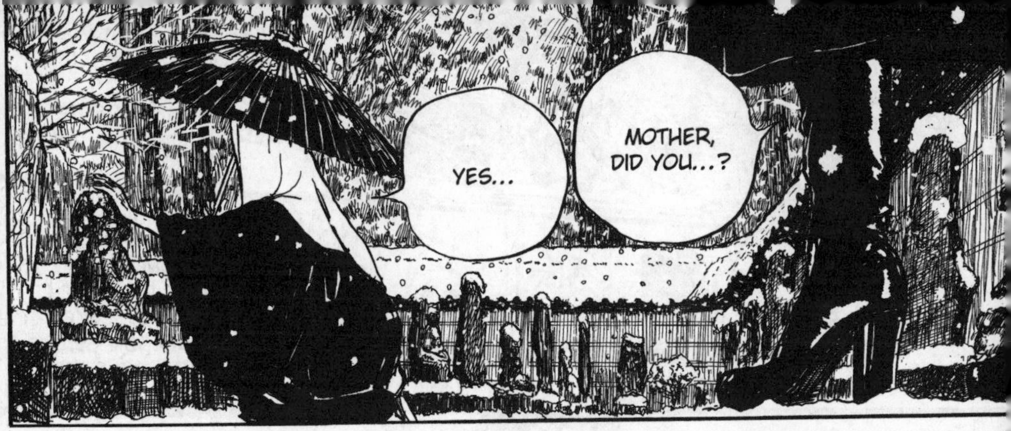
MOTHER, DID YOU...?
YES...

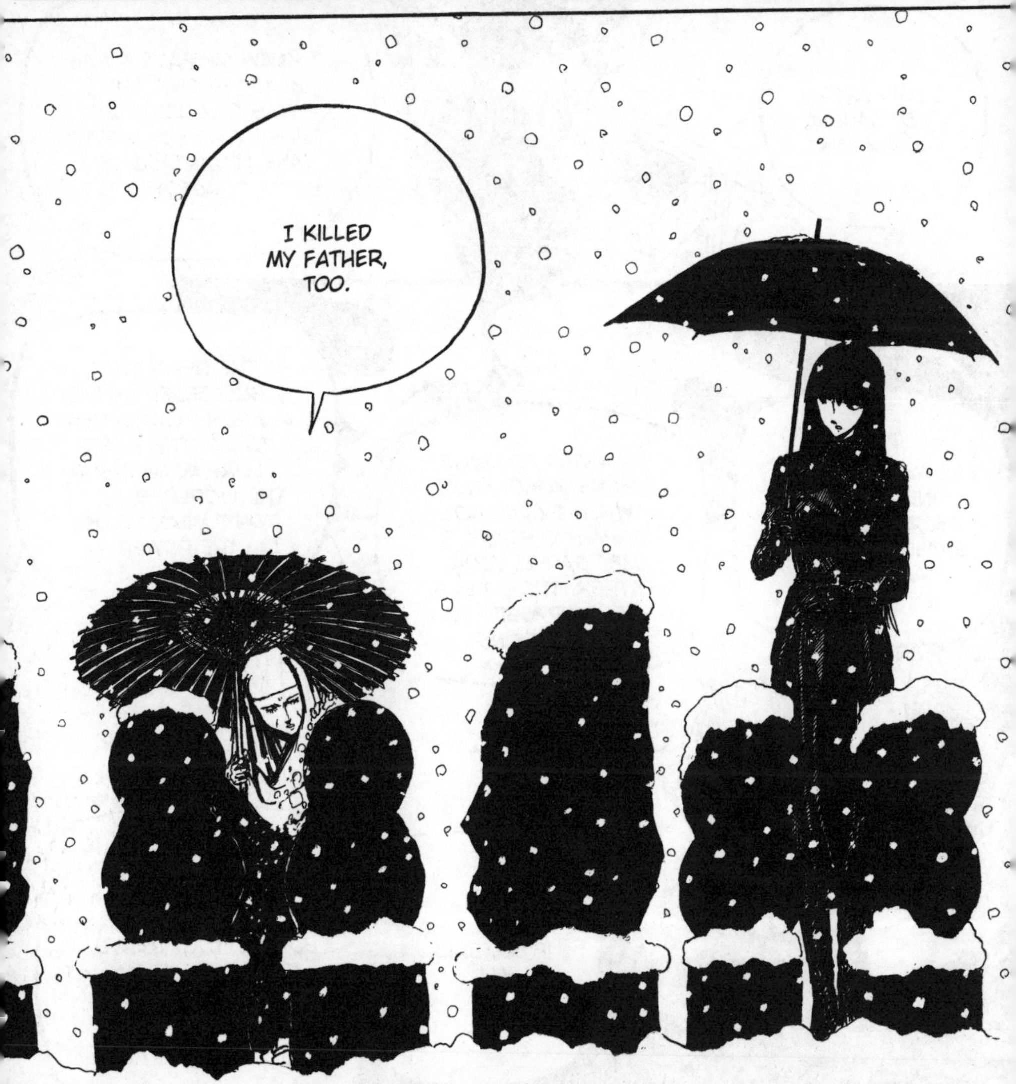
I KILLED MY FATHER, TOO.

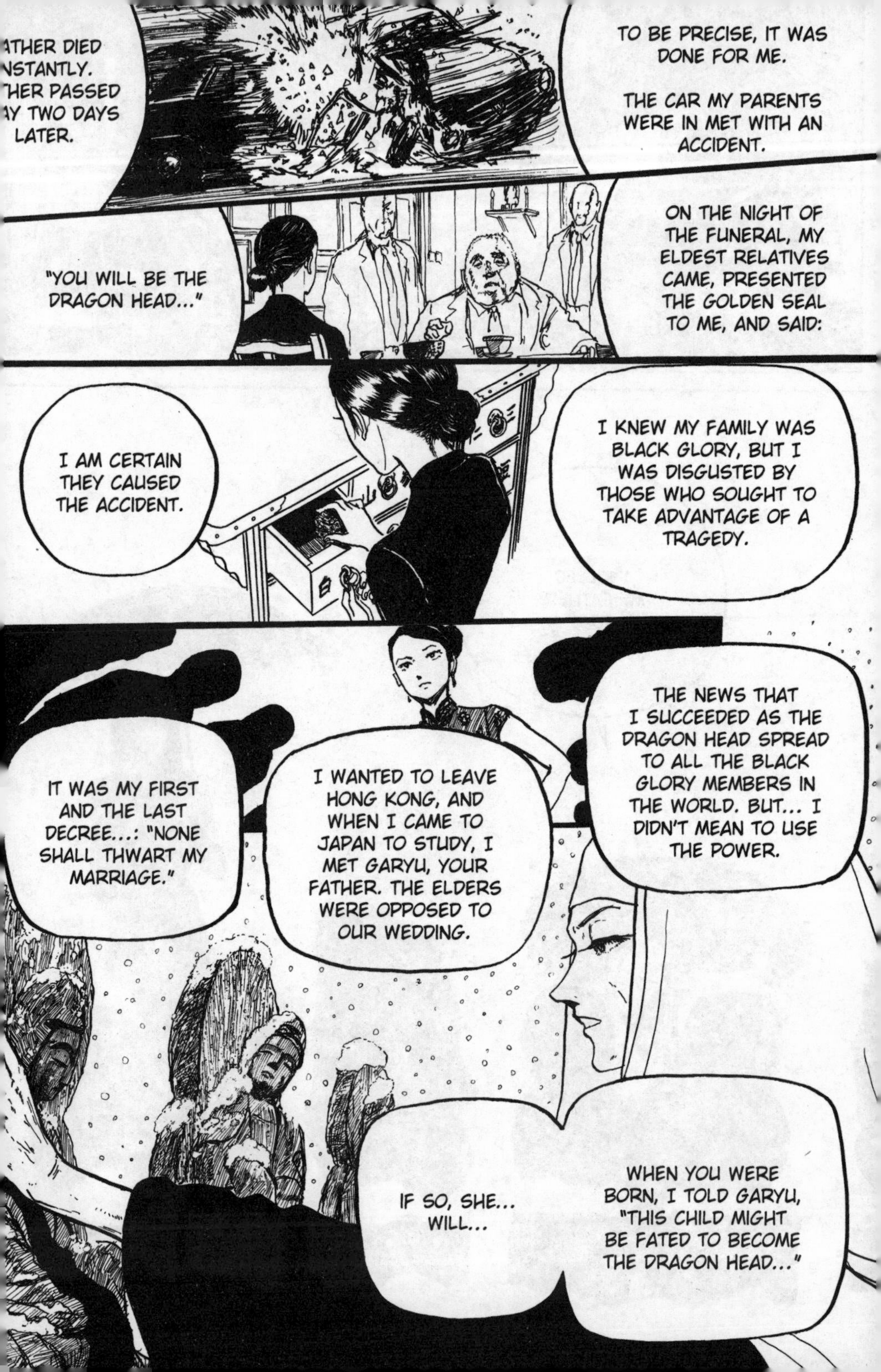

TO BE PRECISE, IT WAS DONE FOR ME.
THE CAR MY PARENTS WERE IN MET WITH AN ACCIDENT.
ATHER DIED NSTANTLY. THER PASSED AY TWO DAYS LATER.
ON THE NIGHT OF THE FUNERAL, MY ELDEST RELATIVES CAME, PRESENTED THE GOLDEN SEAL TO ME, AND SAID:
"YOU WILL BE THE DRAGON HEAD..."
I KNEW MY FAMILY WAS BLACK GLORY, BUT I WAS DISGUSTED BY THOSE WHO SOUGHT TO TAKE ADVANTAGE OF A TRAGEDY.
I AM CERTAIN THEY CAUSED THE ACCIDENT.
THE NEWS THAT I SUCCEEDED AS THE DRAGON HEAD SPREAD TO ALL THE BLACK GLORY MEMBERS IN THE WORLD. BUT... I DIDN'T MEAN TO USE THE POWER.
I WANTED TO LEAVE HONG KONG, AND WHEN I CAME TO JAPAN TO STUDY, I MET GARYU, YOUR FATHER. THE ELDERS WERE OPPOSED TO OUR WEDDING.
IT WAS MY FIRST AND THE LAST DECREE...: "NONE SHALL THWART MY MARRIAGE."
WHEN YOU WERE BORN, I TOLD GARYU, "THIS CHILD MIGHT BE FATED TO BECOME THE DRAGON HEAD..."
IF SO, SHE... WILL...

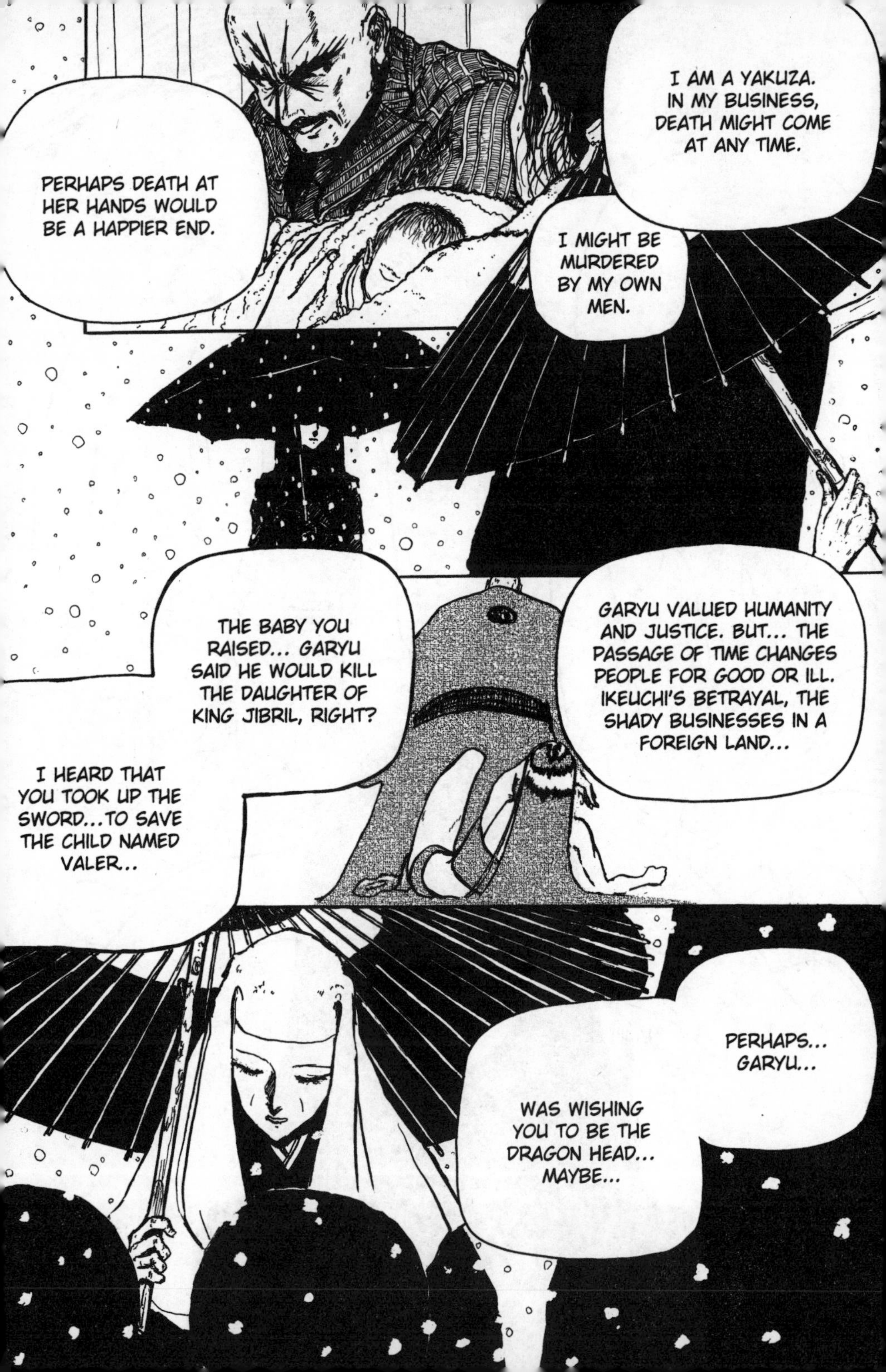
I AM A YAKUZA. IN MY BUSINESS, DEATH MIGHT COME AT ANY TIME.
I MIGHT BE MURDERED BY MY OWN MEN.
PERHAPS DEATH AT HER HANDS WOULD BE A HAPPIER END.
THE BABY YOU RAISED... GARYU SAID HE WOULD KILL THE DAUGHTER OF KING JIBRIL, RIGHT?
I HEARD THAT YOU TOOK UP THE SWORD...TO SAVE THE CHILD NAMED VALER...
GARYU VALUED HUMANITY AND JUSTICE. BUT... THE PASSAGE OF TIME CHANGES PEOPLE FOR GOOD OR ILL. IKEUCHI'S BETRAYAL, THE SHADY BUSINESSES IN A FOREIGN LAND...
PERHAPS... GARYU...
WAS WISHING YOU TO BE THE DRAGON HEAD... MAYBE...

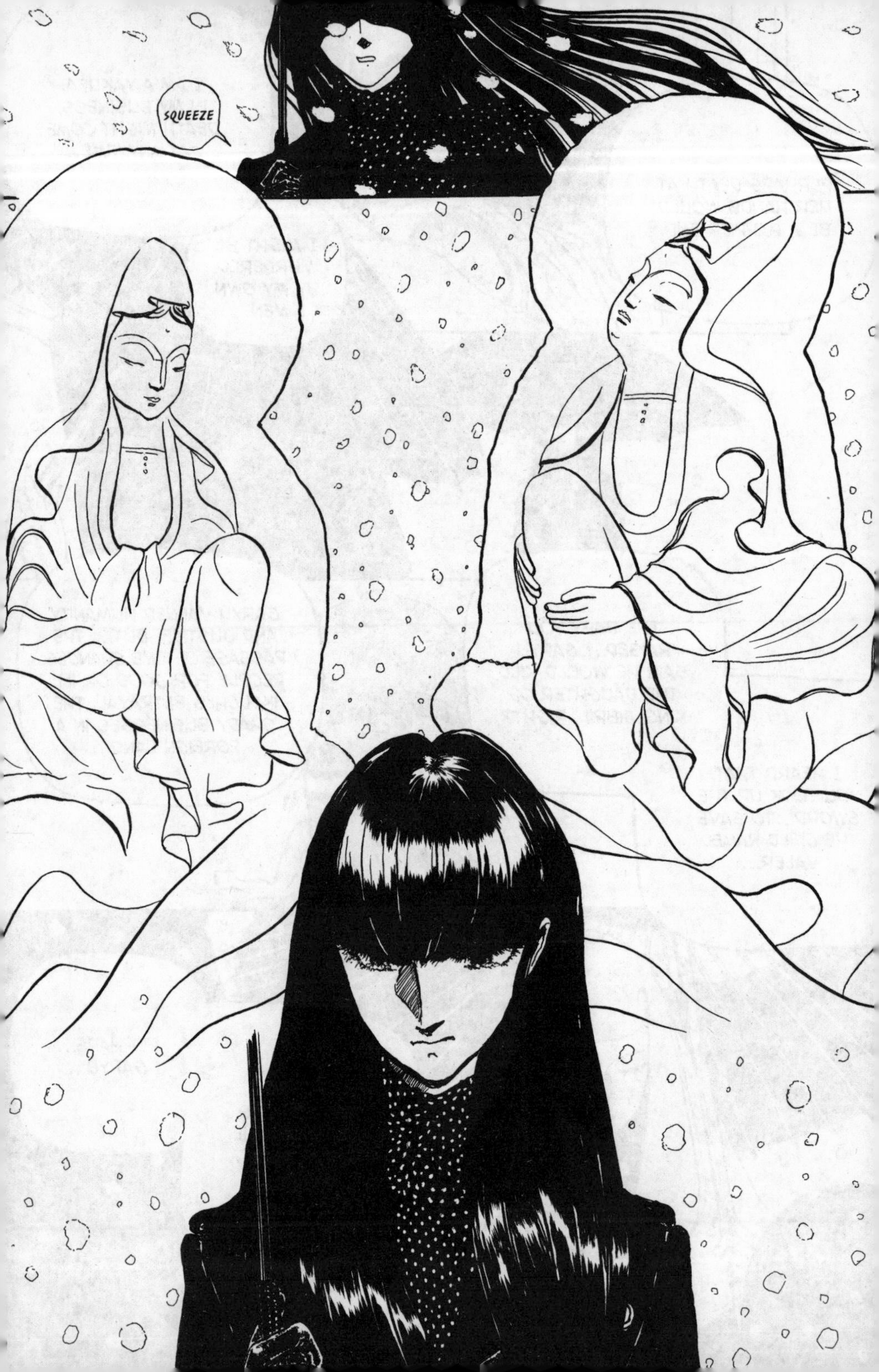
SQUEEZE

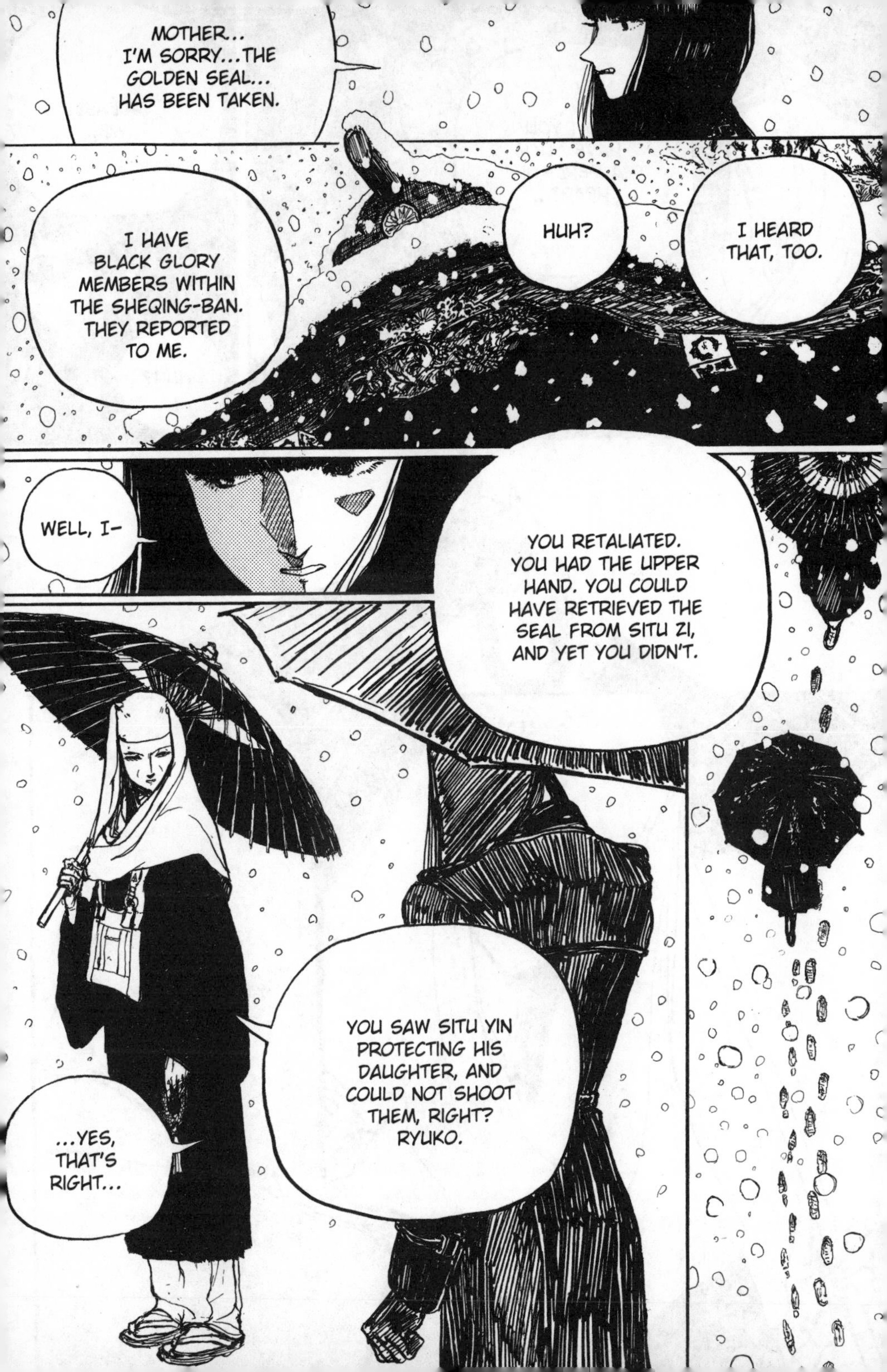
MOTHER... I'M SORRY...THE GOLDEN SEAL... HAS BEEN TAKEN.
I HEARD THAT, TOO.
HUH?
I HAVE BLACK GLORY MEMBERS WITHIN THE SHEQING-BAN. THEY REPORTED TO ME.
YOU RETALIATED. YOU HAD THE UPPER HAND. YOU COULD HAVE RETRIEVED THE SEAL FROM SITU ZI, AND YET YOU DIDN'T.
WELL, I-
YOU SAW SITU YIN PROTECTING HIS DAUGHTER, AND COULD NOT SHOOT THEM, RIGHT? RYUKO.
...YES, THAT'S RIGHT...

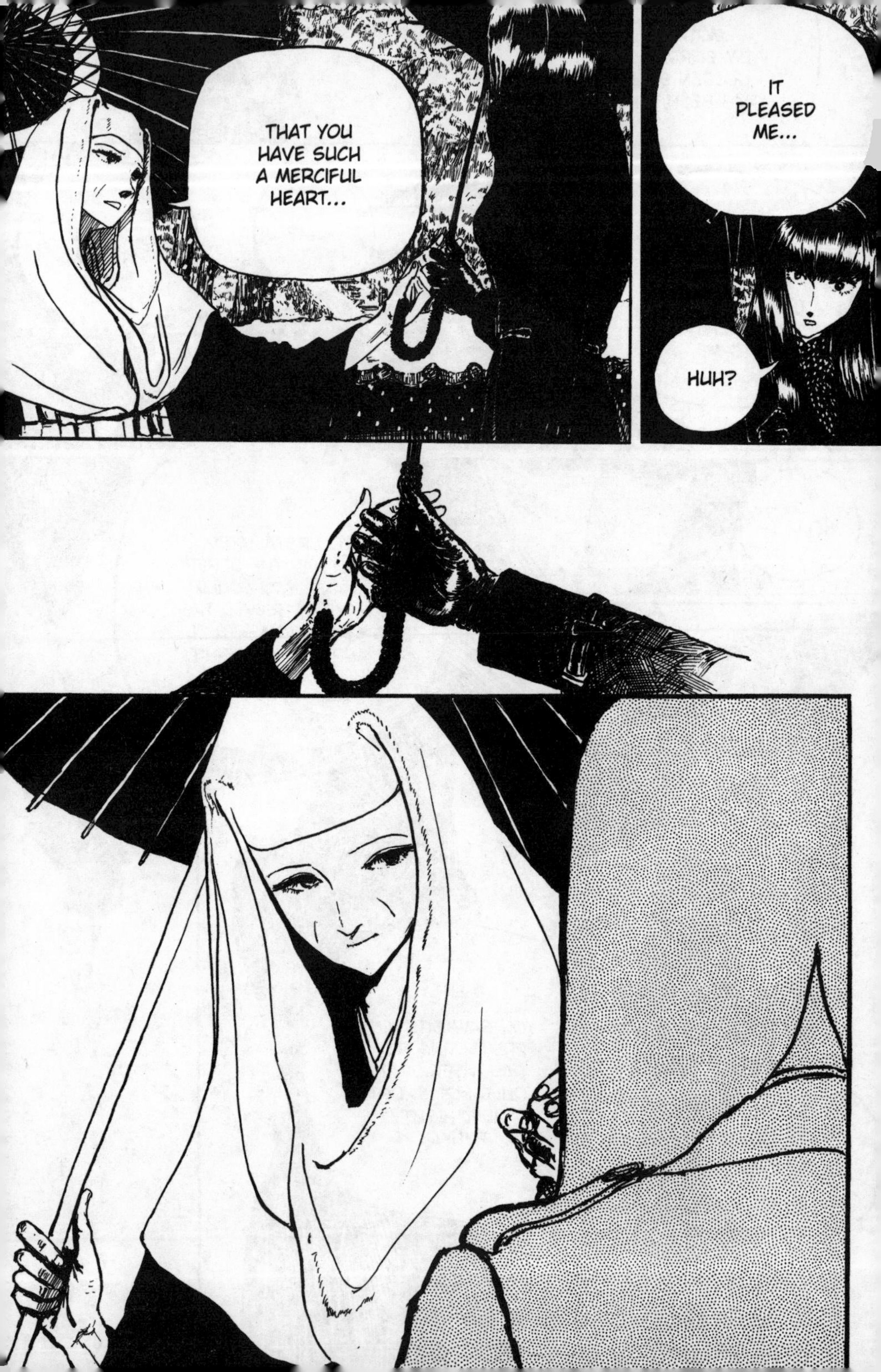
IT PLEASED ME...
HUH?
THAT YOU HAVE SUCH A MERCIFUL HEART...

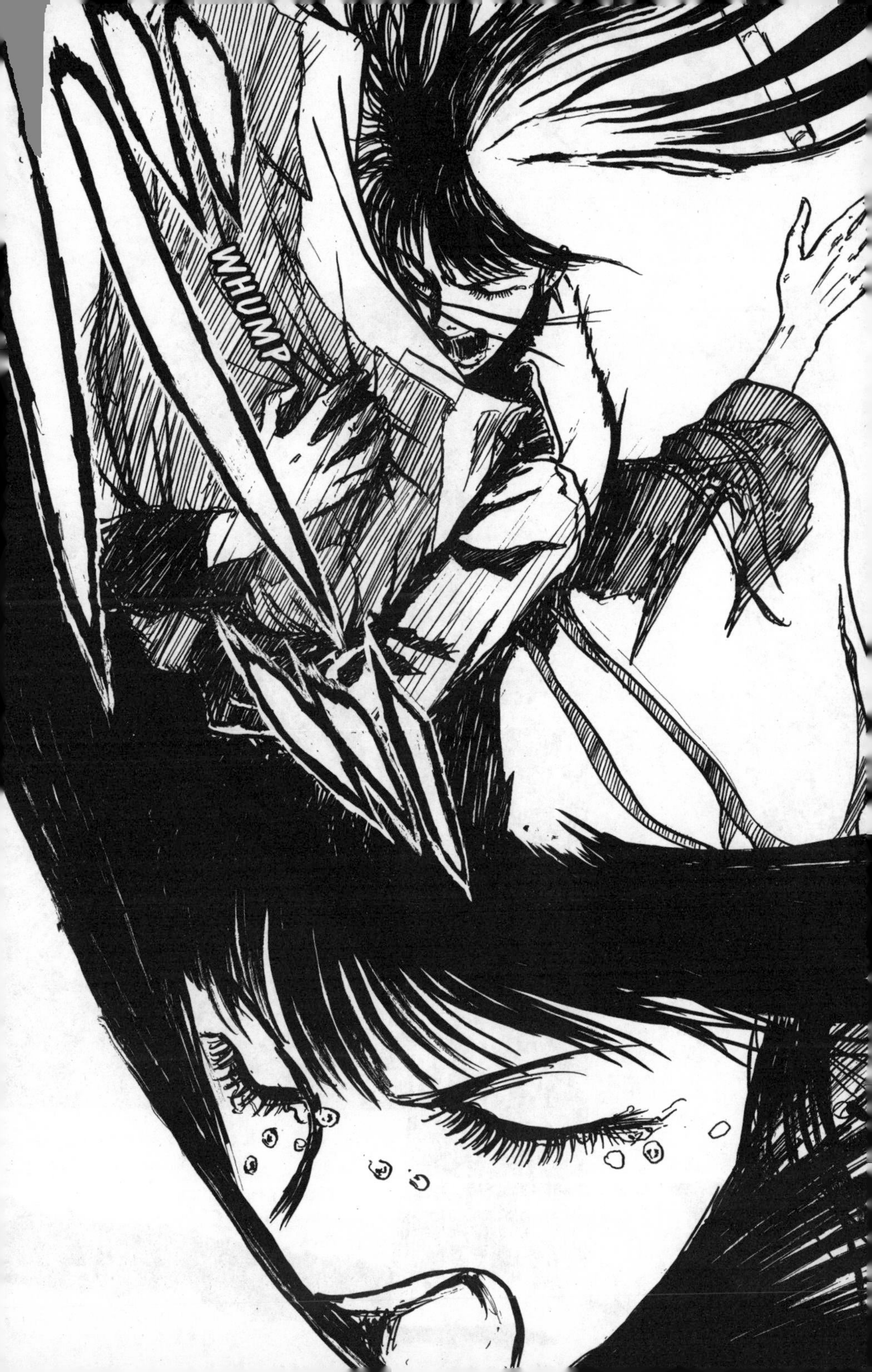
WHUMP

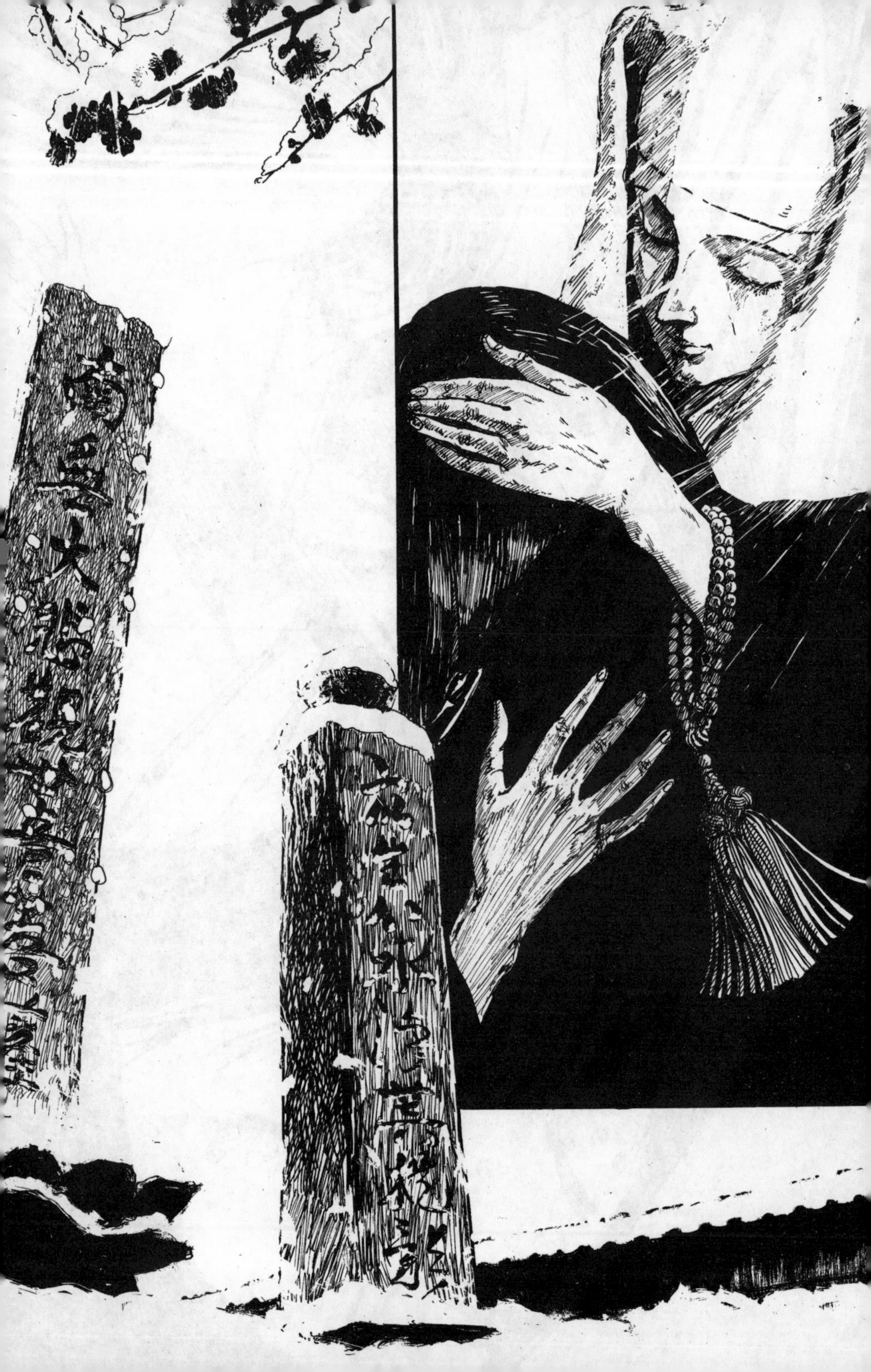

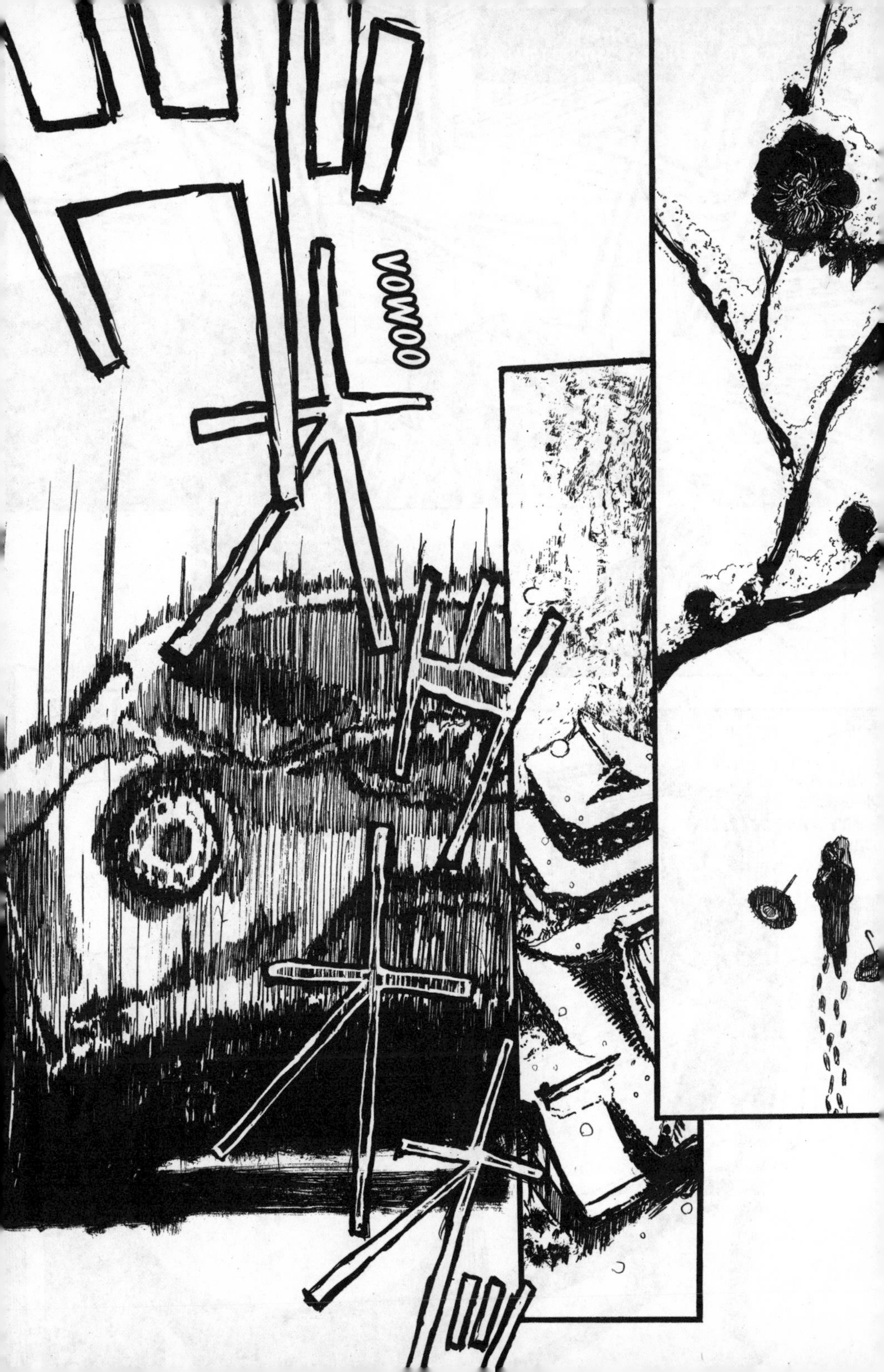
VOWOO

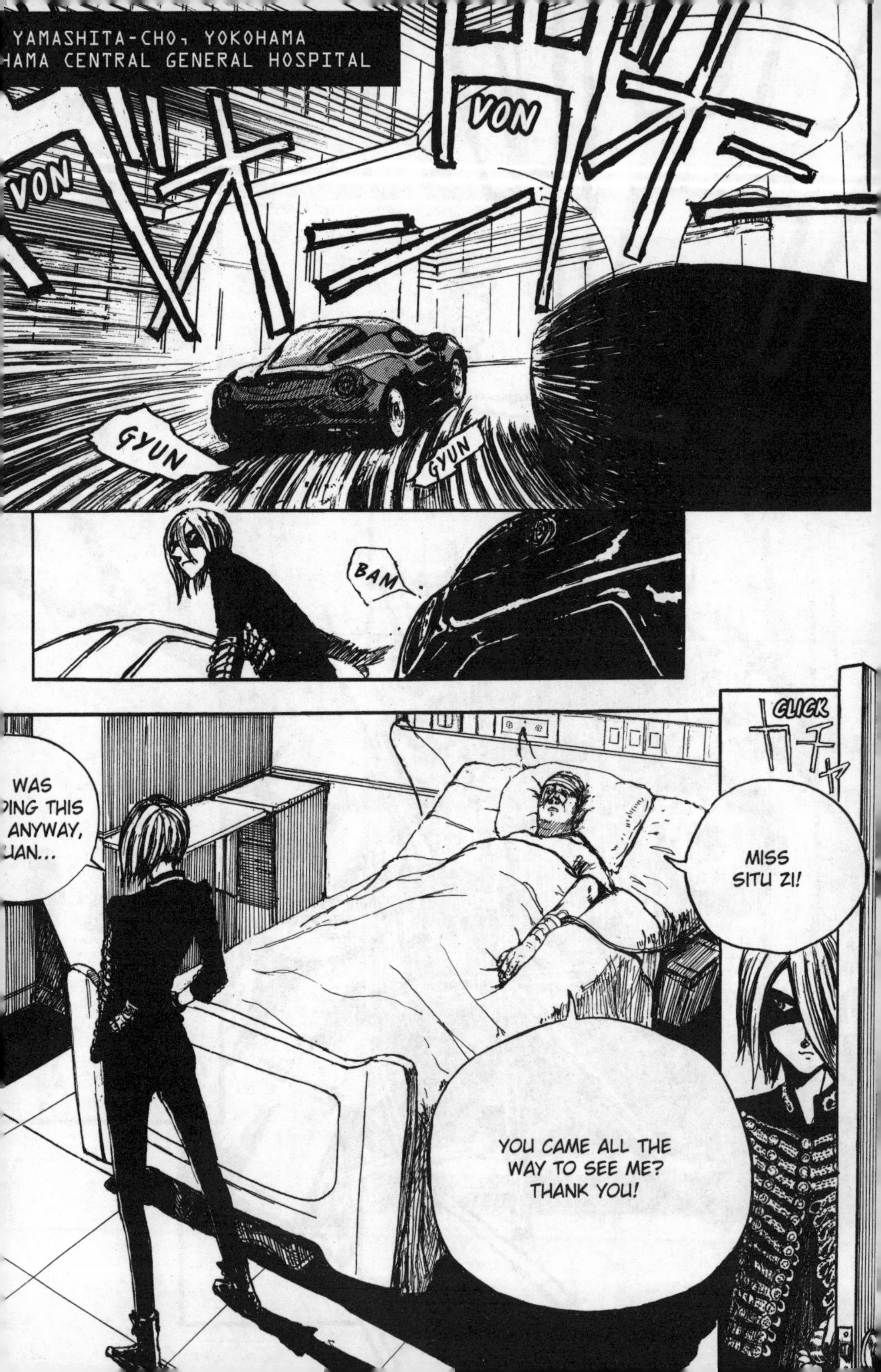
YAMASHITA-CHO, YOKOHAMA
HAMA CENTRAL GENERAL HOSPITAL
VON
VON
GYUN
GYUN
BAM
CLICK
MISS SITU ZI!
YOU CAME ALL THE WAY TO SEE ME? THANK YOU!
WAS DING THIS ANYWAY, UAN...

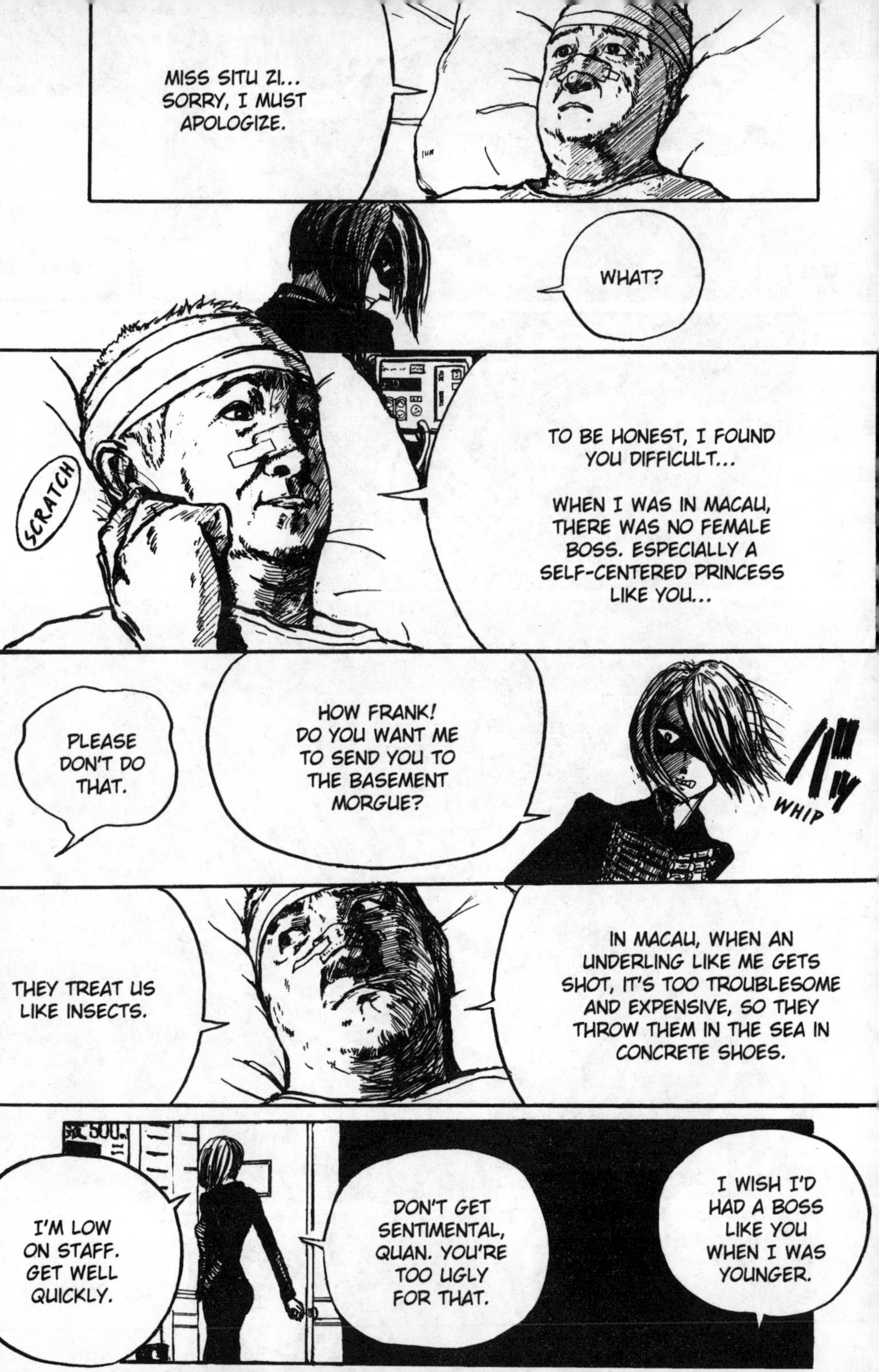
MISS SITU ZI... SORRY, I MUST APOLOGIZE.
WHAT?
TO BE HONEST, I FOUND YOU DIFFICULT...
WHEN I WAS IN MACAU, THERE WAS NO FEMALE BOSS. ESPECIALLY A SELF-CENTERED PRINCESS LIKE YOU...
SCRATCH
WHIP
HOW FRANK! DO YOU WANT ME TO SEND YOU TO THE BASEMENT MORGUE?
PLEASE DON'T DO THAT.
IN MACAU, WHEN AN UNDERLING LIKE ME GETS SHOT, IT'S TOO TROUBLESOME AND EXPENSIVE, SO THEY THROW THEM IN THE SEA IN CONCRETE SHOES.
THEY TREAT US LIKE INSECTS.
I WISH I'D HAD A BOSS LIKE YOU WHEN I WAS YOUNGER.
DON'T GET SENTIMENTAL, QUAN. YOU'RE TOO UGLY FOR THAT.
I'M LOW ON STAFF. GET WELL QUICKLY.

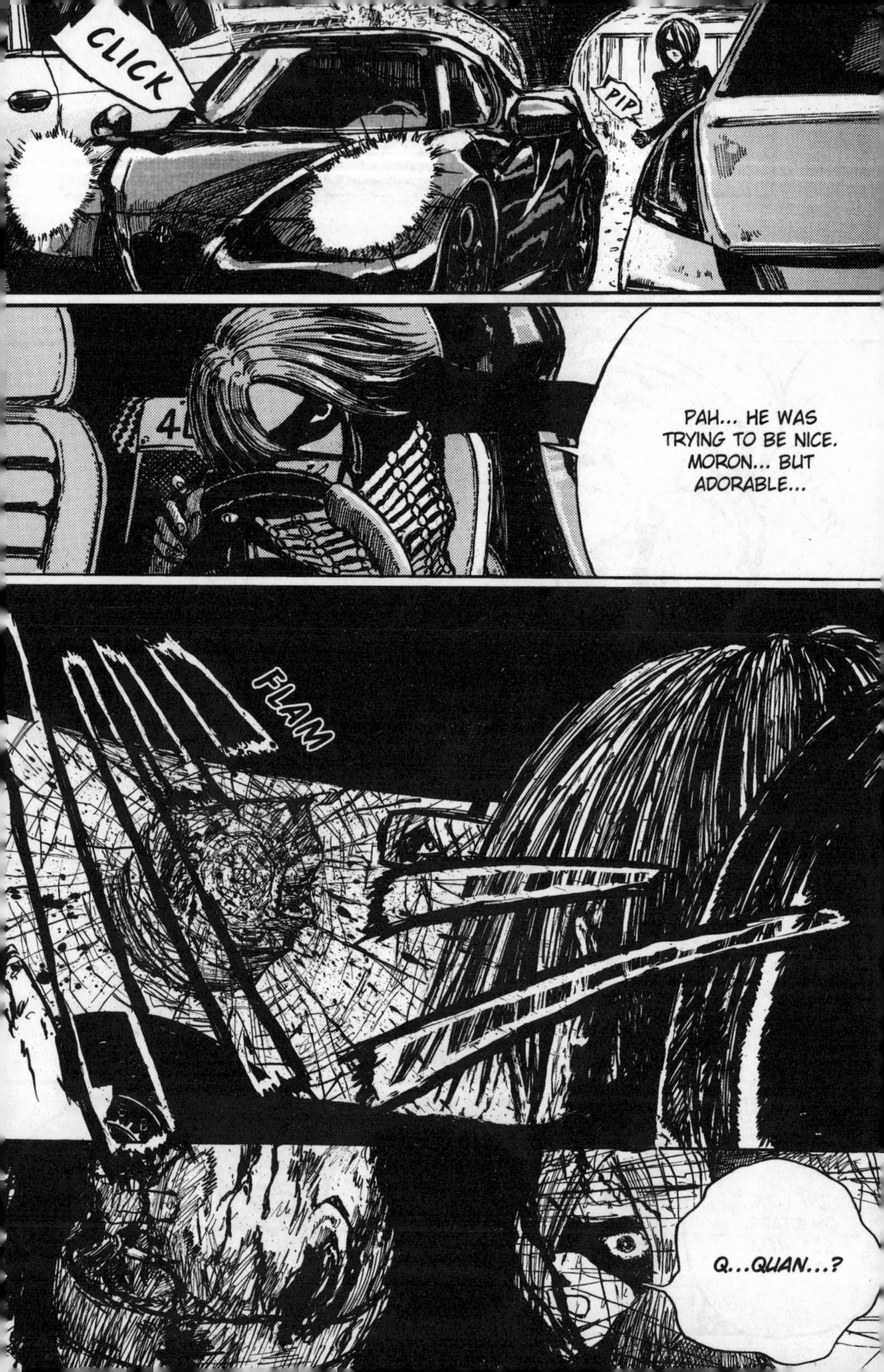
PIP
CLICK
PAH... HE WAS TRYING TO BE NICE. MORON... BUT ADORABLE...
FLAM
Q...QUAN...?

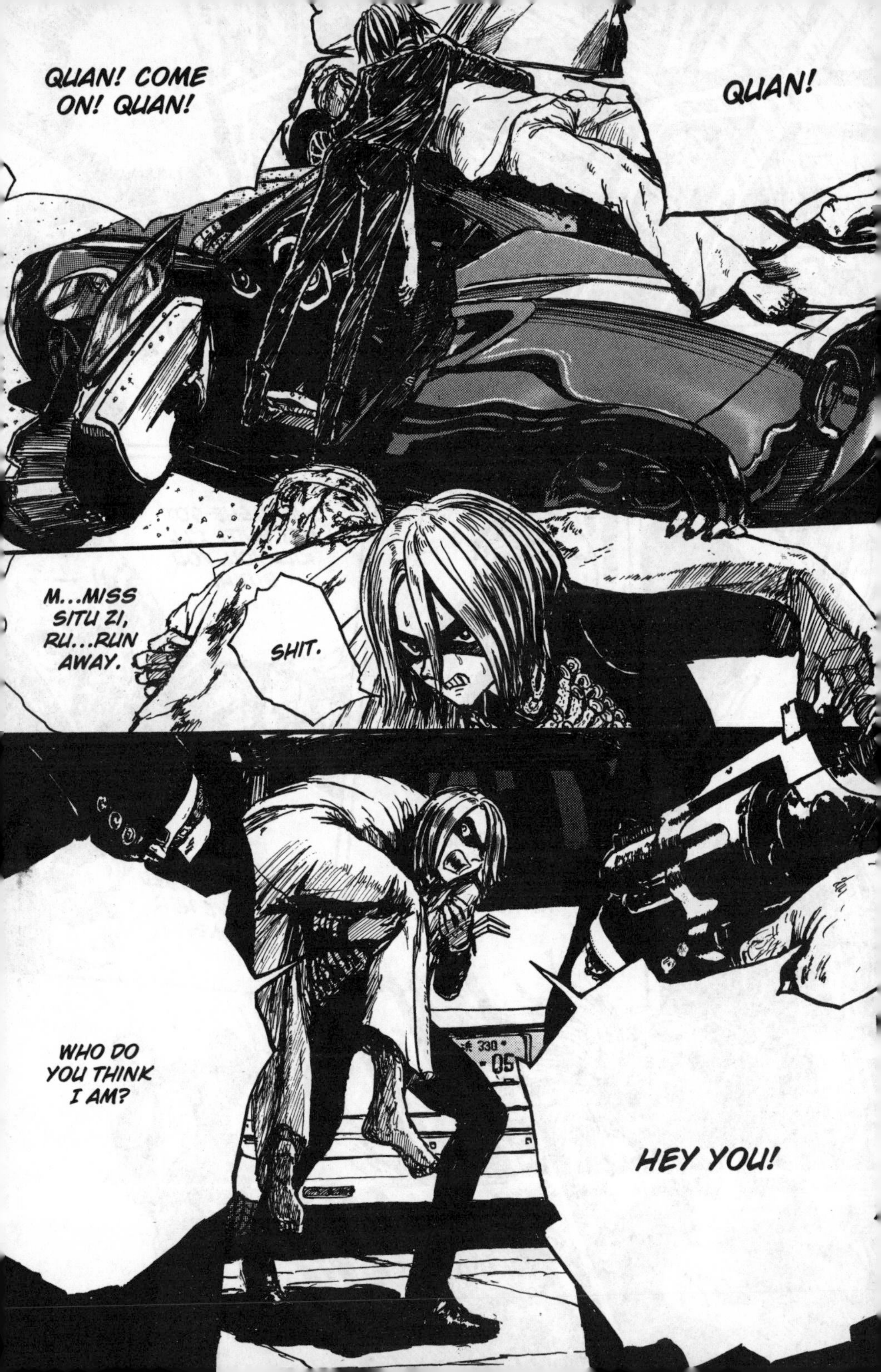
QUAN!
QUAN! COME ON! QUAN!
SHIT.
M...MISS SITU ZI, RU...RUN AWAY.
HEY YOU!
WHO DO YOU THINK I AM?

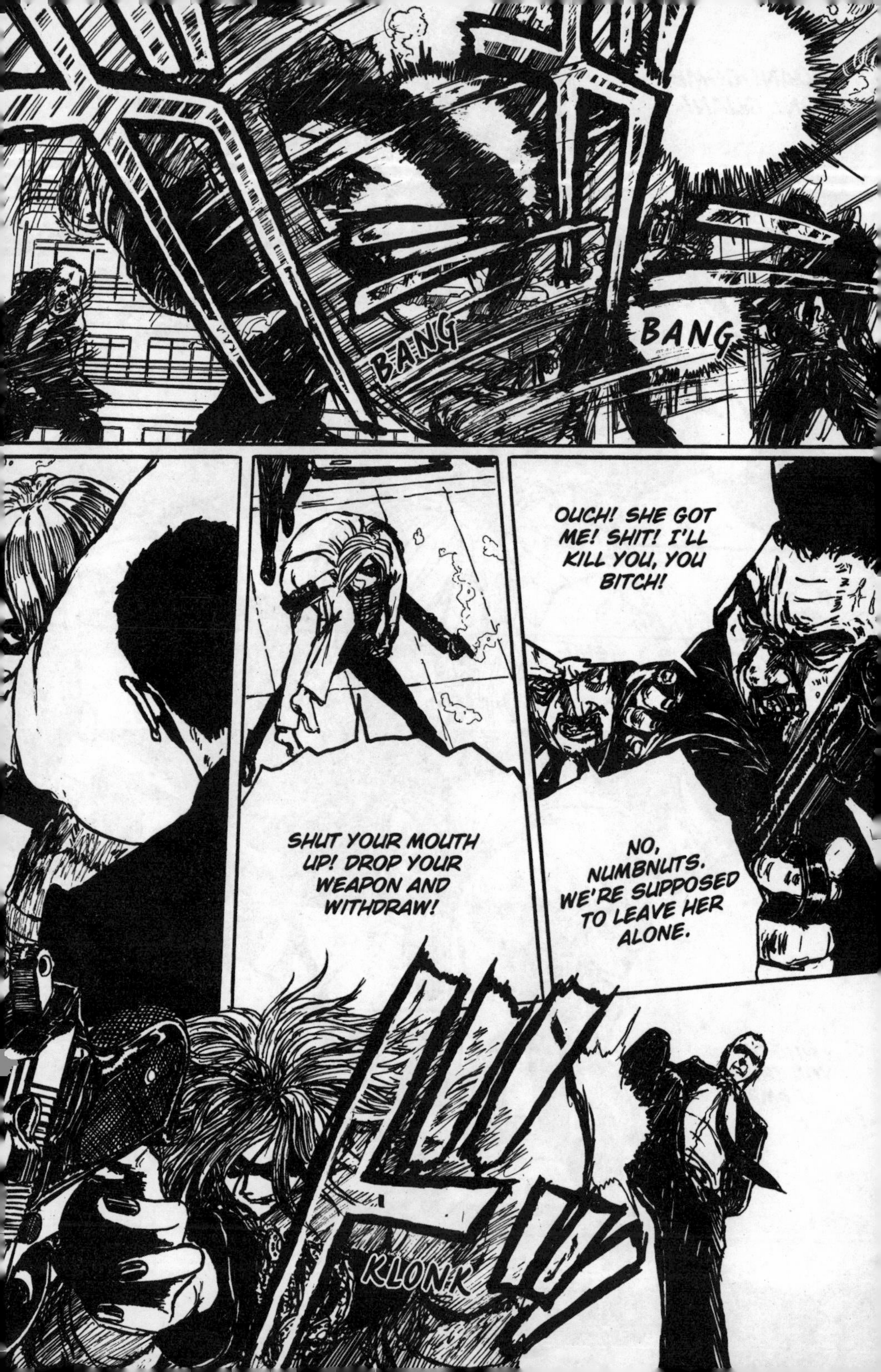
BANG
BANG
OUCH! SHE GOT ME! SHIT! I'LL KILL YOU, YOU BITCH!
NO, NUMBNUTS. WE'RE SUPPOSED TO LEAVE HER ALONE.
SHUT YOUR MOUTH UP! DROP YOUR WEAPON AND WITHDRAW!
KLONK

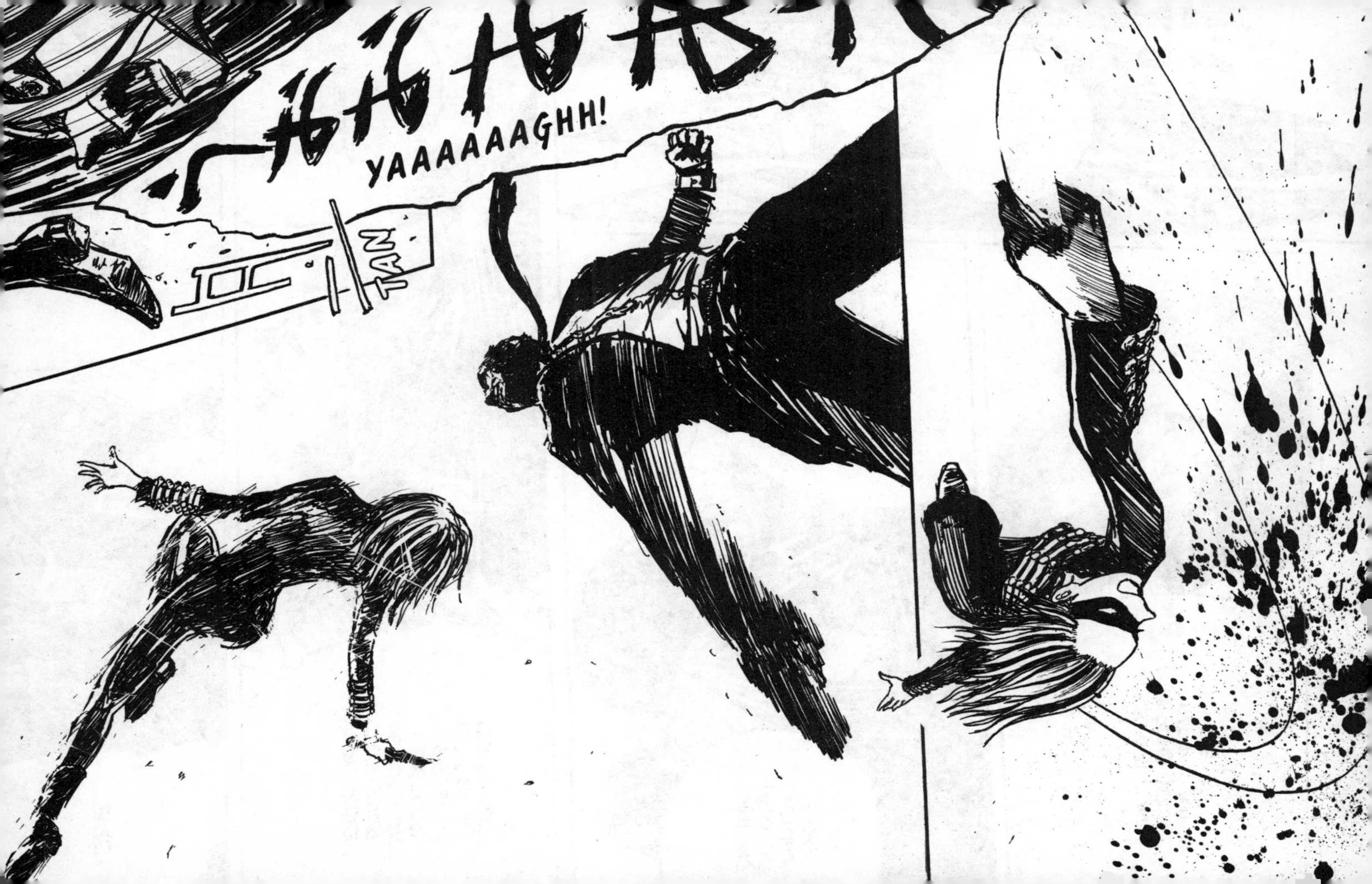
YAAAAAAGHH!
TAN

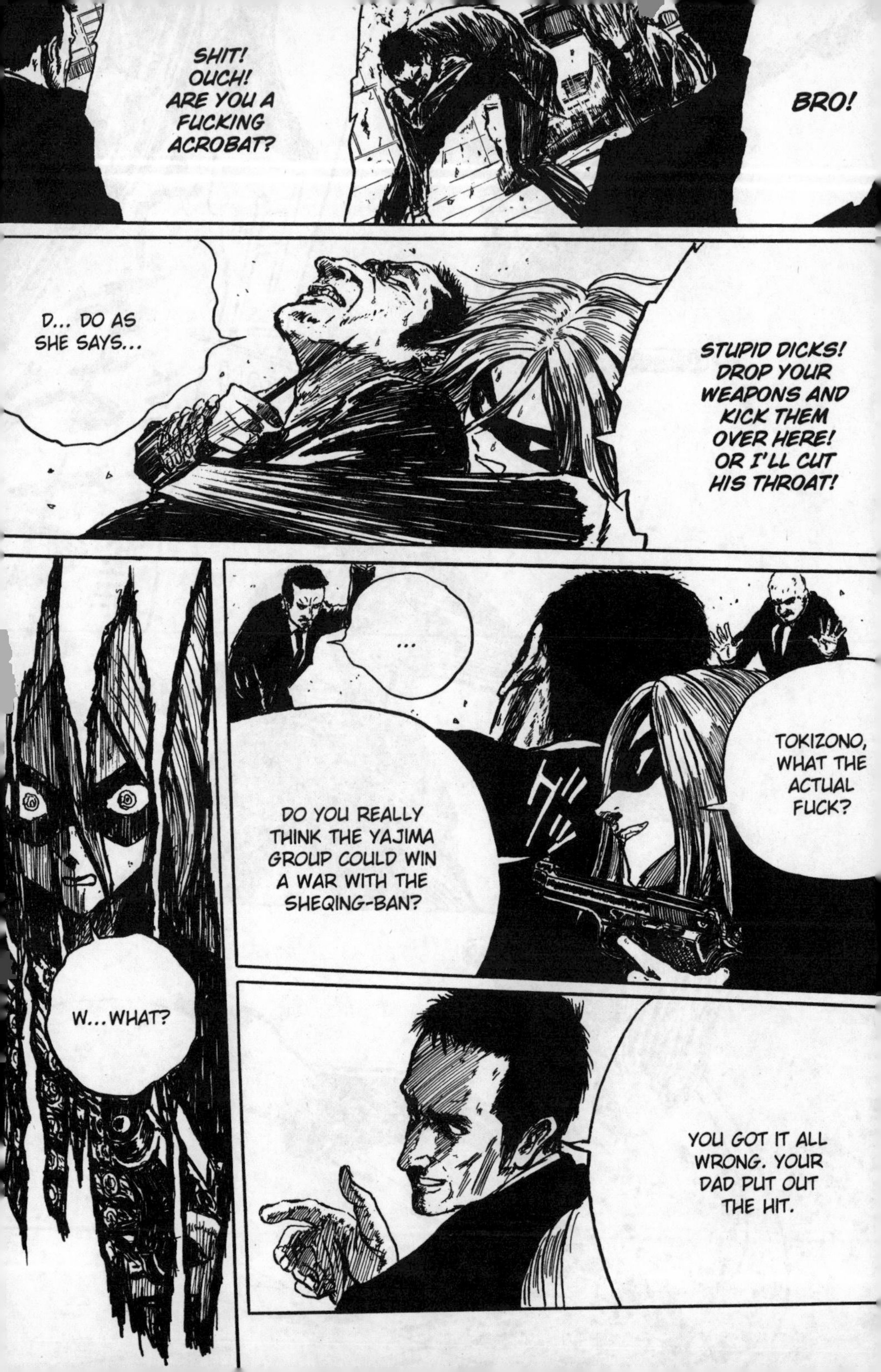
BRO!
SHIT! OUCH! ARE YOU A FUCKING ACROBAT?
STUPID DICKS! DROP YOUR WEAPONS AND KICK THEM OVER HERE! OR I'LL CUT HIS THROAT!
D... DO AS SHE SAYS...
TOKIZONO, WHAT THE ACTUAL FUCK?
...
DO YOU REALLY THINK THE YAJIMA GROUP COULD WIN A WAR WITH THE SHEQING-BAN?
YOU GOT IT ALL WRONG. YOUR DAD PUT OUT THE HIT.
W...WHAT?

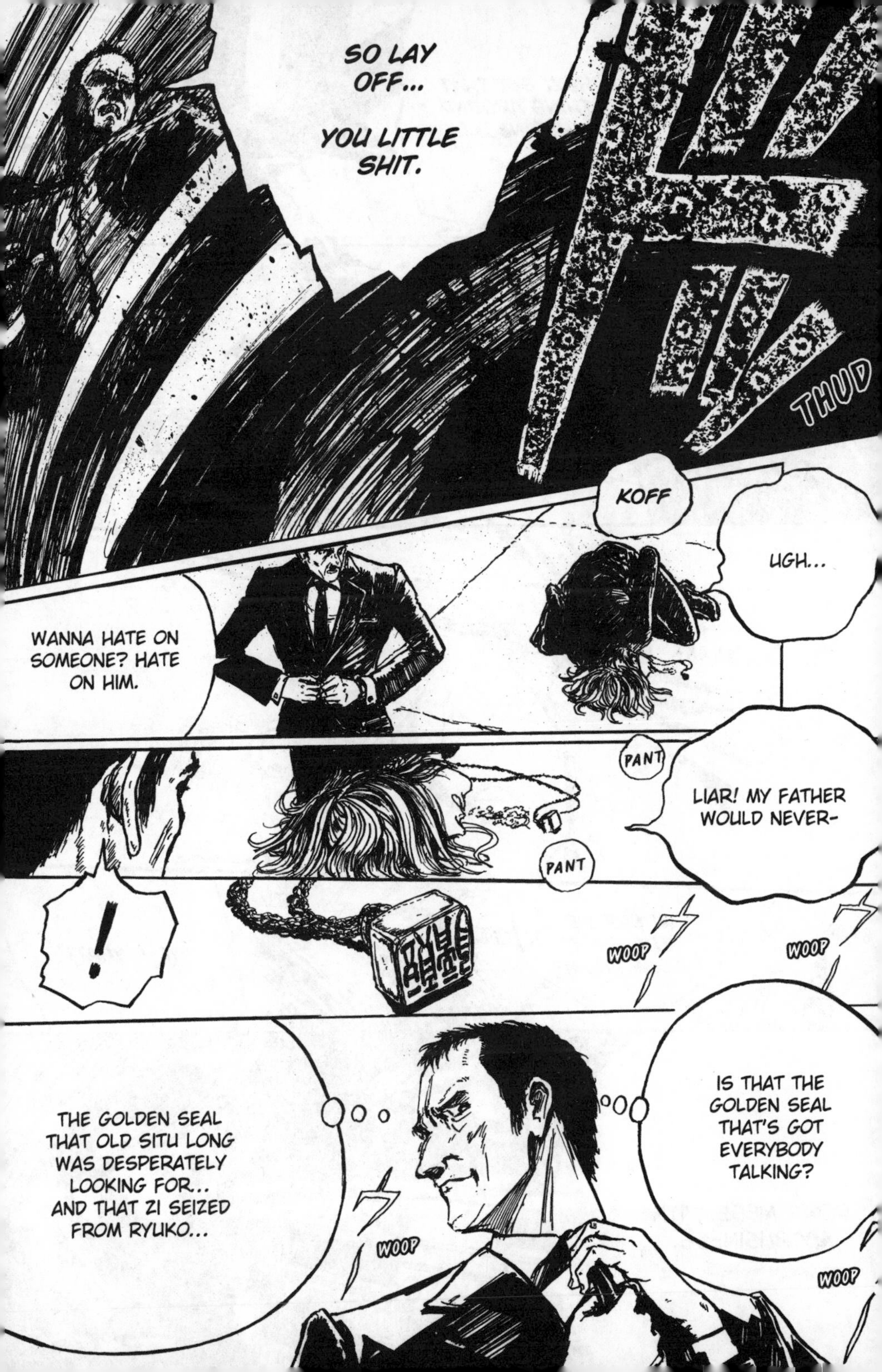
SO LAY OFF... YOU LITTLE SHIT.
THUD
KOFF
UGH...
WANNA HATE ON SOMEONE? HATE ON HIM.
PANT
LIAR! MY FATHER WOULD NEVER-
PANT
WOOP
WOOP
!
IS THAT THE GOLDEN SEAL THAT'S GOT EVERYBODY TALKING?
THE GOLDEN SEAL THAT OLD SITU LONG WAS DESPERATELY LOOKING FOR... AND THAT ZI SEIZED FROM RYUKO...
WOOP
WOOP

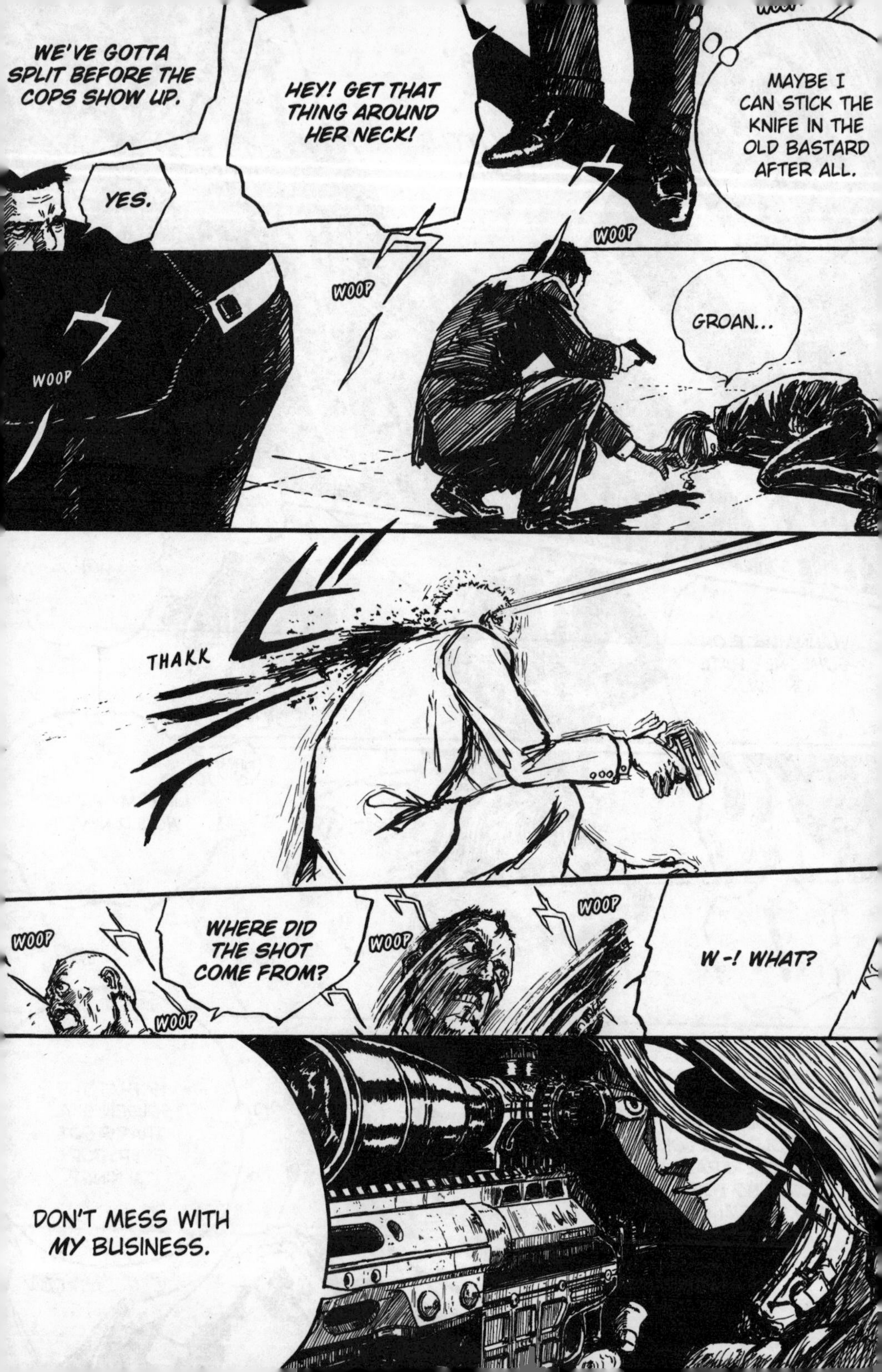
MAYBE I CAN STICK THE KNIFE IN THE OLD BASTARD AFTER ALL.
HEY! GET THAT THING AROUND HER NECK!
WE'VE GOTTA SPLIT BEFORE THE COPS SHOW UP.
YES.
WOOP
WOOP
WOOP
GROAN...
WOOP
THAKK
W -! WHAT?
WOOP
WOOP
WHERE DID THE SHOT COME FROM?
WOOP
WOOP
DON'T MESS WITH MY BUSINESS.

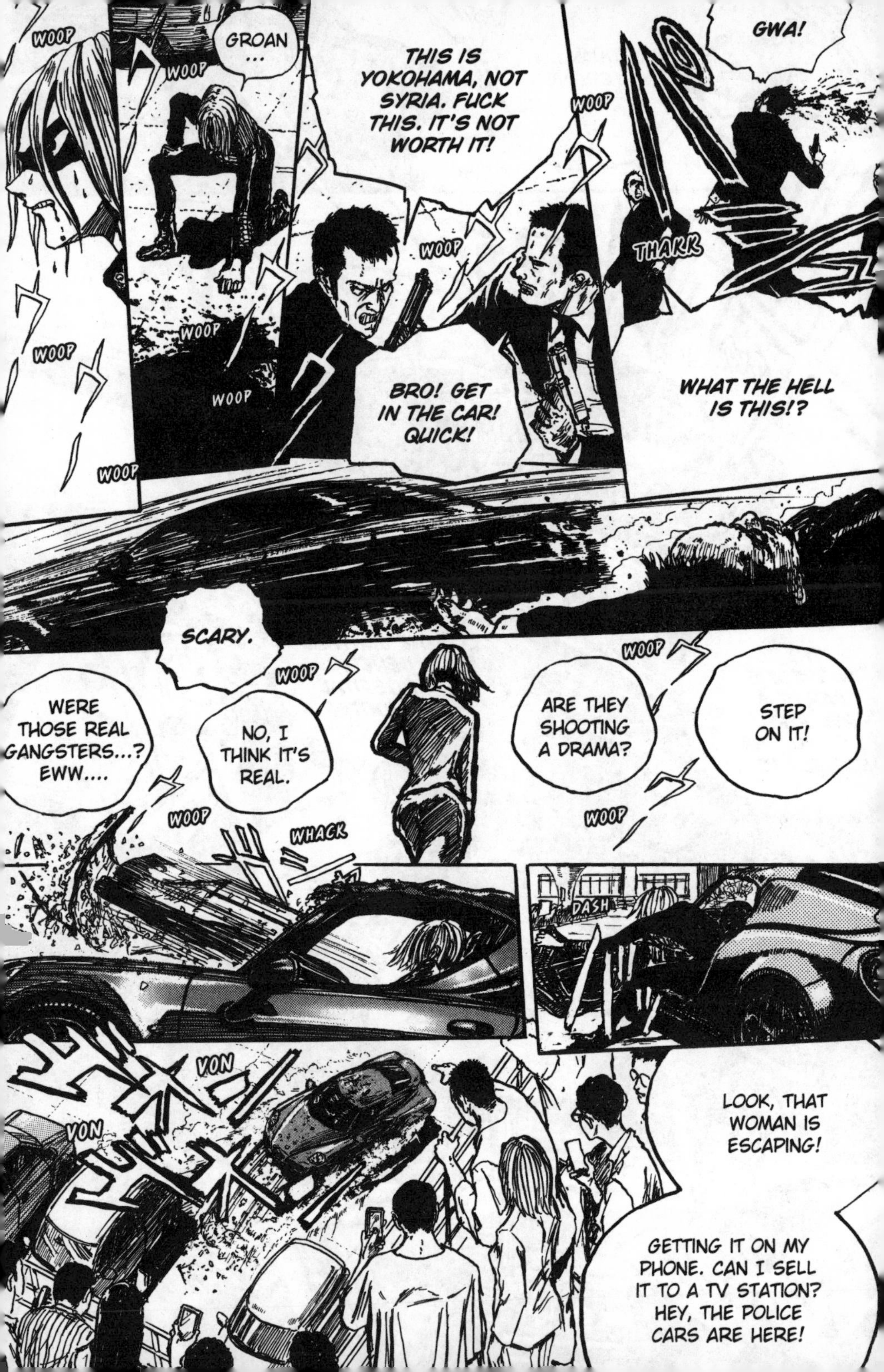
GWA!
THAKK
WHAT THE HELL IS THIS!?
WOOP
THIS IS YOKOHAMA, NOT SYRIA. FUCK THIS. IT'S NOT WORTH IT!
WOOP
BRO! GET IN THE CAR! QUICK!
GROAN ...
WOOP
WOOP
WOOP
WOOP
WOOP
WOOP
SCARY.
WOOP
STEP ON IT!
ARE THEY SHOOTING A DRAMA?
WOOP
WOOP
NO, I THINK IT'S REAL.
WERE THOSE REAL GANGSTERS...? EWW....
WOOP
WHACK
DASH
LOOK, THAT WOMAN IS ESCAPING!
GETTING IT ON MY PHONE. CAN I SELL IT TO A TV STATION? HEY, THE POLICE CARS ARE HERE!
VON
VON

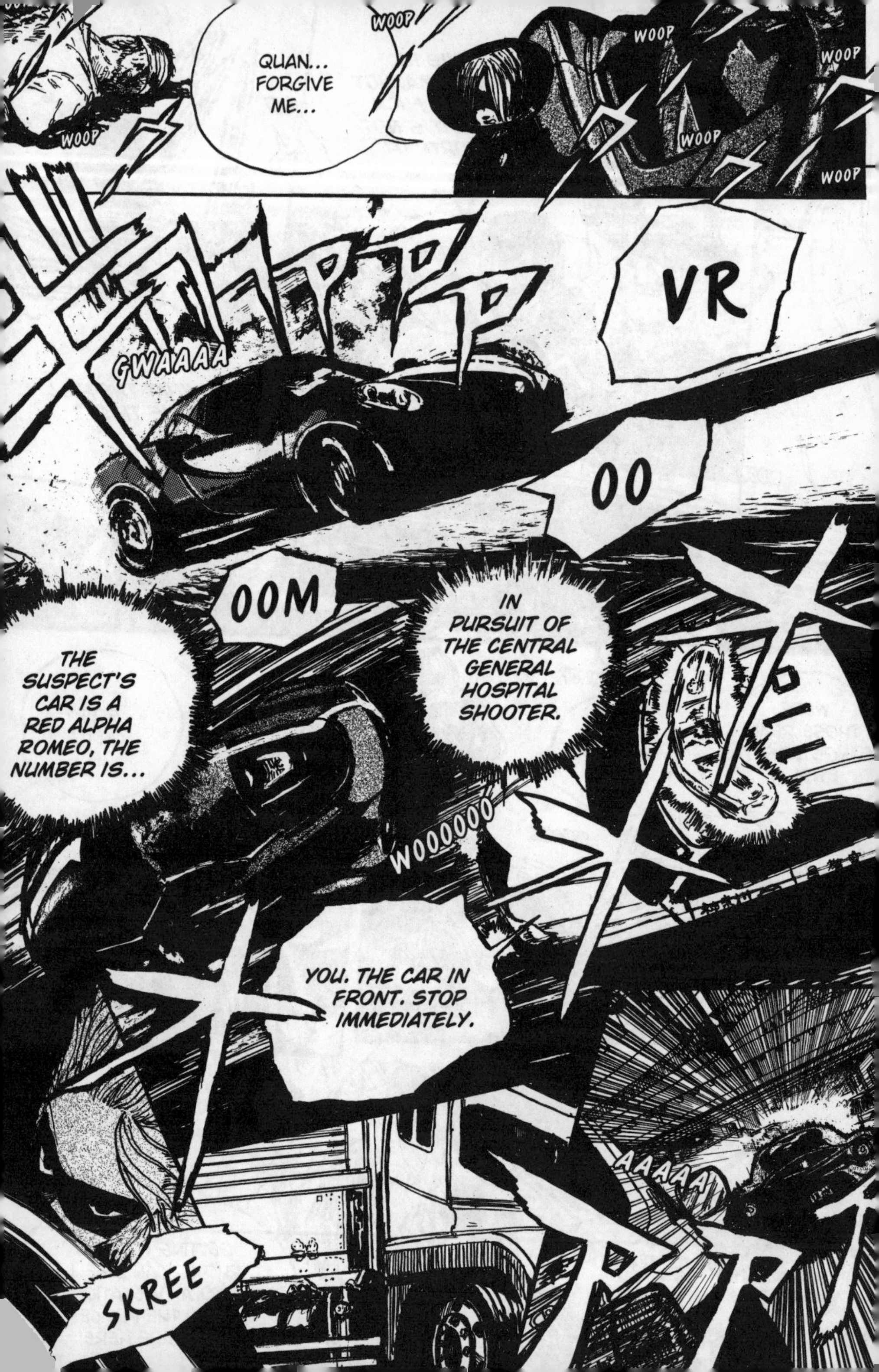
WOOP
WOOP
WOOP
WOOP
WOOP
QUAN... FORGIVE ME...
WOOP
VR
OO
OOM
GWAAAA
IN PURSUIT OF THE CENTRAL GENERAL HOSPITAL SHOOTER.
THE SUSPECT'S CAR IS A RED ALPHA ROMEO, THE NUMBER IS...
WOOOOOO
YOU. THE CAR IN FRONT. STOP IMMEDIATELY.
AAAAA
SKREE

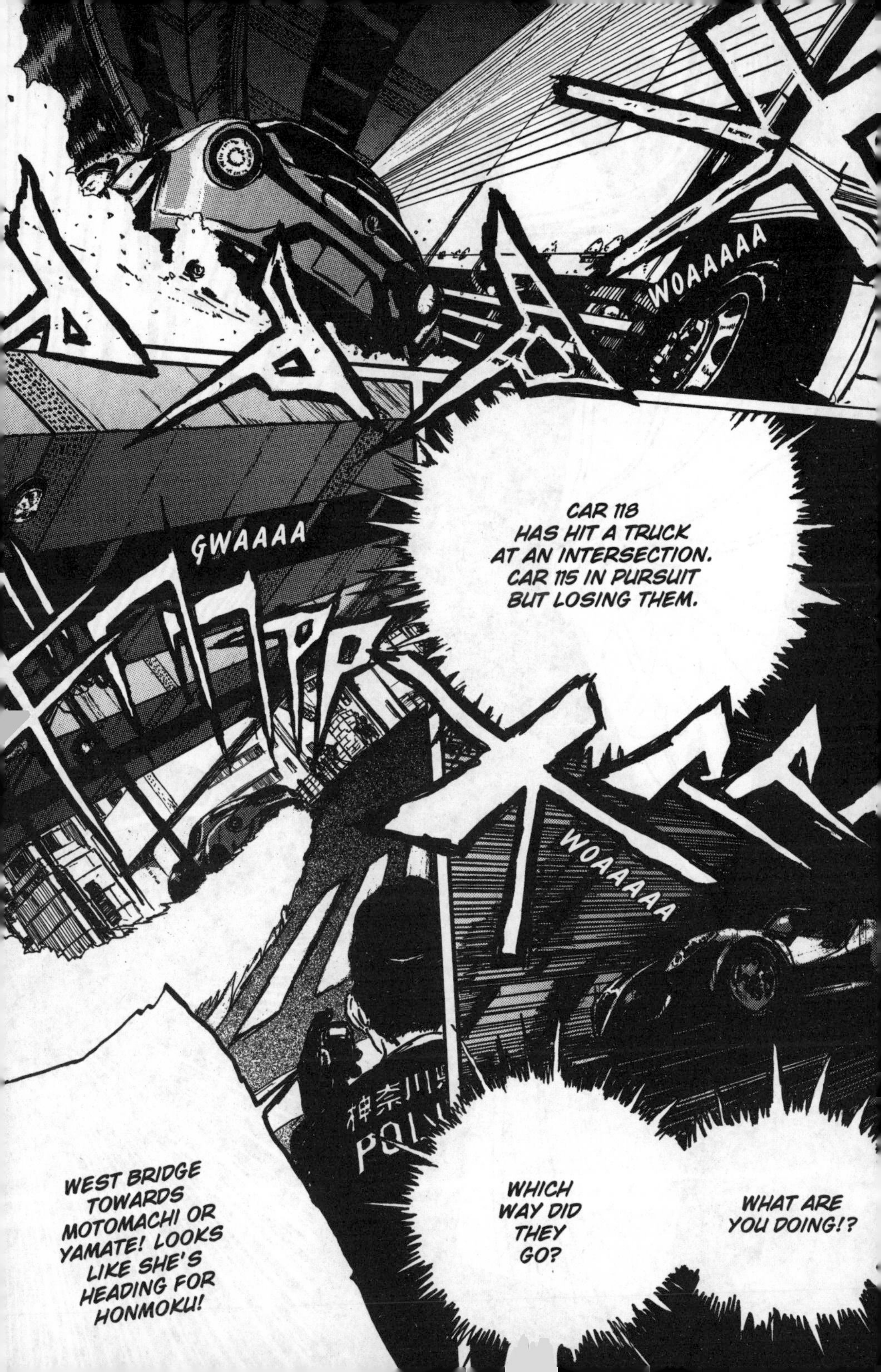
WOAAAAA
GWAAAA
CAR 118 HAS HIT A TRUCK AT AN INTERSECTION. CAR 115 IN PURSUIT BUT LOSING THEM.
WOAAAAA
神奈川県
POLI
WHAT ARE YOU DOING!?
WHICH WAY DID THEY GO?
WEST BRIDGE TOWARDS MOTOMACHI OR YAMATE! LOOKS LIKE SHE'S HEADING FOR HONMOKU!

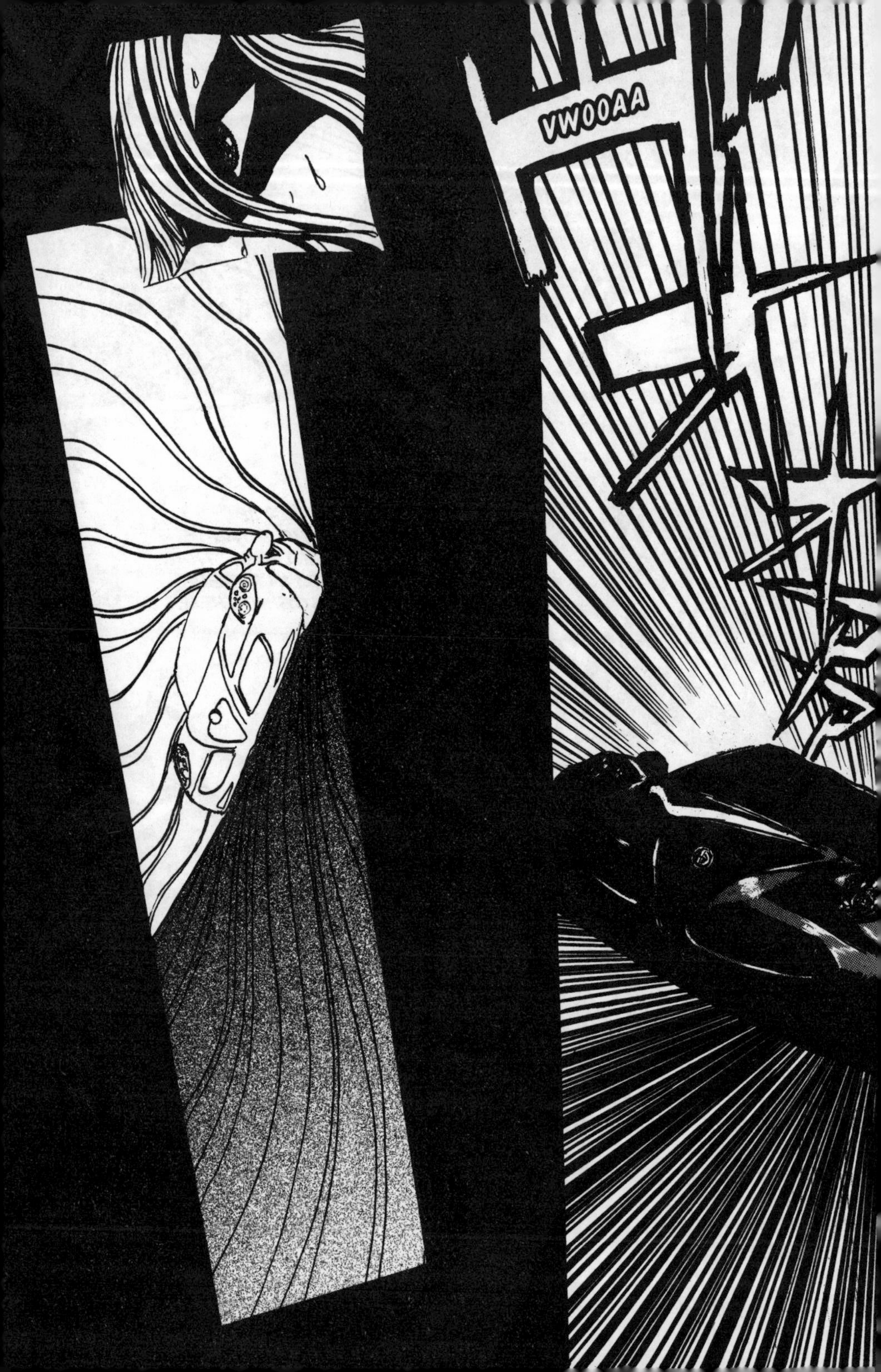
VWOOAA

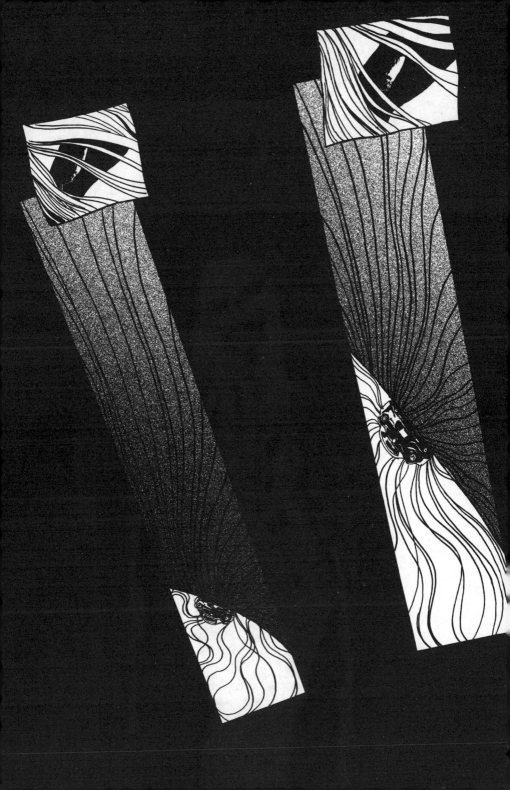

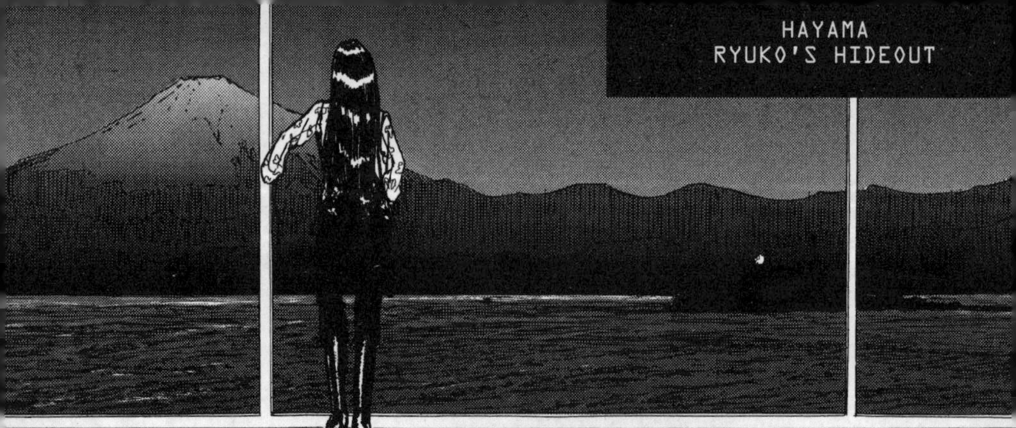
HAYAMA
RYUKO'S HIDEOUT

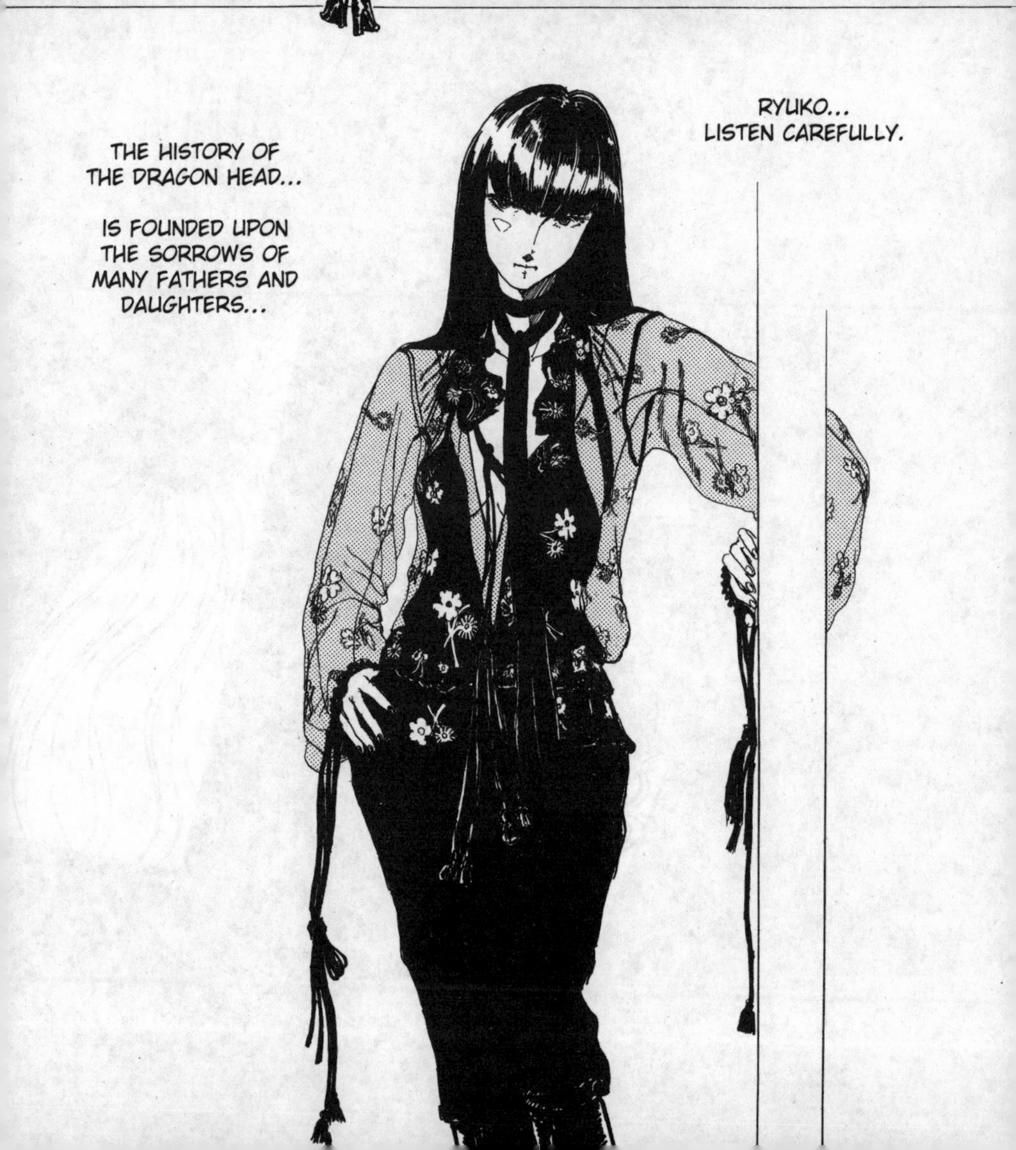
RYUKO... LISTEN CAREFULLY.
THE HISTORY OF THE DRAGON HEAD...
IS FOUNDED UPON THE SORROWS OF MANY FATHERS AND DAUGHTERS...

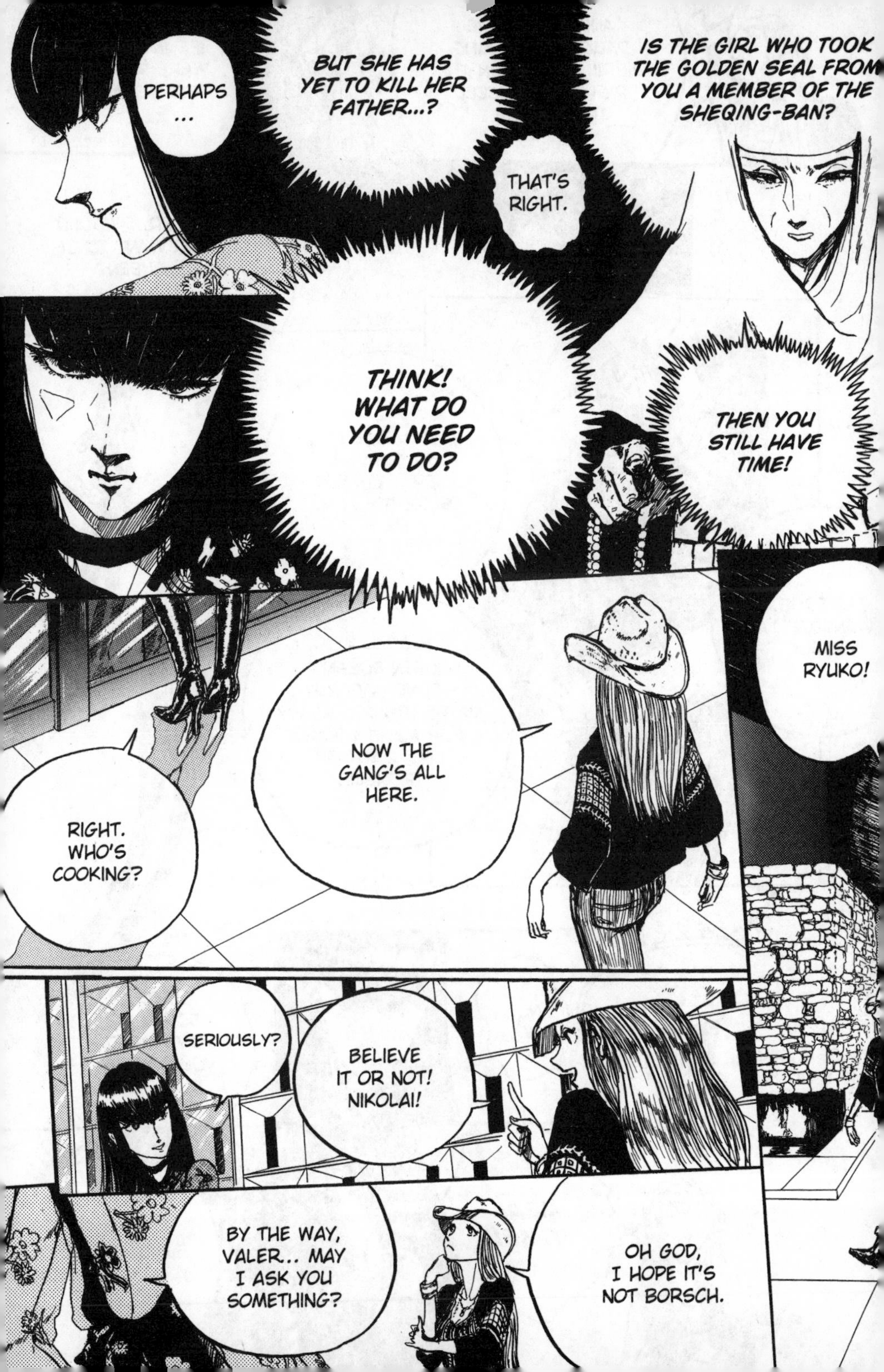
IS THE GIRL WHO TOOK THE GOLDEN SEAL FROM YOU A MEMBER OF THE SHEQING-BAN?
THAT'S RIGHT.
BUT SHE HAS YET TO KILL HER FATHER...?
PERHAPS ...
THEN YOU STILL HAVE TIME!
THINK! WHAT DO YOU NEED TO DO?
MISS RYUKO!
NOW THE GANG'S ALL HERE.
RIGHT. WHO'S COOKING?
BELIEVE IT OR NOT! NIKOLAI!
SERIOUSLY?
OH GOD, I HOPE IT'S NOT BORSCH.
BY THE WAY, VALER... MAY I ASK YOU SOMETHING?

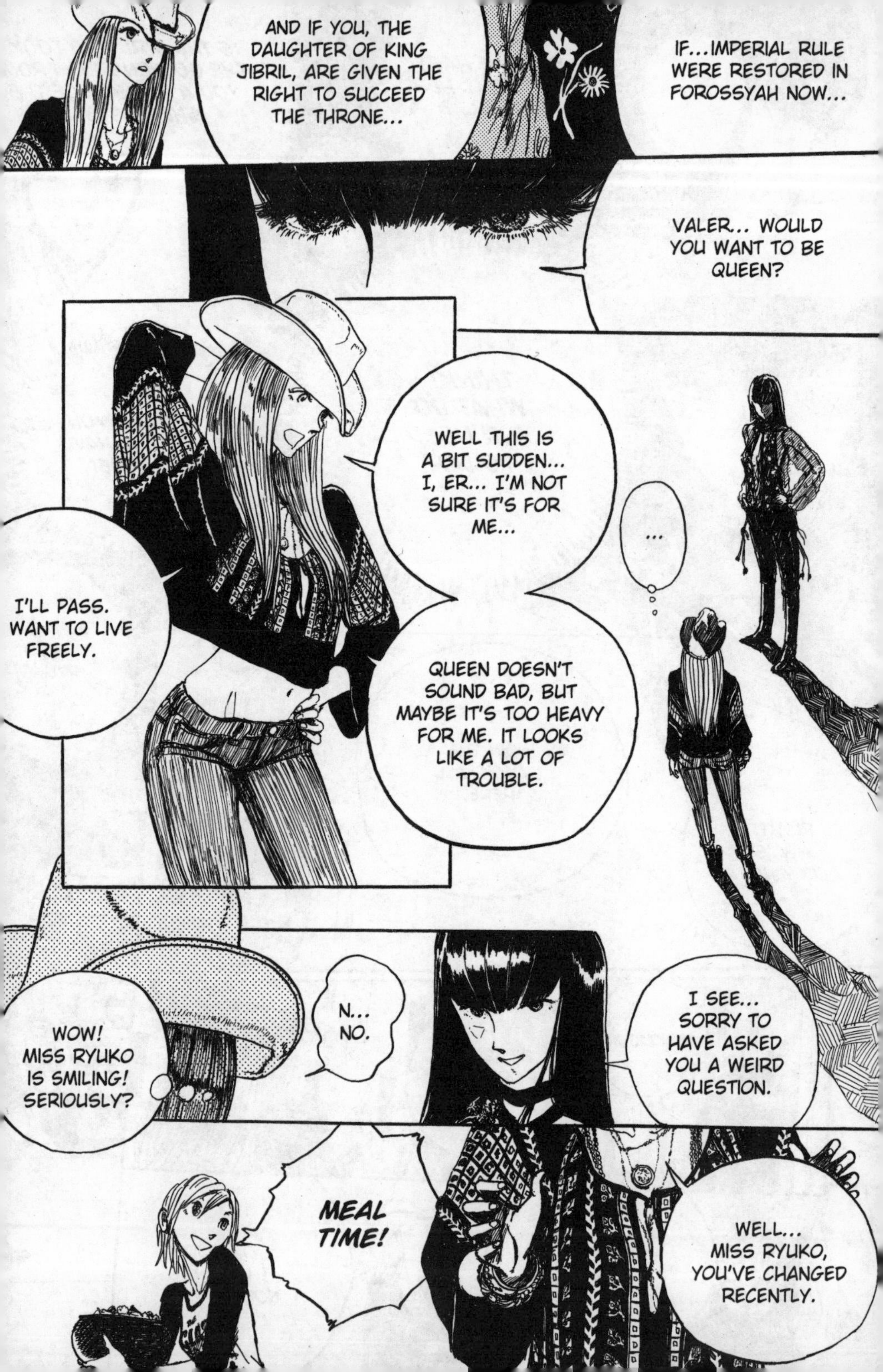
IF...IMPERIAL RULE WERE RESTORED IN FOROSSYAH NOW...
AND IF YOU, THE DAUGHTER OF KING JIBRIL, ARE GIVEN THE RIGHT TO SUCCEED THE THRONE...
VALER... WOULD YOU WANT TO BE QUEEN?
...
WELL THIS IS A BIT SUDDEN... I, ER... I'M NOT SURE IT'S FOR ME...
QUEEN DOESN'T SOUND BAD, BUT MAYBE IT'S TOO HEAVY FOR ME. IT LOOKS LIKE A LOT OF TROUBLE.
I'LL PASS. WANT TO LIVE FREELY.
I SEE... SORRY TO HAVE ASKED YOU A WEIRD QUESTION.
N... NO.
WOW! MISS RYUKO IS SMILING! SERIOUSLY?
WELL... MISS RYUKO, YOU'VE CHANGED RECENTLY.
MEAL TIME!

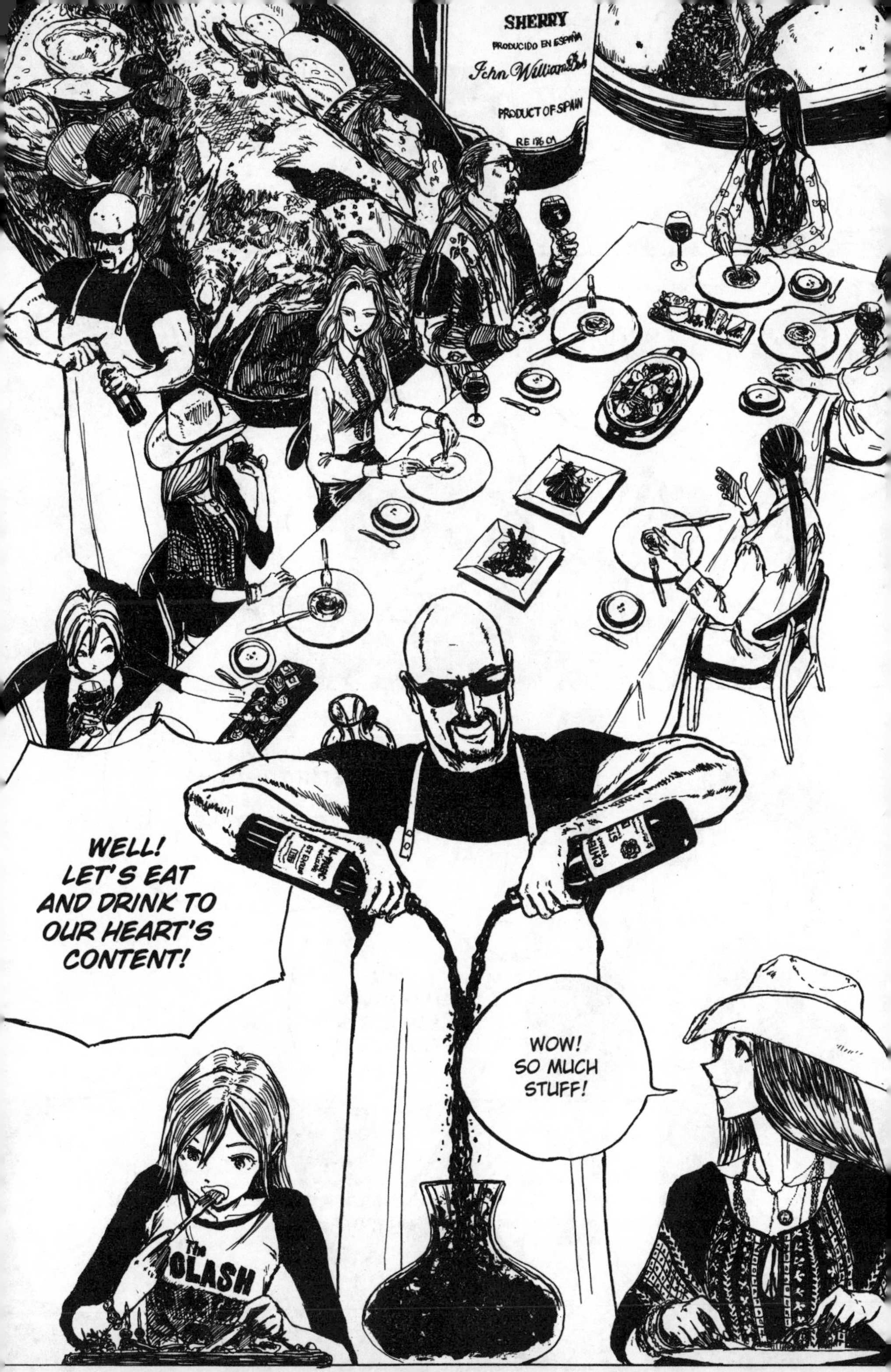
SHERRY
PRODUCIDO EN ESPAÑA
PRODUCT OF SPAIN
WELL! LET'S EAT AND DRINK TO OUR HEART'S CONTENT!
WOW! SO MUCH STUFF!
The CLASH

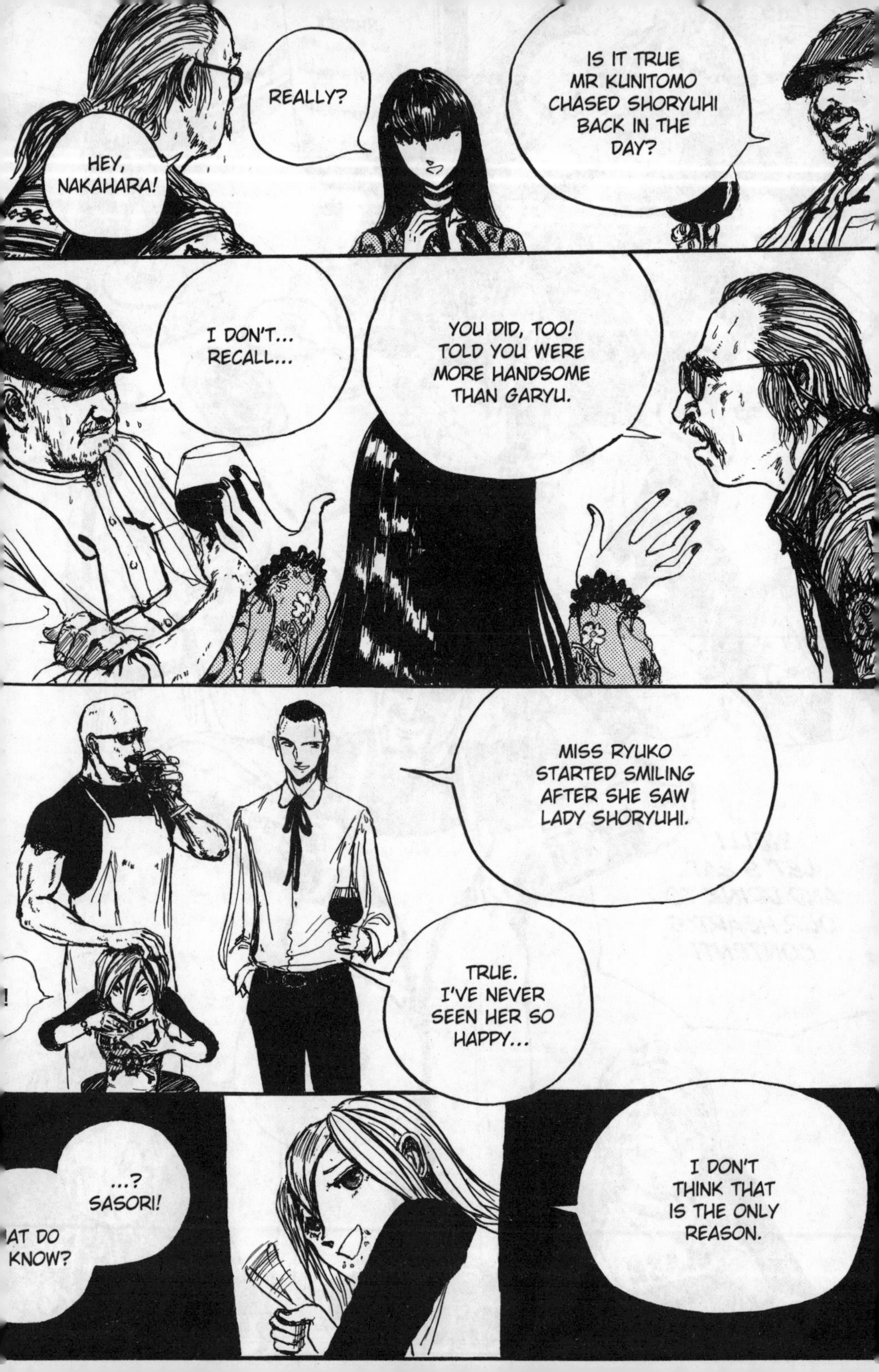
HEY, NAKAHARA!
REALLY?
IS IT TRUE MR KUNITOMO CHASED SHORYUHI BACK IN THE DAY?
I DON'T... RECALL...
YOU DID, TOO! TOLD YOU WERE MORE HANDSOME THAN GARYU.
MISS RYUKO STARTED SMILING AFTER SHE SAW LADY SHORYUHI.
TRUE. I'VE NEVER SEEN HER SO HAPPY...
AT DO KNOW?
...? SASORI!
I DON'T THINK THAT IS THE ONLY REASON.

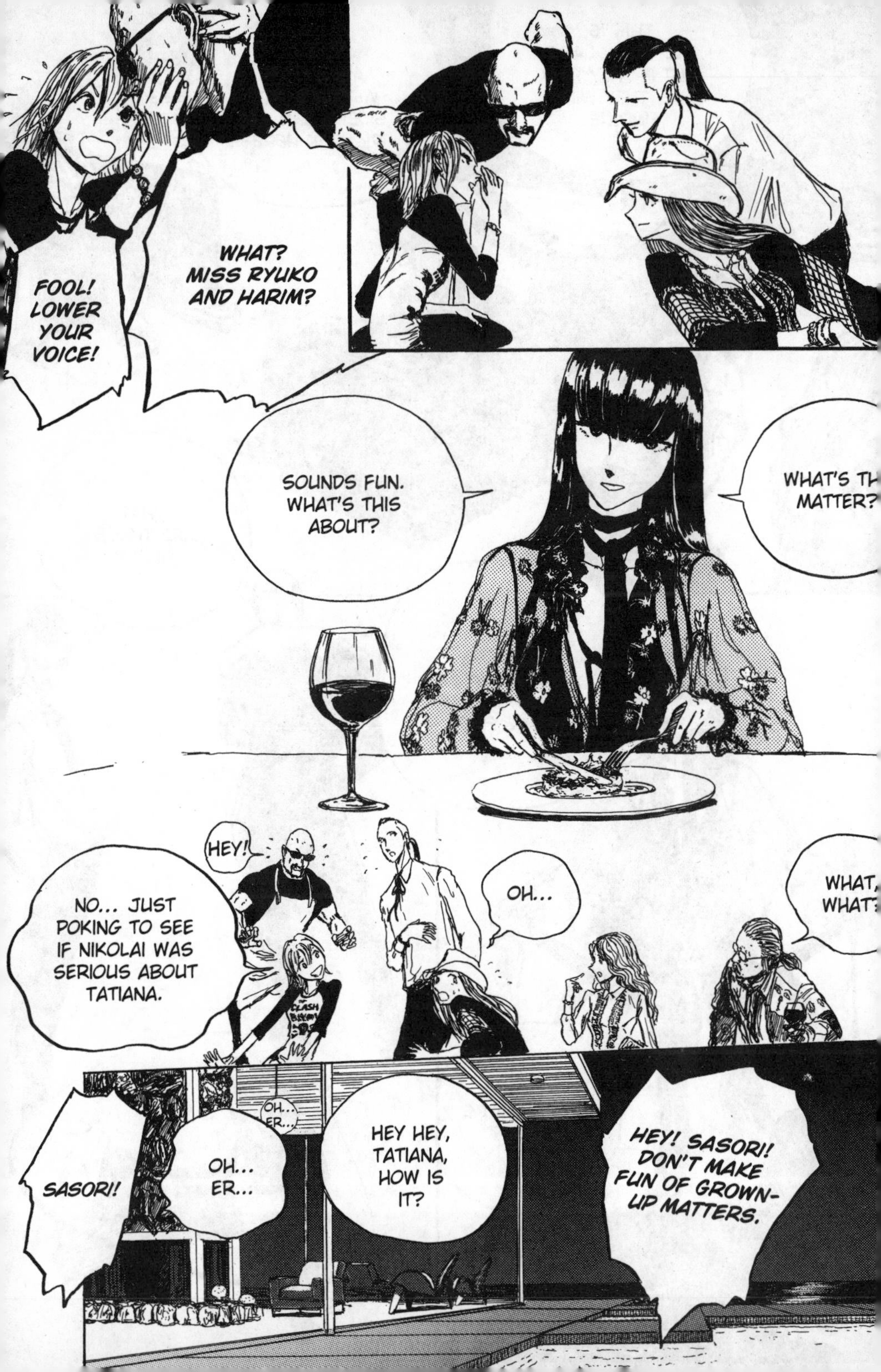
WHAT? MISS RYUKO AND HARIM?
FOOL! LOWER YOUR VOICE!
WHAT'S TH MATTER?
SOUNDS FUN. WHAT'S THIS ABOUT?
WHAT, WHAT?
OH...
HEY!
NO... JUST POKING TO SEE IF NIKOLAI WAS SERIOUS ABOUT TATIANA.
HEY! SASORI! DON'T MAKE FUN OF GROWN-UP MATTERS.
HEY HEY, TATIANA, HOW IS IT?
OH... ER...
OH... ER...
SASORI!

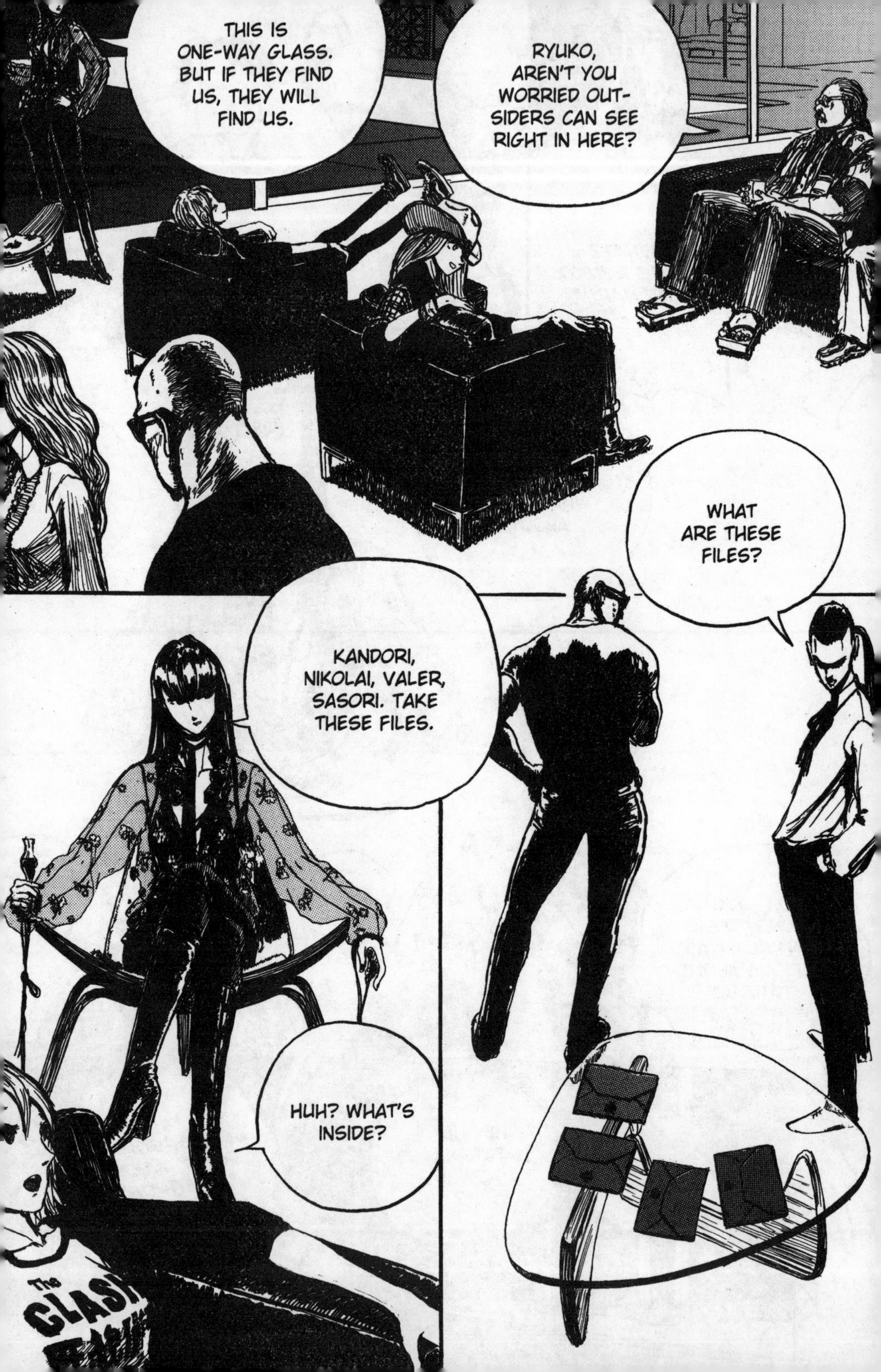
RYUKO, AREN'T YOU WORRIED OUT-SIDERS CAN SEE RIGHT IN HERE?
THIS IS ONE-WAY GLASS. BUT IF THEY FIND US, THEY WILL FIND US.
WHAT ARE THESE FILES?
KANDORI, NIKOLAI, VALER, SASORI. TAKE THESE FILES.
HUH? WHAT'S INSIDE?

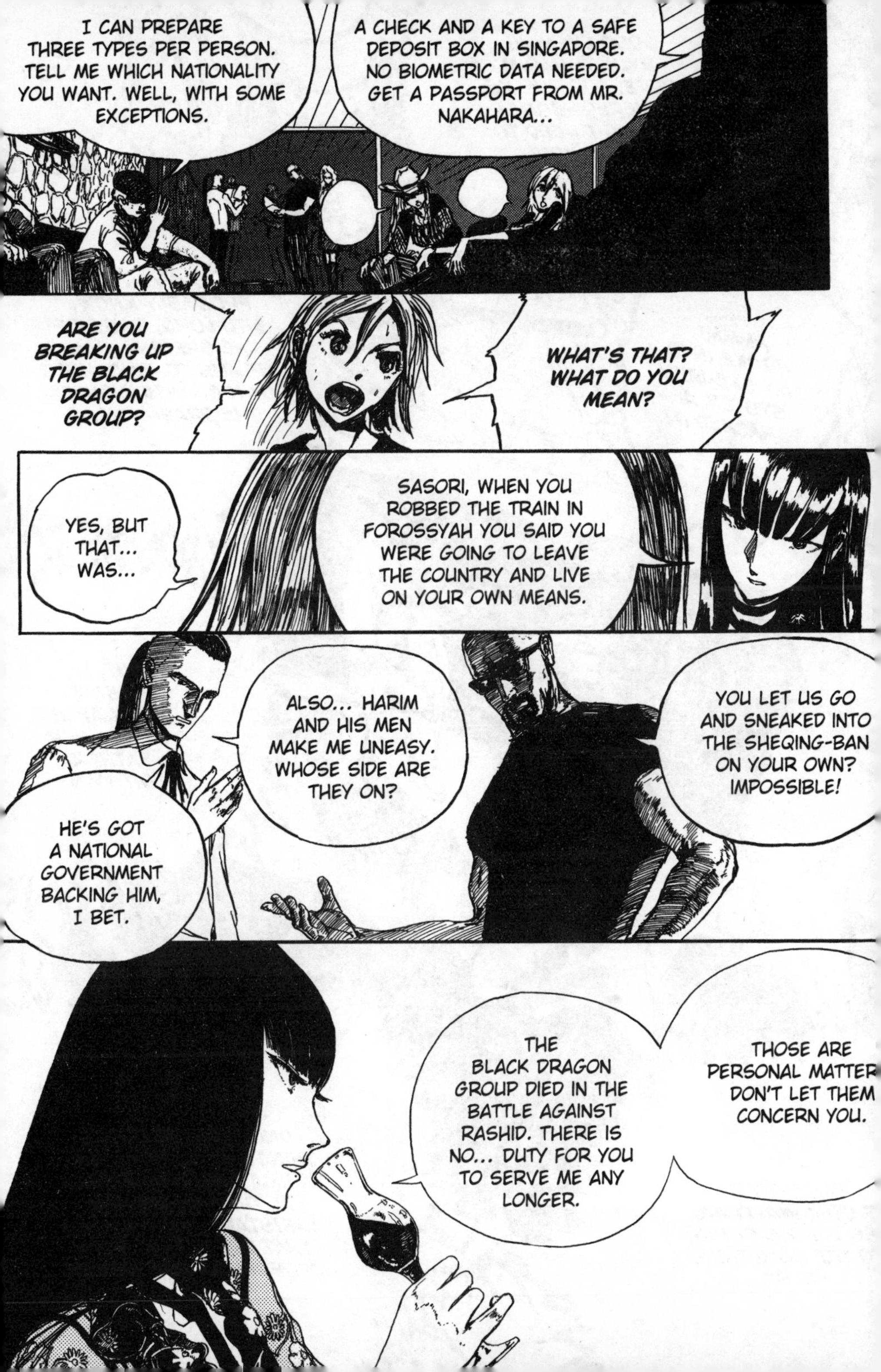
A CHECK AND A KEY TO A SAFE DEPOSIT BOX IN SINGAPORE. NO BIOMETRIC DATA NEEDED. GET A PASSPORT FROM MR. NAKAHARA...
I CAN PREPARE THREE TYPES PER PERSON. TELL ME WHICH NATIONALITY YOU WANT. WELL, WITH SOME EXCEPTIONS.
WHAT'S THAT? WHAT DO YOU MEAN?
ARE YOU BREAKING UP THE BLACK DRAGON GROUP?
SASORI, WHEN YOU ROBBED THE TRAIN IN FOROSSYAH YOU SAID YOU WERE GOING TO LEAVE THE COUNTRY AND LIVE ON YOUR OWN MEANS.
YES, BUT THAT... WAS...
YOU LET US GO AND SNEAKED INTO THE SHEQING-BAN ON YOUR OWN? IMPOSSIBLE!
ALSO... HARIM AND HIS MEN MAKE ME UNEASY. WHOSE SIDE ARE THEY ON?
HE'S GOT A NATIONAL GOVERNMENT BACKING HIM, I BET.
THOSE ARE PERSONAL MATTER DON'T LET THEM CONCERN YOU.
THE BLACK DRAGON GROUP DIED IN THE BATTLE AGAINST RASHID. THERE IS NO... DUTY FOR YOU TO SERVE ME ANY LONGER.

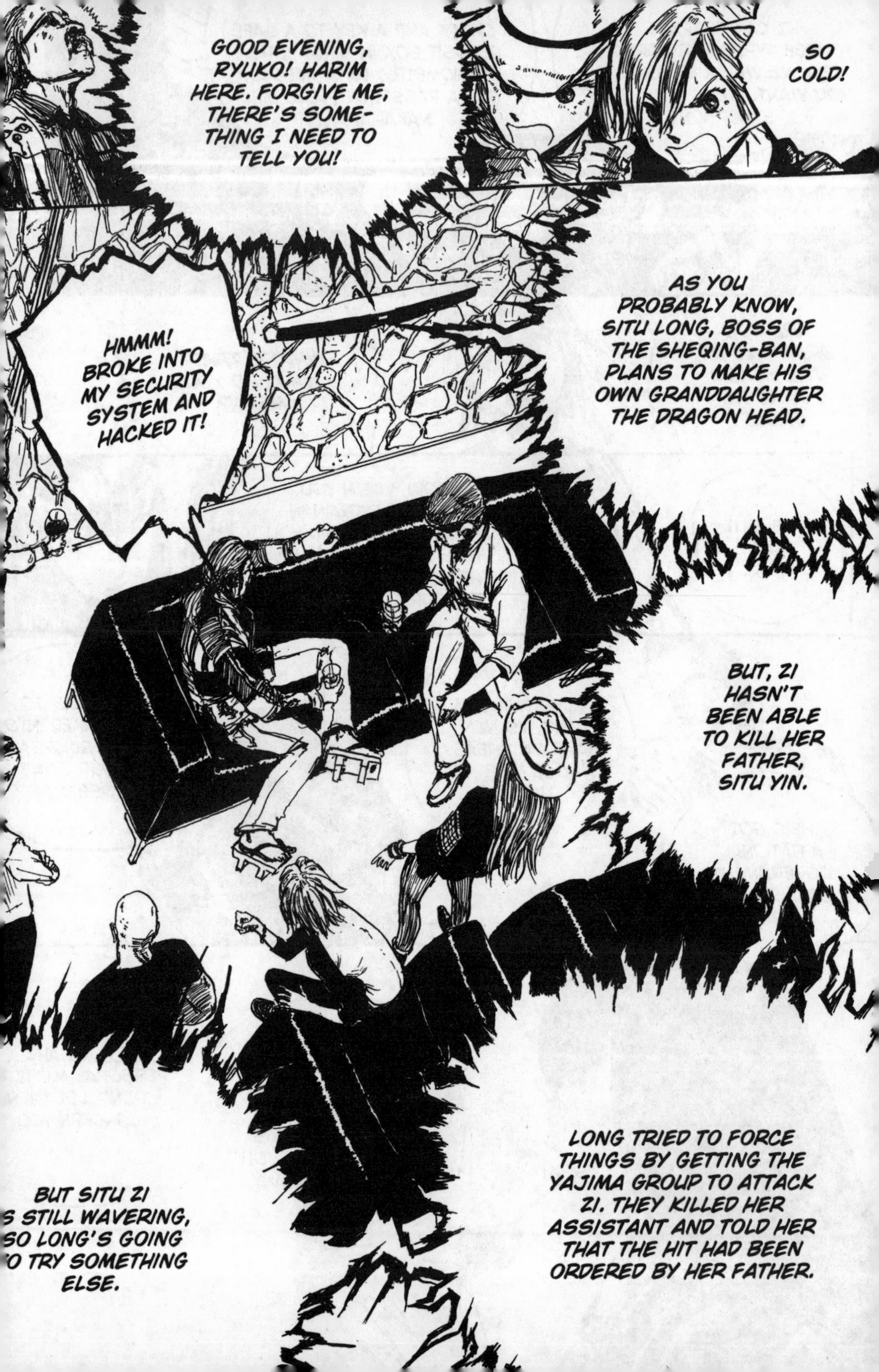
SO COLD!
GOOD EVENING, RYUKO! HARIM HERE. FORGIVE ME, THERE'S SOME-THING I NEED TO TELL YOU!
HMMM! BROKE INTO MY SECURITY SYSTEM AND HACKED IT!
AS YOU PROBABLY KNOW, SITU LONG, BOSS OF THE SHEQING-BAN, PLANS TO MAKE HIS OWN GRANDDAUGHTER THE DRAGON HEAD.
BUT, ZI HASN'T BEEN ABLE TO KILL HER FATHER, SITU YIN.
LONG TRIED TO FORCE THINGS BY GETTING THE YAJIMA GROUP TO ATTACK ZI. THEY KILLED HER ASSISTANT AND TOLD HER THAT THE HIT HAD BEEN ORDERED BY HER FATHER.
BUT SITU ZI S STILL WAVERING, SO LONG'S GOING O TRY SOMETHING ELSE.

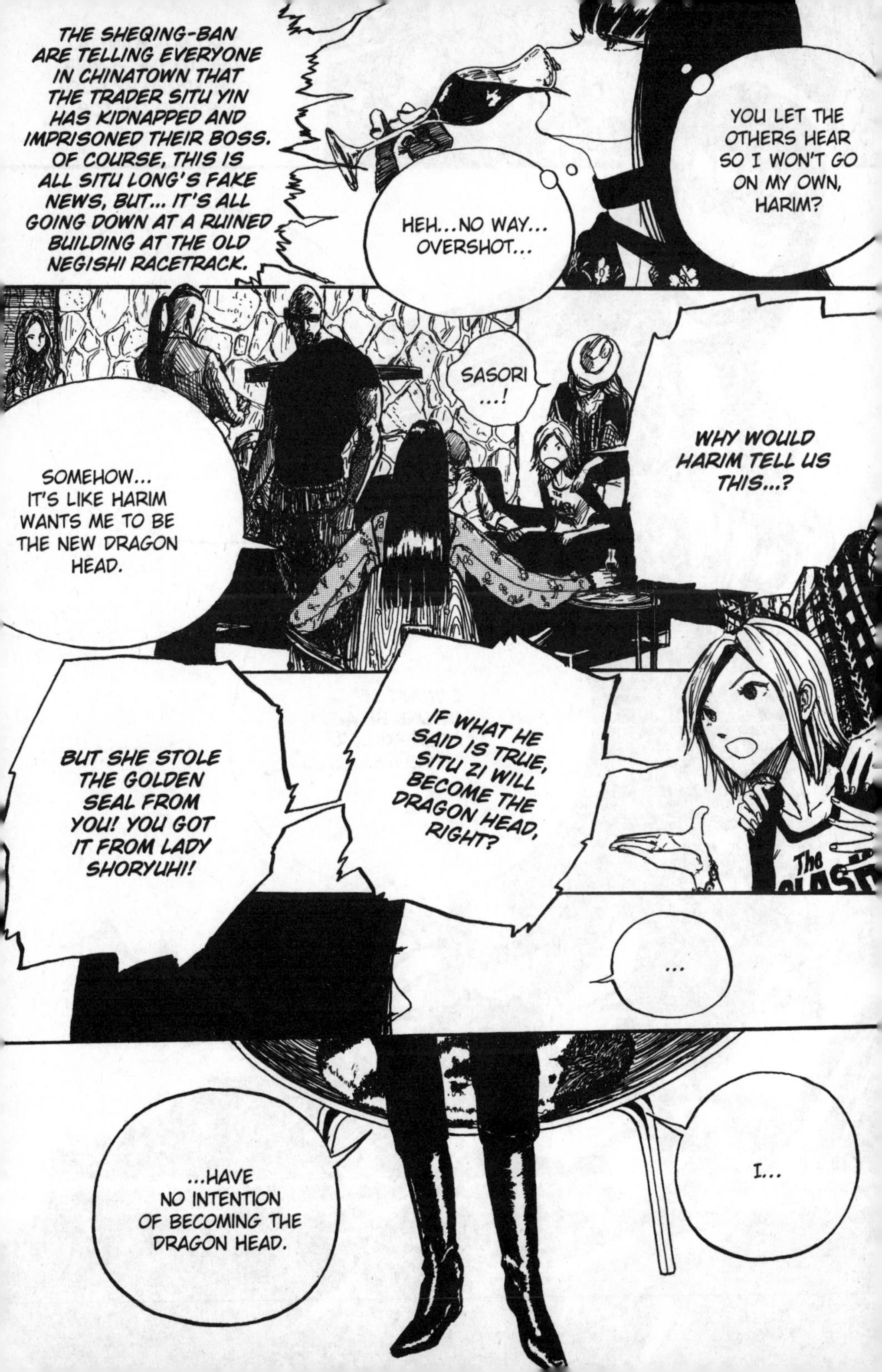
THE SHEQING-BAN ARE TELLING EVERYONE IN CHINATOWN THAT THE TRADER SITU YIN HAS KIDNAPPED AND IMPRISONED THEIR BOSS. OF COURSE, THIS IS ALL SITU LONG'S FAKE NEWS, BUT... IT'S ALL GOING DOWN AT A RUINED BUILDING AT THE OLD NEGISHI RACETRACK.
YOU LET THE OTHERS HEAR SO I WON'T GO ON MY OWN, HARIM?
HEH...NO WAY... OVERSHOT...
SASORI ...!
WHY WOULD HARIM TELL US THIS...?
SOMEHOW... IT'S LIKE HARIM WANTS ME TO BE THE NEW DRAGON HEAD.
IF WHAT HE SAID IS TRUE, SITU ZI WILL BECOME THE DRAGON HEAD, RIGHT?
BUT SHE STOLE THE GOLDEN SEAL FROM YOU! YOU GOT IT FROM LADY SHORYUHI!
...
I...
...HAVE NO INTENTION OF BECOMING THE DRAGON HEAD.

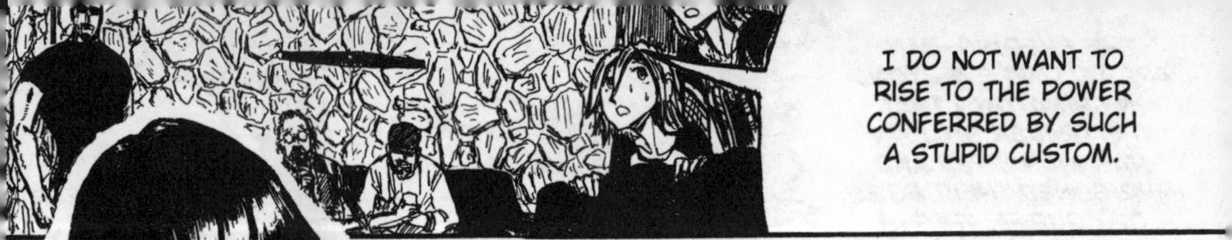
I DO NOT WANT TO RISE TO THE POWER CONFERRED BY SUCH A STUPID CUSTOM.
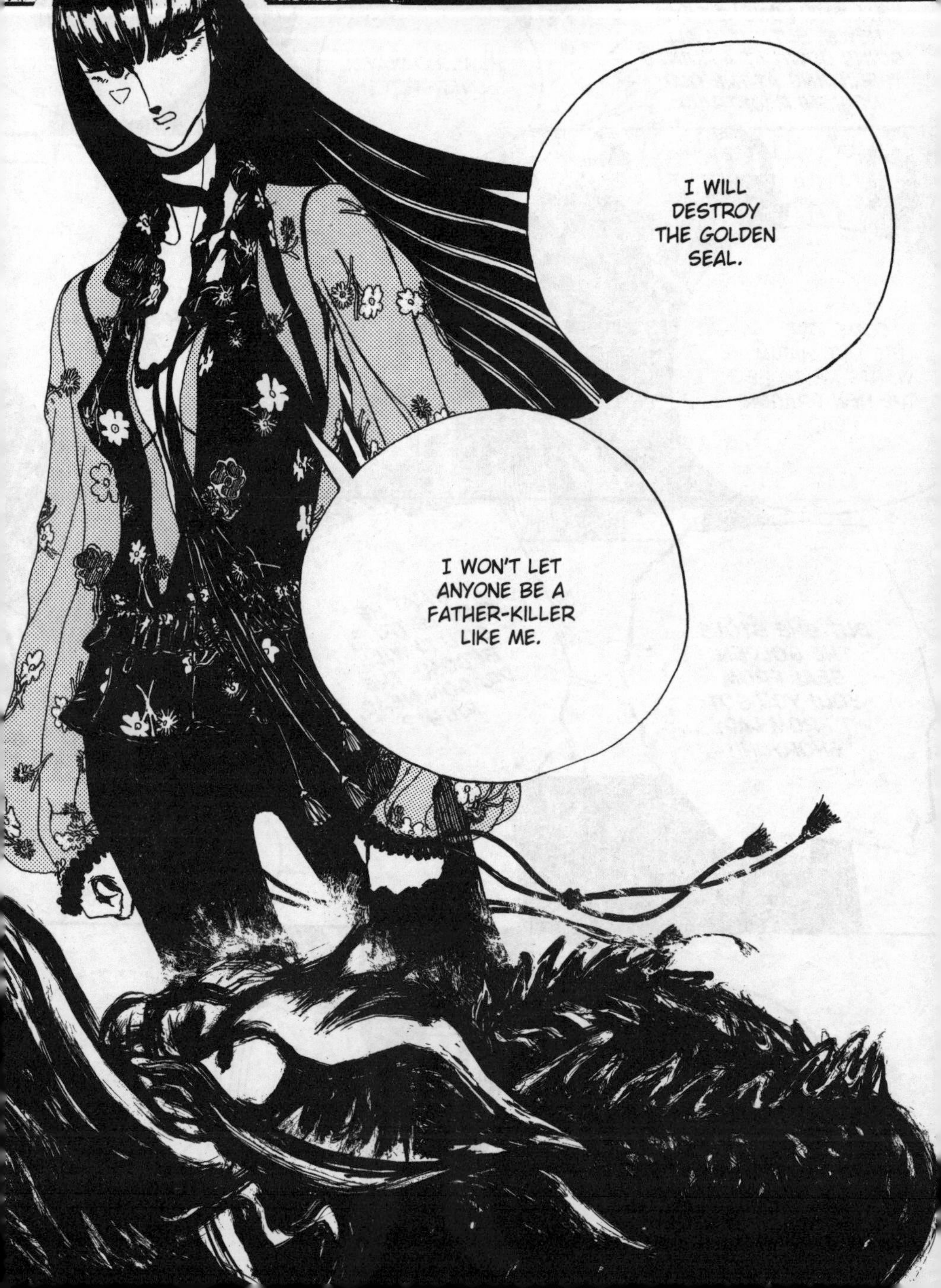
I WILL DESTROY THE GOLDEN SEAL.
I WON'T LET ANYONE BE A FATHER-KILLER LIKE ME.

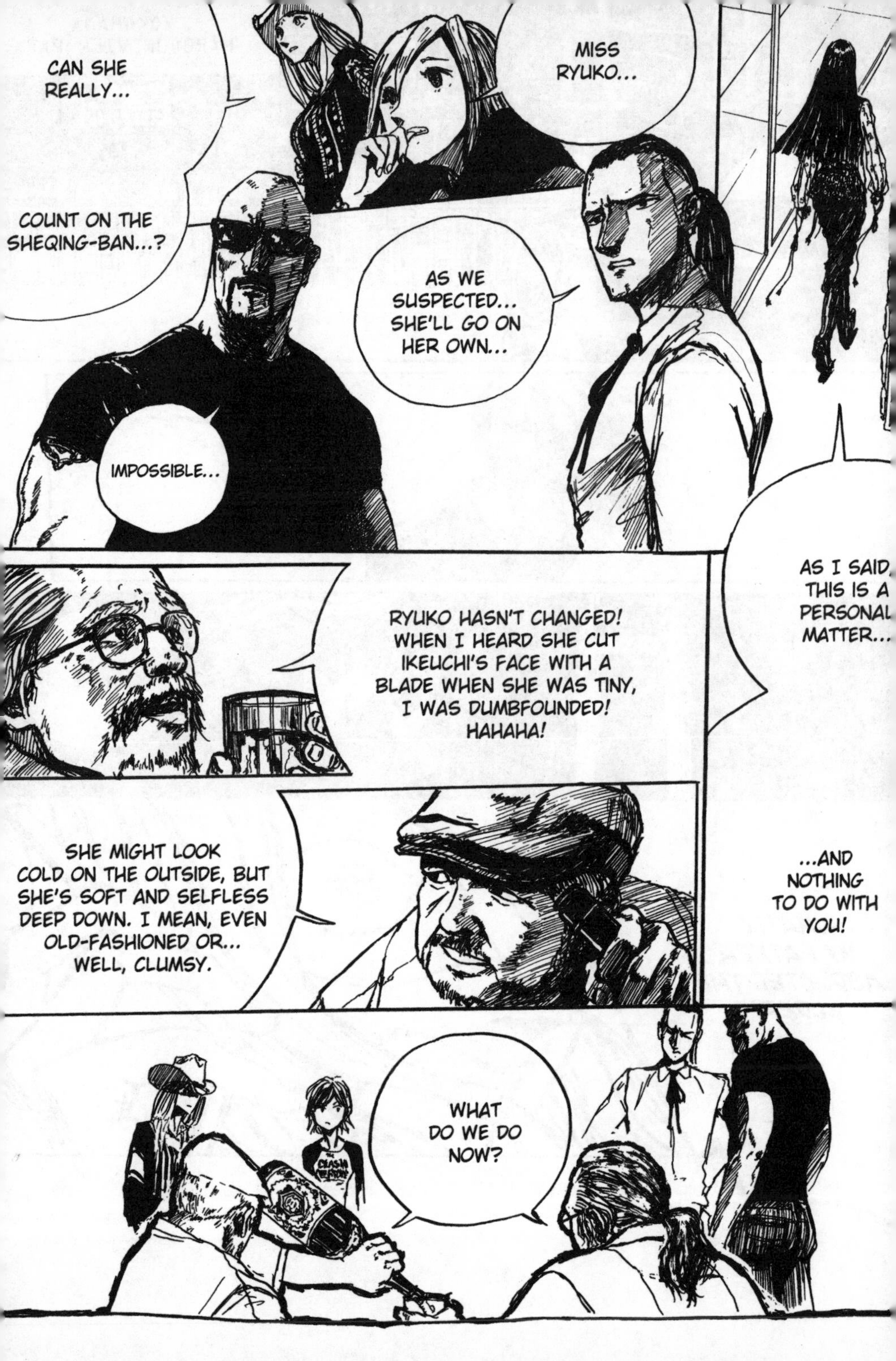
MISS RYUKO...
CAN SHE REALLY...
COUNT ON THE SHEQING-BAN...?
AS WE SUSPECTED... SHE'LL GO ON HER OWN...
IMPOSSIBLE...
AS I SAID THIS IS A PERSONAL MATTER...
...AND NOTHING TO DO WITH YOU!
RYUKO HASN'T CHANGED! WHEN I HEARD SHE CUT IKEUCHI'S FACE WITH A BLADE WHEN SHE WAS TINY, I WAS DUMBFOUNDED! HAHAHA!
SHE MIGHT LOOK COLD ON THE OUTSIDE, BUT SHE'S SOFT AND SELFLESS DEEP DOWN. I MEAN, EVEN OLD-FASHIONED OR... WELL, CLUMSY.
WHAT DO WE DO NOW?

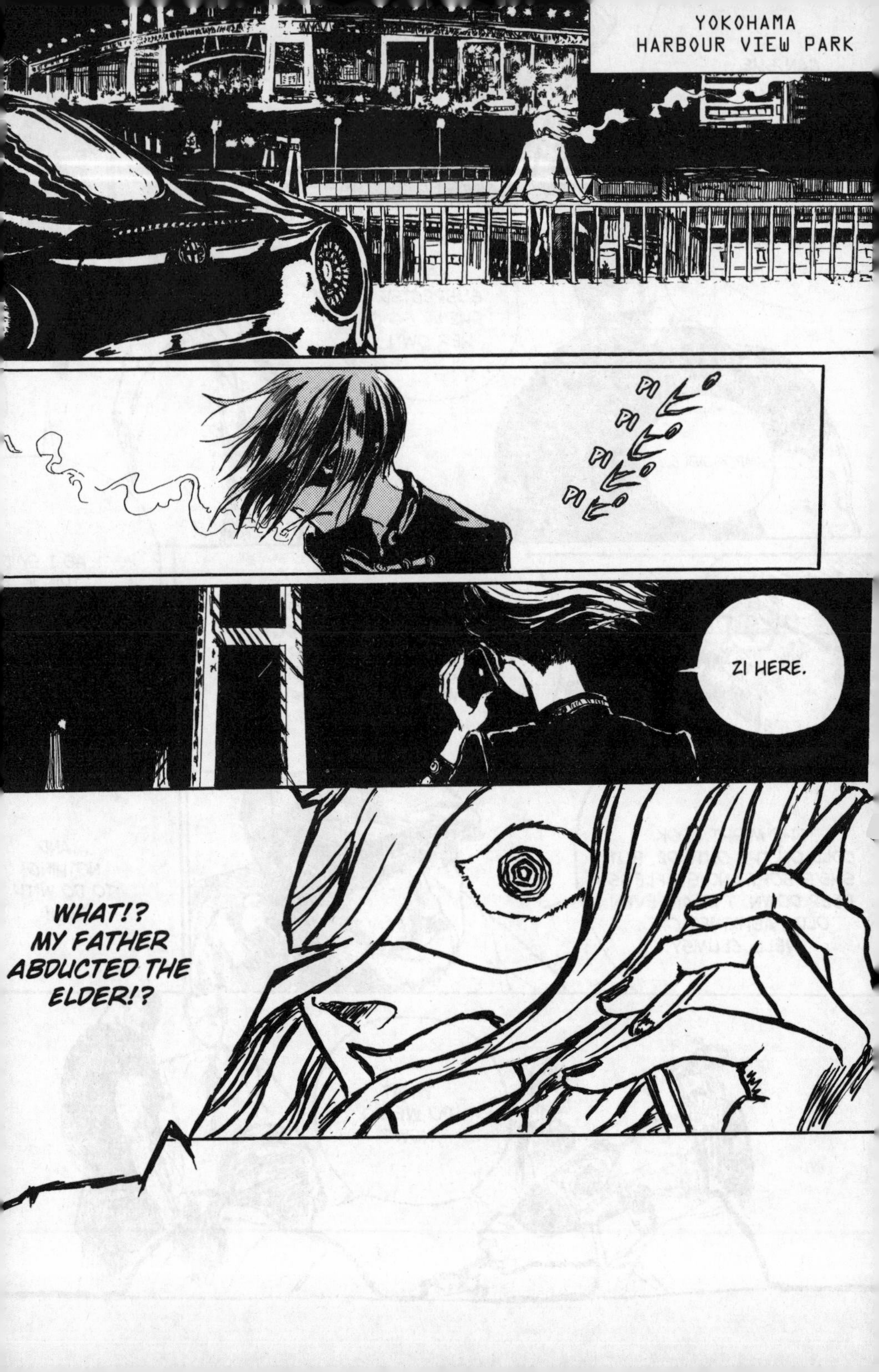
YOKOHAMA
HARBOUR VIEW PARK
PI PI PI PI
ZI HERE.
WHAT!? MY FATHER ABDUCTED THE ELDER!?

CHAPTER 9:
BLOODSHED

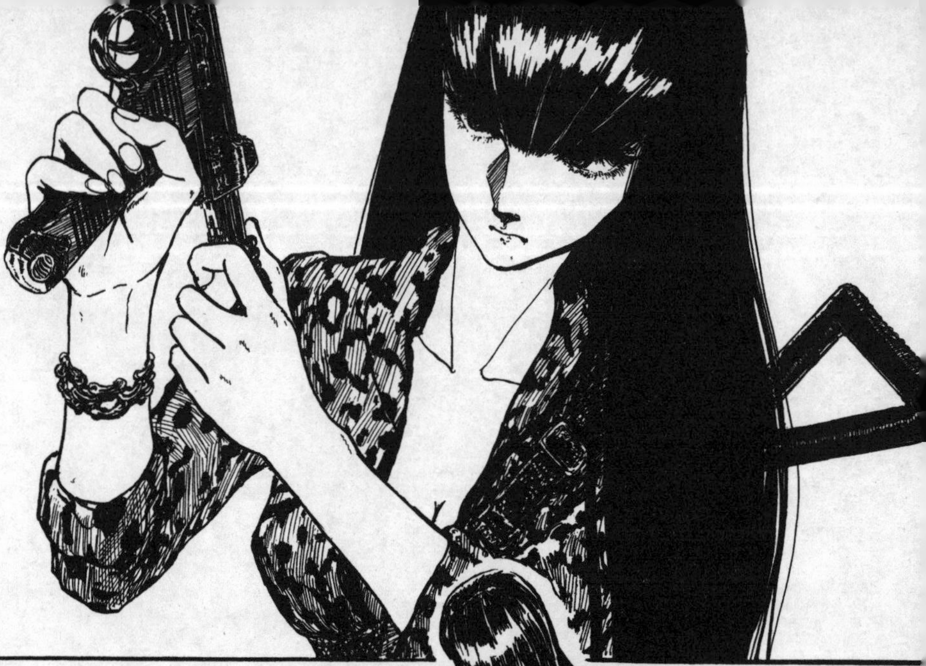
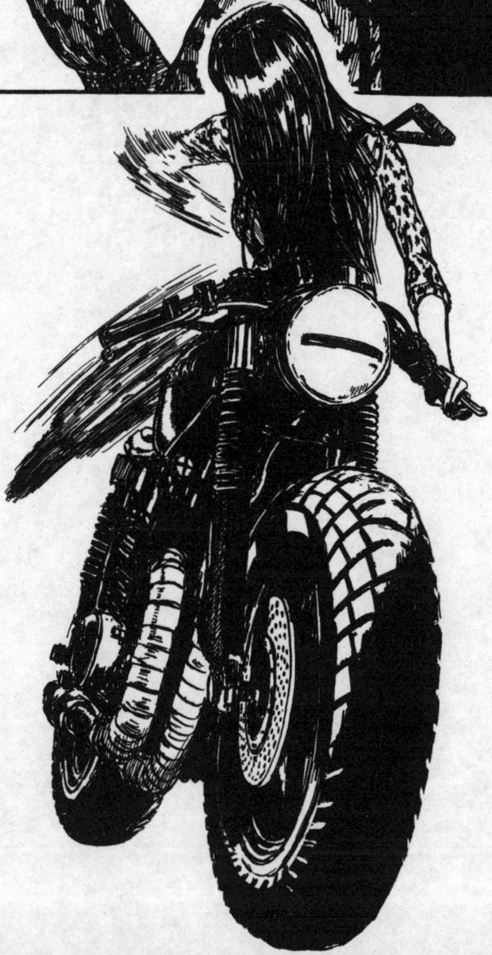

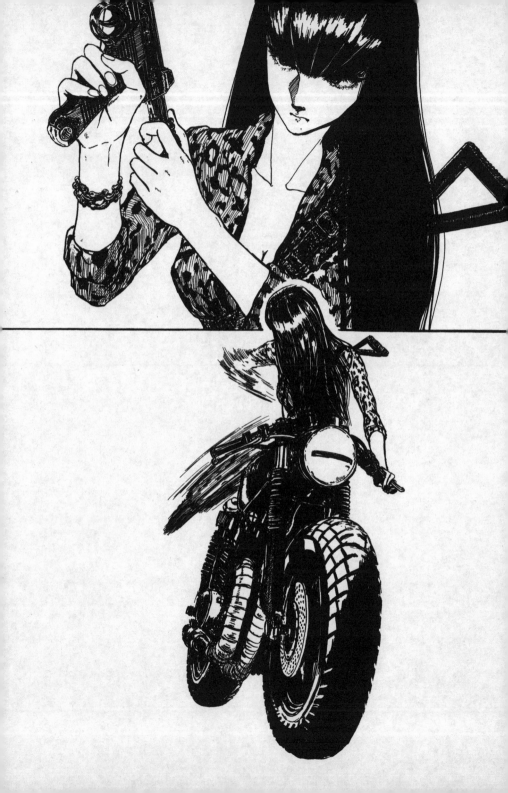

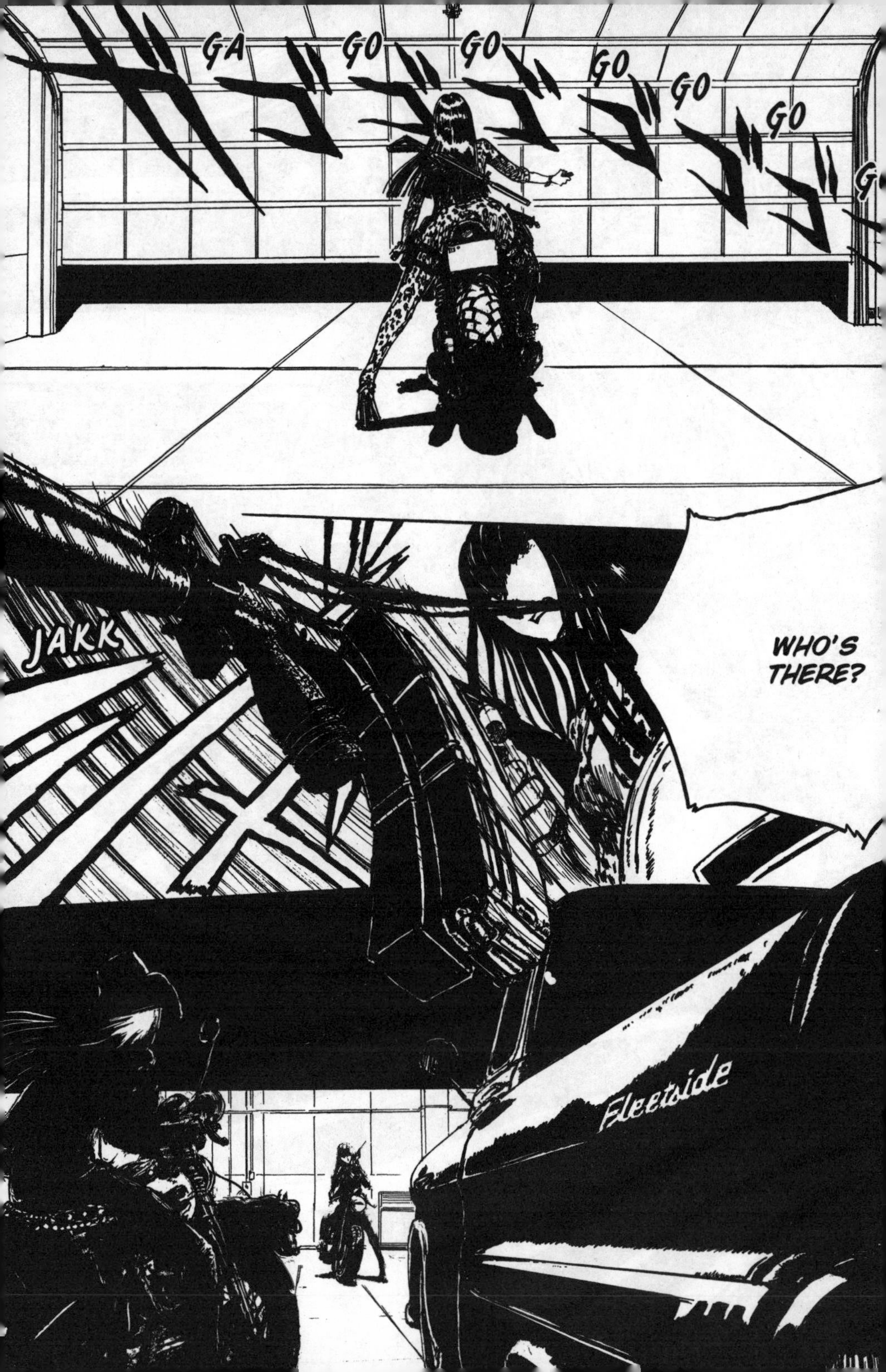
GA
GO
GO
GO
GO
GO
WHO'S THERE?
JAKK
Fleetside

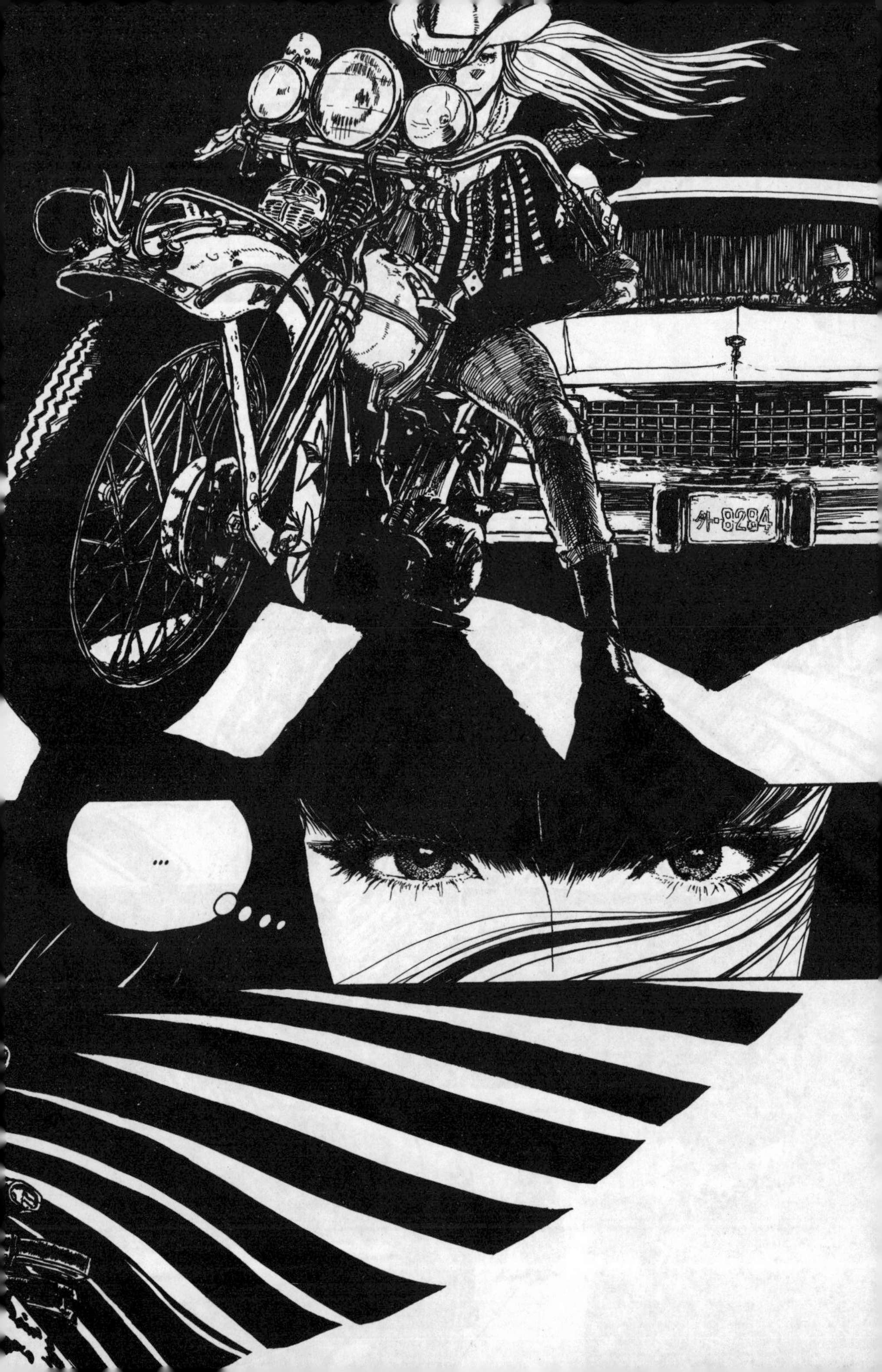
...

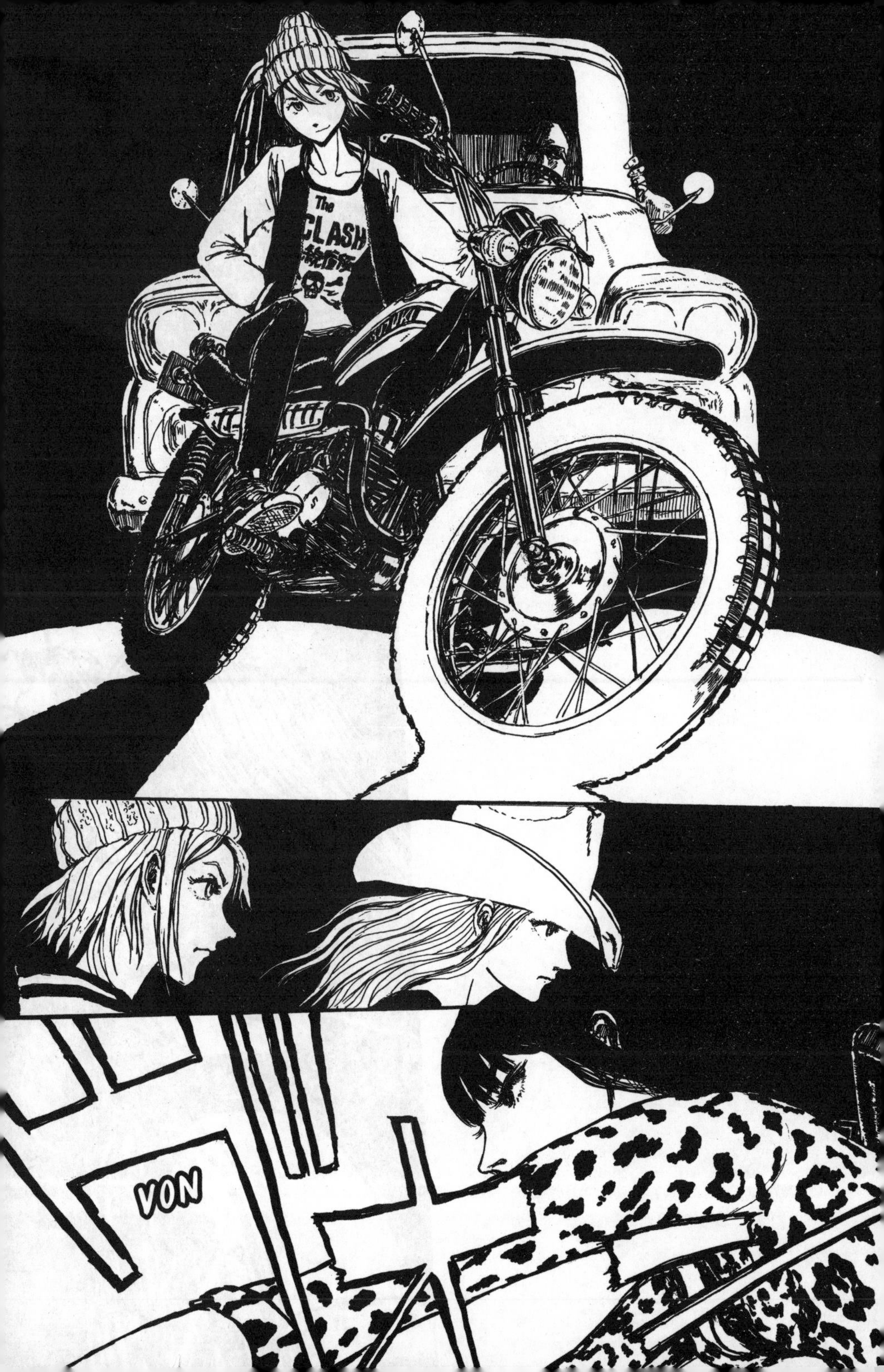
The CLASH
VON

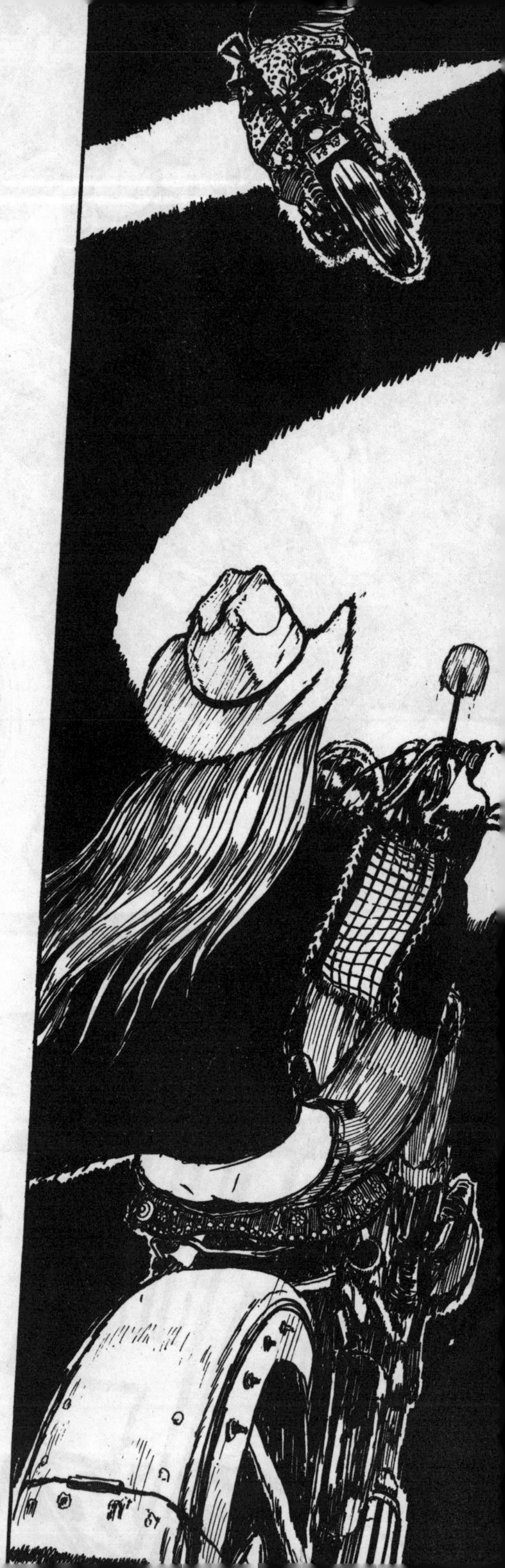

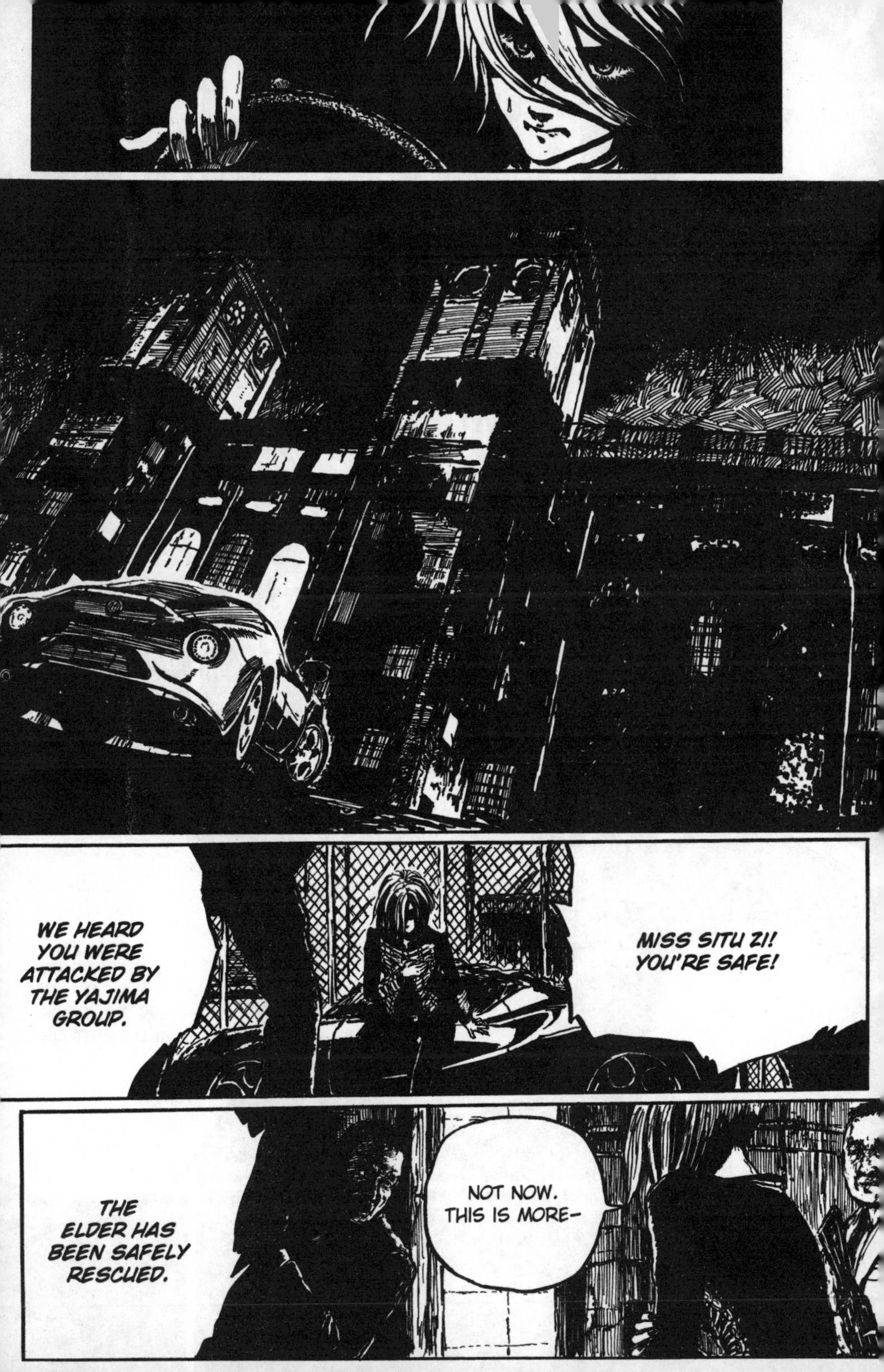
MISS SITU ZI! YOU'RE SAFE!
WE HEARD YOU WERE ATTACKED BY THE YAJIMA GROUP.
NOT NOW. THIS IS MORE-
THE ELDER HAS BEEN SAFELY RESCUED.

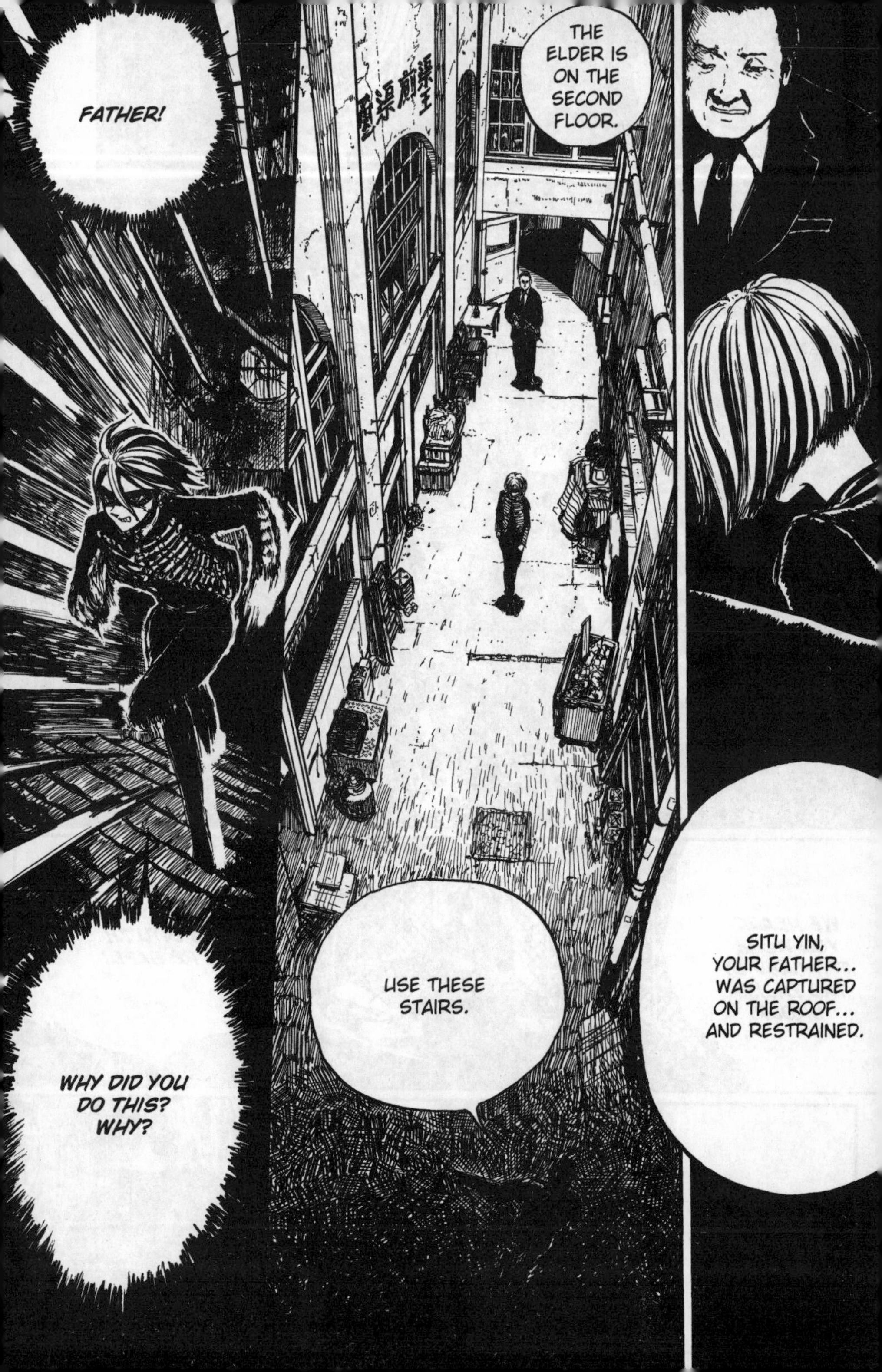
SITU YIN, YOUR FATHER... WAS CAPTURED ON THE ROOF... AND RESTRAINED.
THE ELDER IS ON THE SECOND FLOOR.
USE THESE STAIRS.
FATHER!
WHY DID YOU DO THIS? WHY?

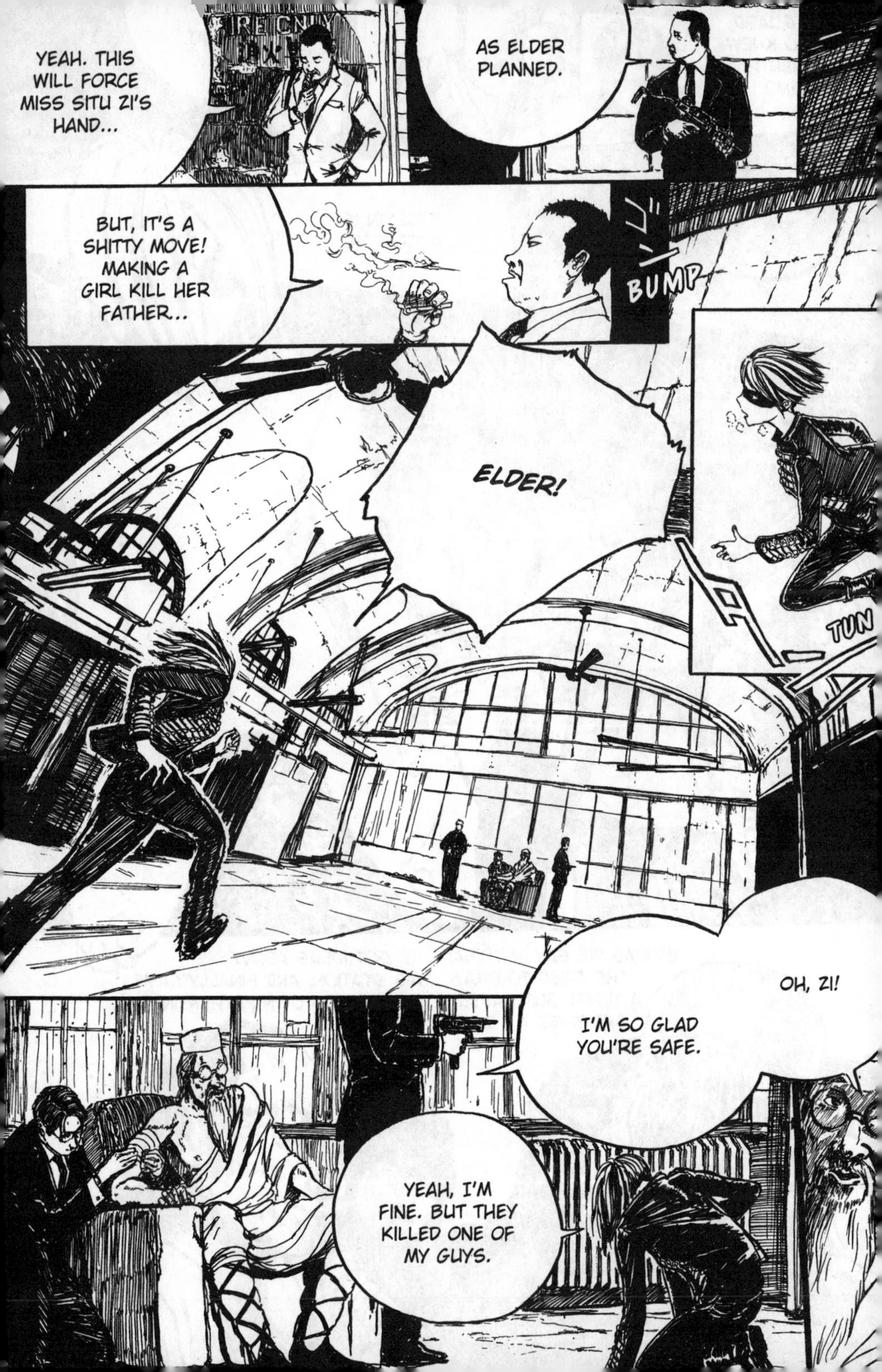
YEAH. THIS WILL FORCE MISS SITU ZI'S HAND...
AS ELDER PLANNED.
BUT, IT'S A SHITTY MOVE! MAKING A GIRL KILL HER FATHER...
BUMP
ELDER!
TUN
OH, ZI!
I'M SO GLAD YOU'RE SAFE.
YEAH, I'M FINE. BUT THEY KILLED ONE OF MY GUYS.

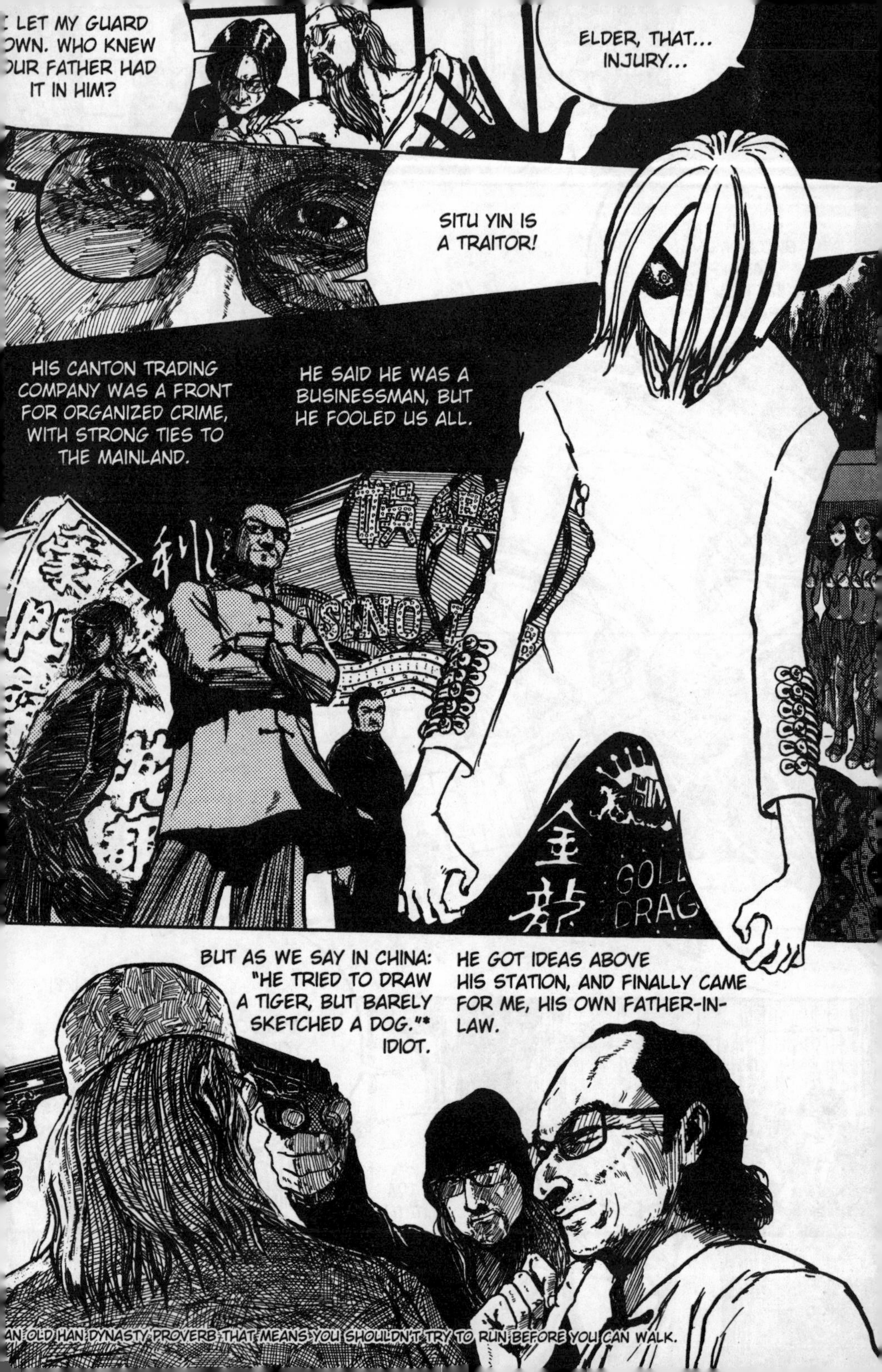
ELDER, THAT... INJURY...
LET MY GUARD OWN. WHO KNEW OUR FATHER HAD IT IN HIM?
SITU YIN IS A TRAITOR!
HE SAID HE WAS A BUSINESSMAN, BUT HE FOOLED US ALL.
HIS CANTON TRADING COMPANY WAS A FRONT FOR ORGANIZED CRIME, WITH STRONG TIES TO THE MAINLAND.
HE GOT IDEAS ABOVE HIS STATION, AND FINALLY CAME FOR ME, HIS OWN FATHER-IN-LAW.
BUT AS WE SAY IN CHINA: "HE TRIED TO DRAW A TIGER, BUT BARELY SKETCHED A DOG."* IDIOT.
AN OLD HAN DYNASTY PROVERB THAT MEANS YOU SHOULDN'T TRY TO RUN BEFORE YOU CAN WALK.

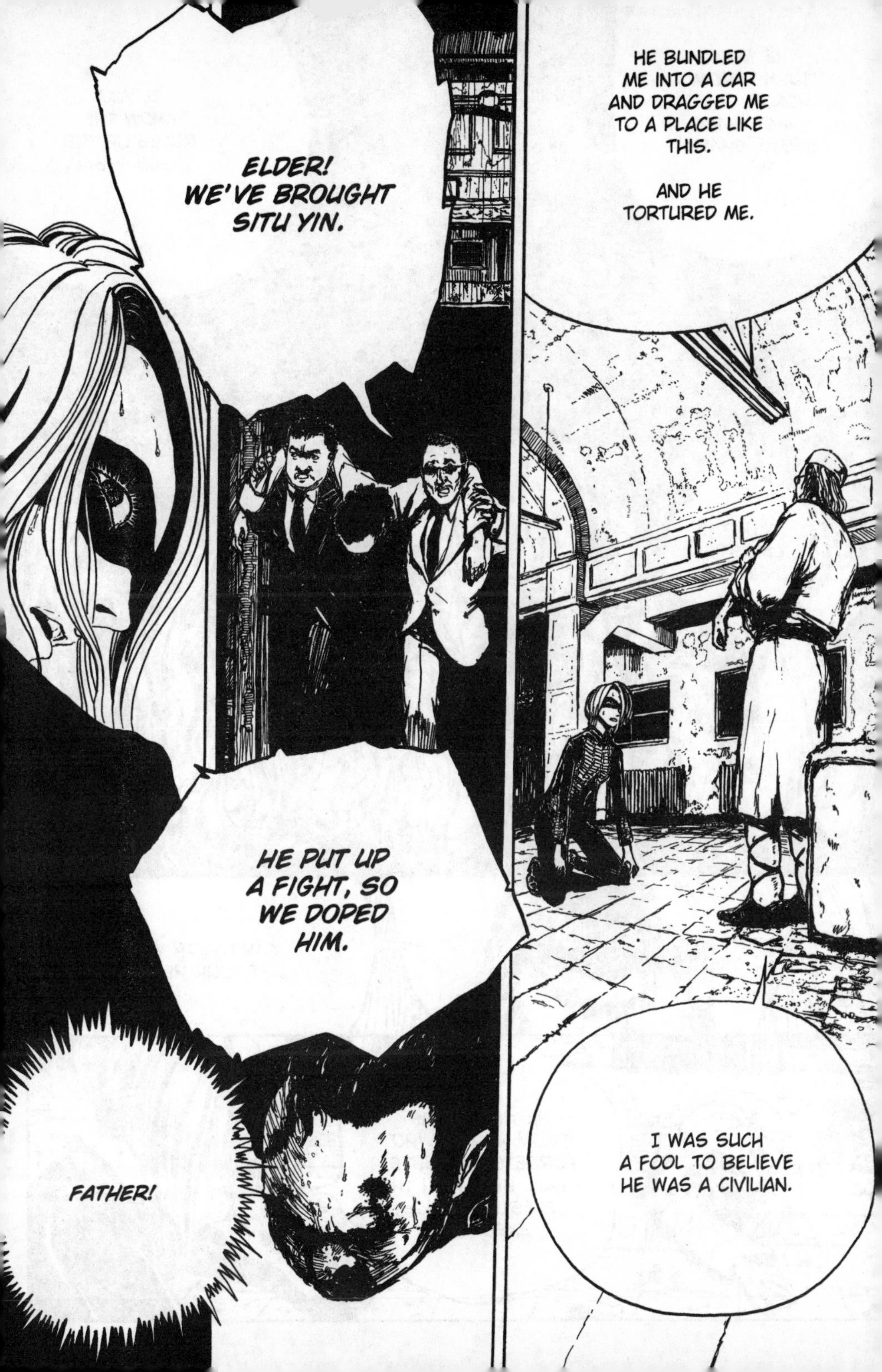
HE BUNDLED ME INTO A CAR AND DRAGGED ME TO A PLACE LIKE THIS.
AND HE TORTURED ME.
I WAS SUCH A FOOL TO BELIEVE HE WAS A CIVILIAN.
ELDER! WE'VE BROUGHT SITU YIN.
HE PUT UP A FIGHT, SO WE DOPED HIM.
FATHER!

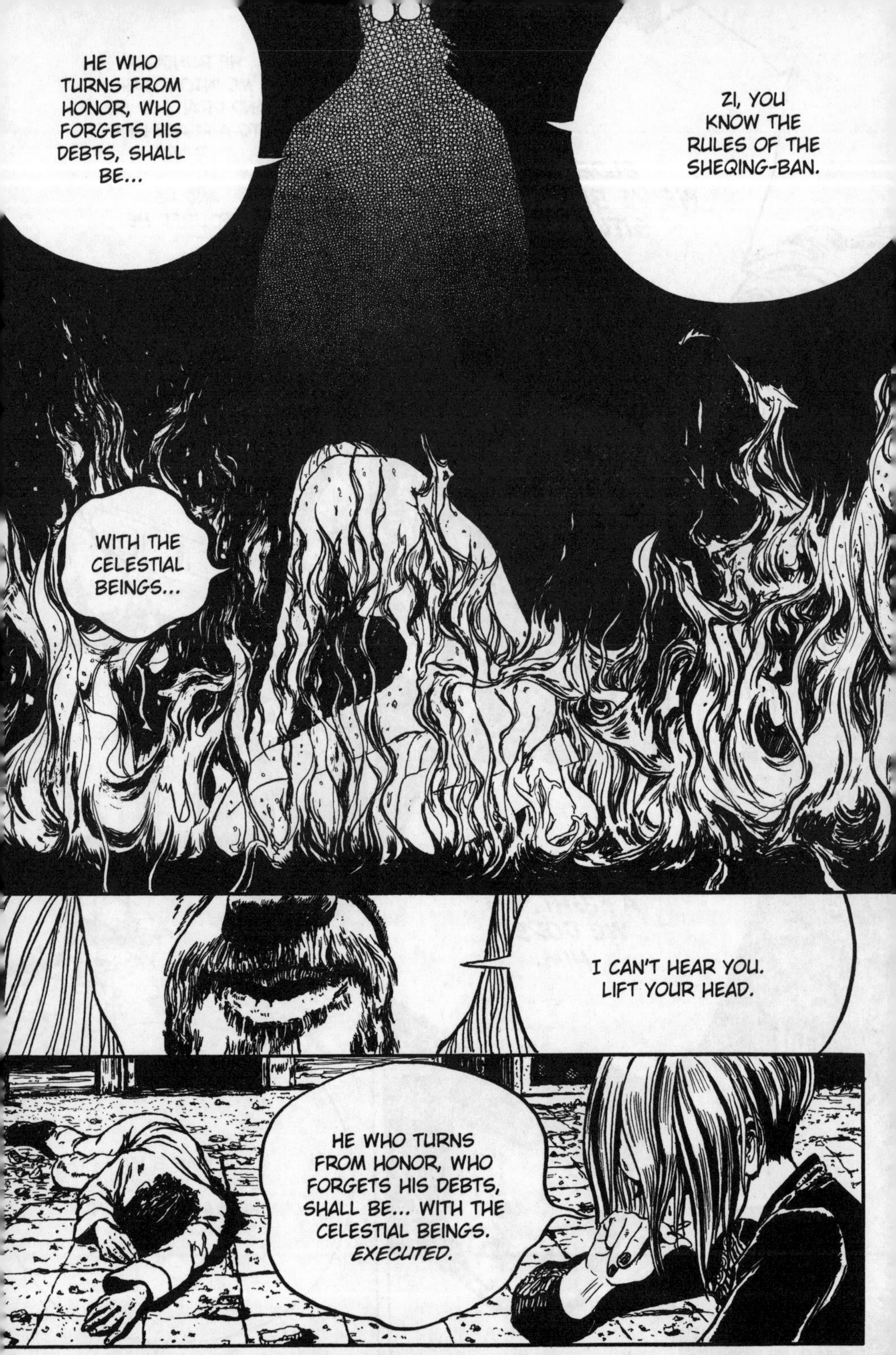
ZI, YOU KNOW THE RULES OF THE SHEQING-BAN.
HE WHO TURNS FROM HONOR, WHO FORGETS HIS DEBTS, SHALL BE...
WITH THE CELESTIAL BEINGS...
I CAN'T HEAR YOU. LIFT YOUR HEAD.
HE WHO TURNS FROM HONOR, WHO FORGETS HIS DEBTS, SHALL BE... WITH THE CELESTIAL BEINGS. *EXECUTED.*

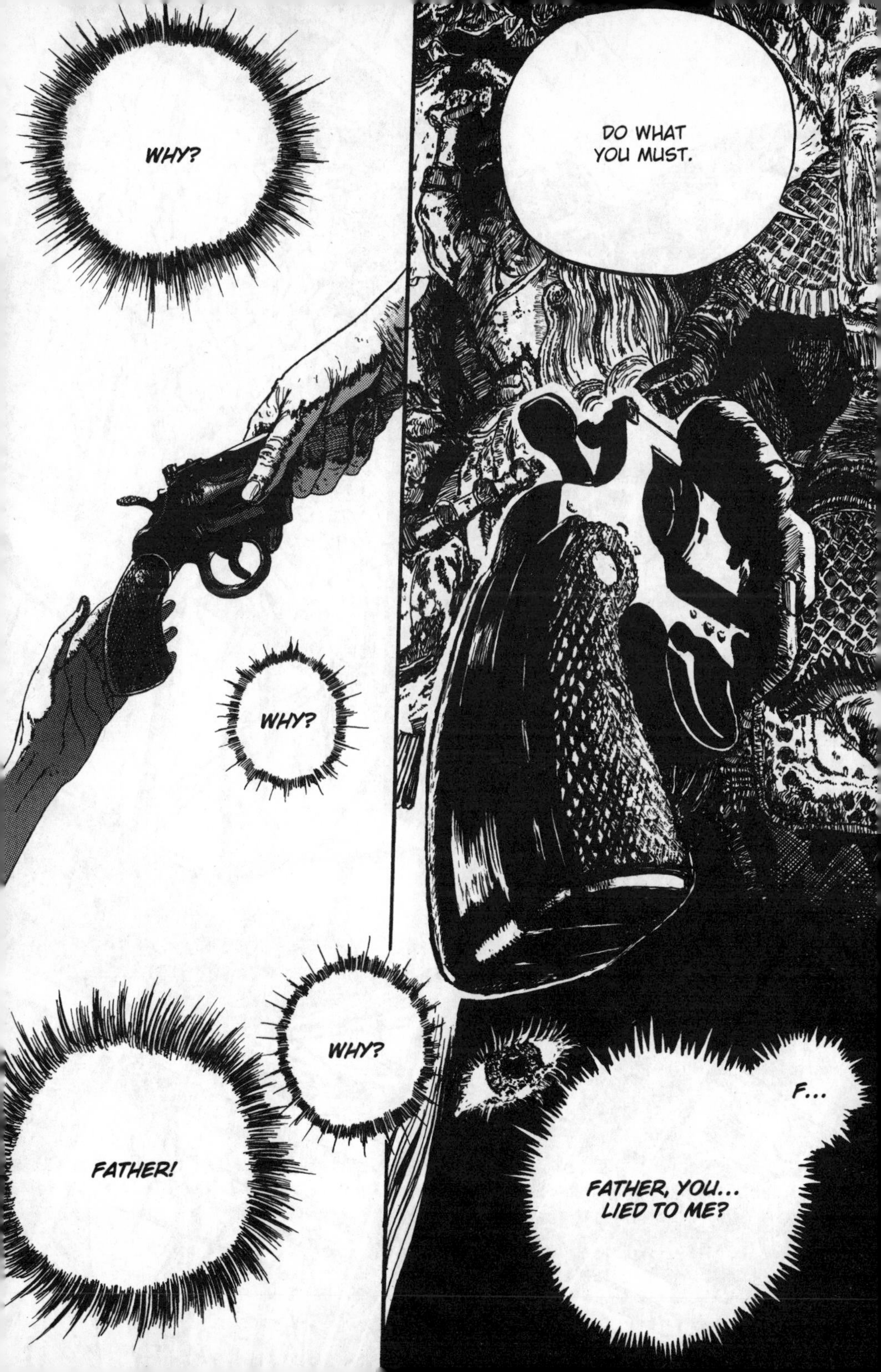
DO WHAT YOU MUST.
WHY?
WHY?
WHY?
FATHER!
F...
FATHER, YOU... LIED TO ME?

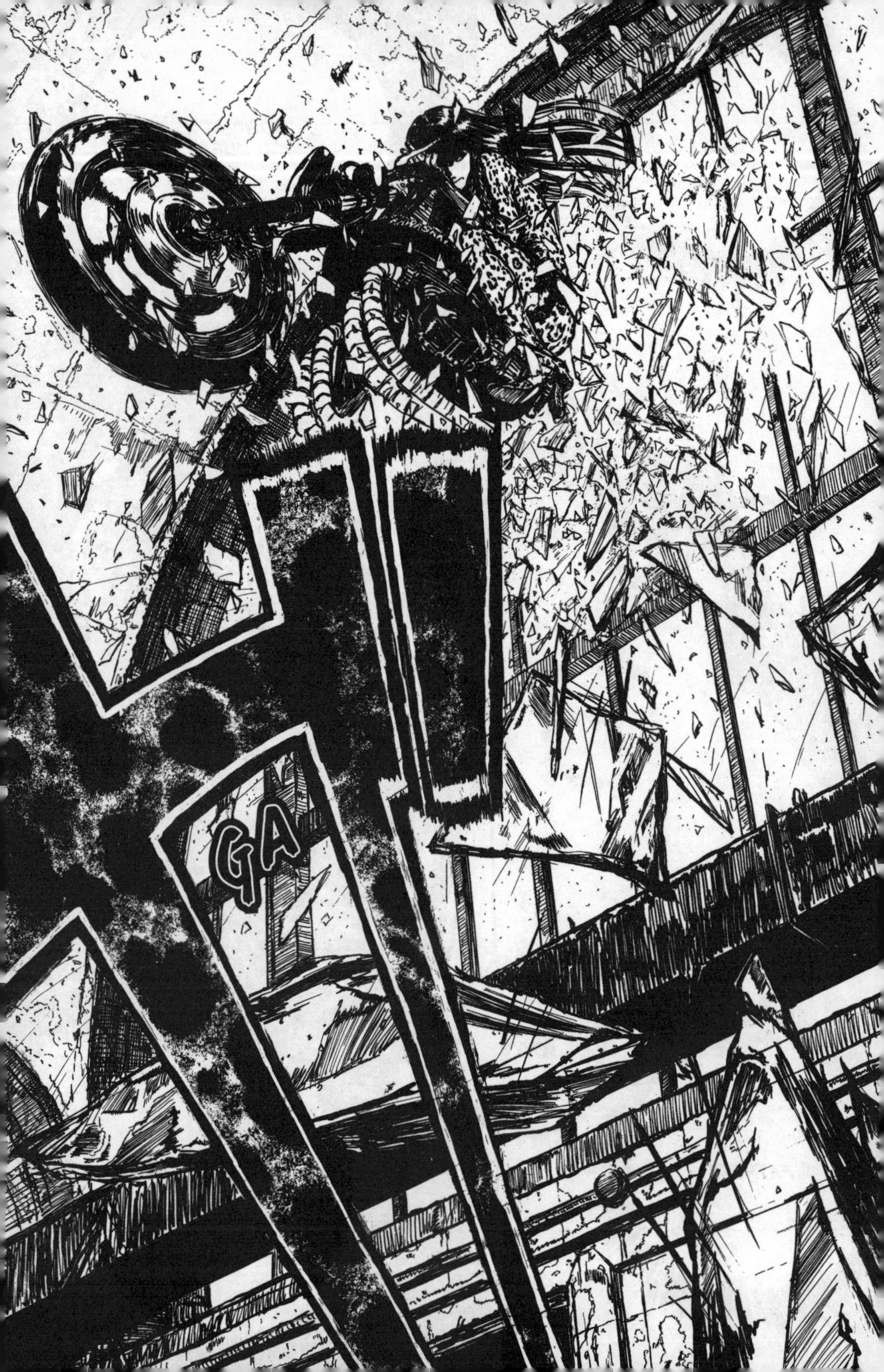
GA

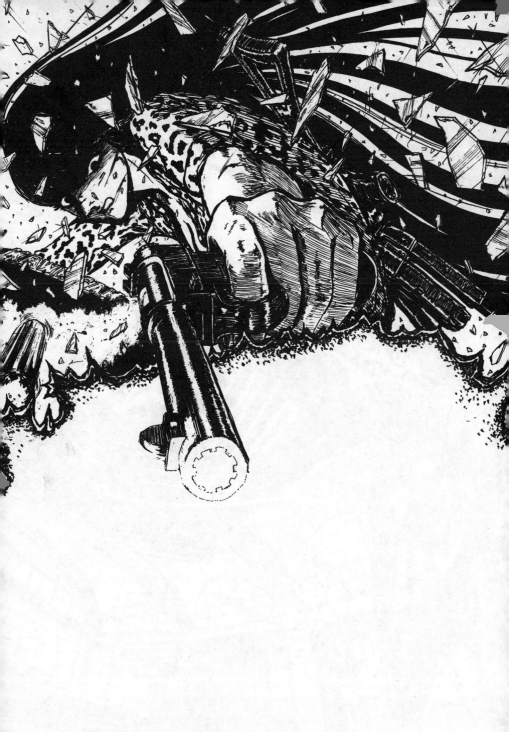

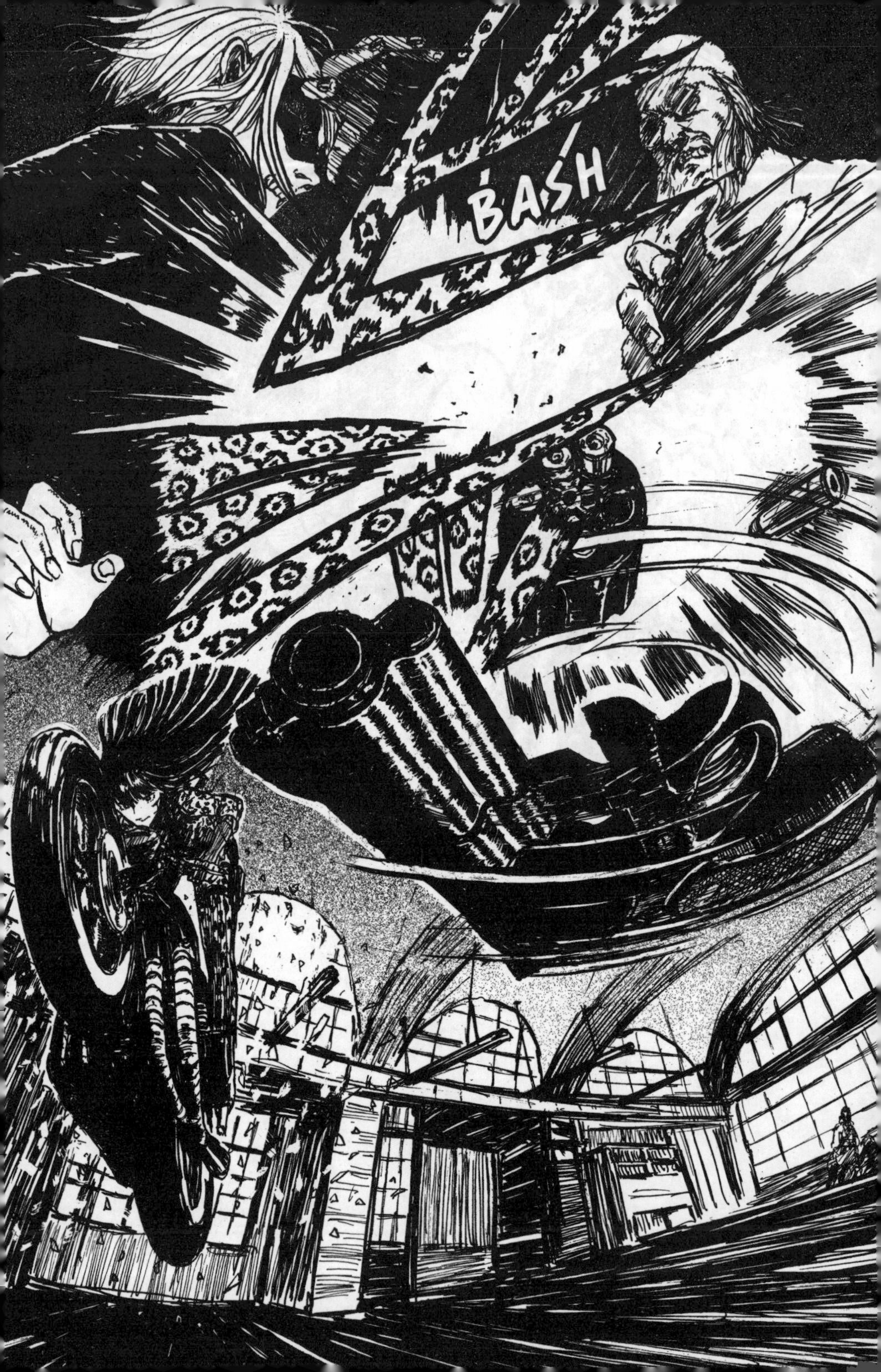
BASH

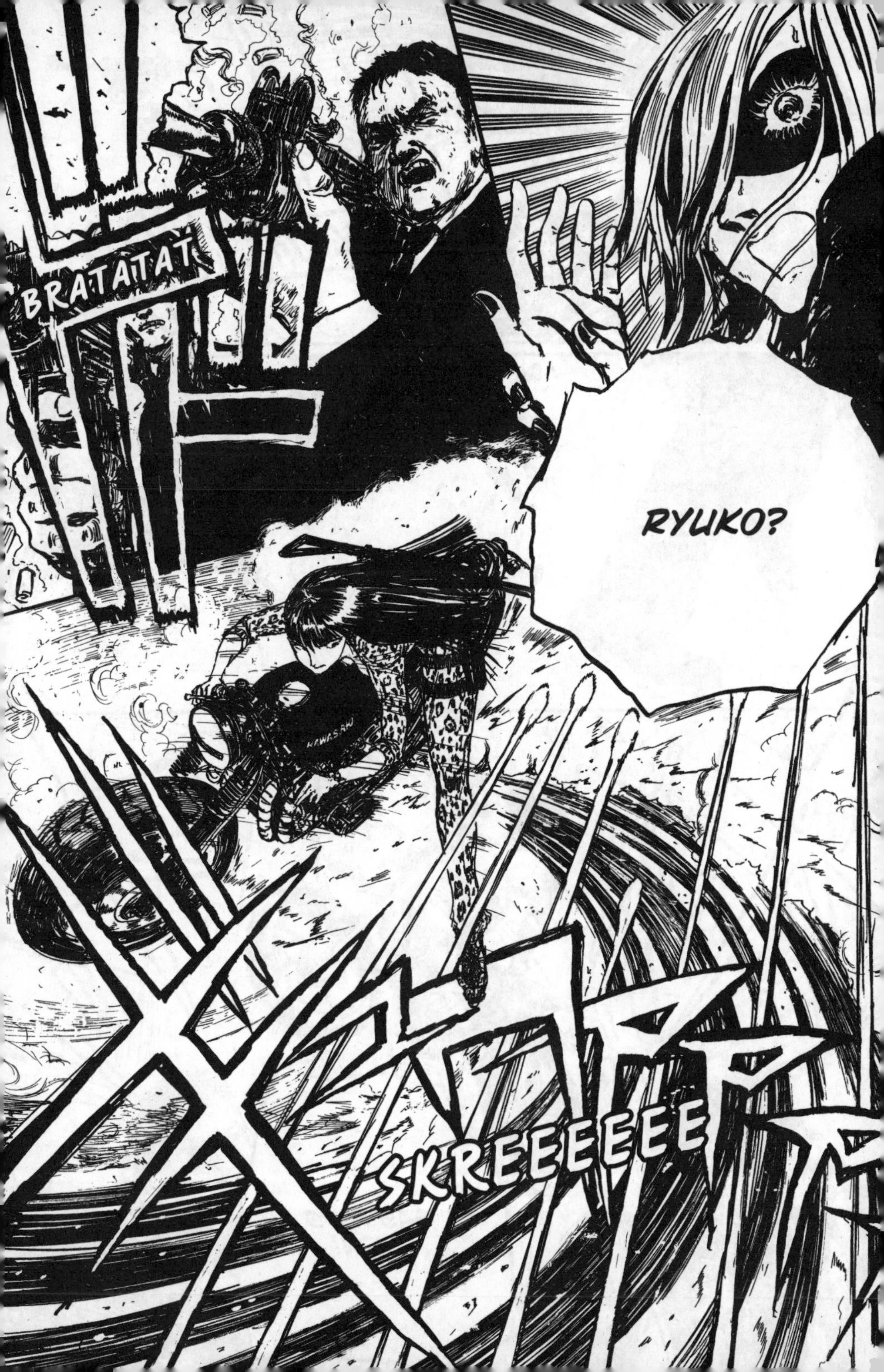
RYUKO?
BRATATAT
KAWASAKI
SKREEEEEEE

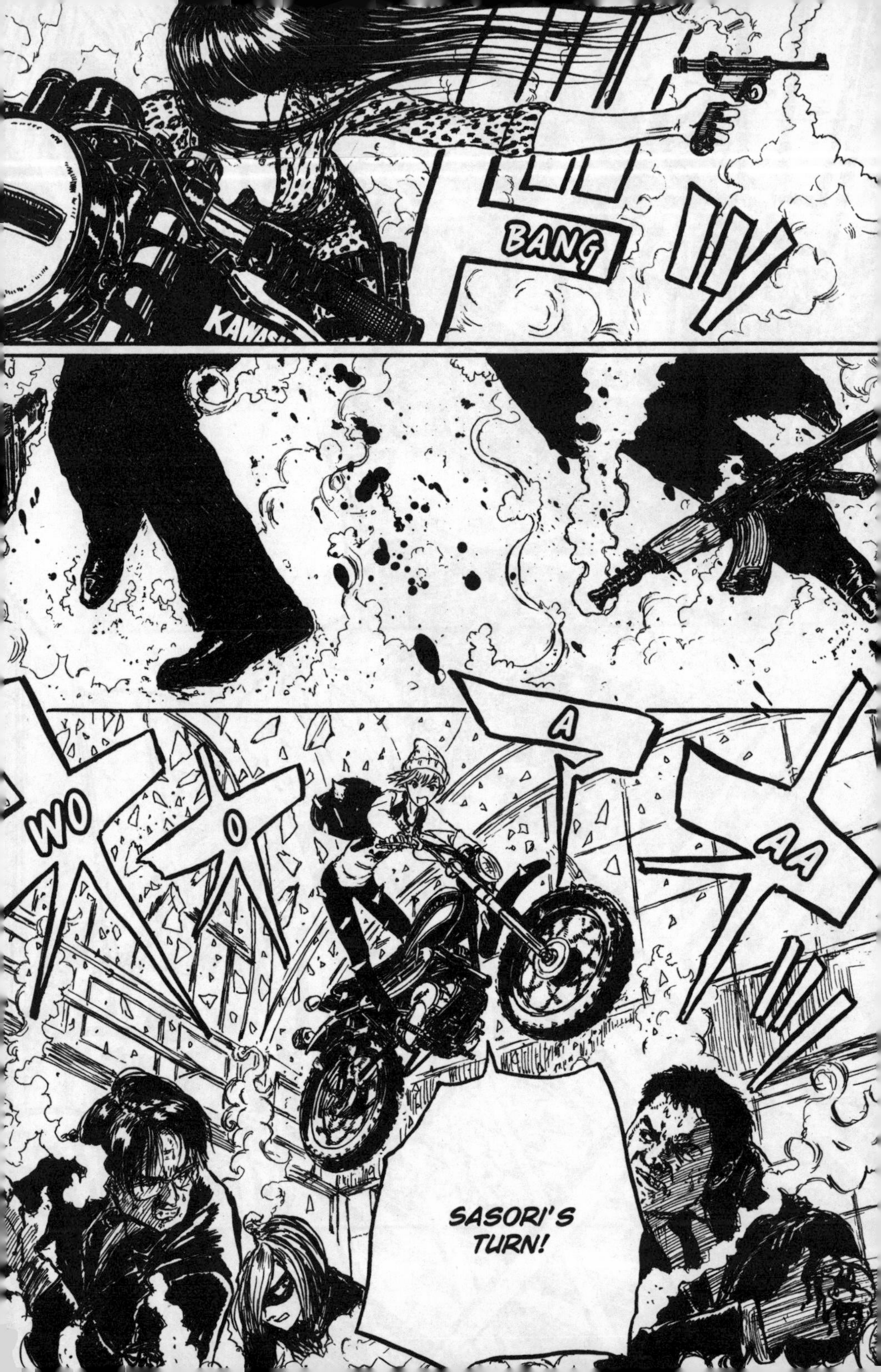
BANG
WO
O
A
AA
SASORI'S TURN!

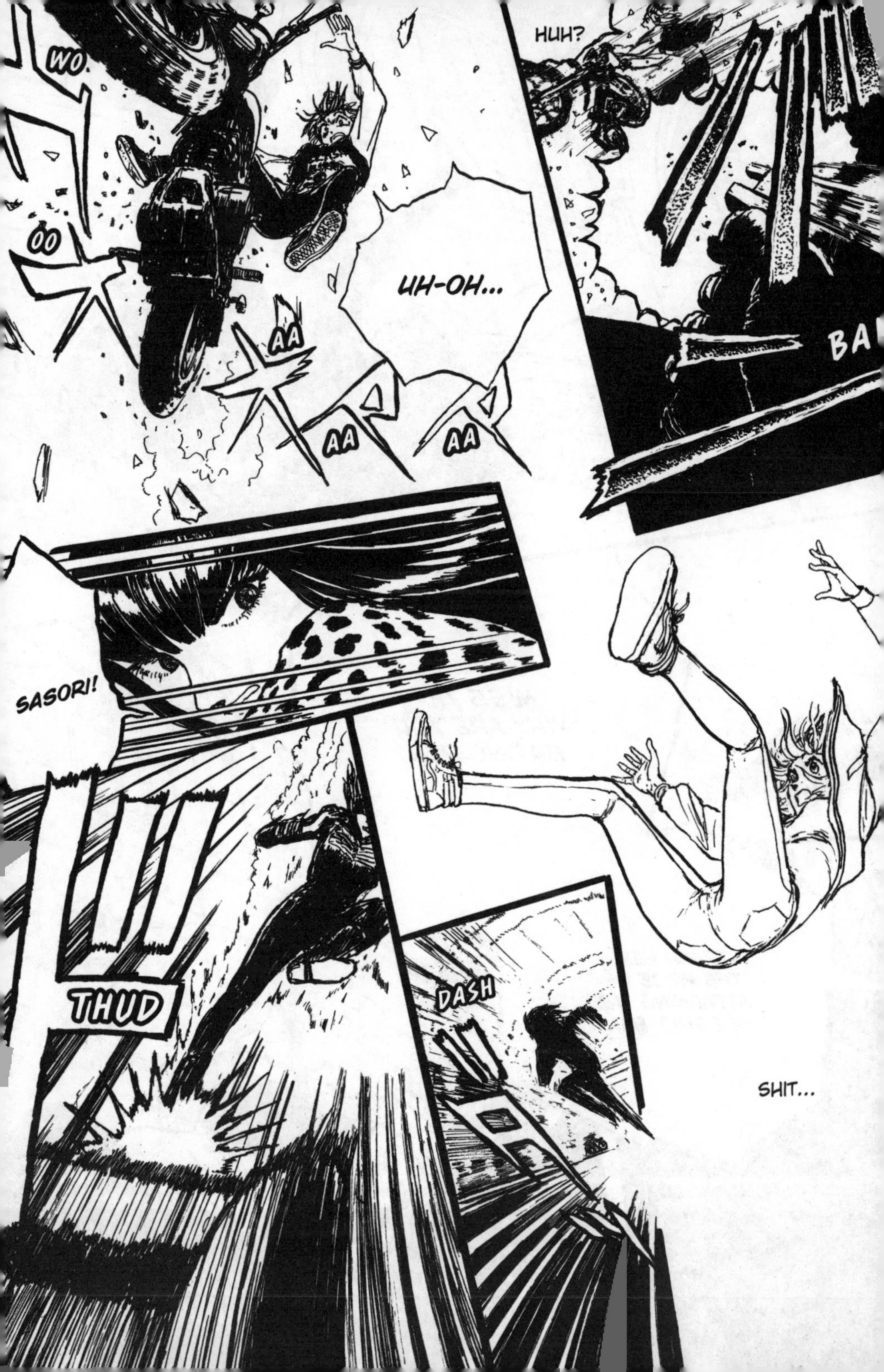
HUH?
BA
WO
OO
AA
AA
AA
UH-OH...
SHIT...
SASORI!
THUD
DASH

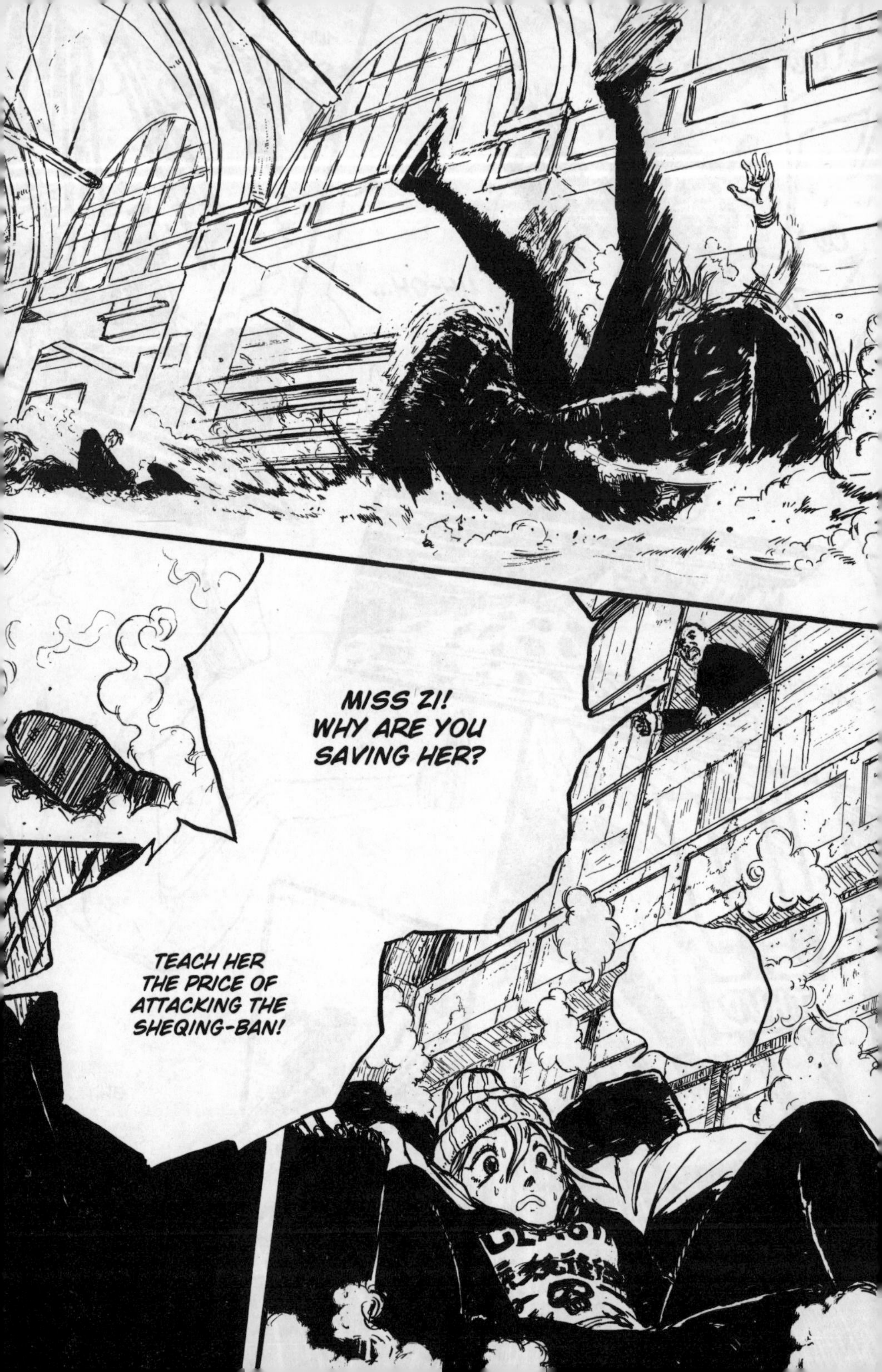
MISS ZI! WHY ARE YOU SAVING HER?
TEACH HER THE PRICE OF ATTACKING THE SHEQING-BAN!

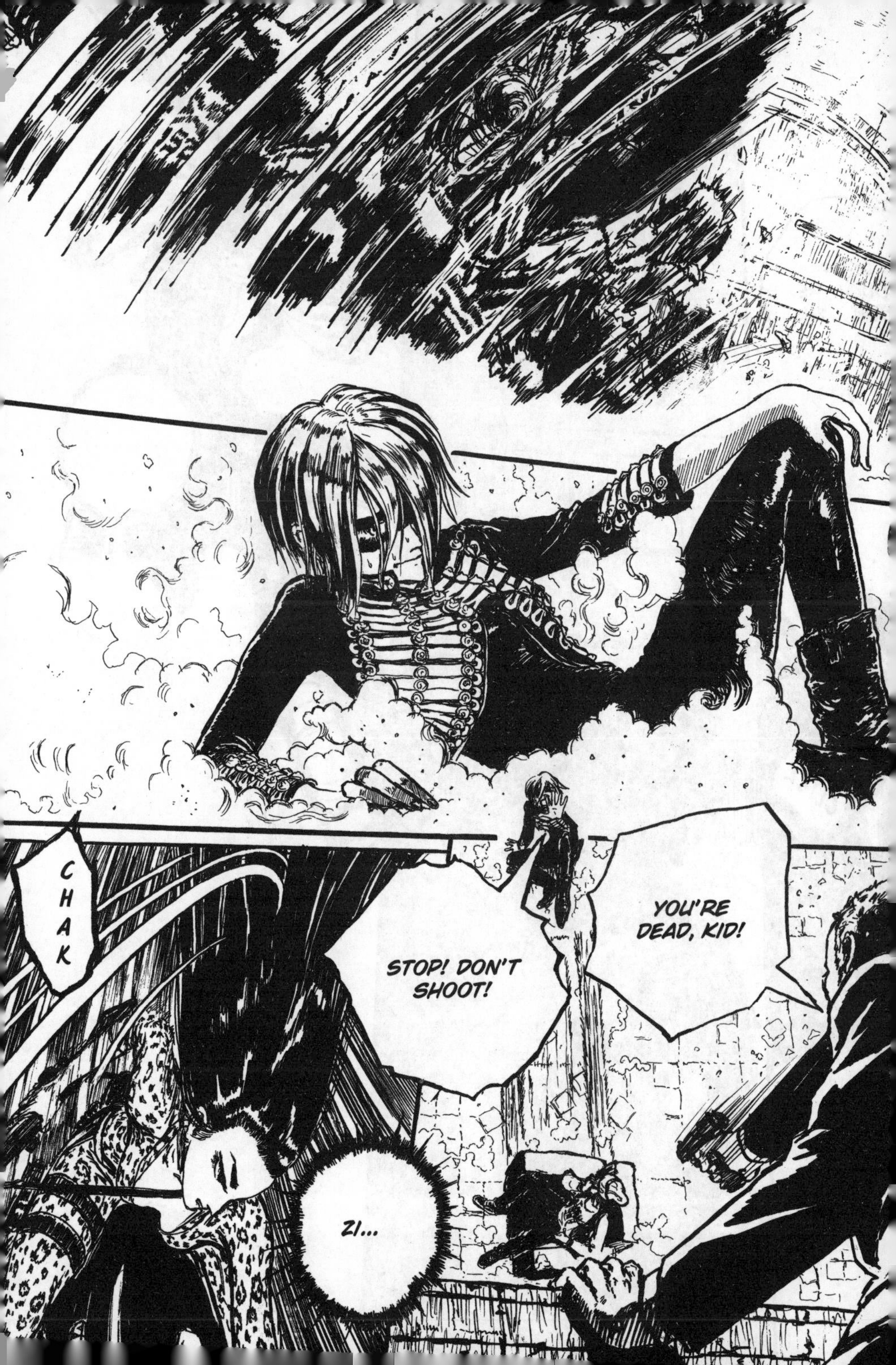
YOU'RE DEAD, KID!
STOP! DON'T SHOOT!
CHAK
ZI...

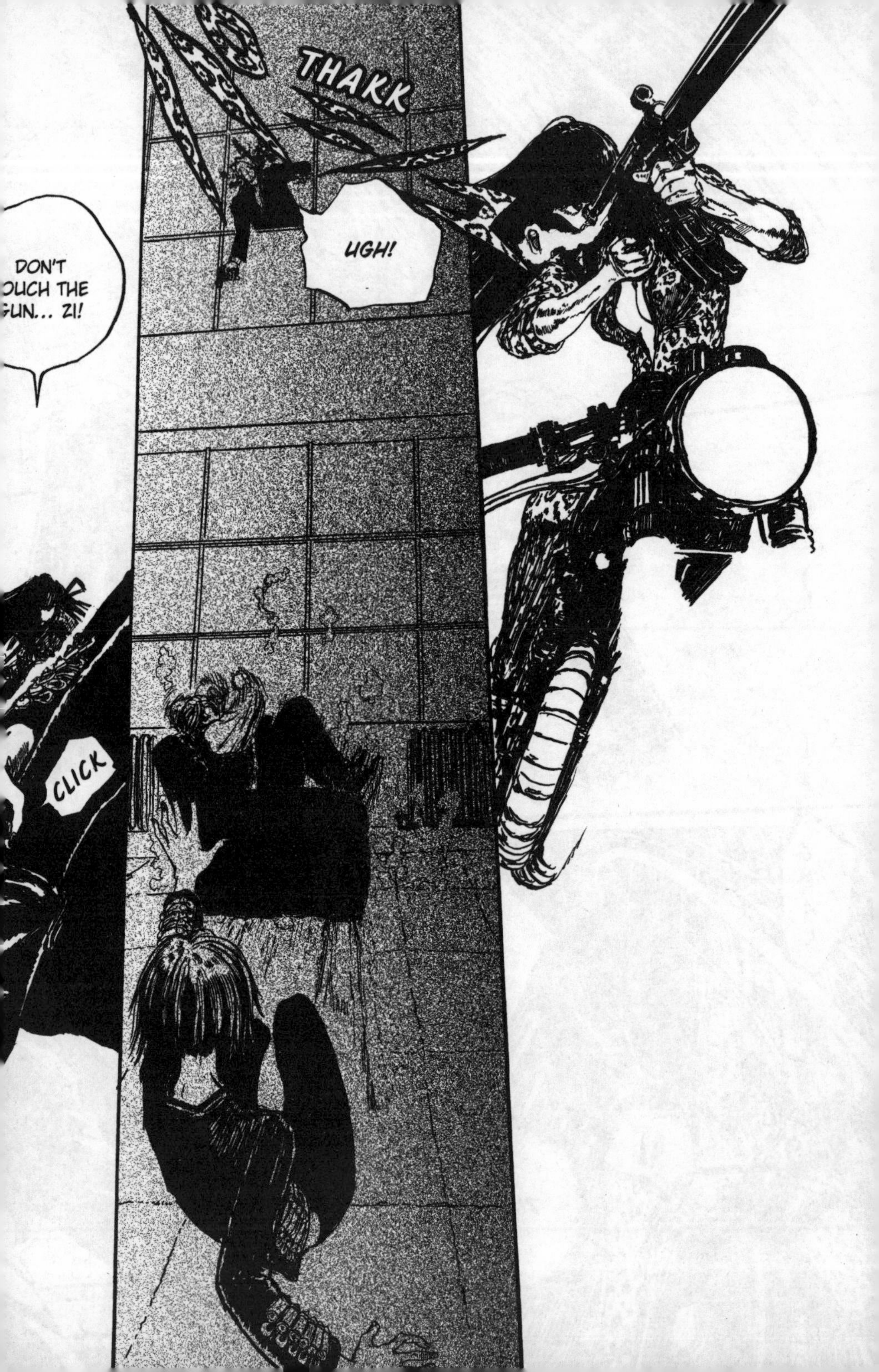
THAKK
UGH!
DON'T OUCH THE GUN... ZI!
CLICK

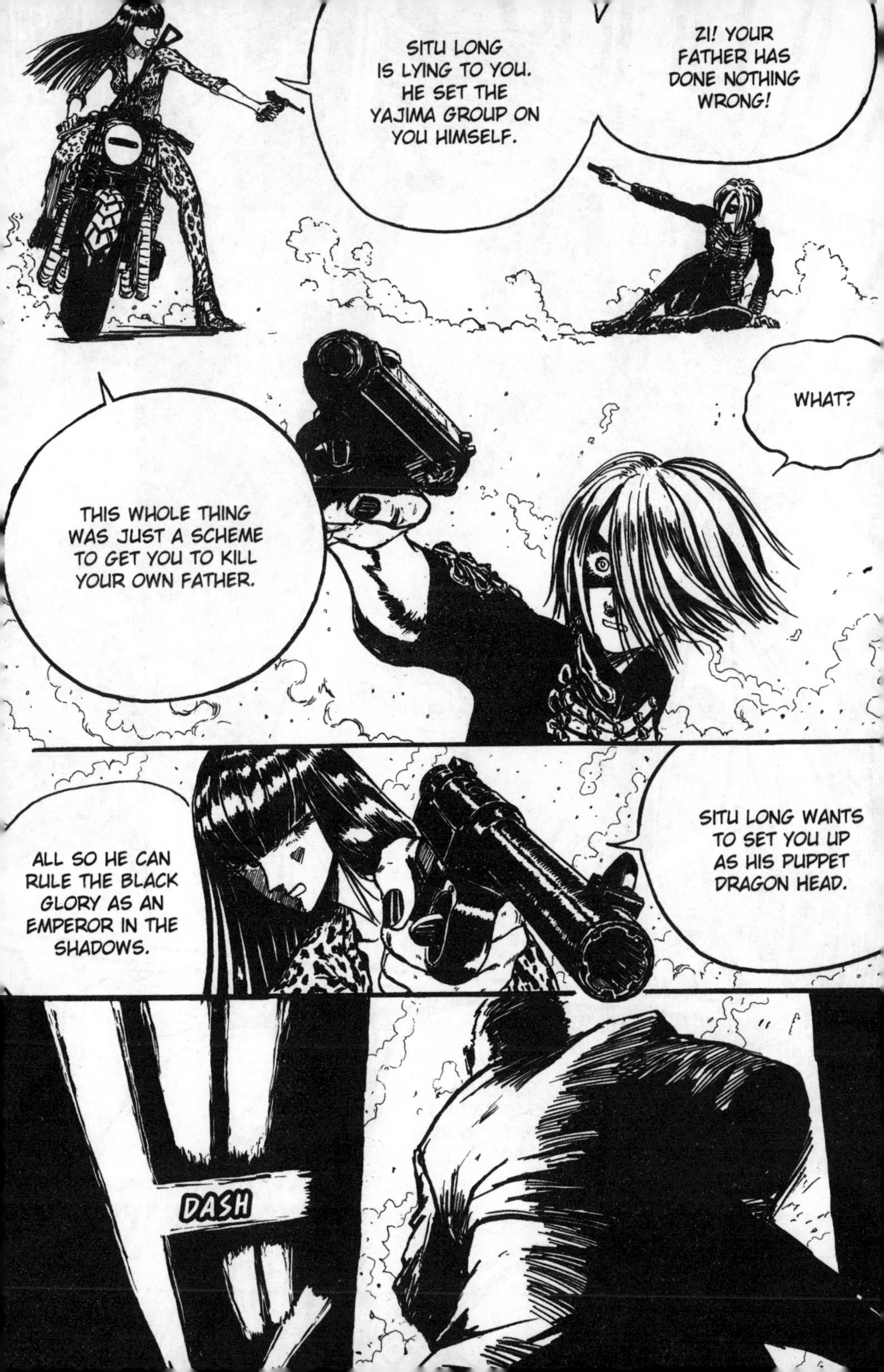
ZI! YOUR FATHER HAS DONE NOTHING WRONG!
SITU LONG IS LYING TO YOU. HE SET THE YAJIMA GROUP ON YOU HIMSELF.
WHAT?
THIS WHOLE THING WAS JUST A SCHEME TO GET YOU TO KILL YOUR OWN FATHER.
SITU LONG WANTS TO SET YOU UP AS HIS PUPPET DRAGON HEAD.
ALL SO HE CAN RULE THE BLACK GLORY AS AN EMPEROR IN THE SHADOWS.
DASH

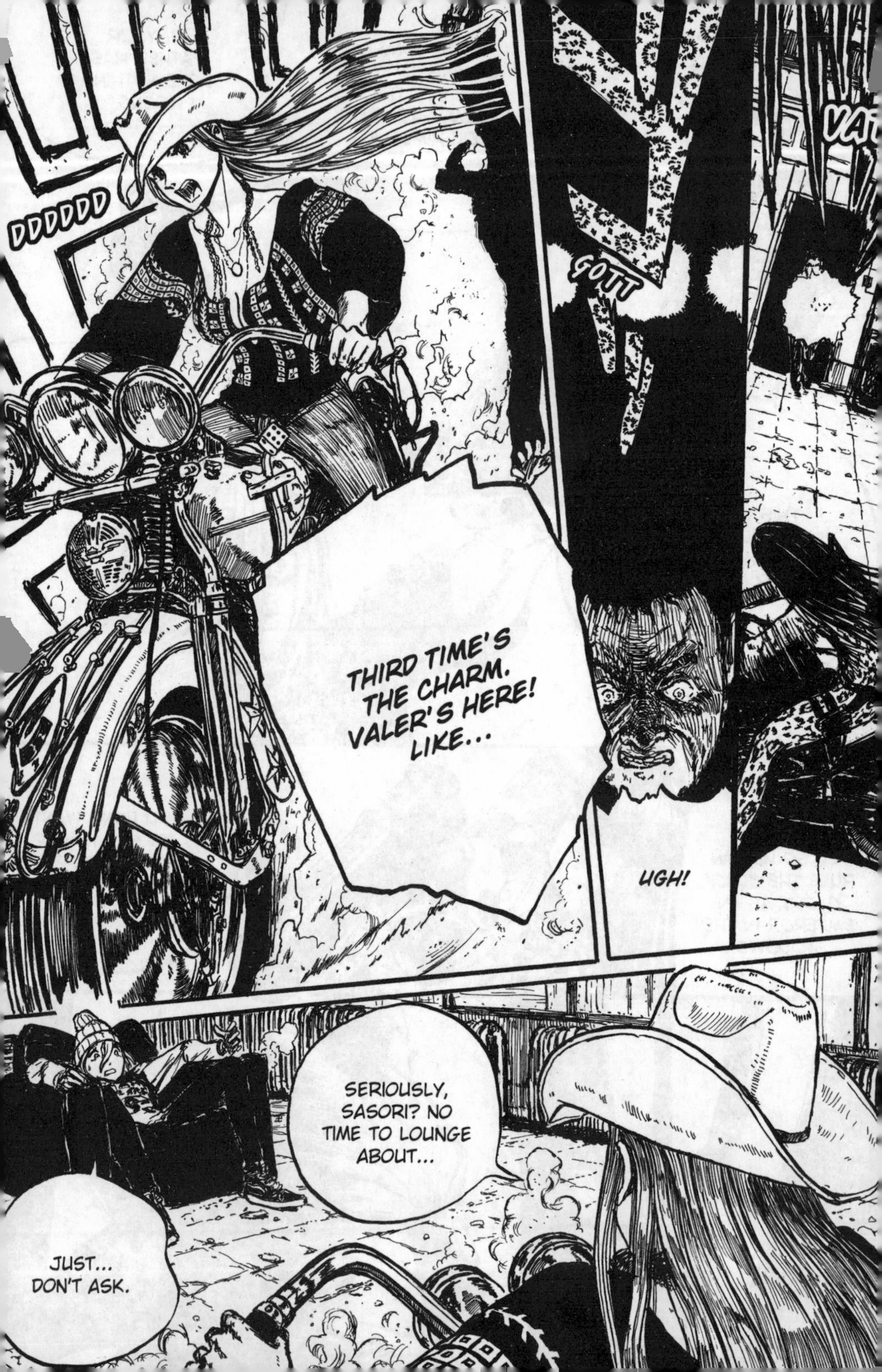
VA
GOTT
THIRD TIME'S THE CHARM. VALER'S HERE! LIKE...
UGH!
DDDDDD
SERIOUSLY, SASORI? NO TIME TO LOUNGE ABOUT...
JUST... DON'T ASK.

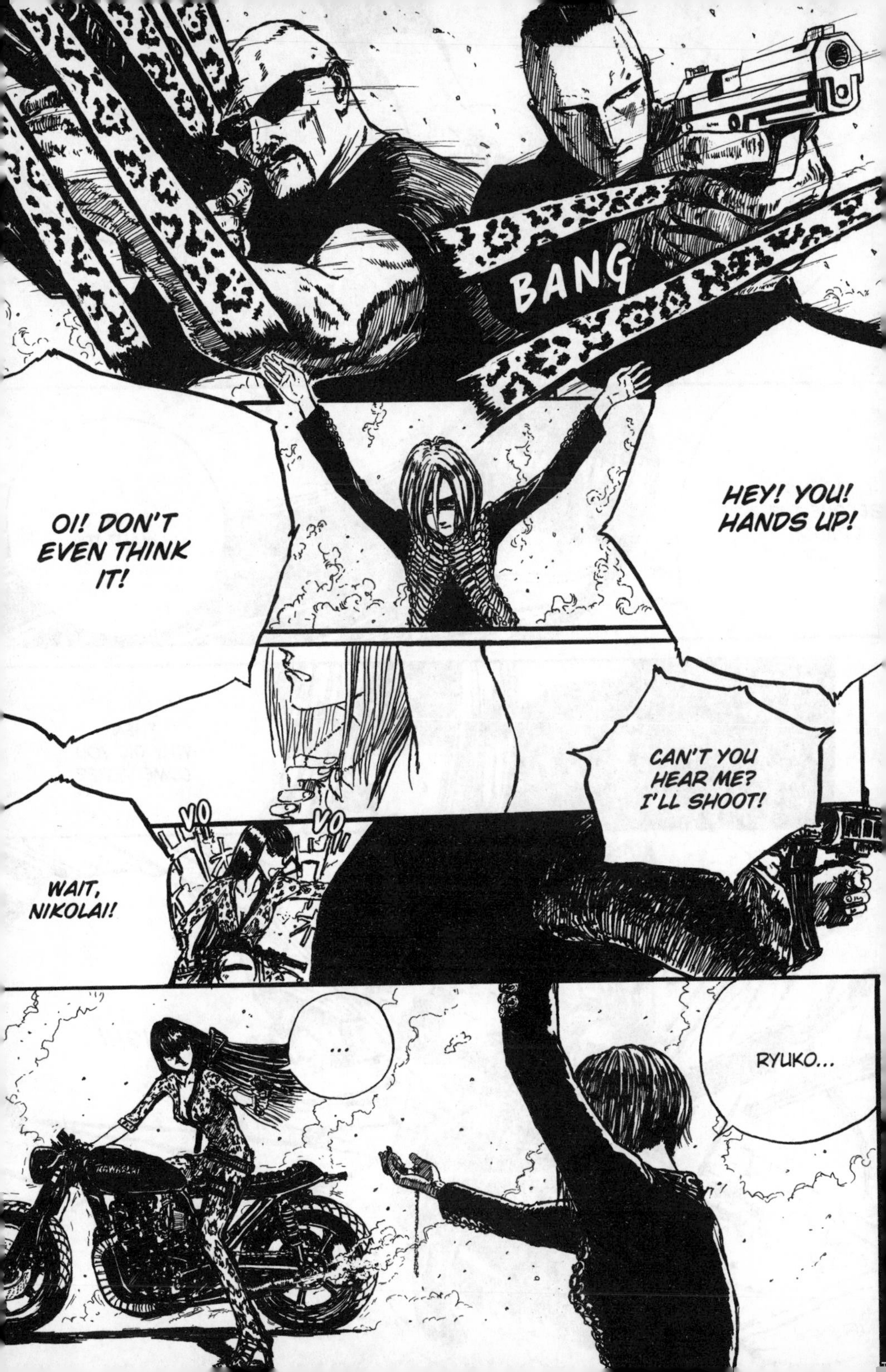
BANG
HEY! YOU! HANDS UP!
OI! DON'T EVEN THINK IT!
CAN'T YOU HEAR ME? I'LL SHOOT!
VO
VO
WAIT, NIKOLAI!
RYUKO...
...

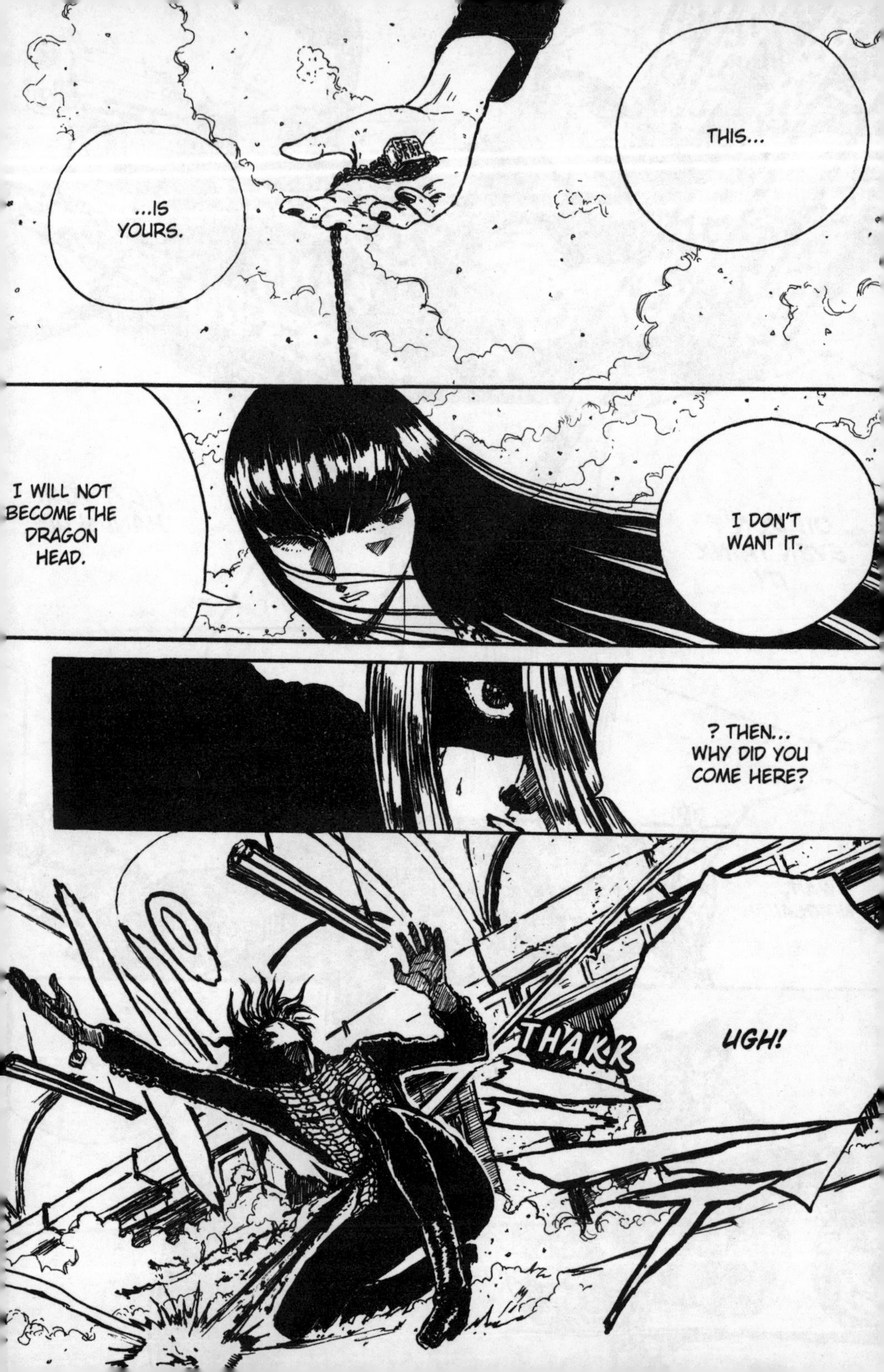
THIS...
...IS YOURS.
I DON'T WANT IT.
I WILL NOT BECOME THE DRAGON HEAD.
? THEN... WHY DID YOU COME HERE?
UGH!
THAKK

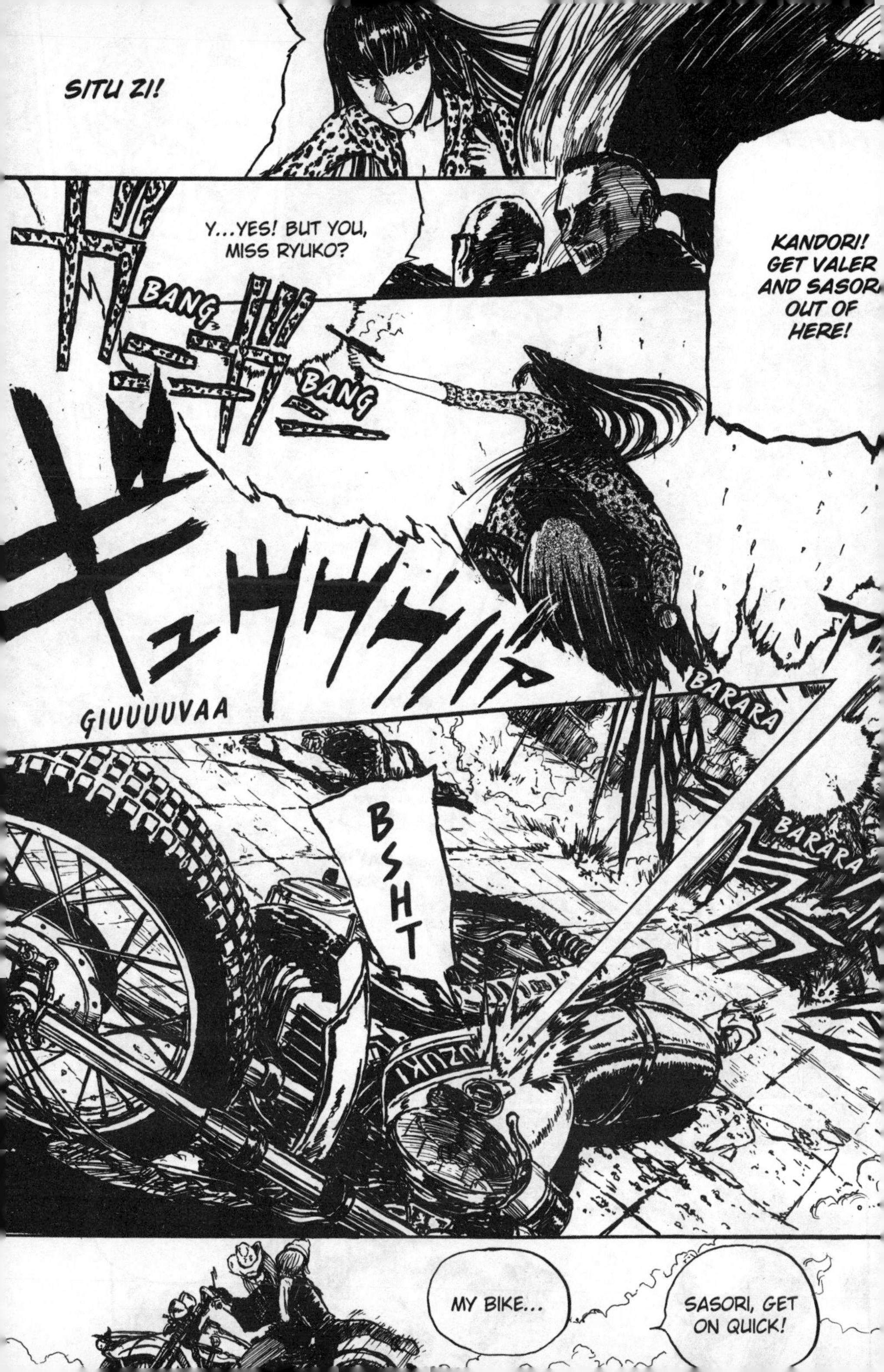
SITU ZI!
KANDORI! GET VALER AND SASOR OUT OF HERE!
Y...YES! BUT YOU, MISS RYUKO?
BANG
BANG
BARARA
GIUUUUVAA
BARARA
BSHT
SASORI, GET ON QUICK!
MY BIKE...

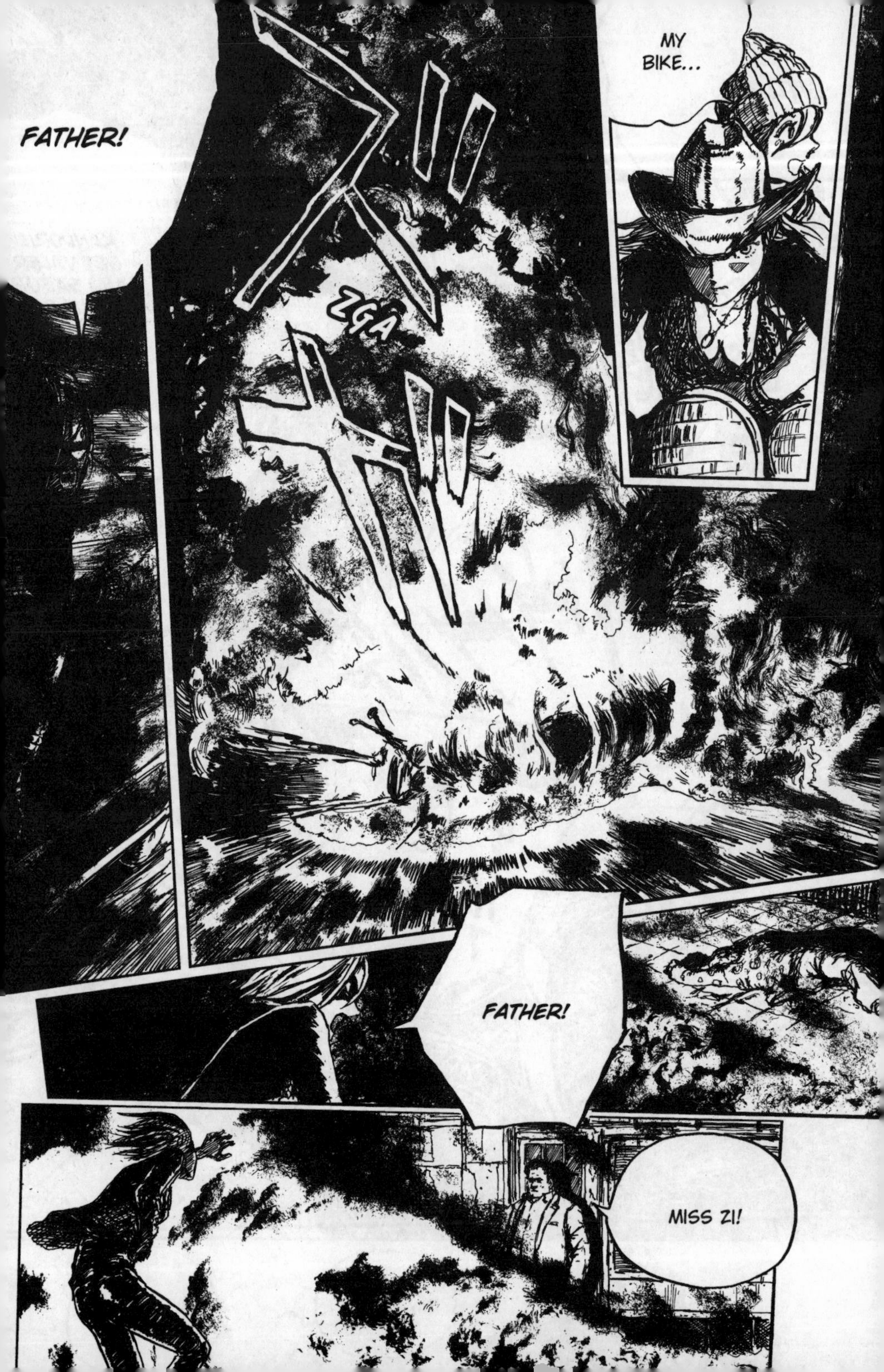
MY BIKE...
ZGA
FATHER!
FATHER!
MISS ZI!

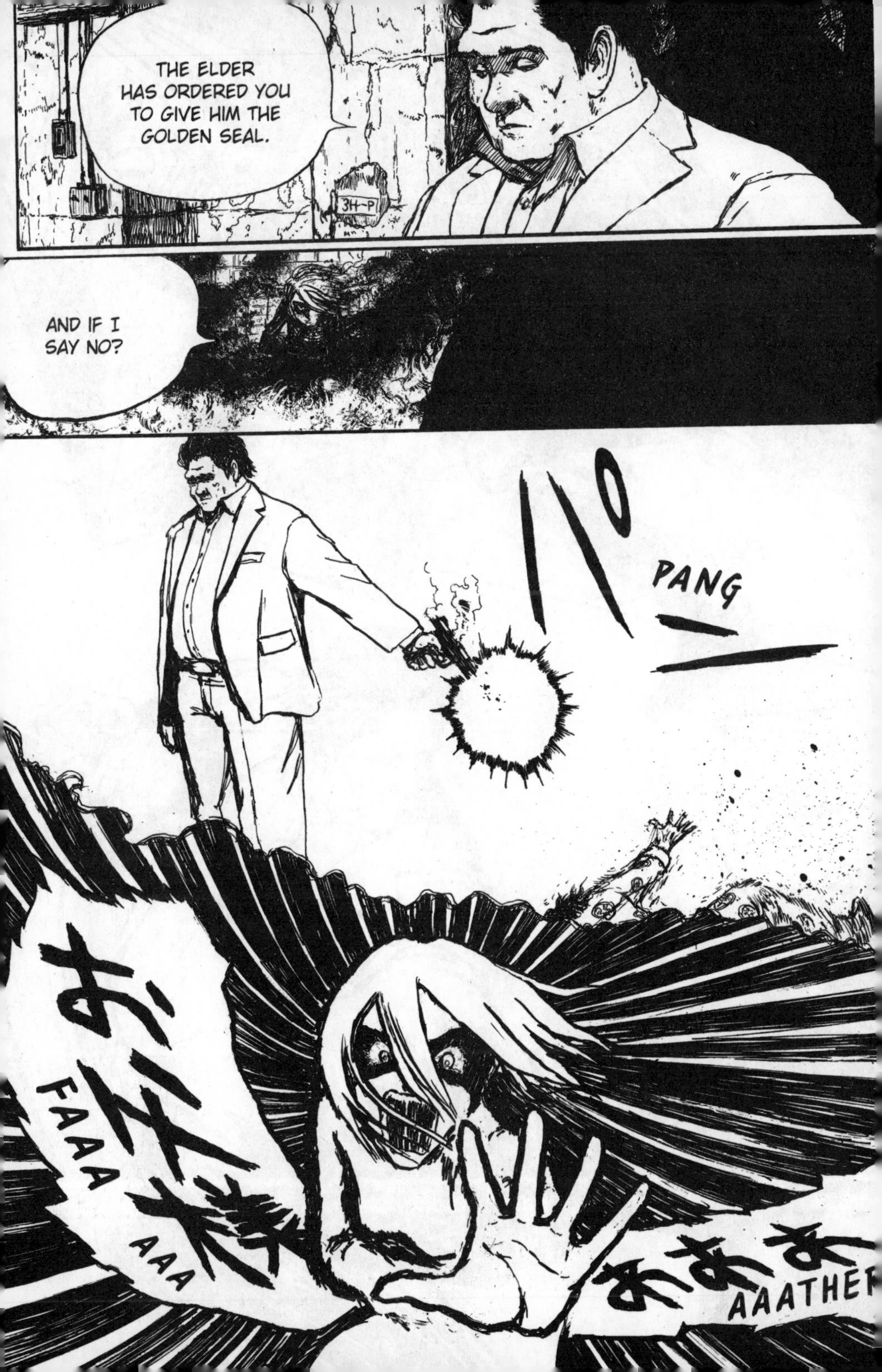
THE ELDER HAS ORDERED YOU TO GIVE HIM THE GOLDEN SEAL.
3H-P
AND IF I SAY NO?
PANG
FAAA
AAA
AAATHER

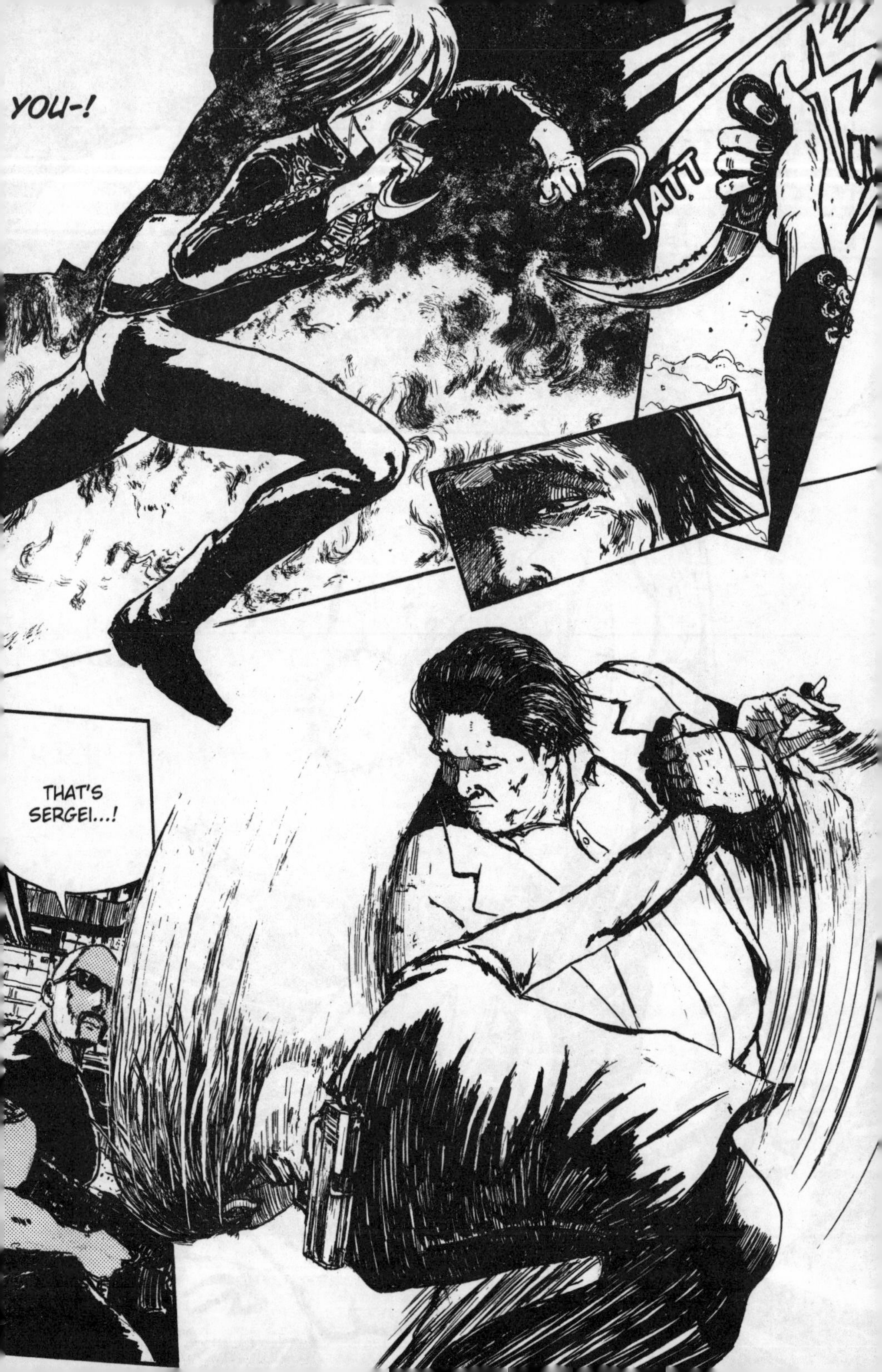
YOU-!
JATT
THAT'S SERGEI...!

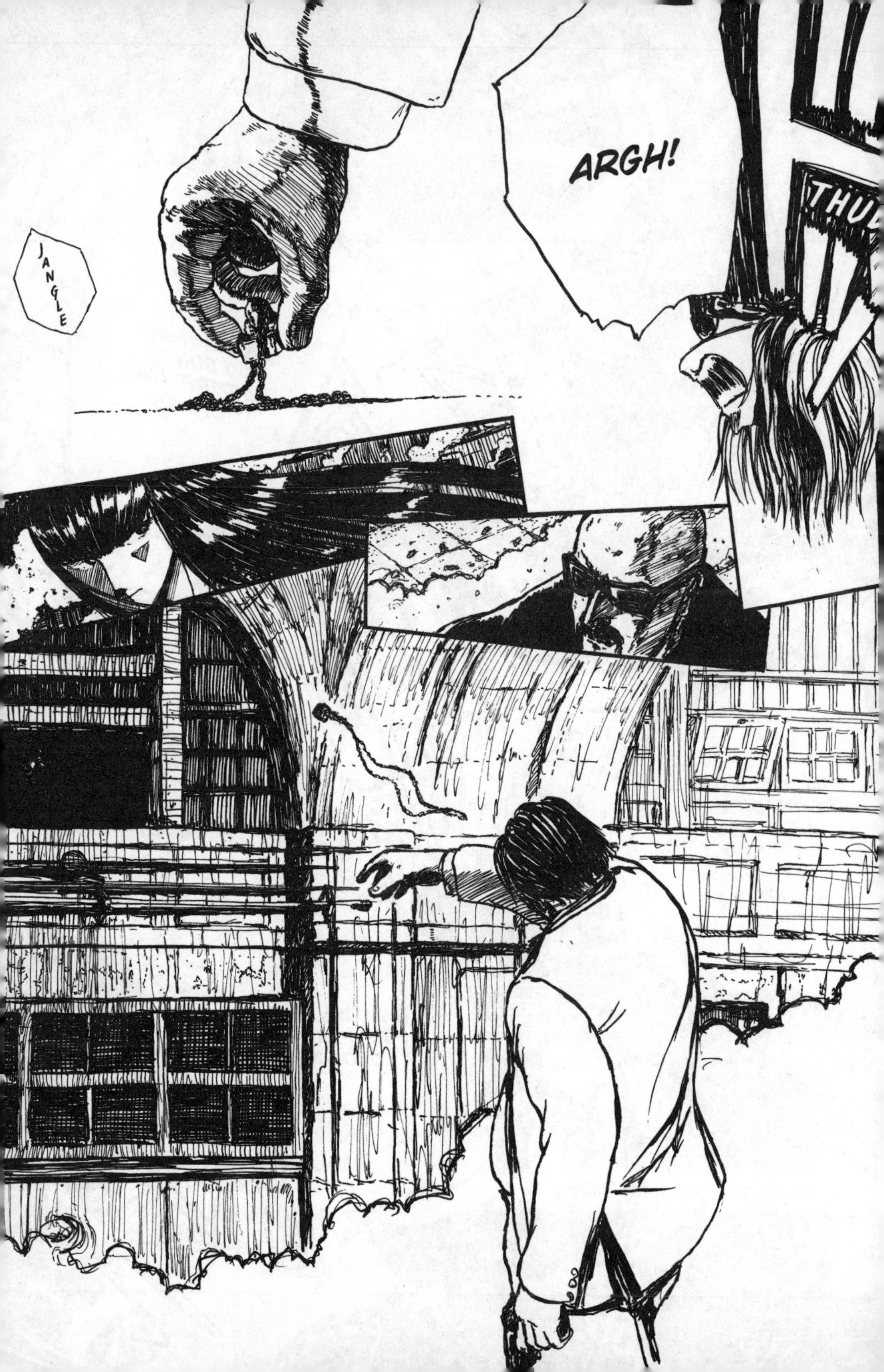
THUD
ARGH!
JANGLE

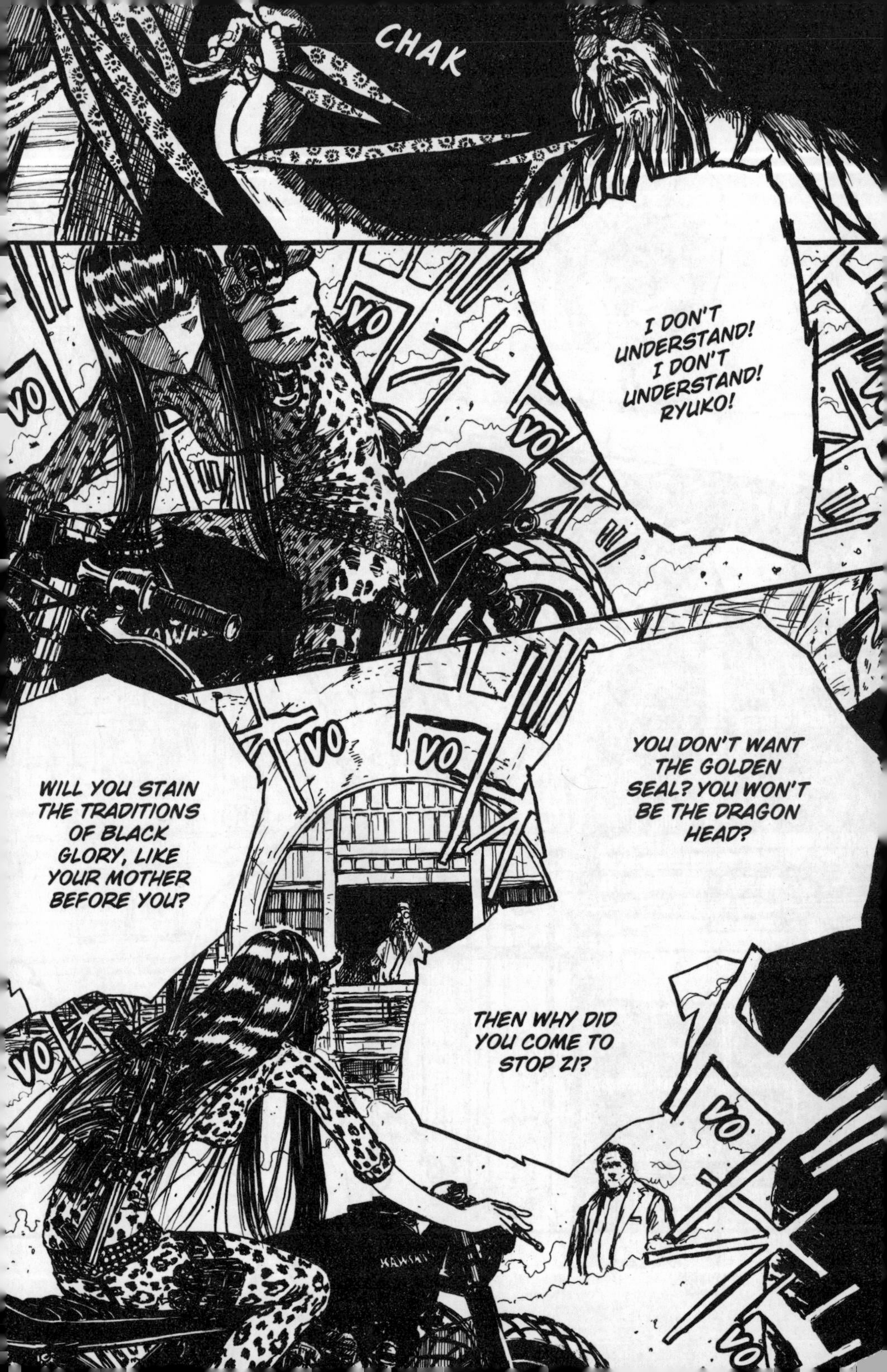
CHAK
I DON'T UNDERSTAND! I DON'T UNDERSTAND! RYUKO!
VO
VO
VO
YOU DON'T WANT THE GOLDEN SEAL? YOU WON'T BE THE DRAGON HEAD?
VO
VO
WILL YOU STAIN THE TRADITIONS OF BLACK GLORY, LIKE YOUR MOTHER BEFORE YOU?
VO
THEN WHY DID YOU COME TO STOP ZI?
VO
VO

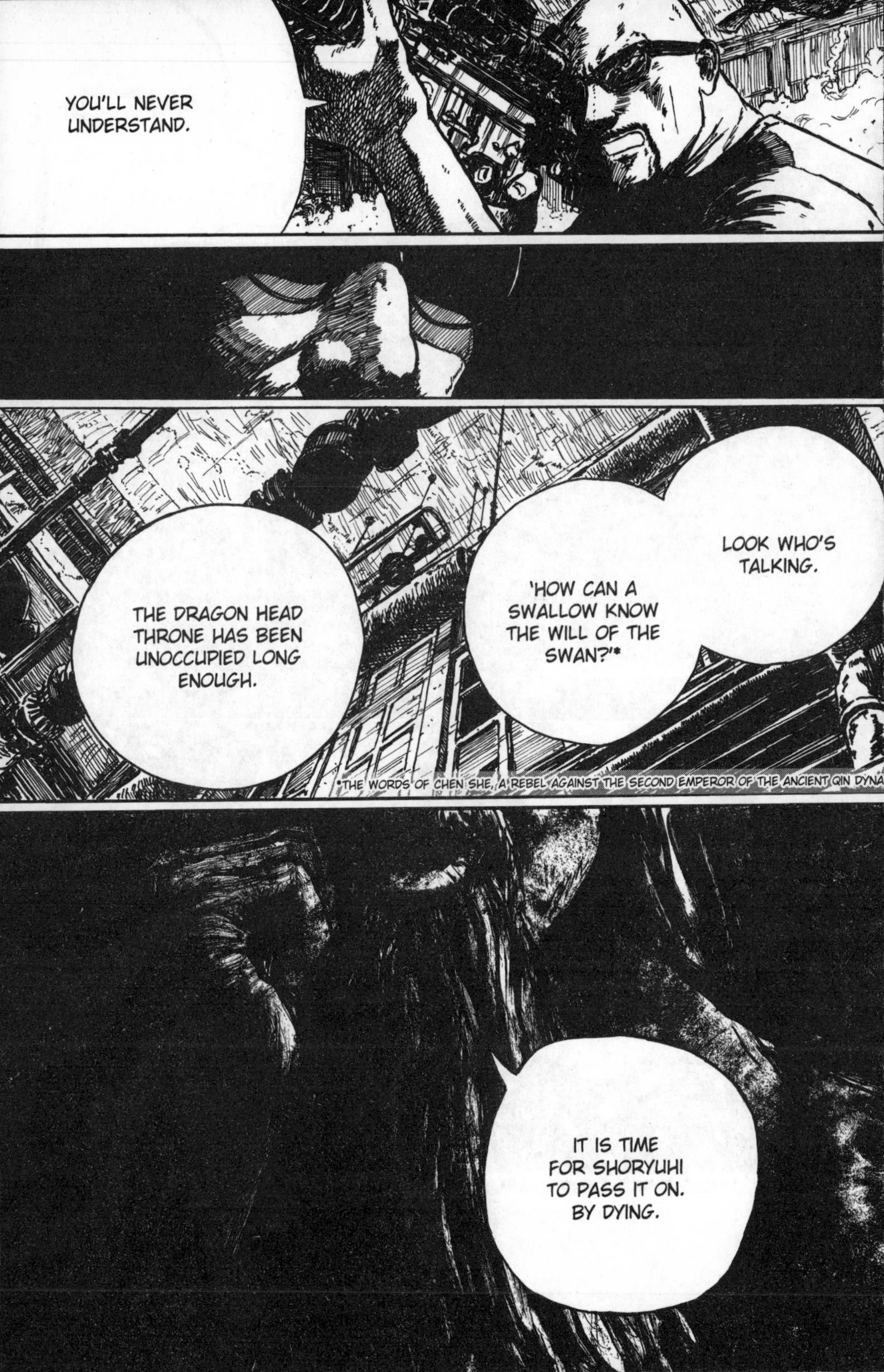
YOU'LL NEVER UNDERSTAND.
LOOK WHO'S TALKING.
'HOW CAN A SWALLOW KNOW THE WILL OF THE SWAN?'*
THE DRAGON HEAD THRONE HAS BEEN UNOCCUPIED LONG ENOUGH.
*THE WORDS OF CHEN SHE, A REBEL AGAINST THE SECOND EMPEROR OF THE ANCIENT QIN DYNA
IT IS TIME FOR SHORYUHI TO PASS IT ON. BY DYING.

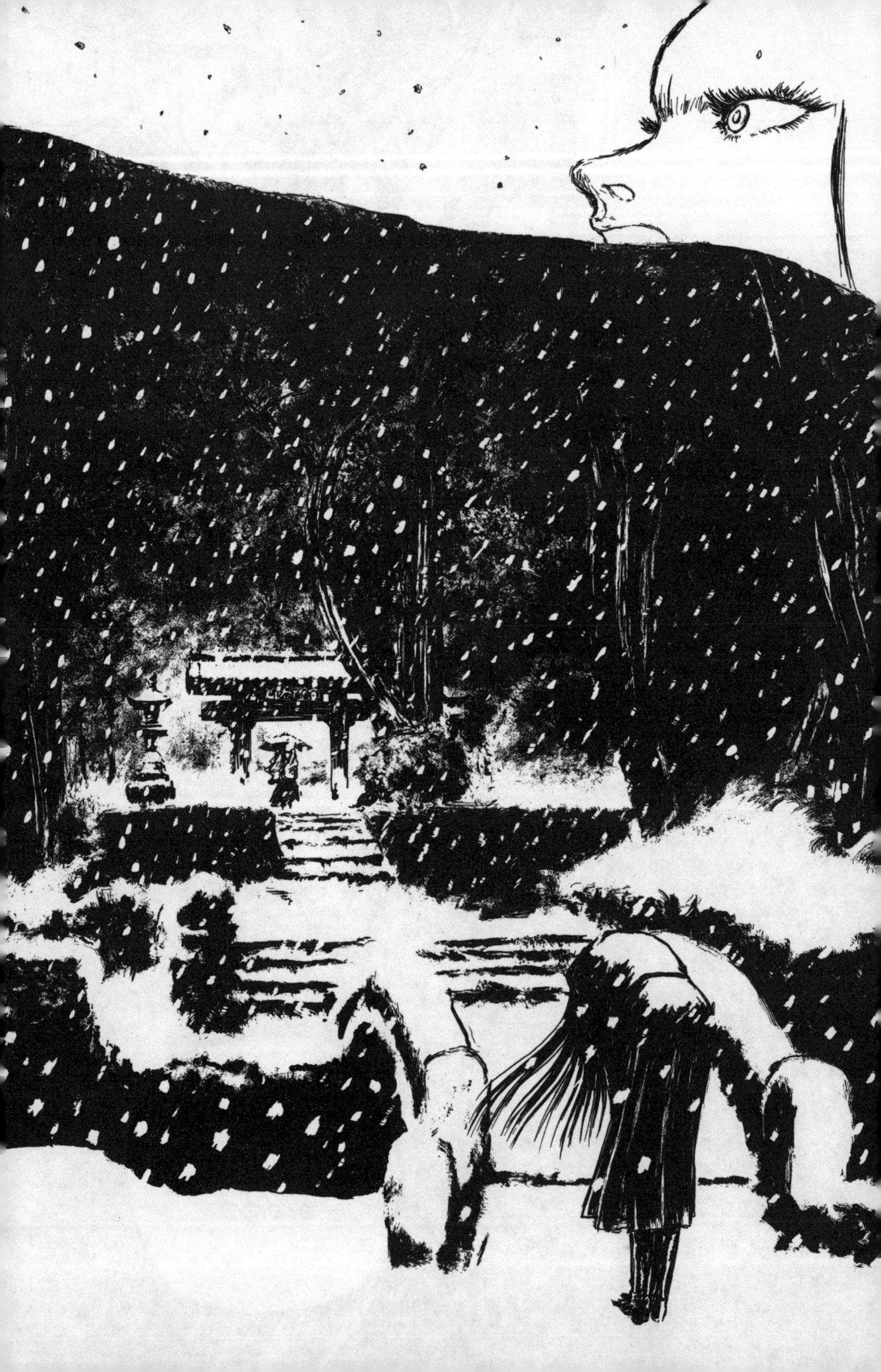

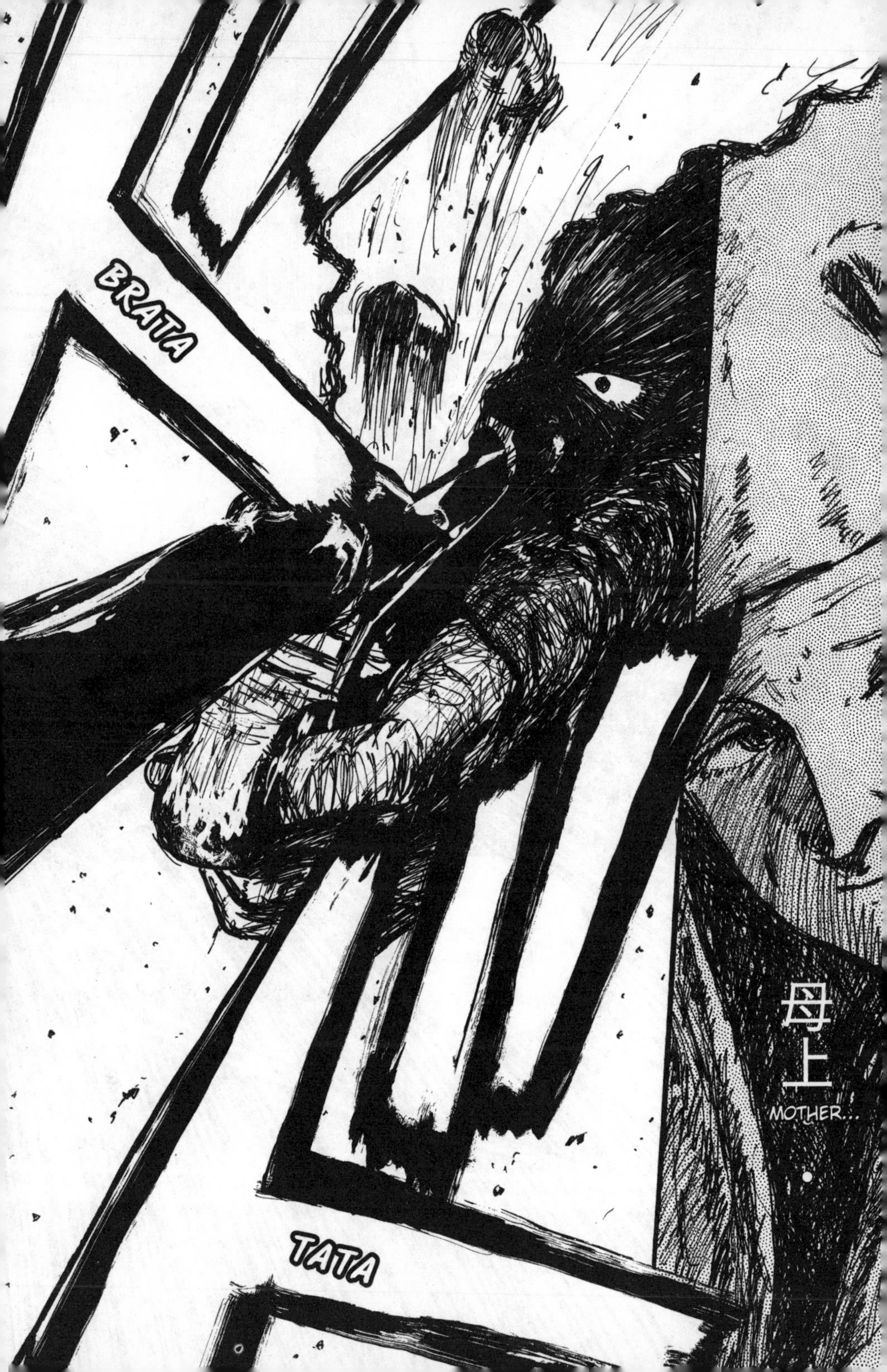
母上
MOTHER...
BRATA
TATA

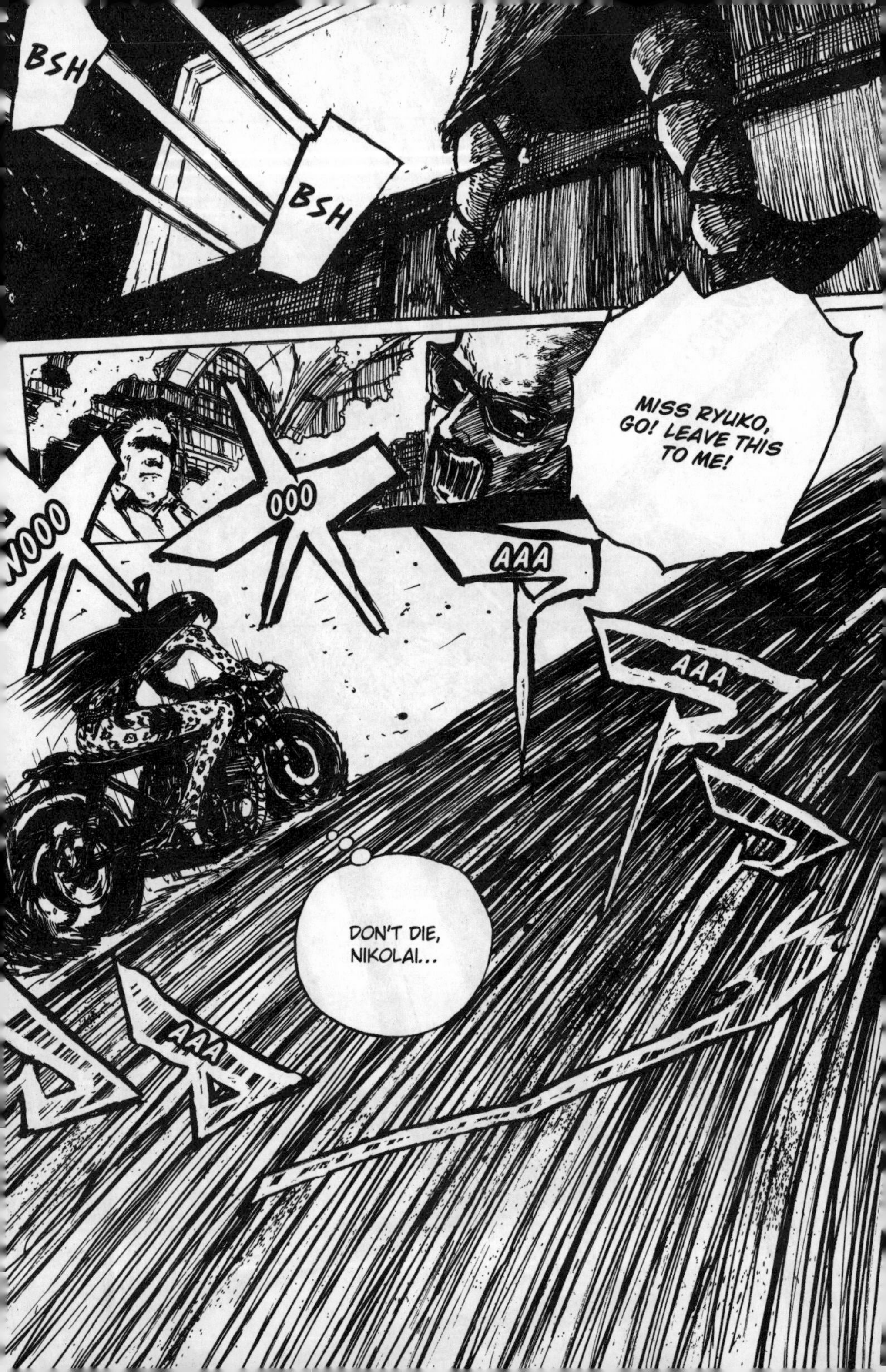
BSH
BSH
MISS RYUKO, GO! LEAVE THIS TO ME!
AAA
OOO
NOOO
AAA
DON'T DIE, NIKOLAI...
AAA

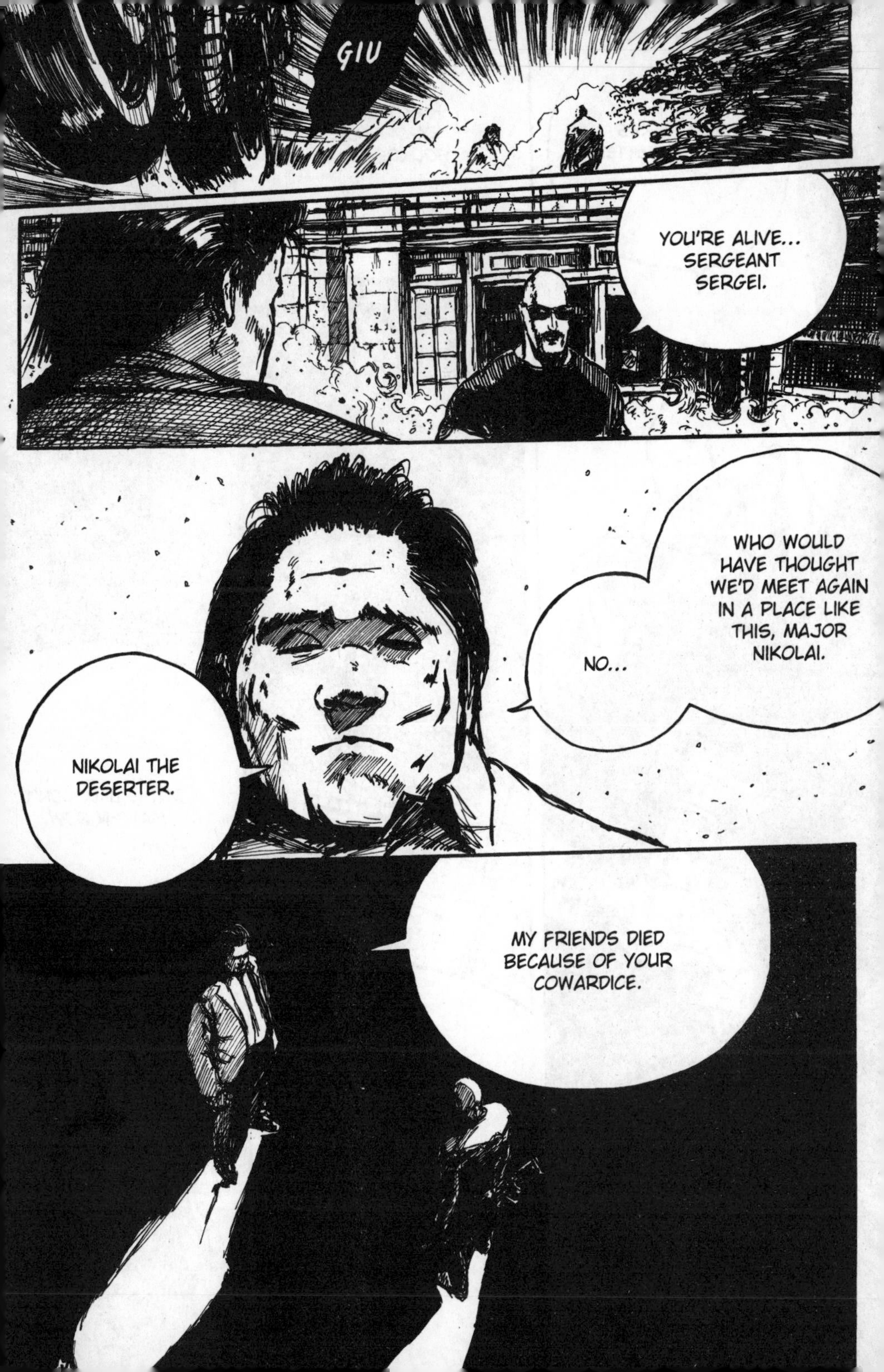
GIU
YOU'RE ALIVE... SERGEANT SERGEI.
WHO WOULD HAVE THOUGHT WE'D MEET AGAIN IN A PLACE LIKE THIS, MAJOR NIKOLAI.
NO...
NIKOLAI THE DESERTER.
MY FRIENDS DIED BECAUSE OF YOUR COWARDICE.

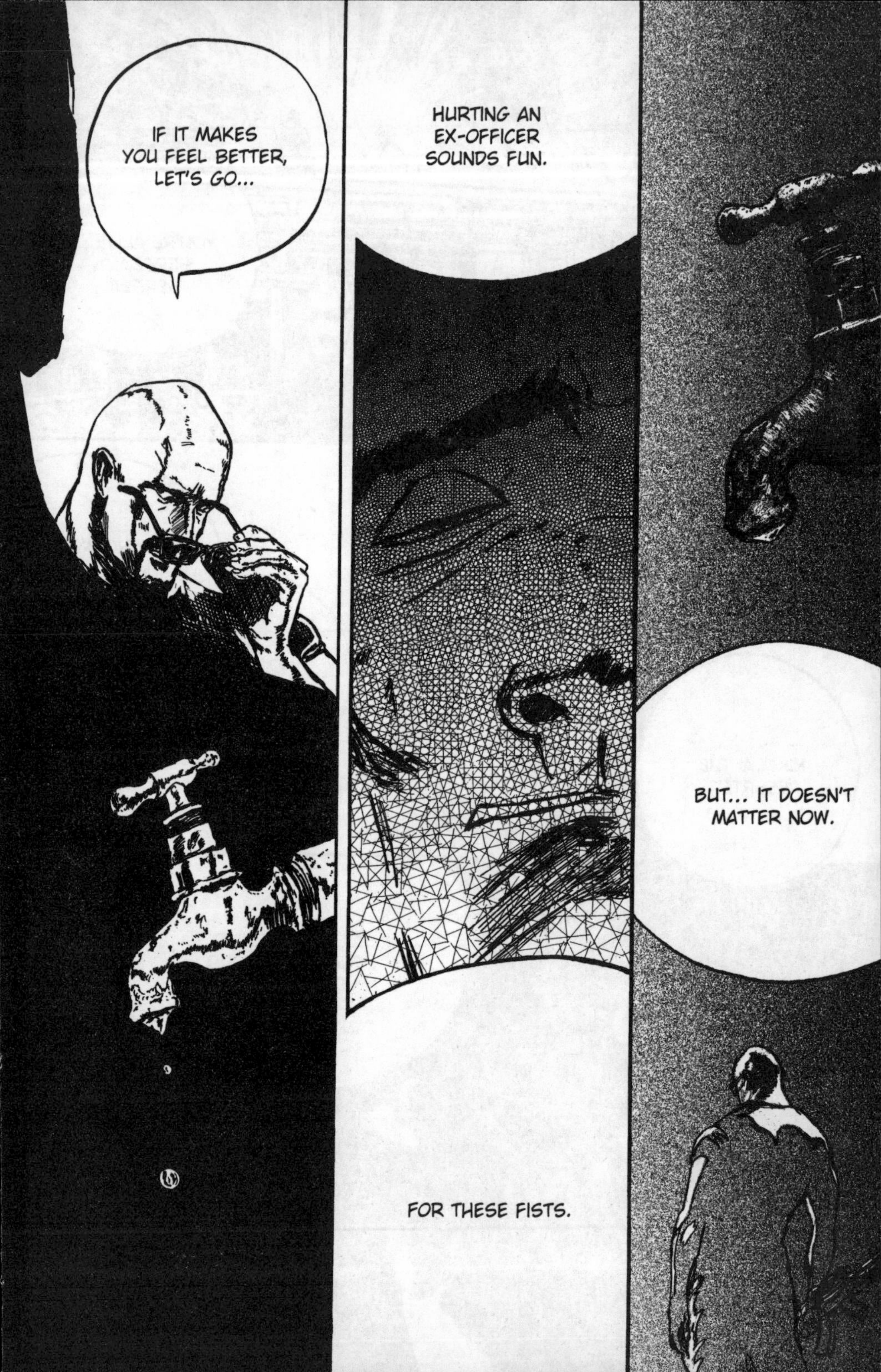
IF IT MAKES YOU FEEL BETTER, LET'S GO...
HURTING AN EX-OFFICER SOUNDS FUN.
FOR THESE FISTS.
BUT... IT DOESN'T MATTER NOW.

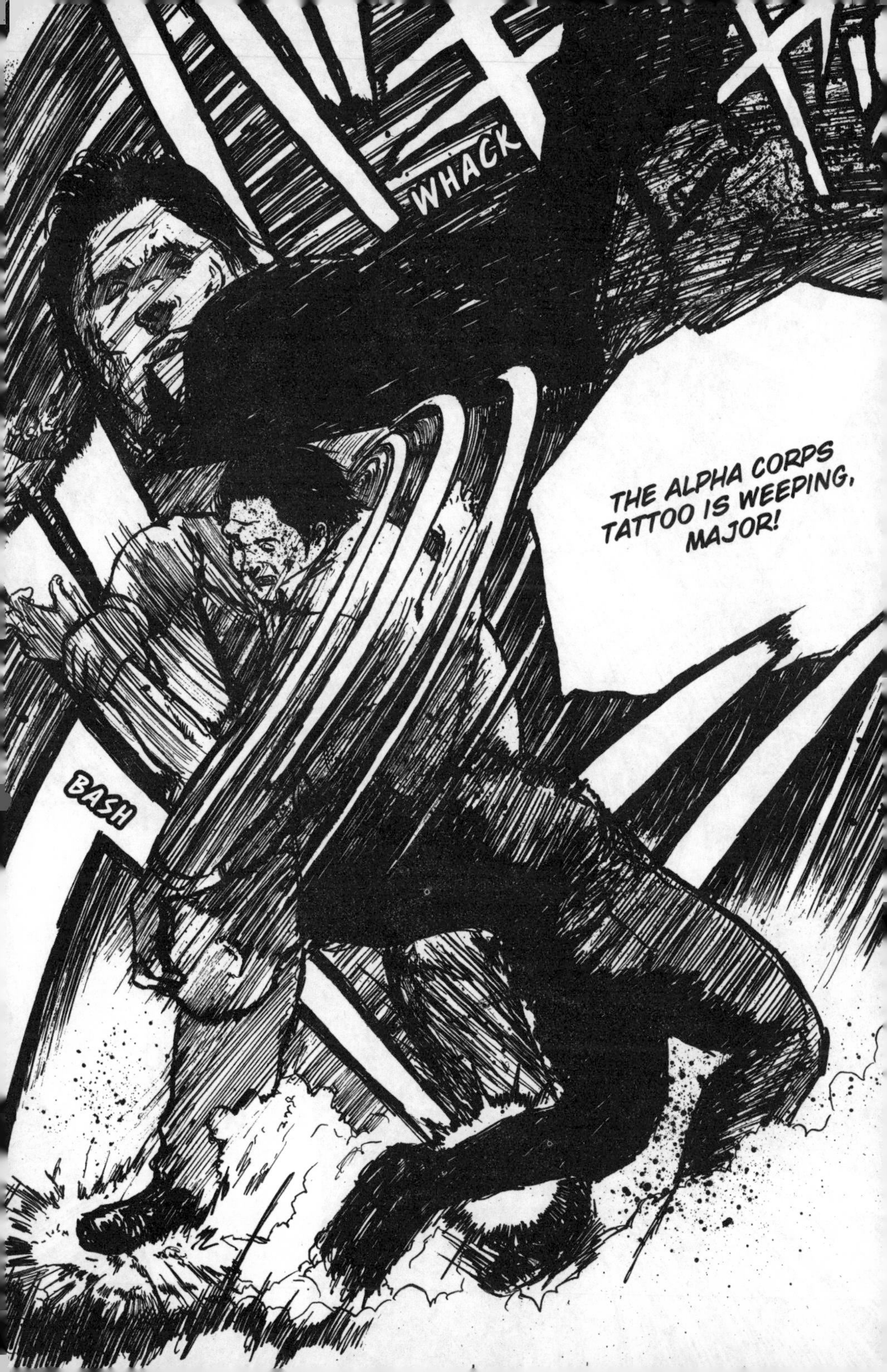
THE ALPHA CORPS TATTOO IS WEEPING, MAJOR!
WHACK
BASH

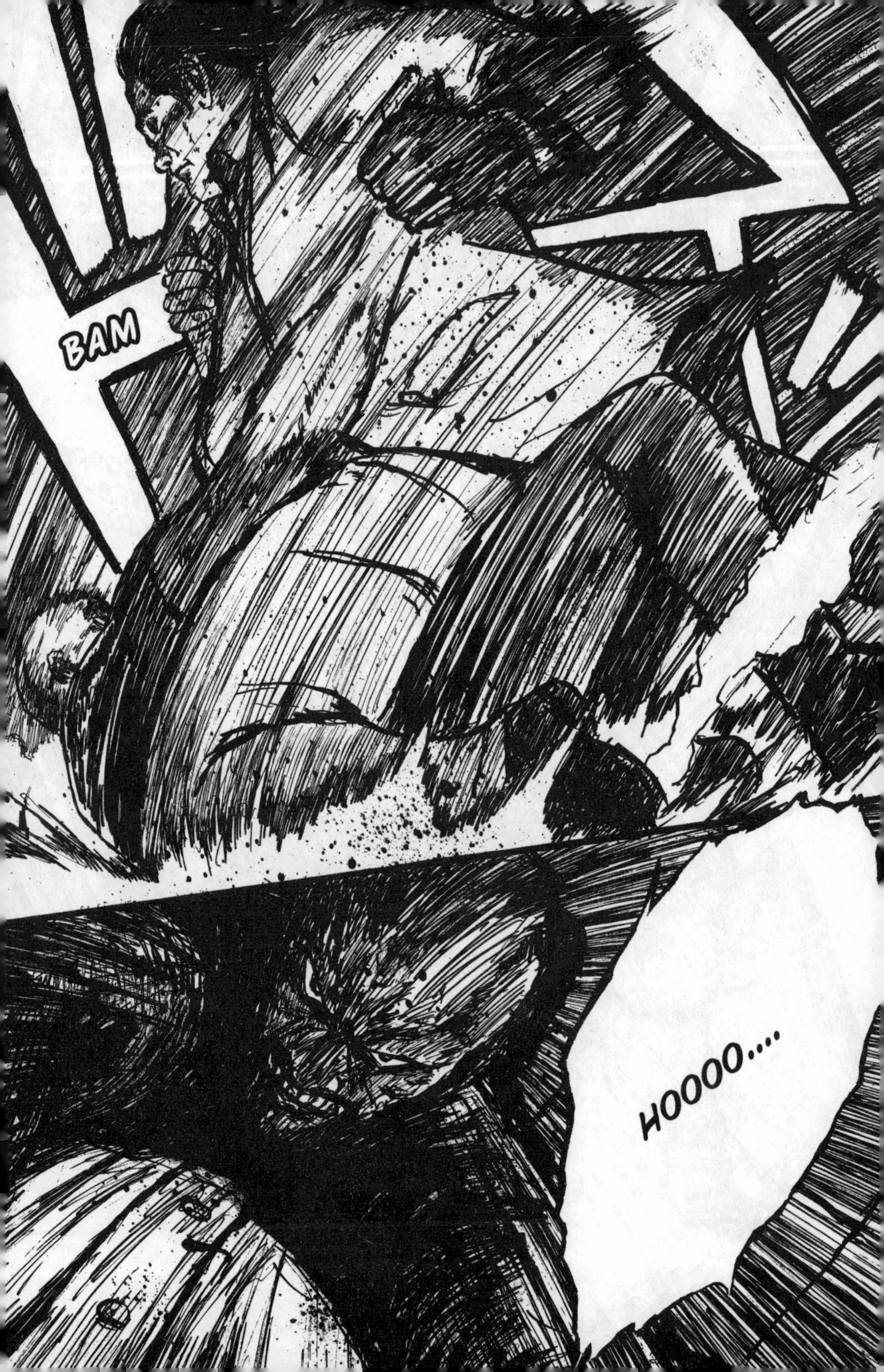
BAM
HOOOO....

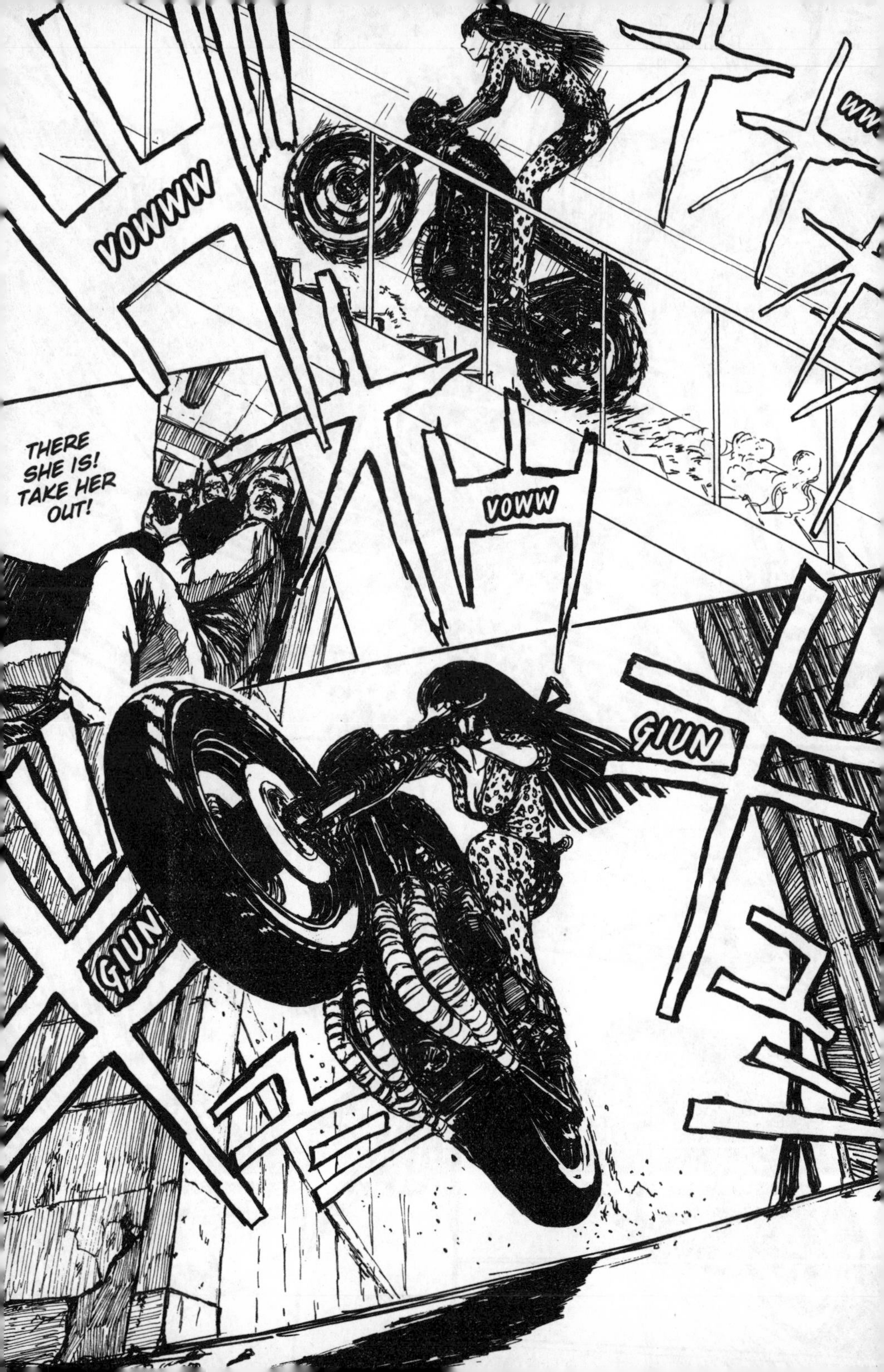
WW
VOWWW
VOWW
THERE SHE IS! TAKE HER OUT!
GIUN
GIUN

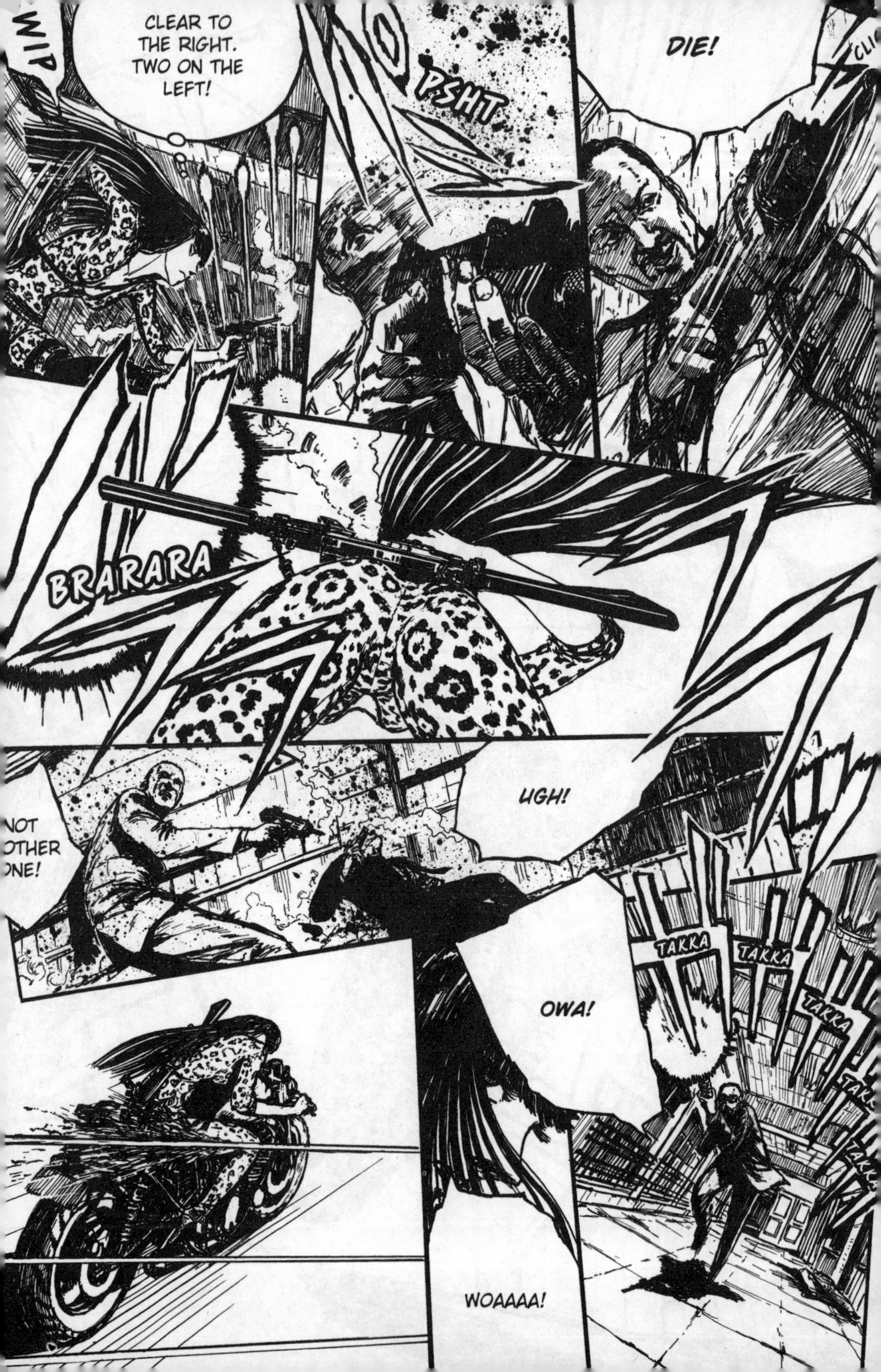
DIE!
PSHT
WIP
CLEAR TO THE RIGHT. TWO ON THE LEFT!
BRARARA
UGH!
TAKKA
TAKKA
TAKKA
TAKKA
TAKKA
OWA!
WOAAAA!
NOT OTHER ONE!

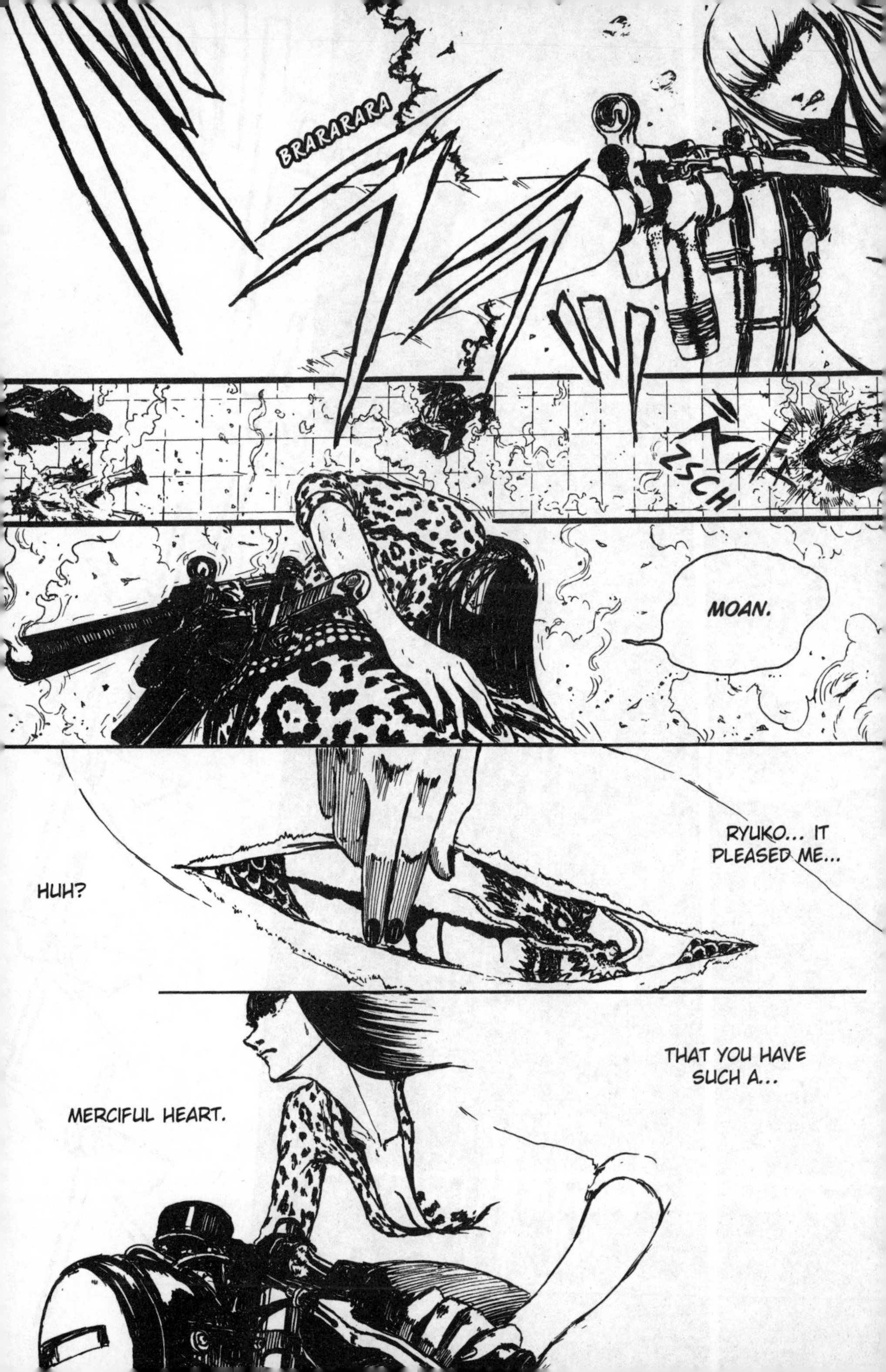
BRARARARA
ZSCH
MOAN.
RYUKO... IT PLEASED ME...
HUH?
THAT YOU HAVE SUCH A...
MERCIFUL HEART.

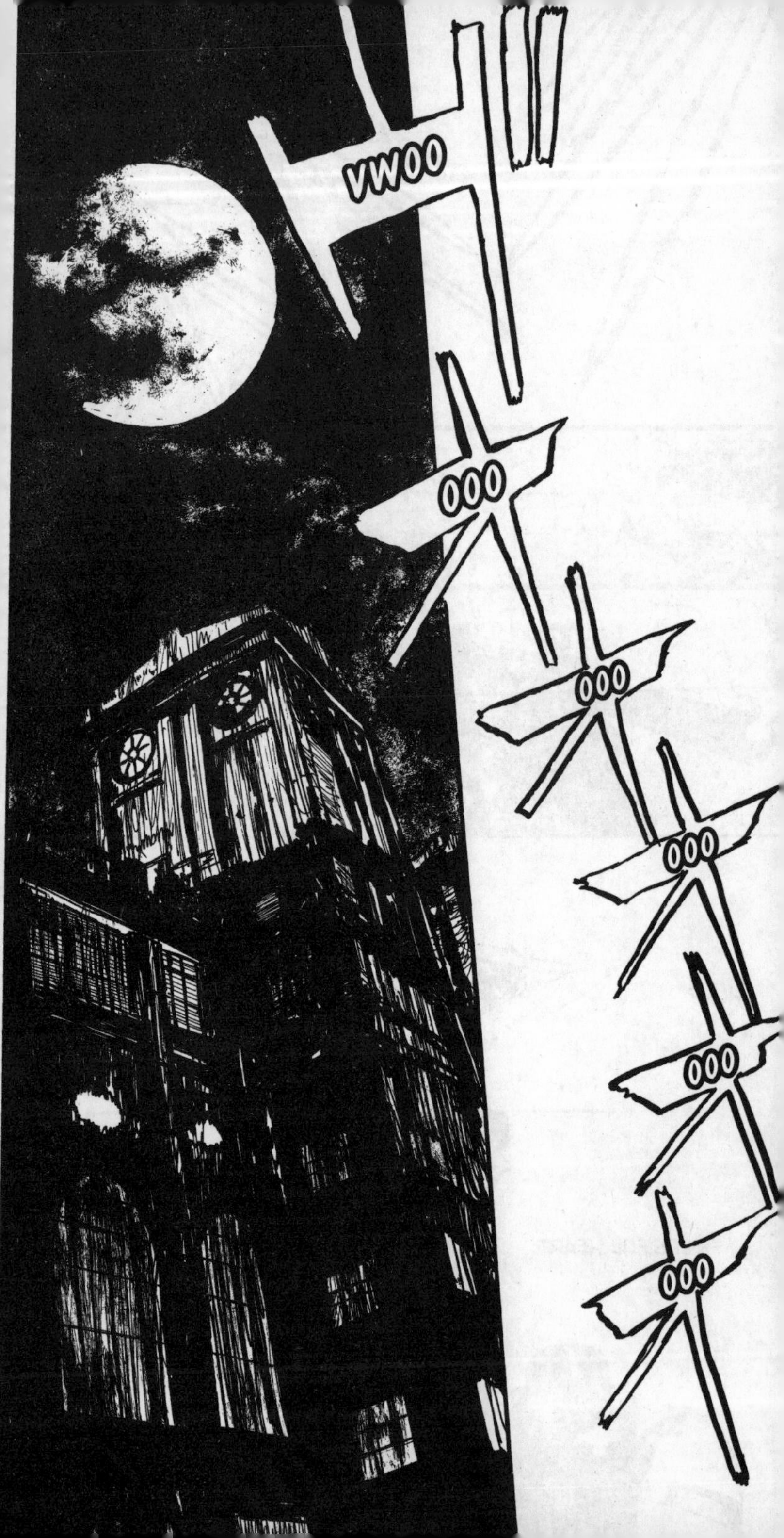
VWOO
OOO
OOO
OOO
OOO
OOO

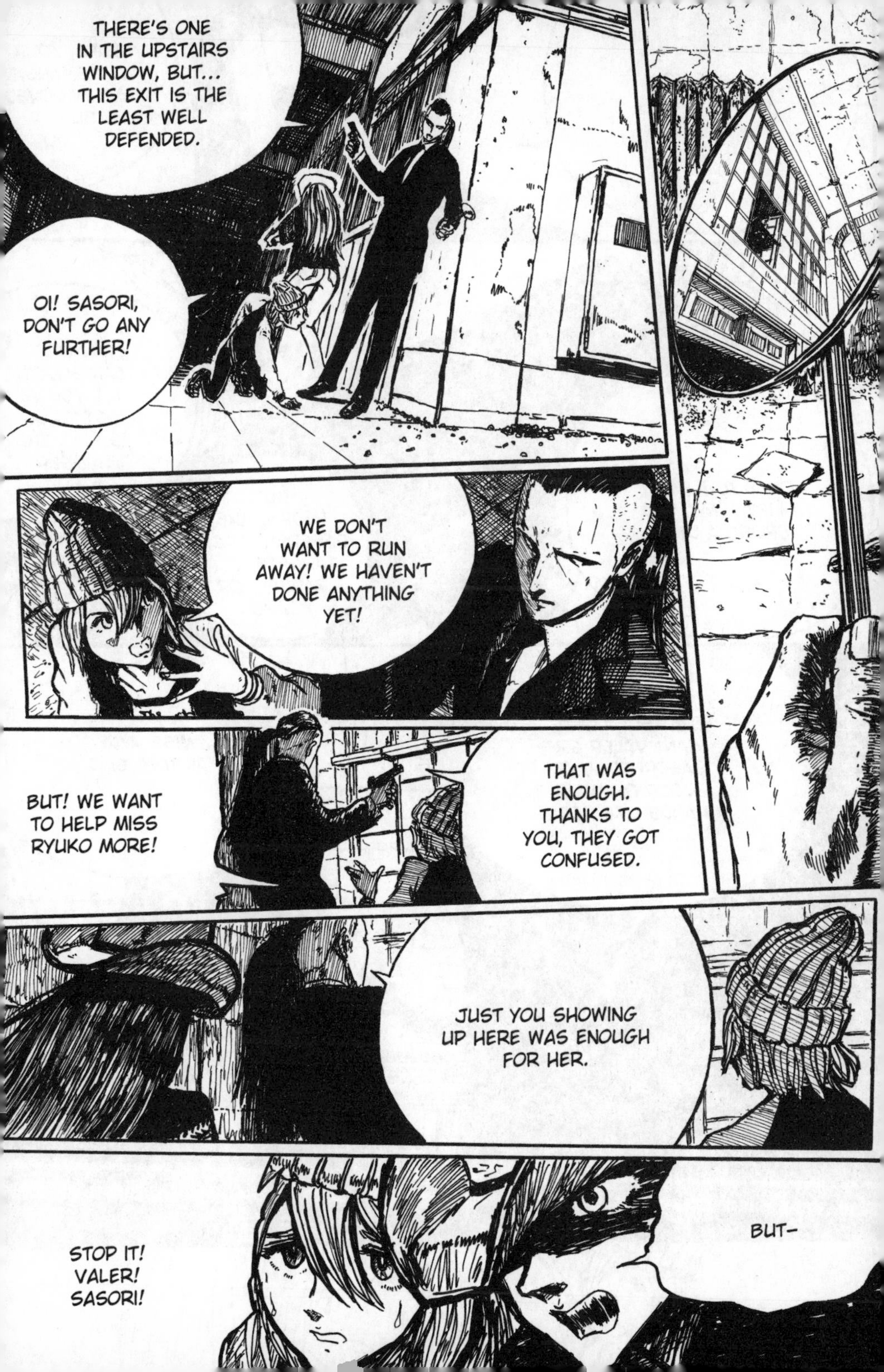

THERE'S ONE IN THE UPSTAIRS WINDOW, BUT... THIS EXIT IS THE LEAST WELL DEFENDED.
OI! SASORI, DON'T GO ANY FURTHER!
WE DON'T WANT TO RUN AWAY! WE HAVEN'T DONE ANYTHING YET!
THAT WAS ENOUGH. THANKS TO YOU, THEY GOT CONFUSED.
BUT! WE WANT TO HELP MISS RYUKO MORE!
JUST YOU SHOWING UP HERE WAS ENOUGH FOR HER.
BUT–
STOP IT! VALER! SASORI!

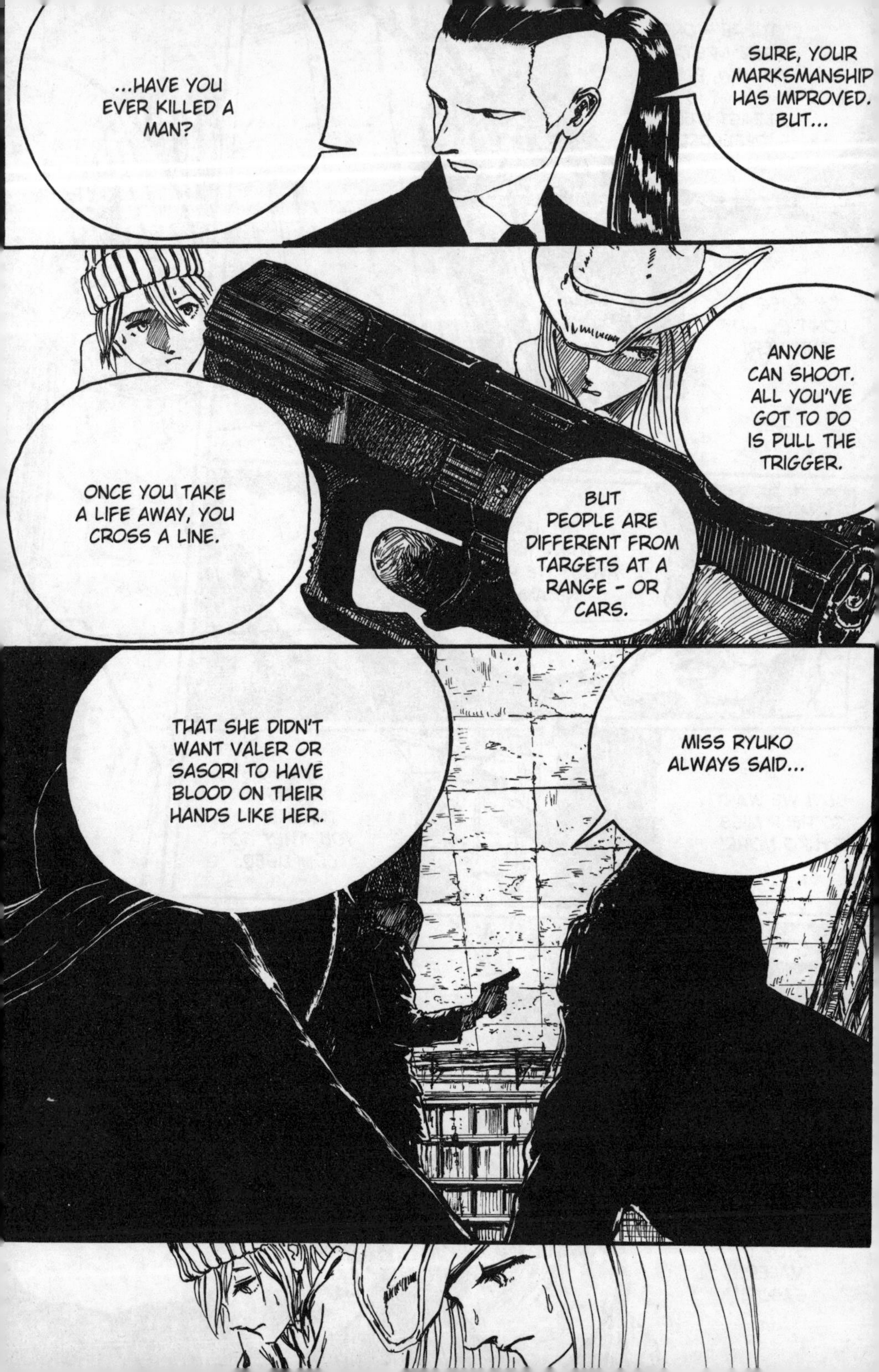
SURE, YOUR MARKSMANSHIP HAS IMPROVED. BUT...
...HAVE YOU EVER KILLED A MAN?
ANYONE CAN SHOOT. ALL YOU'VE GOT TO DO IS PULL THE TRIGGER.
BUT PEOPLE ARE DIFFERENT FROM TARGETS AT A RANGE - OR CARS.
ONCE YOU TAKE A LIFE AWAY, YOU CROSS A LINE.
MISS RYUKO ALWAYS SAID...
THAT SHE DIDN'T WANT VALER OR SASORI TO HAVE BLOOD ON THEIR HANDS LIKE HER.

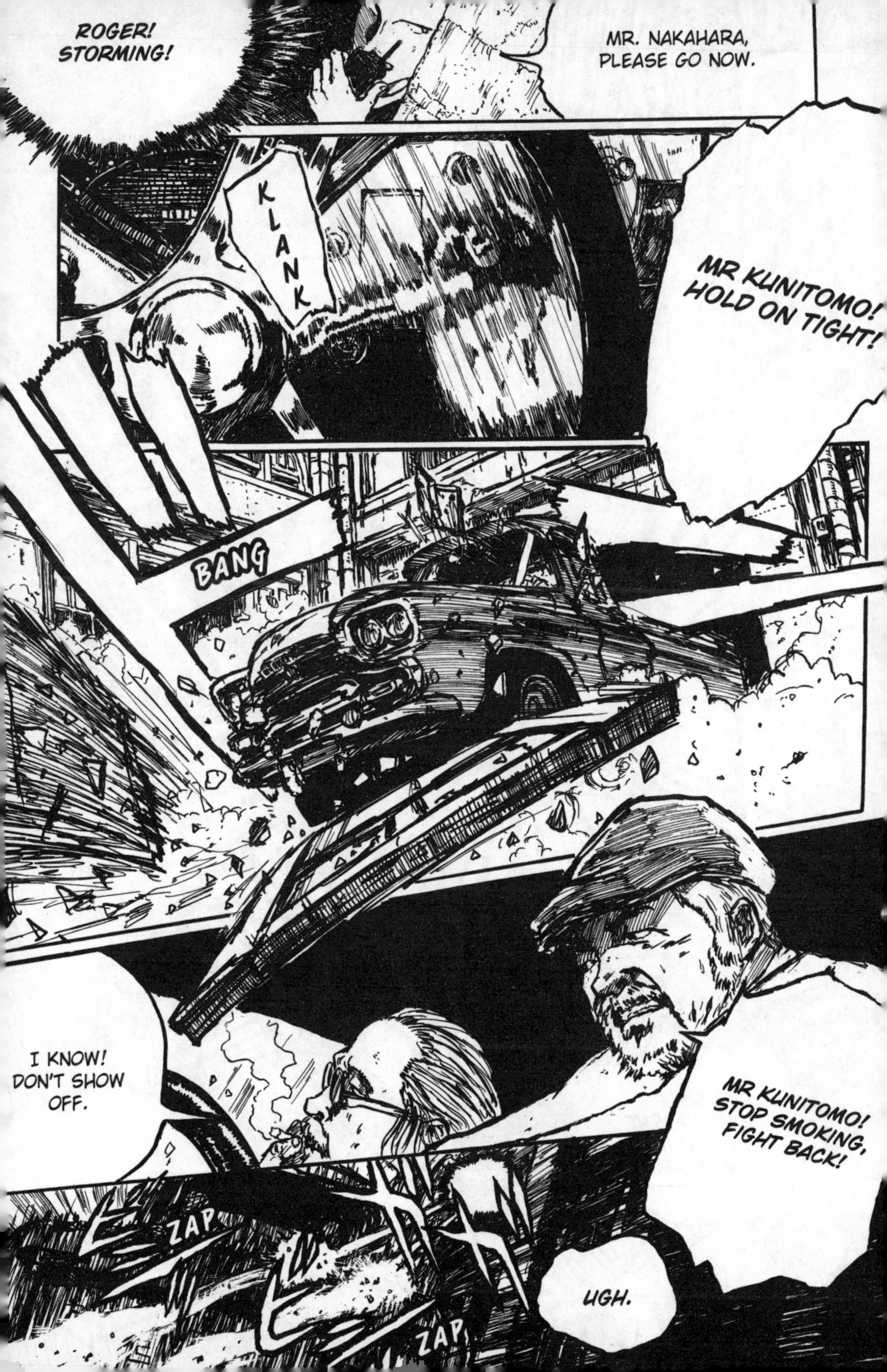
MR. NAKAHARA, PLEASE GO NOW.
ROGER! STORMING!
MR KUNITOMO! HOLD ON TIGHT!
KLANK
BANG
MR KUNITOMO! STOP SMOKING, FIGHT BACK!
I KNOW! DON'T SHOW OFF.
ZAP
UGH.
ZAP

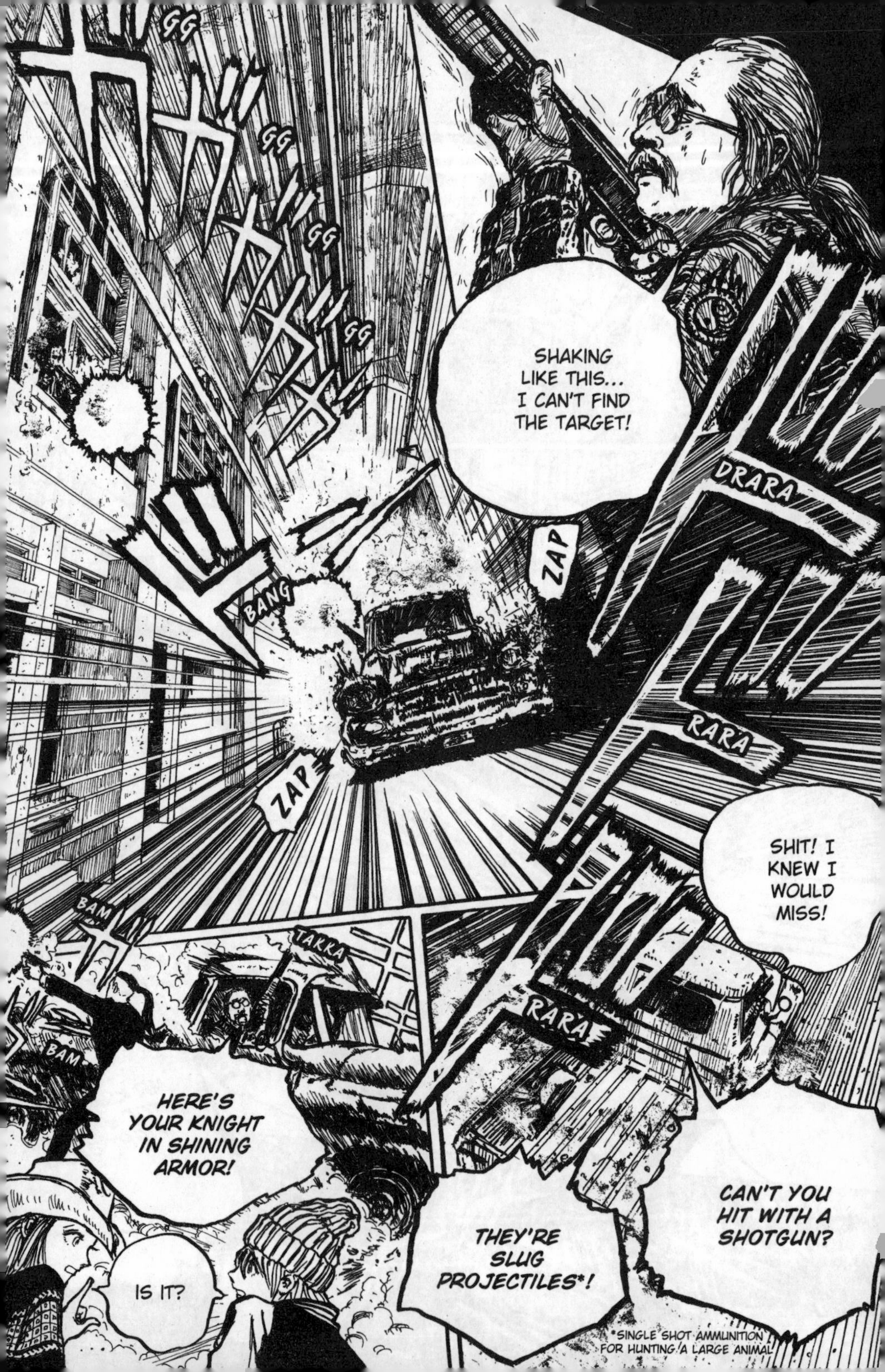
GG
GG
GG
GG
SHAKING LIKE THIS... I CAN'T FIND THE TARGET!
DRARA
ZAP
BANG
RARA
ZAP
SHIT! I KNEW I WOULD MISS!
BAM
TAKKA
RARA
BAM
HERE'S YOUR KNIGHT IN SHINING ARMOR!
CAN'T YOU HIT WITH A SHOTGUN?
THEY'RE SLUG PROJECTILES*!
IS IT?
*SINGLE SHOT AMMUNITION FOR HUNTING A LARGE ANIMAL

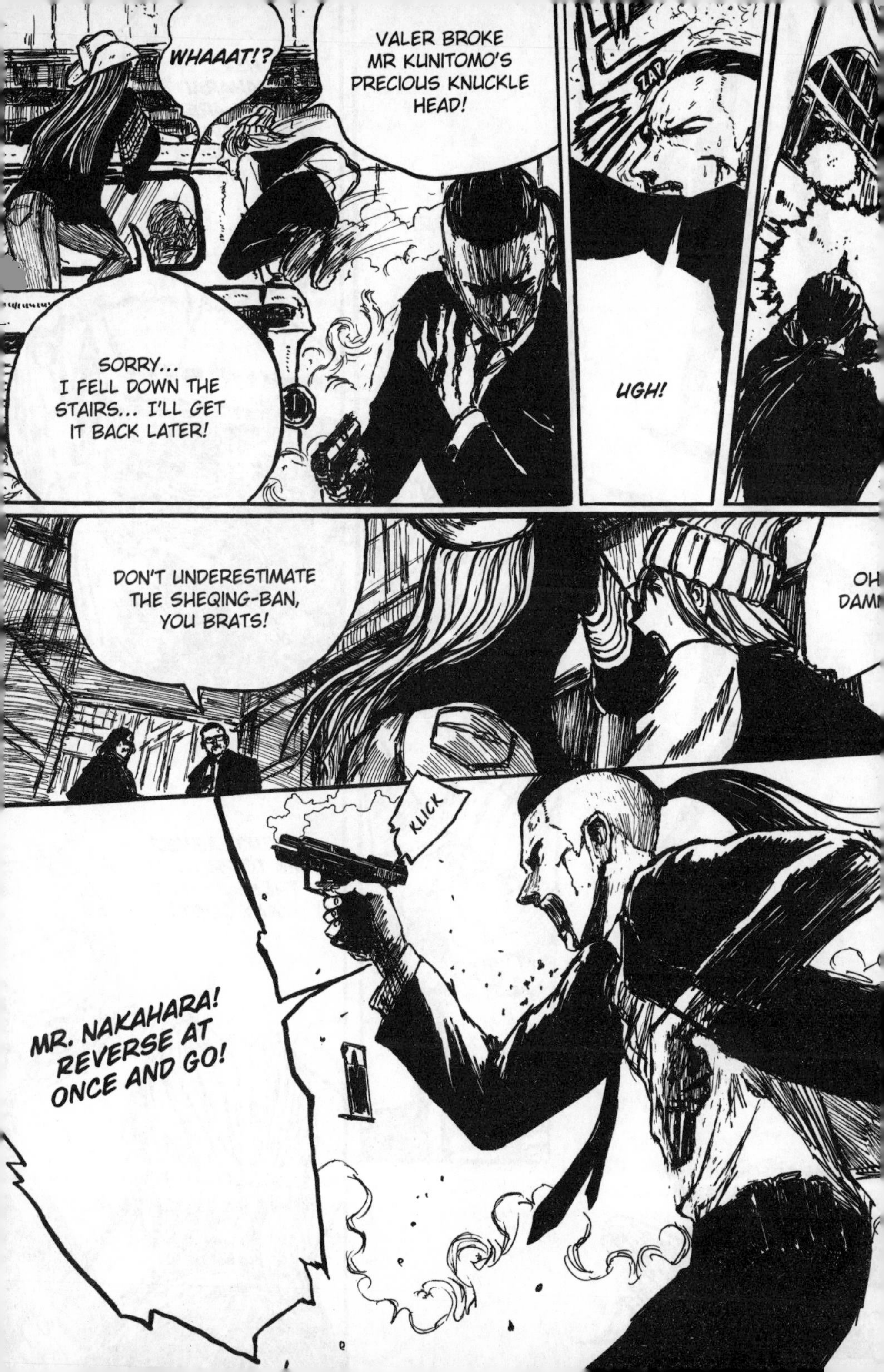
ZAP
UGH!
VALER BROKE MR KUNITOMO'S PRECIOUS KNUCKLE HEAD!
WHAAAT!?
SORRY... I FELL DOWN THE STAIRS... I'LL GET IT BACK LATER!
OH DAM
DON'T UNDERESTIMATE THE SHEQING-BAN, YOU BRATS!
KLICK
MR. NAKAHARA! REVERSE AT ONCE AND GO!

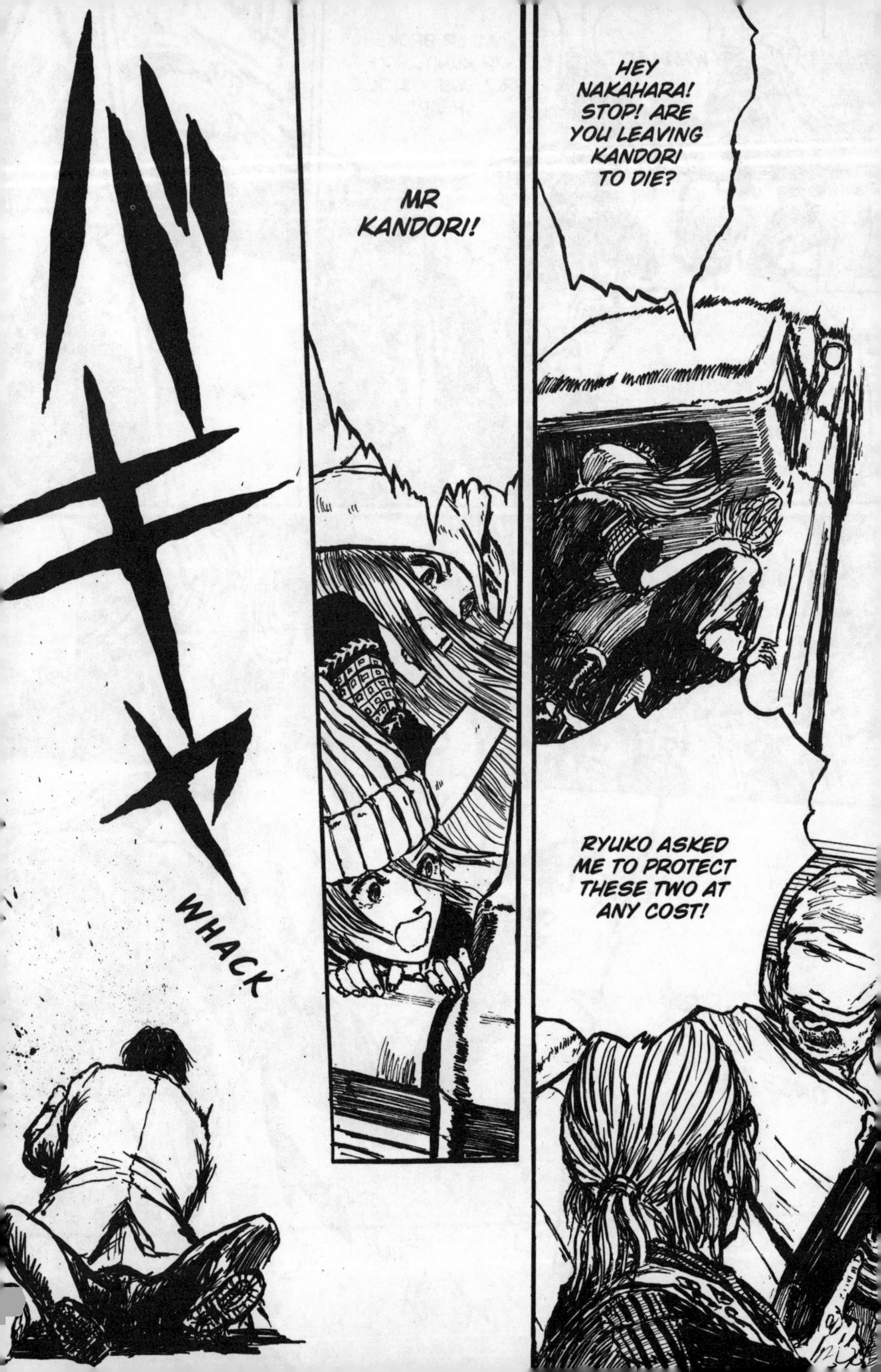
HEY NAKAHARA! STOP! ARE YOU LEAVING KANDORI TO DIE?
RYUKO ASKED ME TO PROTECT THESE TWO AT ANY COST!
MR KANDORI!
WHACK

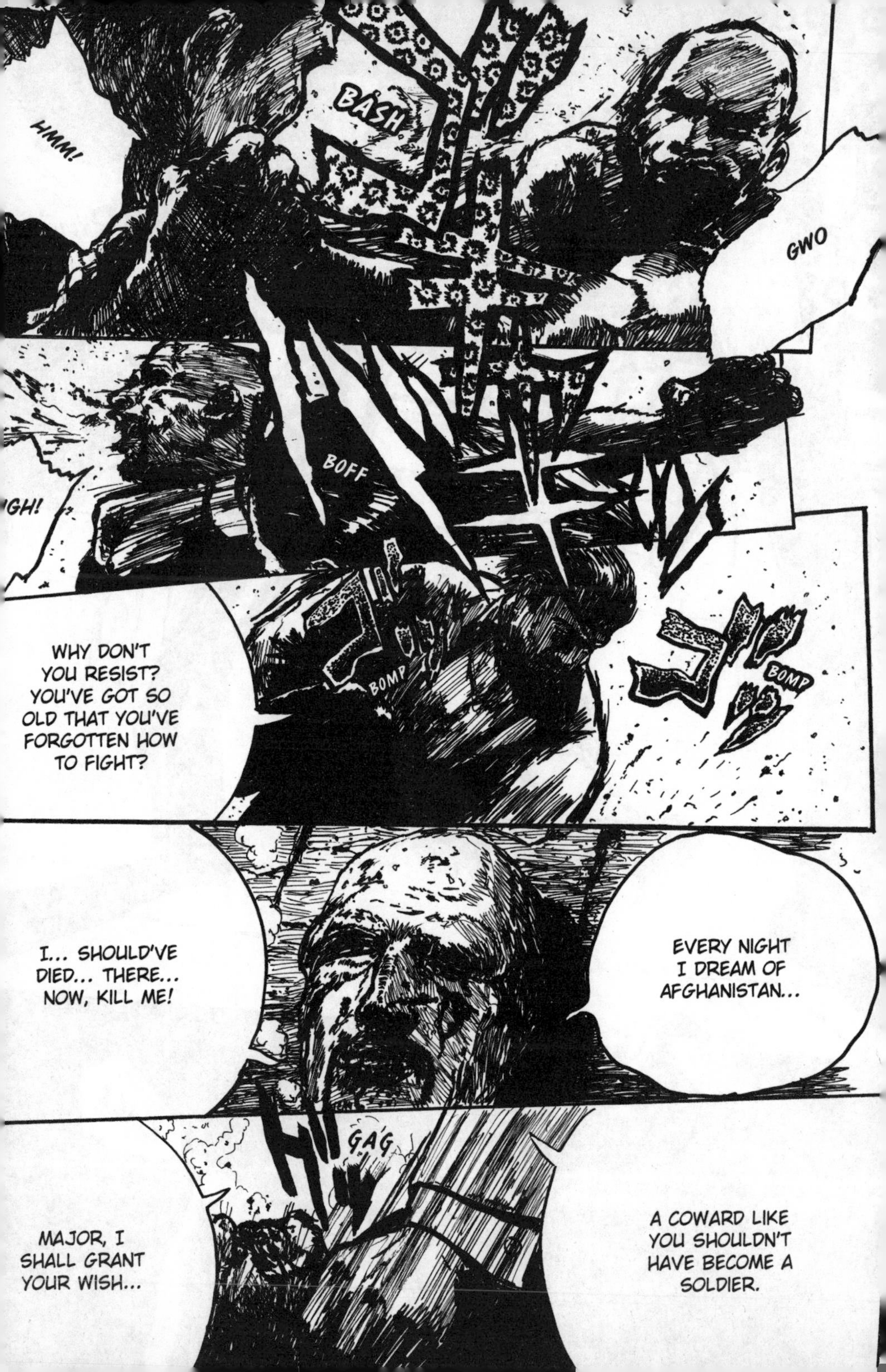
GWO
BASH
HMM!
BOFF
GH!
BOMP
BOMP
WHY DON'T YOU RESIST? YOU'VE GOT SO OLD THAT YOU'VE FORGOTTEN HOW TO FIGHT?
EVERY NIGHT I DREAM OF AFGHANISTAN...
I... SHOULD'VE DIED... THERE... NOW, KILL ME!
A COWARD LIKE YOU SHOULDN'T HAVE BECOME A SOLDIER.
GAG
MAJOR, I SHALL GRANT YOUR WISH...

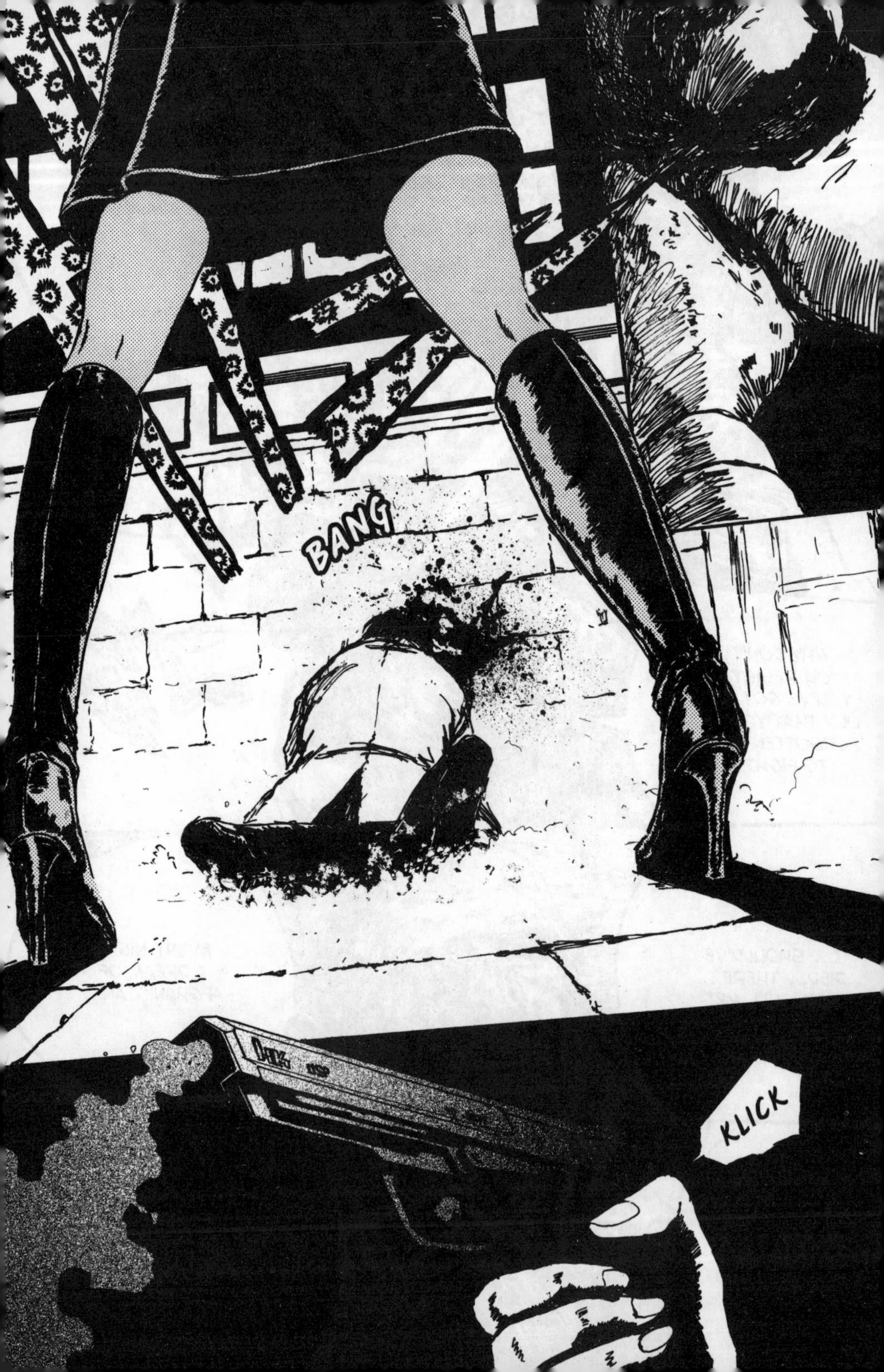
BANG
KLICK

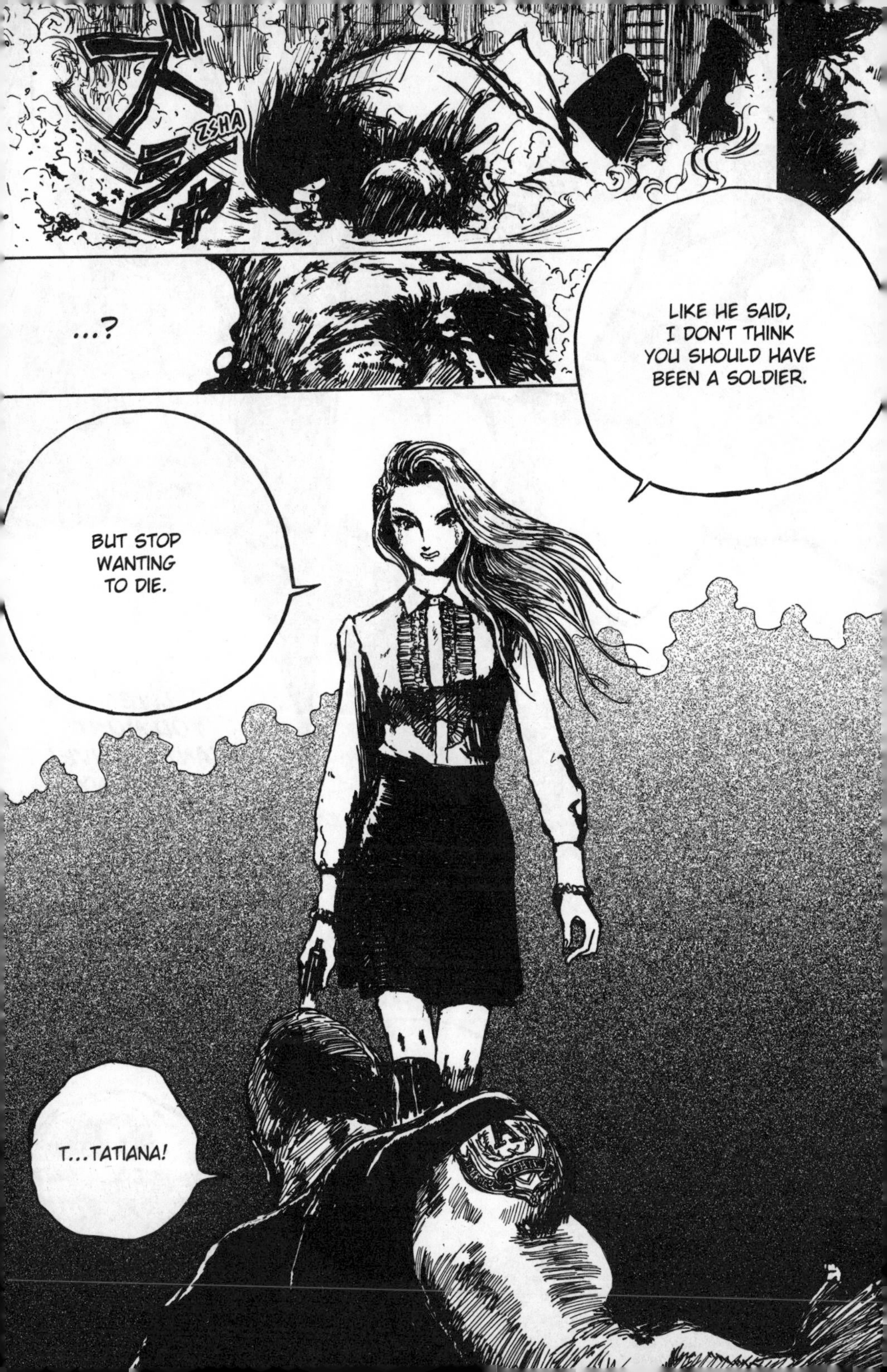
ZSHA
LIKE HE SAID, I DON'T THINK YOU SHOULD HAVE BEEN A SOLDIER.
...?
BUT STOP WANTING TO DIE.
T...TATIANA!

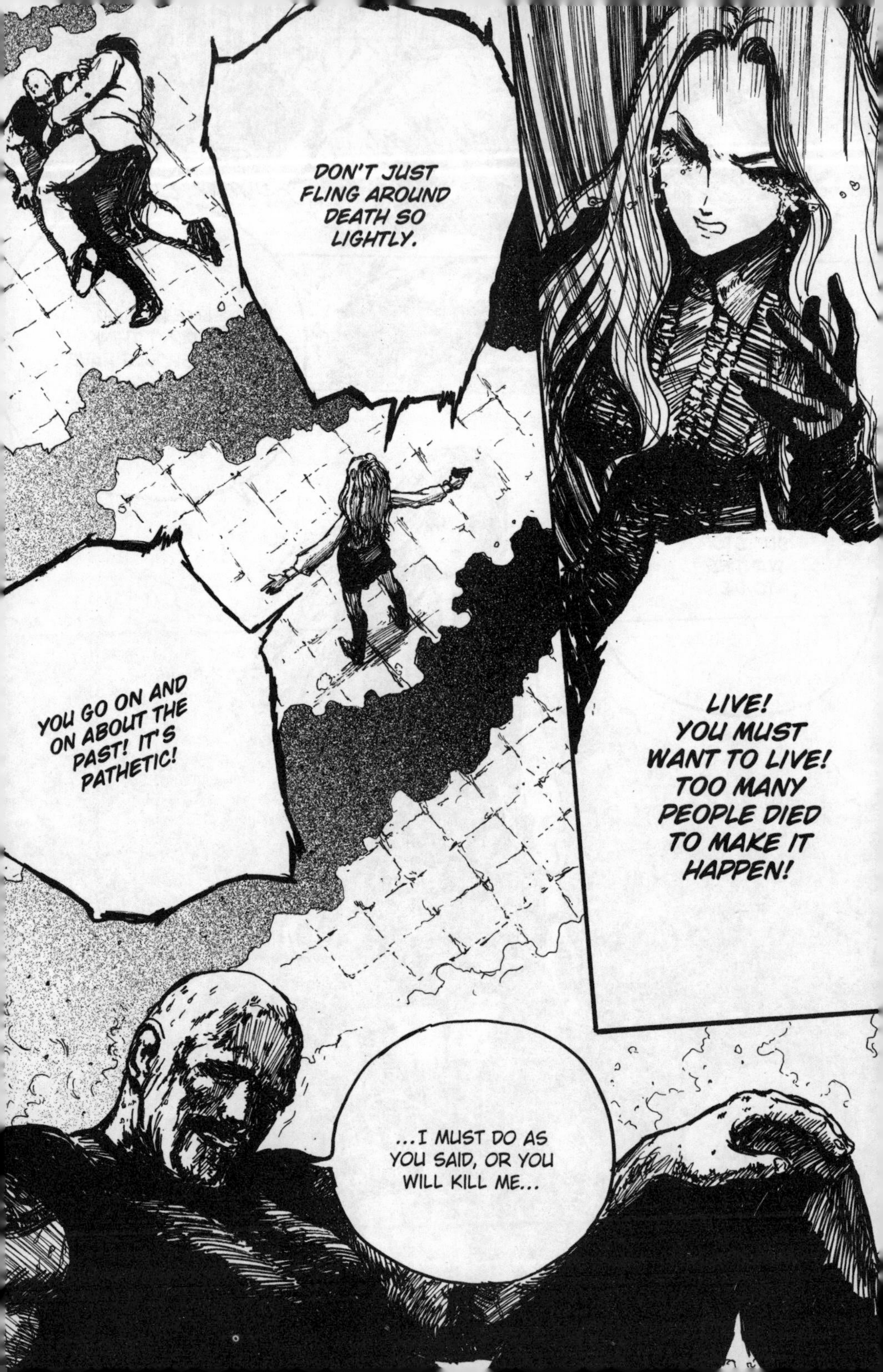
LIVE! YOU MUST WANT TO LIVE! TOO MANY PEOPLE DIED TO MAKE IT HAPPEN!
DON'T JUST FLING AROUND DEATH SO LIGHTLY.
YOU GO ON AND ON ABOUT THE PAST! IT'S PATHETIC!
...I MUST DO AS YOU SAID, OR YOU WILL KILL ME...

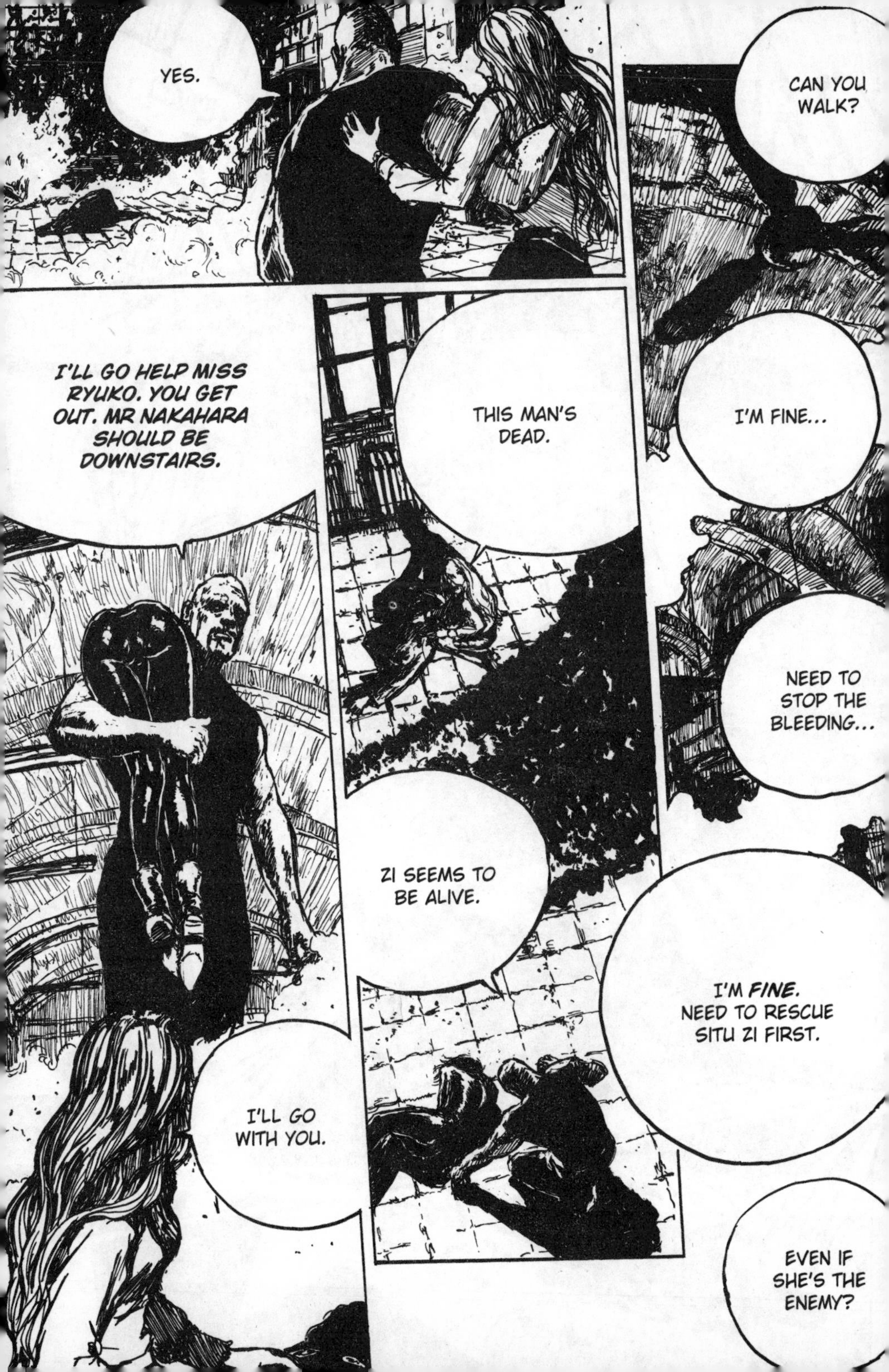
CAN YOU WALK?
I'M FINE...
NEED TO STOP THE BLEEDING...
I'M *FINE.* NEED TO RESCUE SITU ZI FIRST.
EVEN IF SHE'S THE ENEMY?
THIS MAN'S DEAD.
ZI SEEMS TO BE ALIVE.
YES.
I'LL GO HELP MISS RYUKO. YOU GET OUT. MR NAKAHARA SHOULD BE DOWNSTAIRS.
I'LL GO WITH YOU.

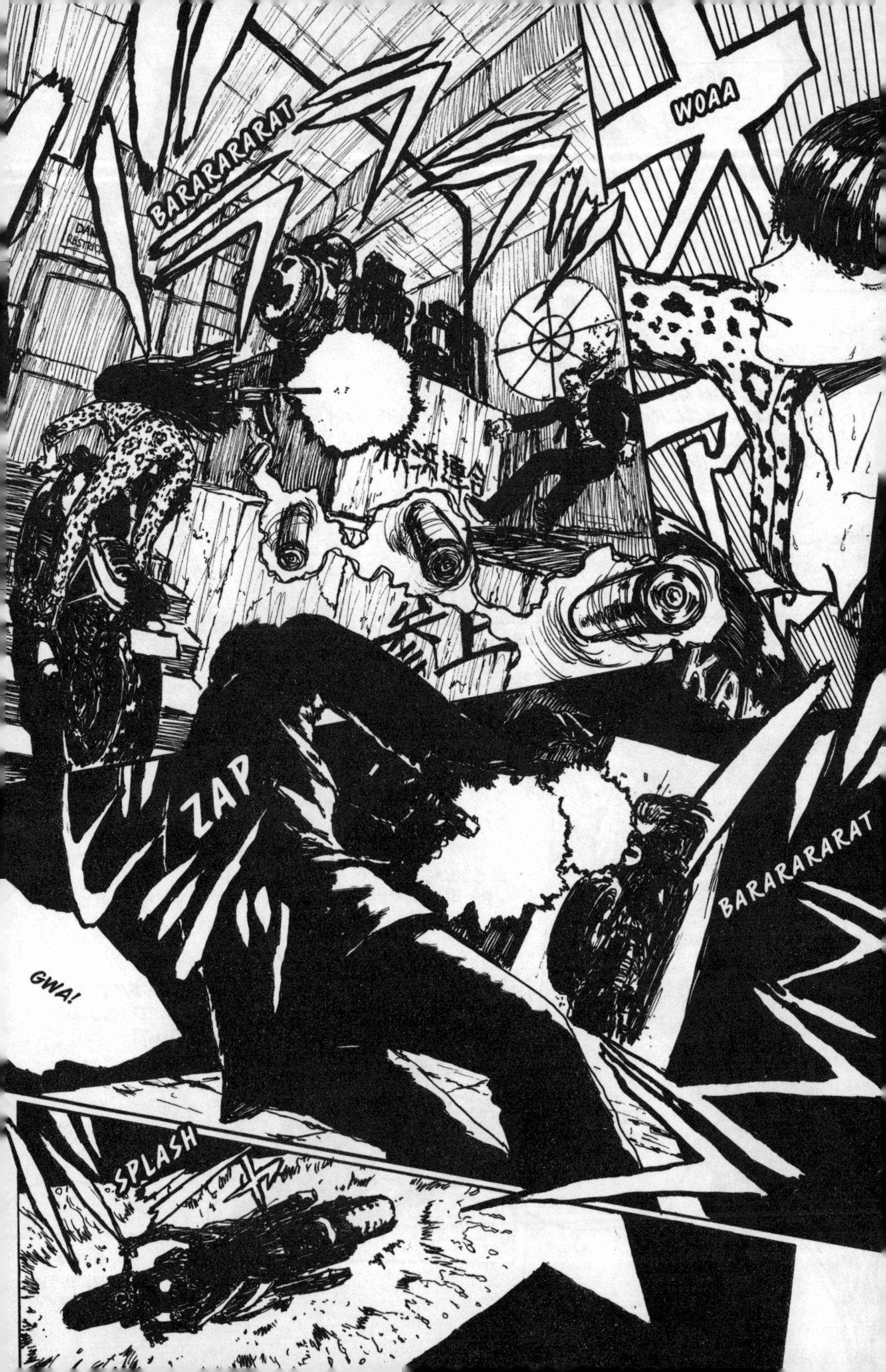
WOAA
BARARARARAT
BARARARARAT
ZAP
GWA!
SPLASH

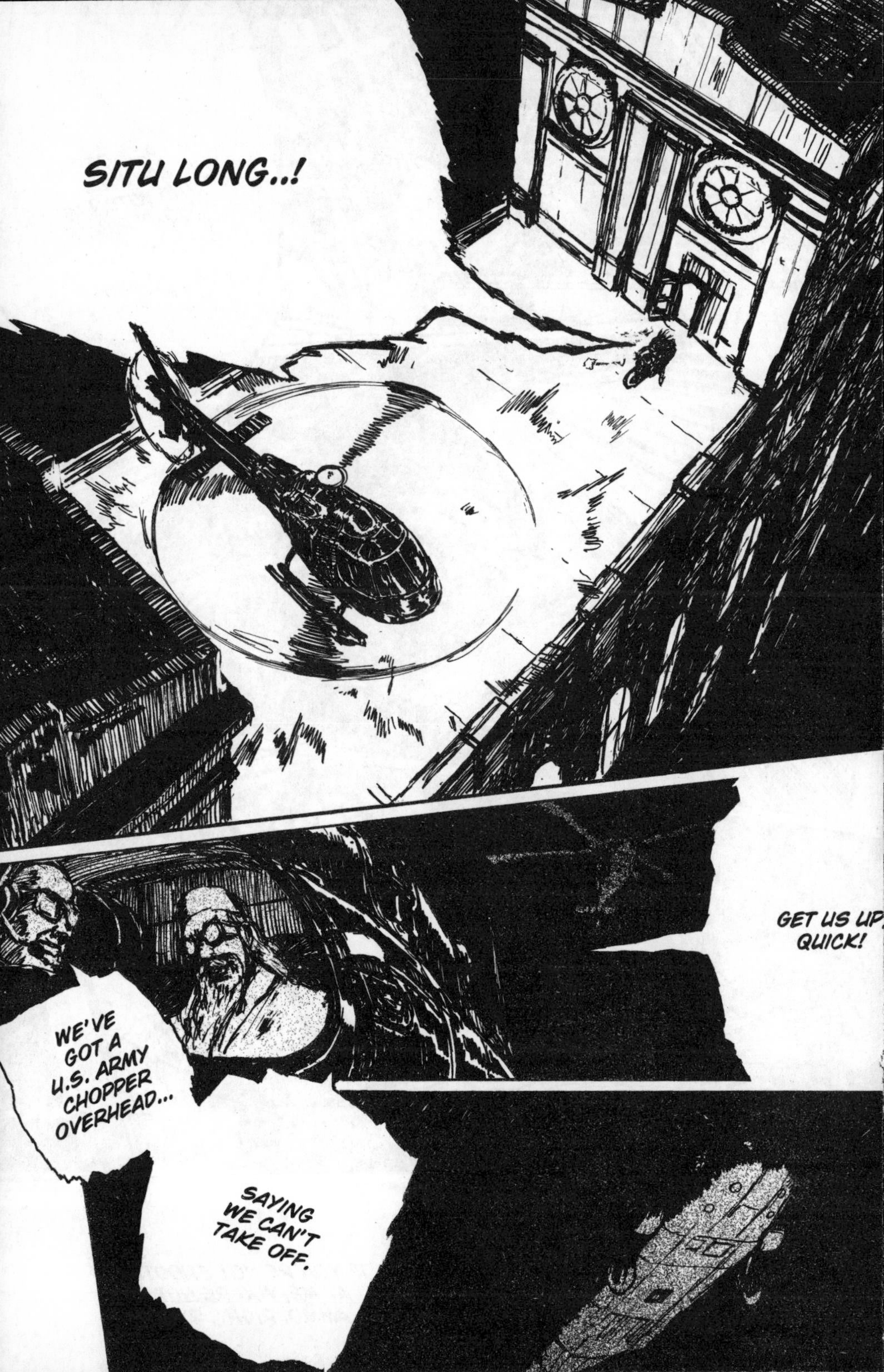
SITU LONG..!
GET US UP, QUICK!
WE'VE GOT A U.S. ARMY CHOPPER OVERHEAD...
SAYING WE CAN'T TAKE OFF.

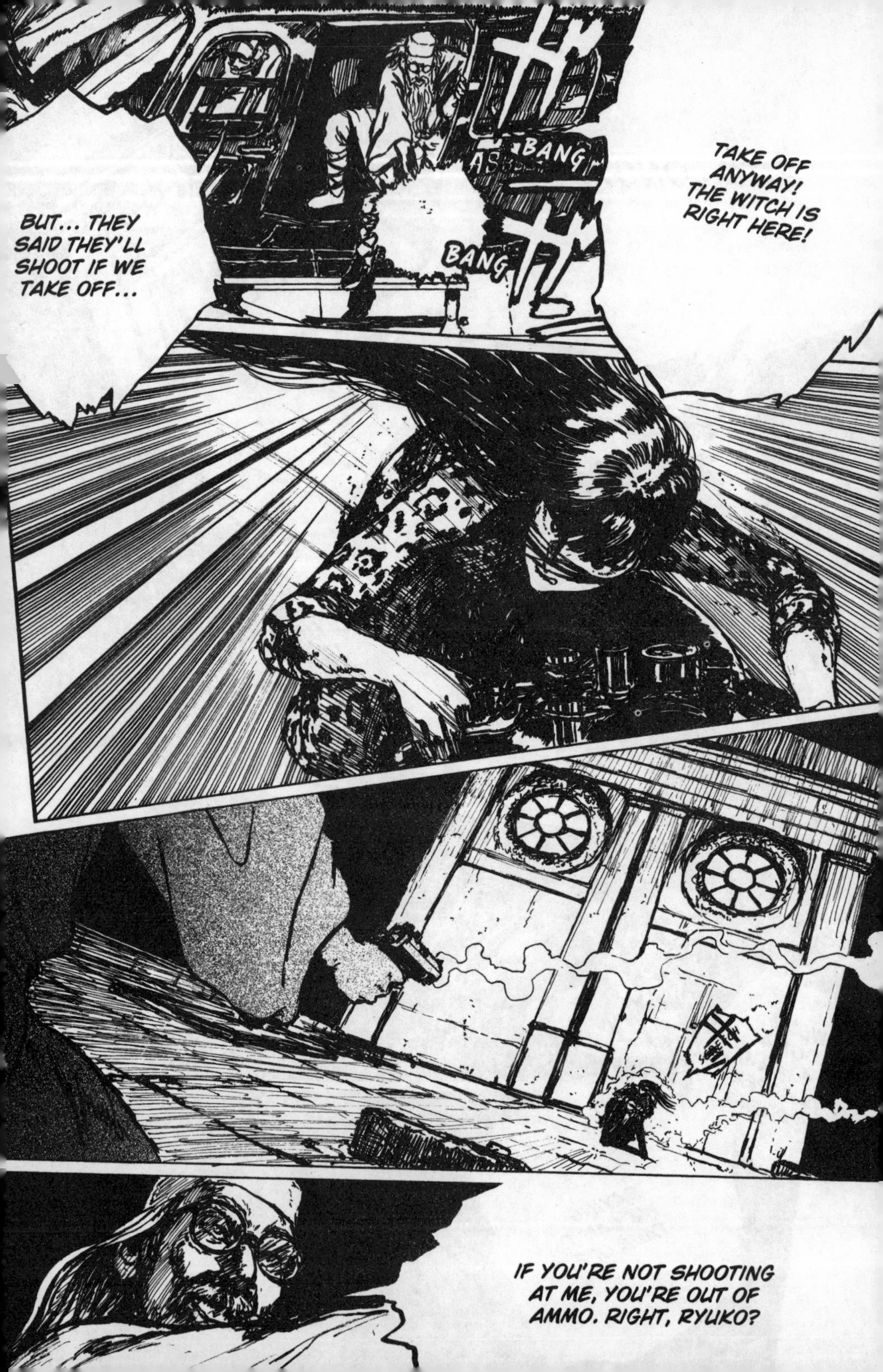
TAKE OFF ANYWAY! THE WITCH IS RIGHT HERE!
BANG
BANG
BUT... THEY SAID THEY'LL SHOOT IF WE TAKE OFF...
IF YOU'RE NOT SHOOTING AT ME, YOU'RE OUT OF AMMO. RIGHT, RYUKO?

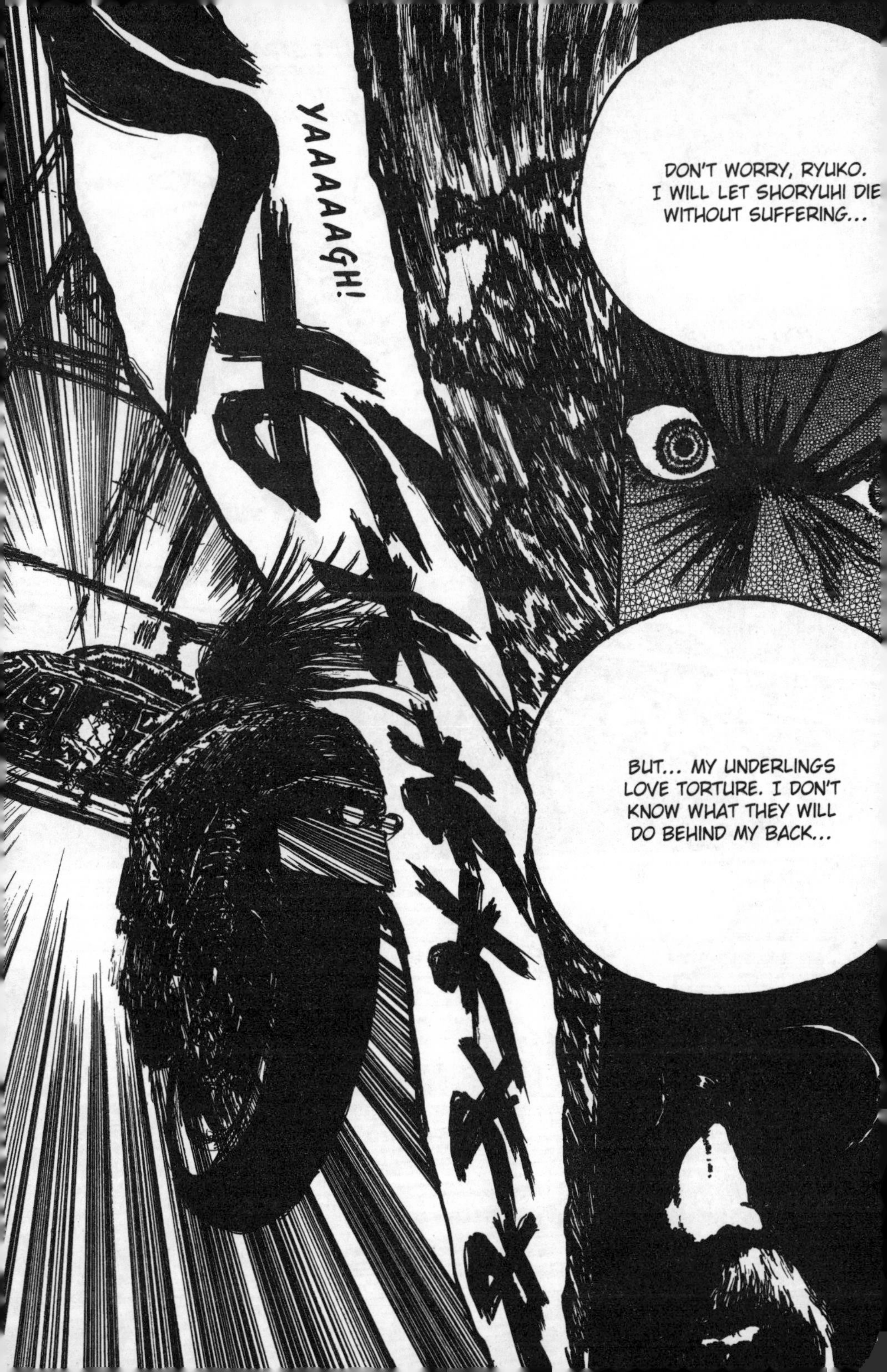
DON'T WORRY, RYUKO. I WILL LET SHORYUHI DIE WITHOUT SUFFERING...
BUT... MY UNDERLINGS LOVE TORTURE. I DON'T KNOW WHAT THEY WILL DO BEHIND MY BACK...
YAAAAAGH!

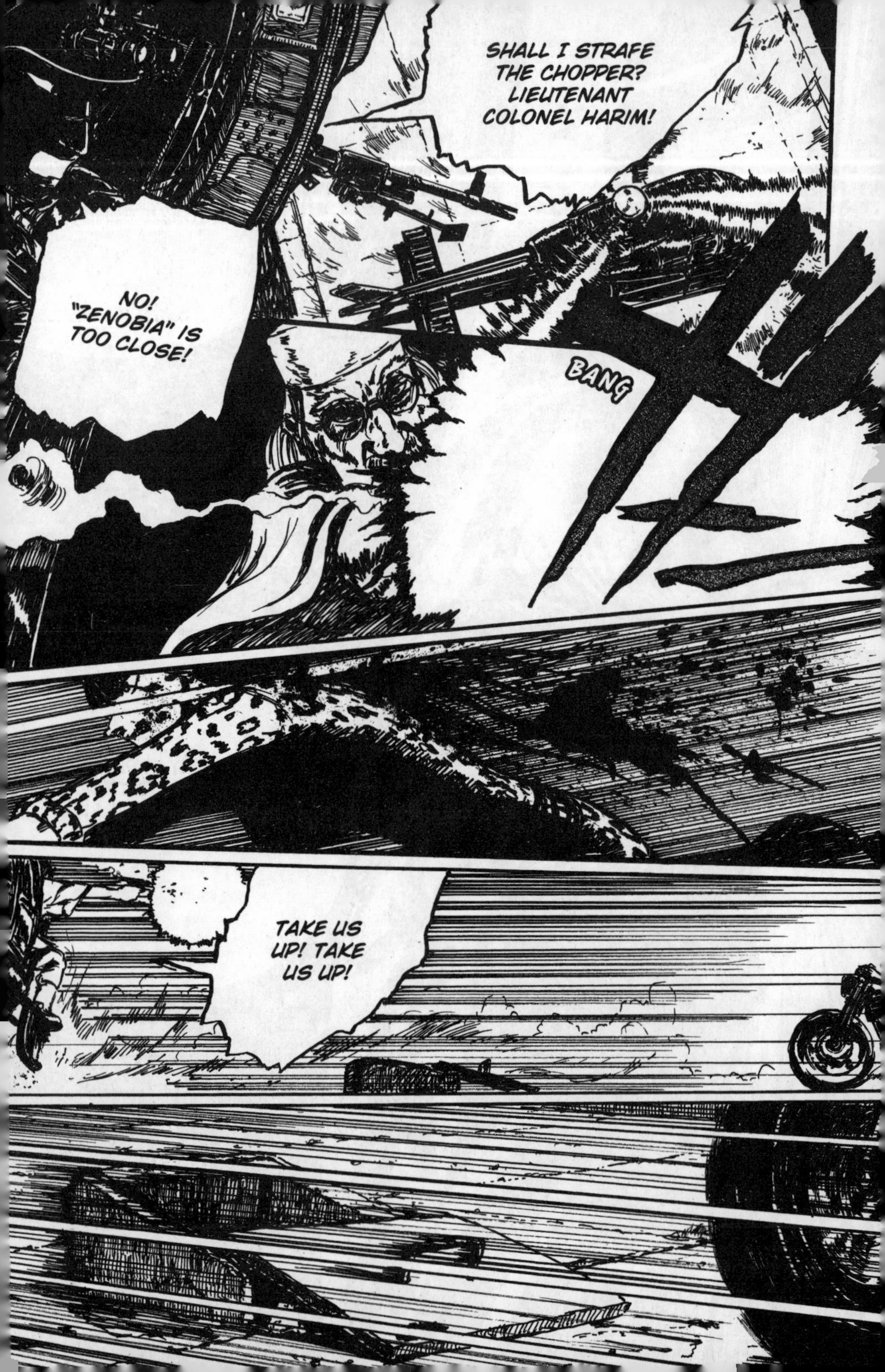
SHALL I STRAFE THE CHOPPER? LIEUTENANT COLONEL HARIM!
NO! "ZENOBIA" IS TOO CLOSE!
BANG
TAKE US UP! TAKE US UP!

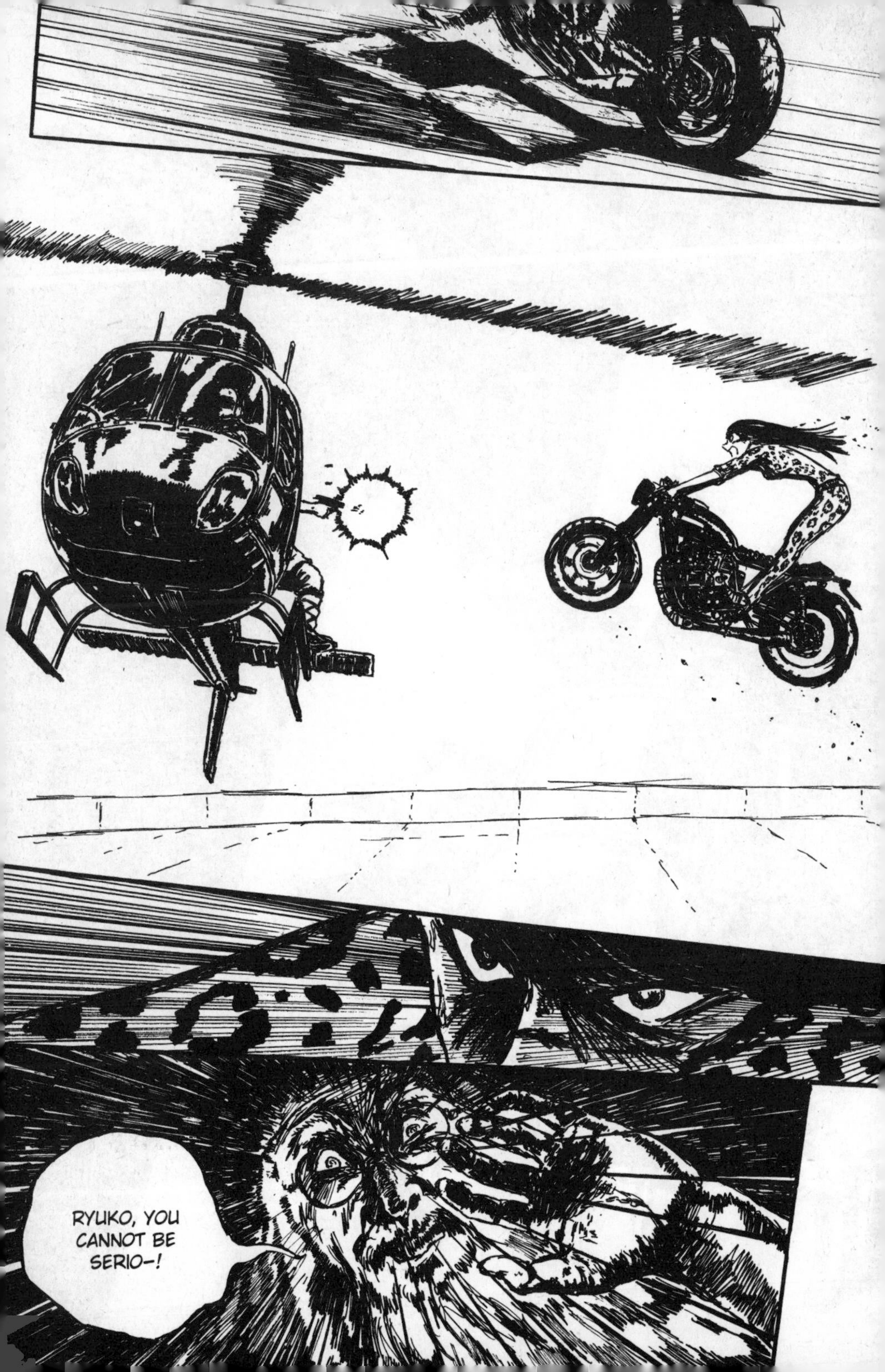
RYUKO, YOU CANNOT BE SERIO-!

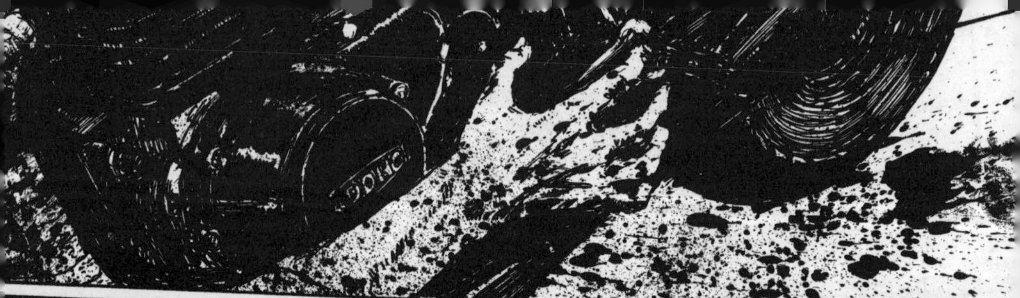
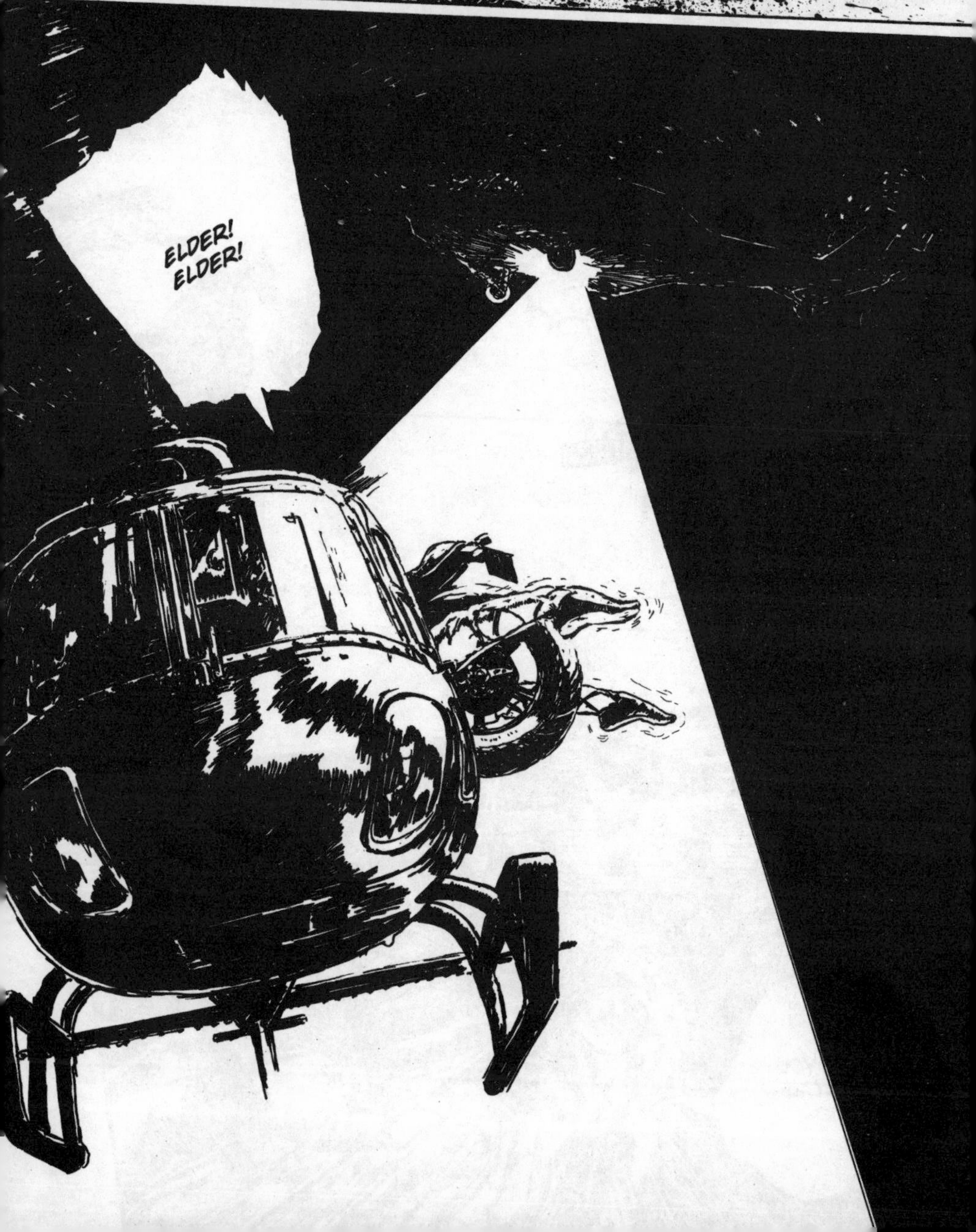
ELDER!
ELDER!

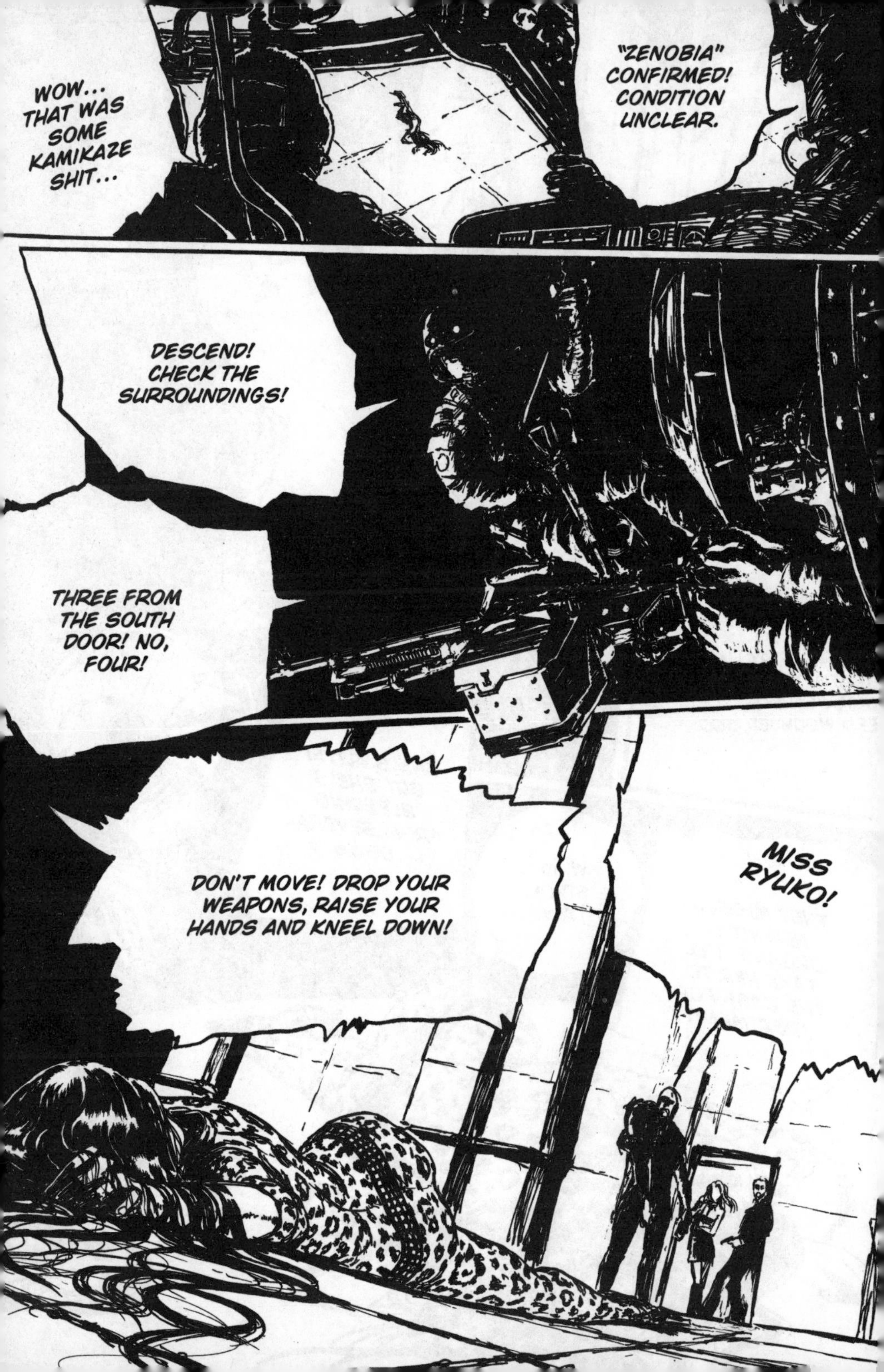
"ZENOBIA" CONFIRMED! CONDITION UNCLEAR.
WOW... THAT WAS SOME KAMIKAZE SHIT...
DESCEND! CHECK THE SURROUNDINGS!
THREE FROM THE SOUTH DOOR! NO, FOUR!
MISS RYUKO!
DON'T MOVE! DROP YOUR WEAPONS, RAISE YOUR HANDS AND KNEEL DOWN!

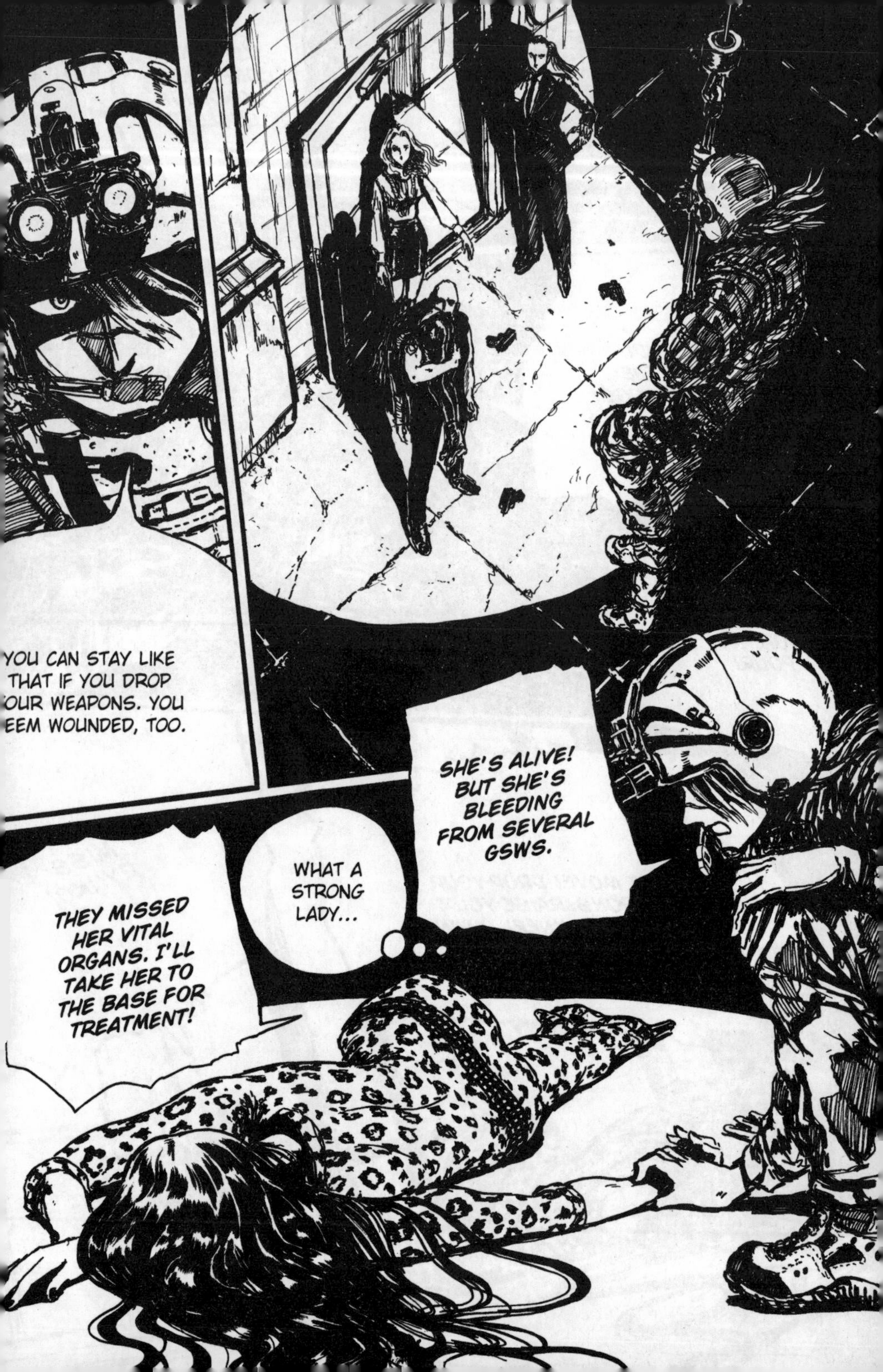

YOU CAN STAY LIKE THAT IF YOU DROP OUR WEAPONS. YOU EEM WOUNDED, TOO.
SHE'S ALIVE! BUT SHE'S BLEEDING FROM SEVERAL GSWS.
WHAT A STRONG LADY...
THEY MISSED HER VITAL ORGANS. I'LL TAKE HER TO THE BASE FOR TREATMENT!

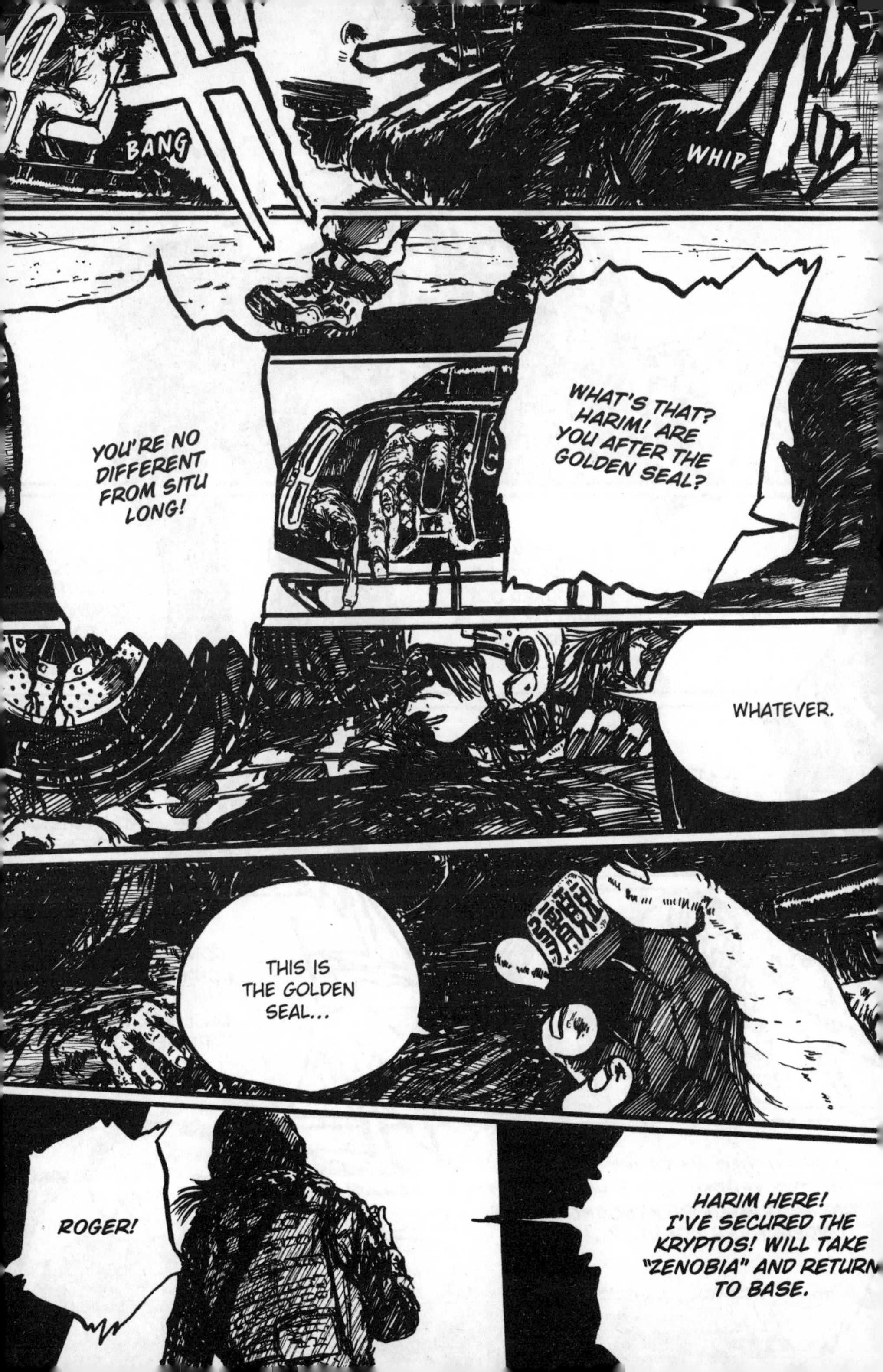
WHIP
BANG
WHAT'S THAT? HARIM! ARE YOU AFTER THE GOLDEN SEAL?
YOU'RE NO DIFFERENT FROM SITU LONG!
WHATEVER.
THIS IS THE GOLDEN SEAL...
HARIM HERE! I'VE SECURED THE KRYPTOS! WILL TAKE "ZENOBIA" AND RETURN TO BASE.
ROGER!

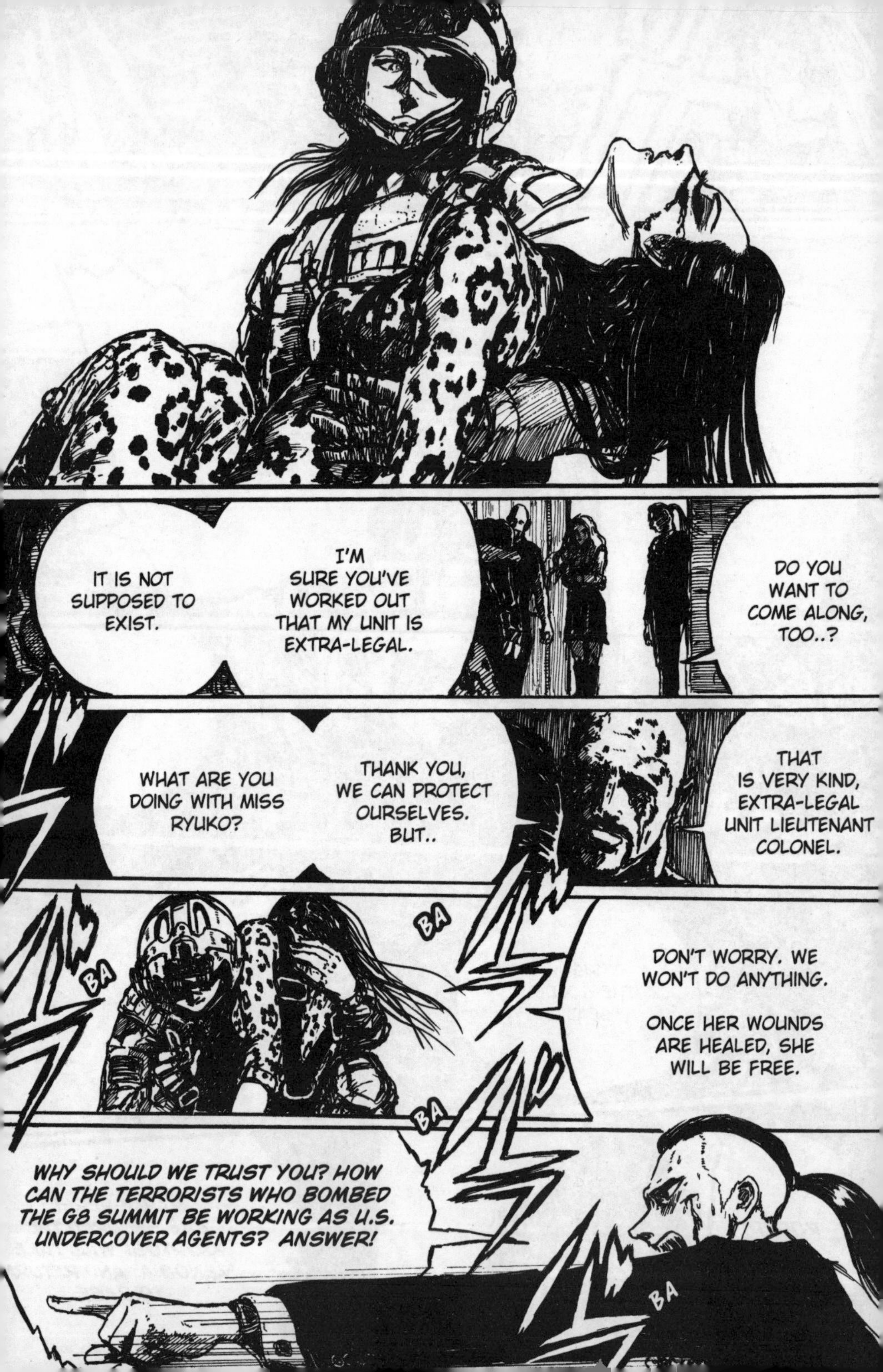
DO YOU WANT TO COME ALONG, TOO..?
I'M SURE YOU'VE WORKED OUT THAT MY UNIT IS EXTRA-LEGAL.
IT IS NOT SUPPOSED TO EXIST.
THAT IS VERY KIND, EXTRA-LEGAL UNIT LIEUTENANT COLONEL.
THANK YOU, WE CAN PROTECT OURSELVES. BUT..
WHAT ARE YOU DOING WITH MISS RYUKO?
DON'T WORRY. WE WON'T DO ANYTHING.
ONCE HER WOUNDS ARE HEALED, SHE WILL BE FREE.
BA
BA
BA
WHY SHOULD WE TRUST YOU? HOW CAN THE TERRORISTS WHO BOMBED THE G8 SUMMIT BE WORKING AS U.S. UNDERCOVER AGENTS? ANSWER!
BA

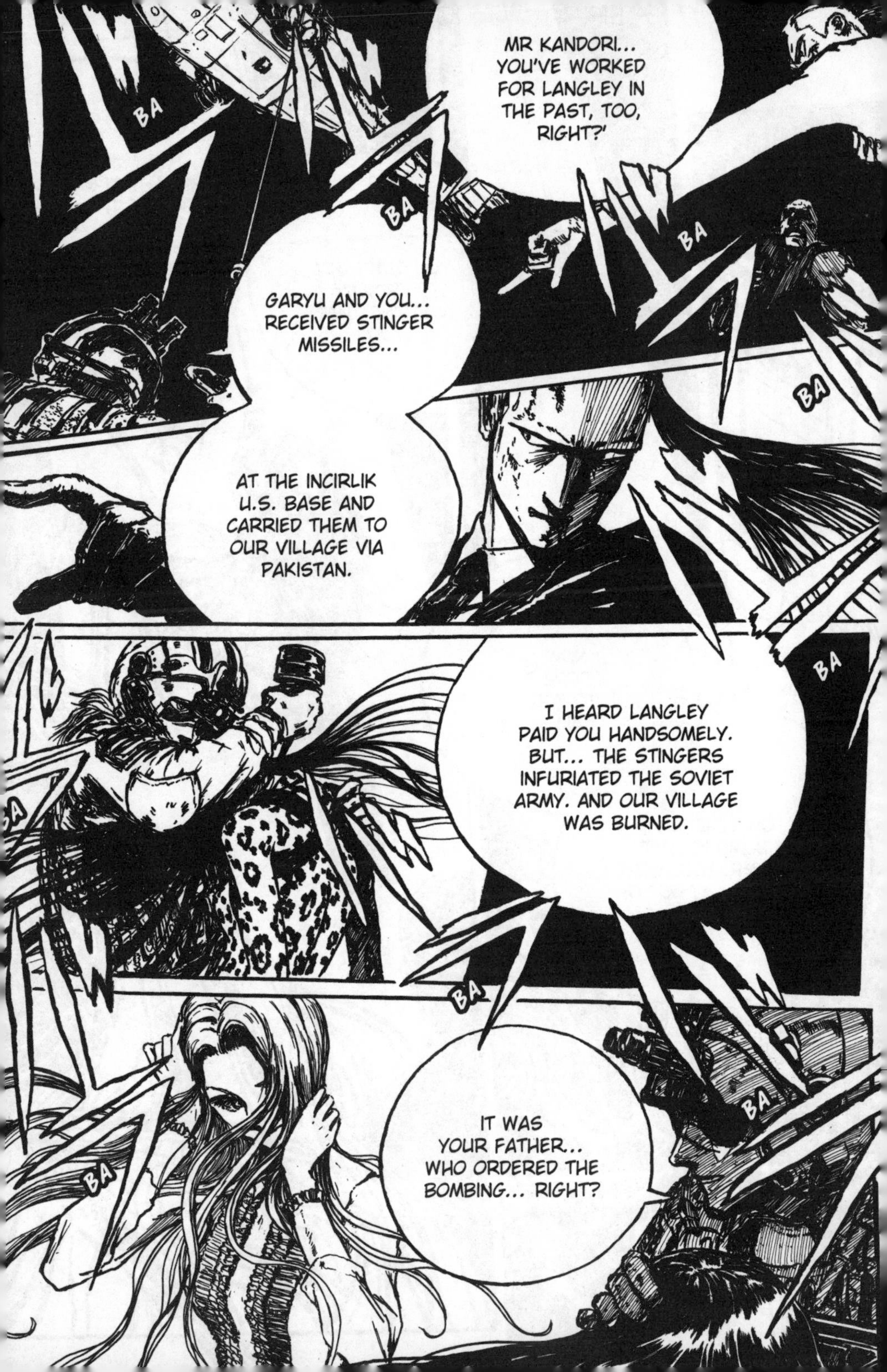
MR KANDORI... YOU'VE WORKED FOR LANGLEY IN THE PAST, TOO, RIGHT?'
BA
BA
BA
GARYU AND YOU... RECEIVED STINGER MISSILES...
AT THE INCIRLIK U.S. BASE AND CARRIED THEM TO OUR VILLAGE VIA PAKISTAN.
BA
BA
I HEARD LANGLEY PAID YOU HANDSOMELY. BUT... THE STINGERS INFURIATED THE SOVIET ARMY. AND OUR VILLAGE WAS BURNED.
BA
BA
IT WAS YOUR FATHER... WHO ORDERED THE BOMBING... RIGHT?
BA

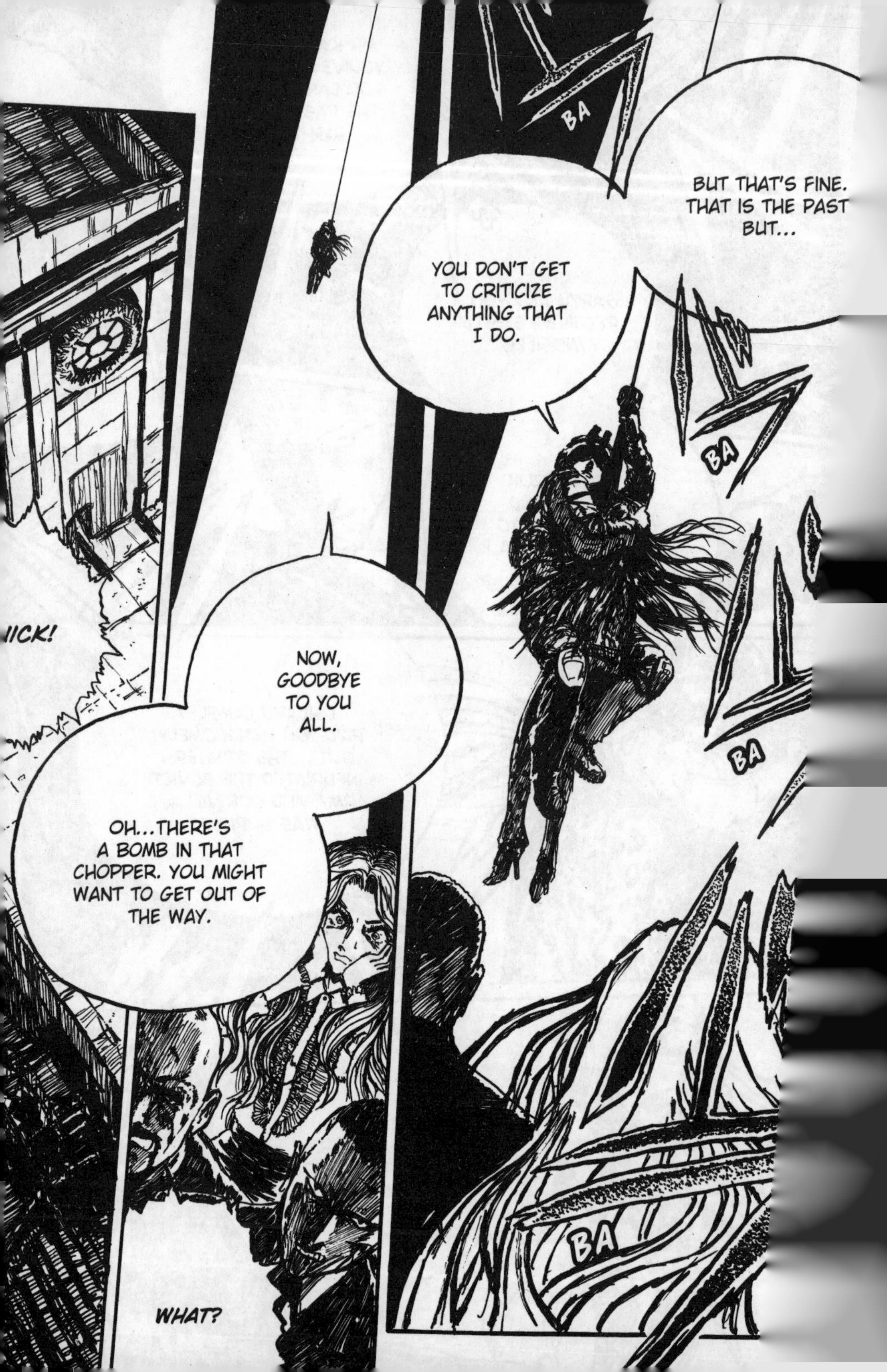
BA
BUT THAT'S FINE. THAT IS THE PAST BUT...
YOU DON'T GET TO CRITICIZE ANYTHING THAT I DO.
BA
BA
BA
NOW, GOODBYE TO YOU ALL.
OH...THERE'S A BOMB IN THAT CHOPPER. YOU MIGHT WANT TO GET OUT OF THE WAY.
WHAT?

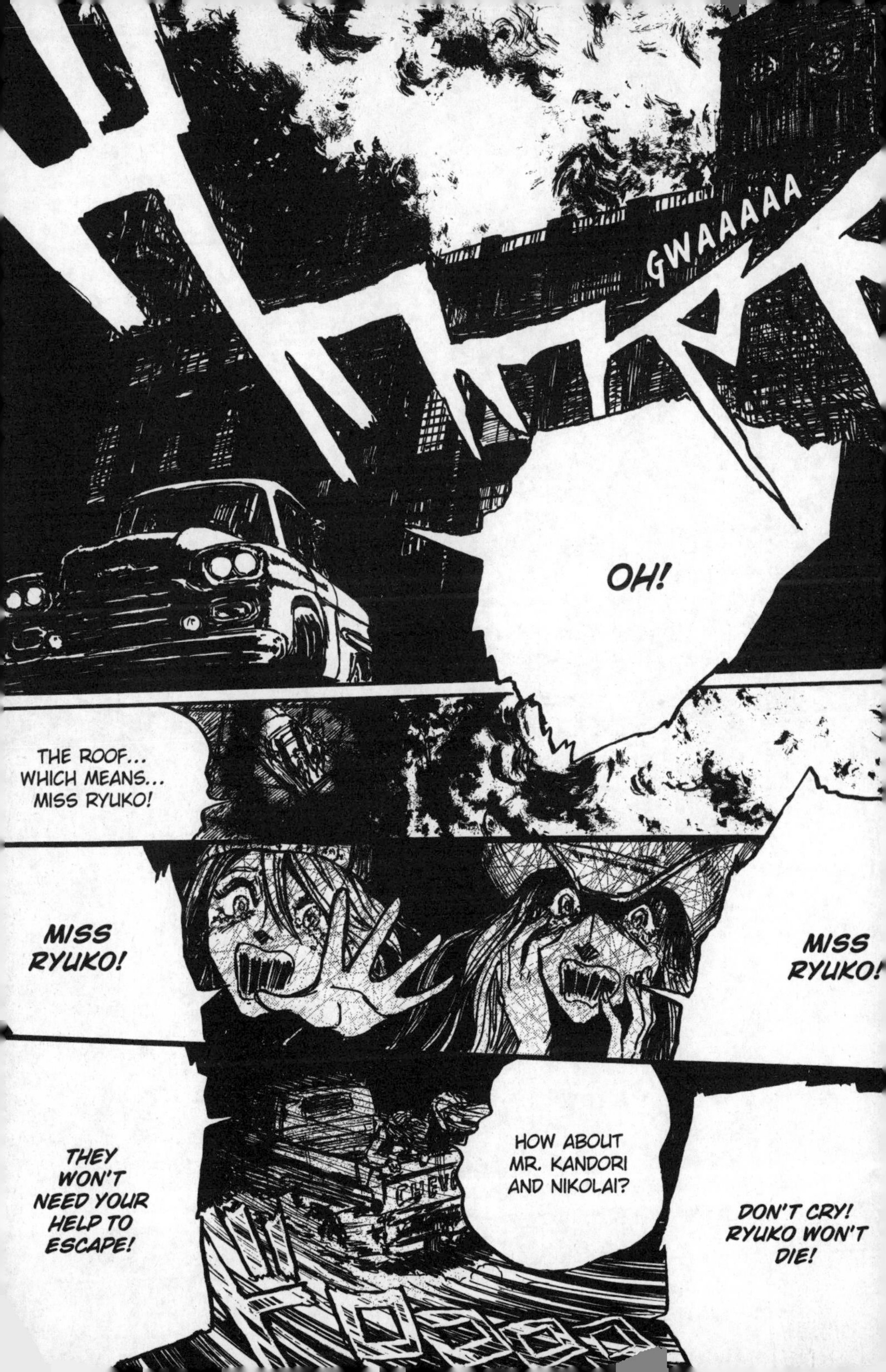
GWAAAAA
OH!
THE ROOF... WHICH MEANS... MISS RYUKO!
MISS RYUKO!
MISS RYUKO!
DON'T CRY! RYUKO WON'T DIE!
HOW ABOUT MR. KANDORI AND NIKOLAI?
THEY WON'T NEED YOUR HELP TO ESCAPE!
CHEVO

CHAPTER 10:
WORD OF HONOR

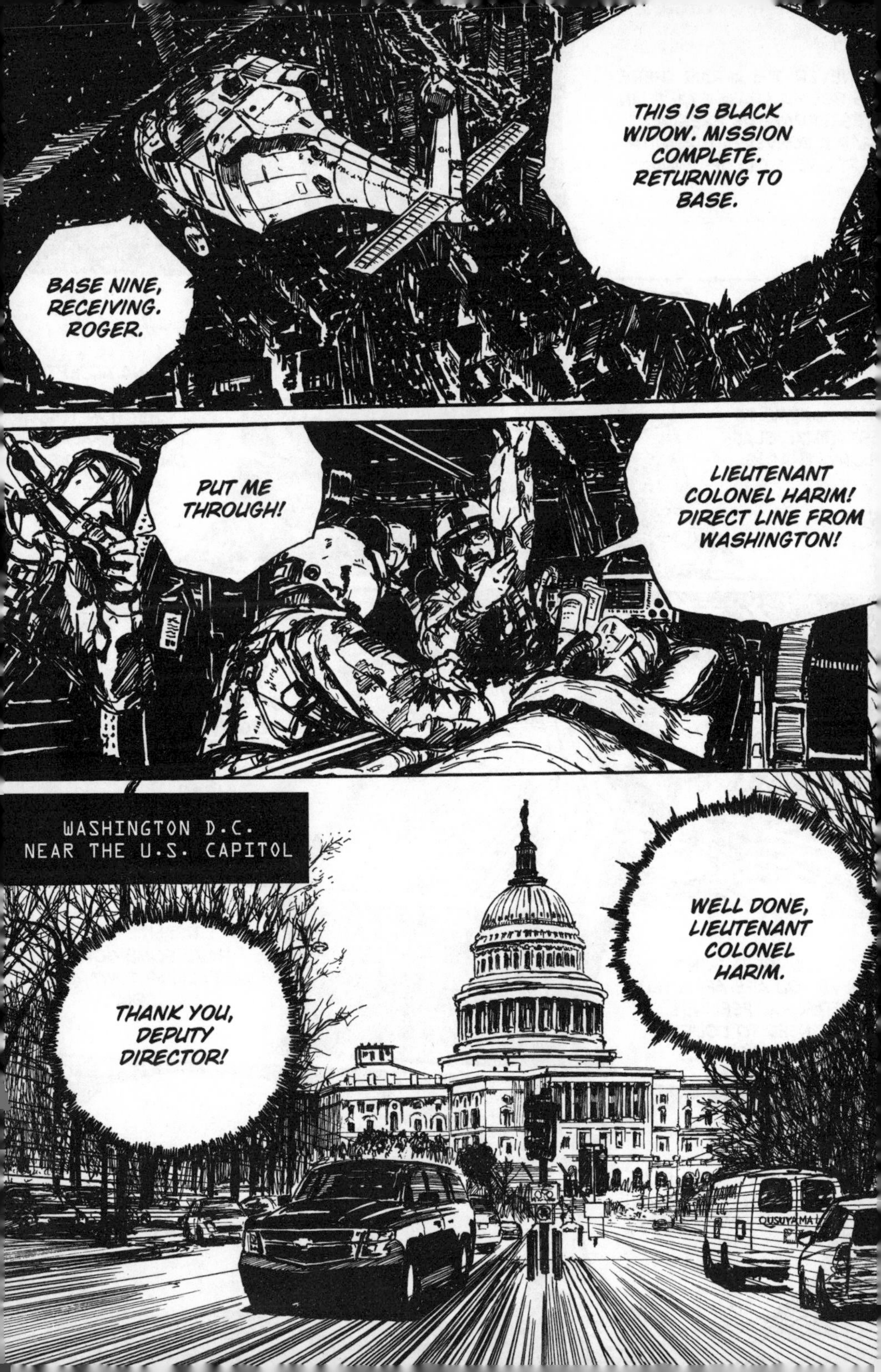
THIS IS BLACK WIDOW. MISSION COMPLETE. RETURNING TO BASE.
BASE NINE, RECEIVING. ROGER.
LIEUTENANT COLONEL HARIM! DIRECT LINE FROM WASHINGTON!
PUT ME THROUGH!
WASHINGTON D.C. NEAR THE U.S. CAPITOL
WELL DONE, LIEUTENANT COLONEL HARIM.
THANK YOU, DEPUTY DIRECTOR!

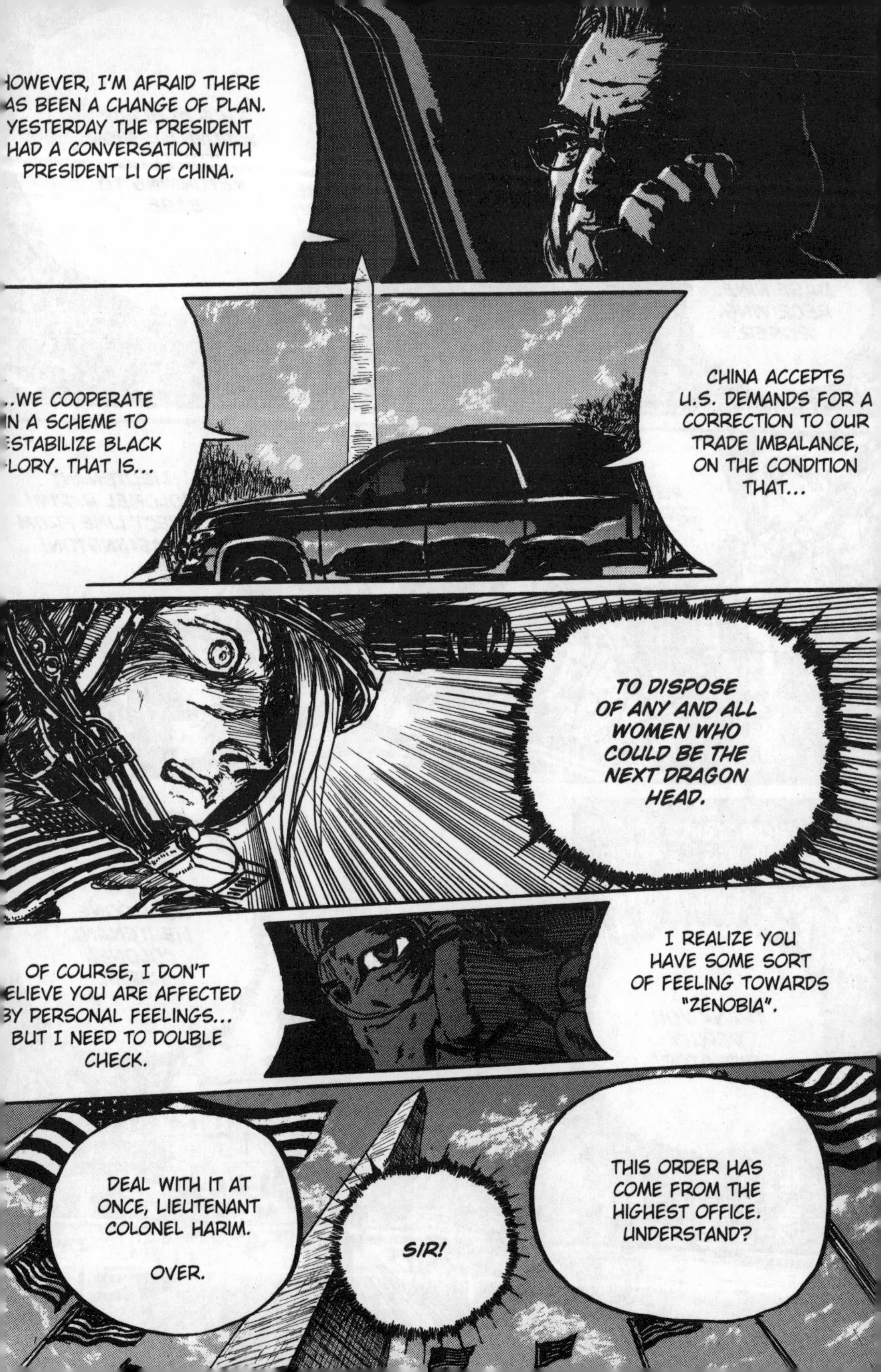
OWEVER, I'M AFRAID THERE AS BEEN A CHANGE OF PLAN. YESTERDAY THE PRESIDENT HAD A CONVERSATION WITH PRESIDENT LI OF CHINA.
CHINA ACCEPTS U.S. DEMANDS FOR A CORRECTION TO OUR TRADE IMBALANCE, ON THE CONDITION THAT...
..WE COOPERATE N A SCHEME TO STABILIZE BLACK LORY. THAT IS...
TO DISPOSE OF ANY AND ALL WOMEN WHO COULD BE THE NEXT DRAGON HEAD.
I REALIZE YOU HAVE SOME SORT OF FEELING TOWARDS "ZENOBIA".
OF COURSE, I DON'T ELIEVE YOU ARE AFFECTED Y PERSONAL FEELINGS... BUT I NEED TO DOUBLE CHECK.
THIS ORDER HAS COME FROM THE HIGHEST OFFICE. UNDERSTAND?
SIR!
DEAL WITH IT AT ONCE, LIEUTENANT COLONEL HARIM.
OVER.

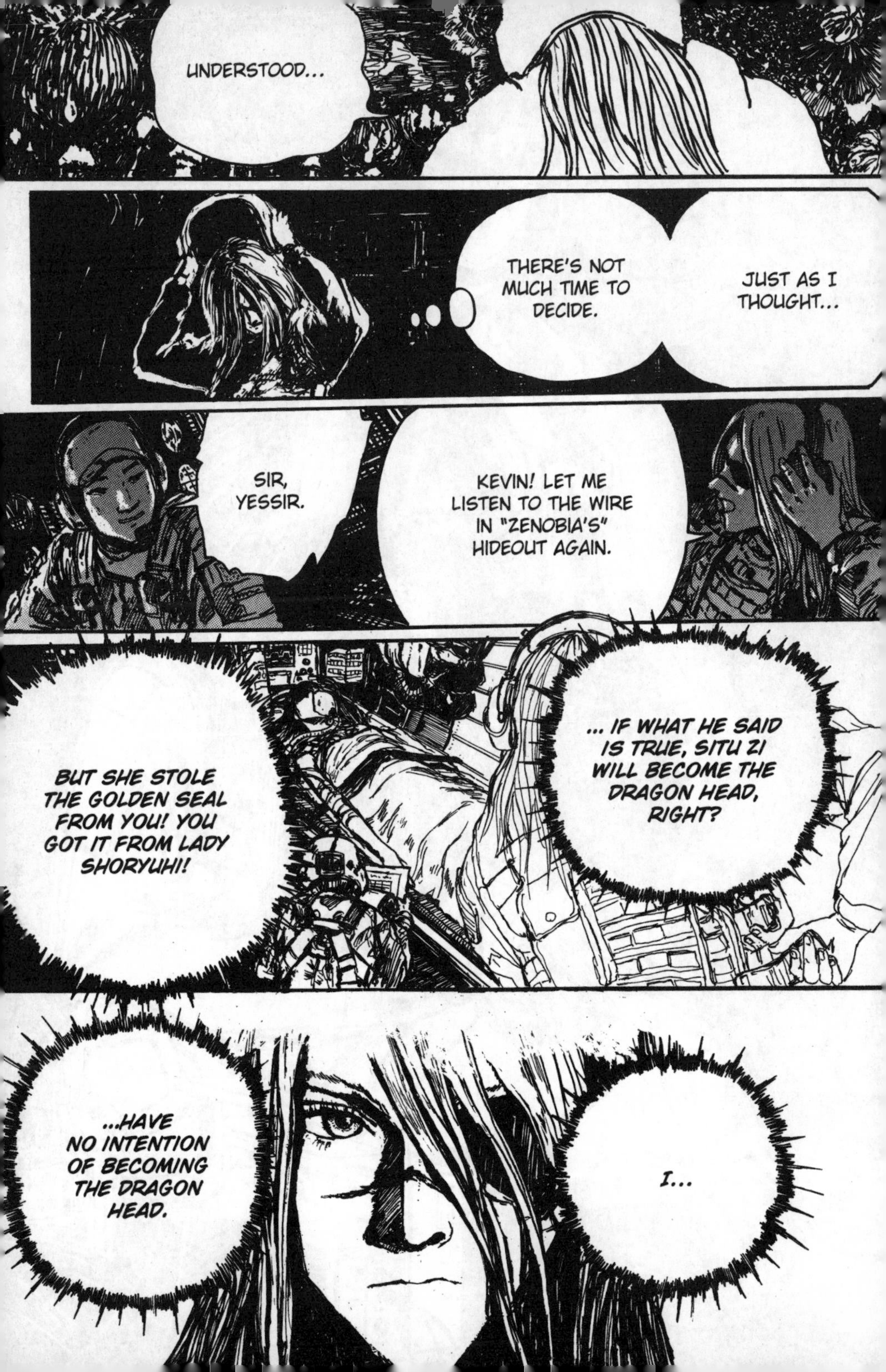
UNDERSTOOD...
JUST AS I THOUGHT...
THERE'S NOT MUCH TIME TO DECIDE.
KEVIN! LET ME LISTEN TO THE WIRE IN "ZENOBIA'S" HIDEOUT AGAIN.
SIR, YESSIR.
... IF WHAT HE SAID IS TRUE, SITU ZI WILL BECOME THE DRAGON HEAD, RIGHT?
BUT SHE STOLE THE GOLDEN SEAL FROM YOU! YOU GOT IT FROM LADY SHORYUHI!
I...
...HAVE NO INTENTION OF BECOMING THE DRAGON HEAD.

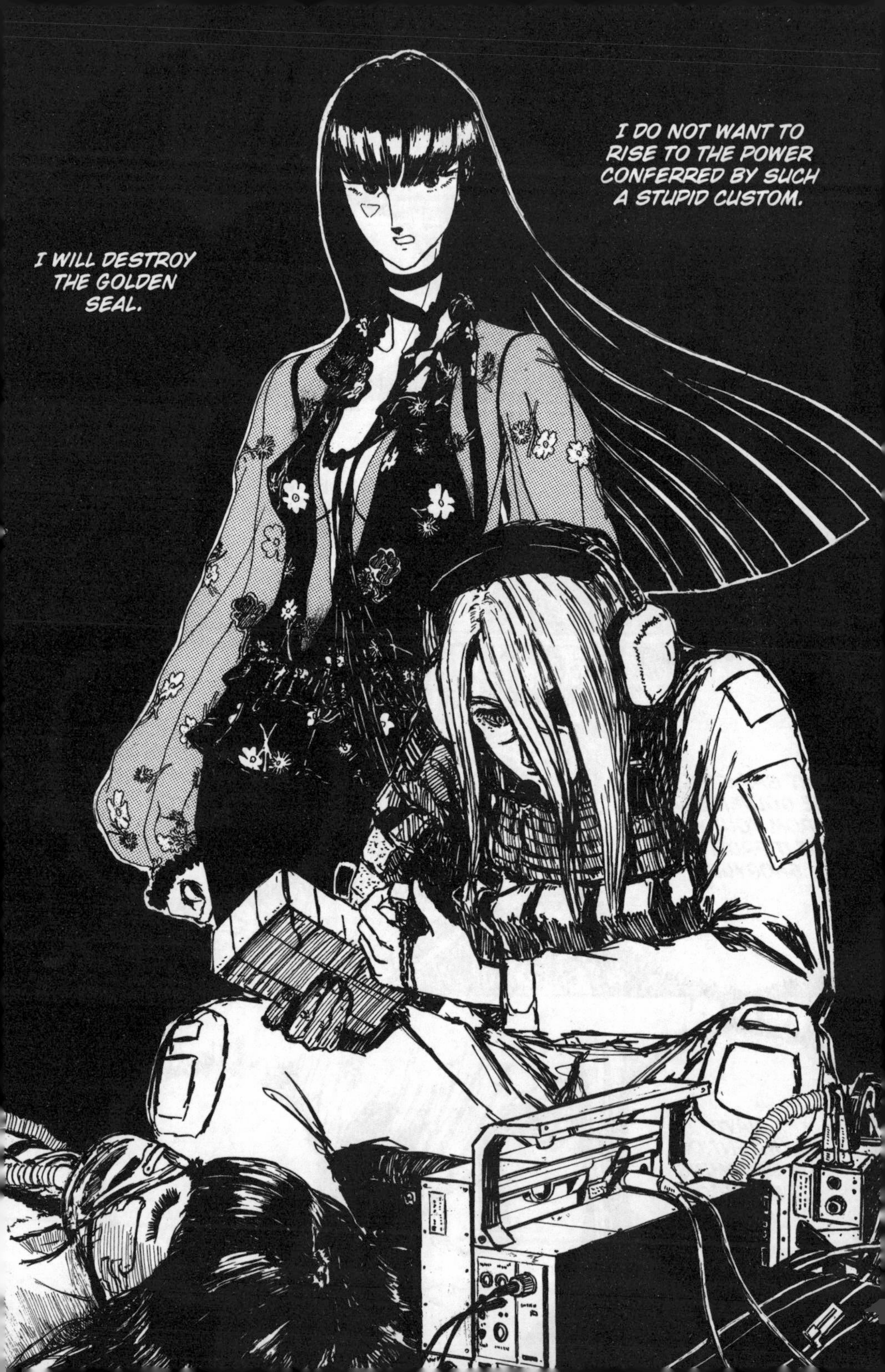
I DO NOT WANT TO RISE TO THE POWER CONFERRED BY SUCH A STUPID CUSTOM.
I WILL DESTROY THE GOLDEN SEAL.

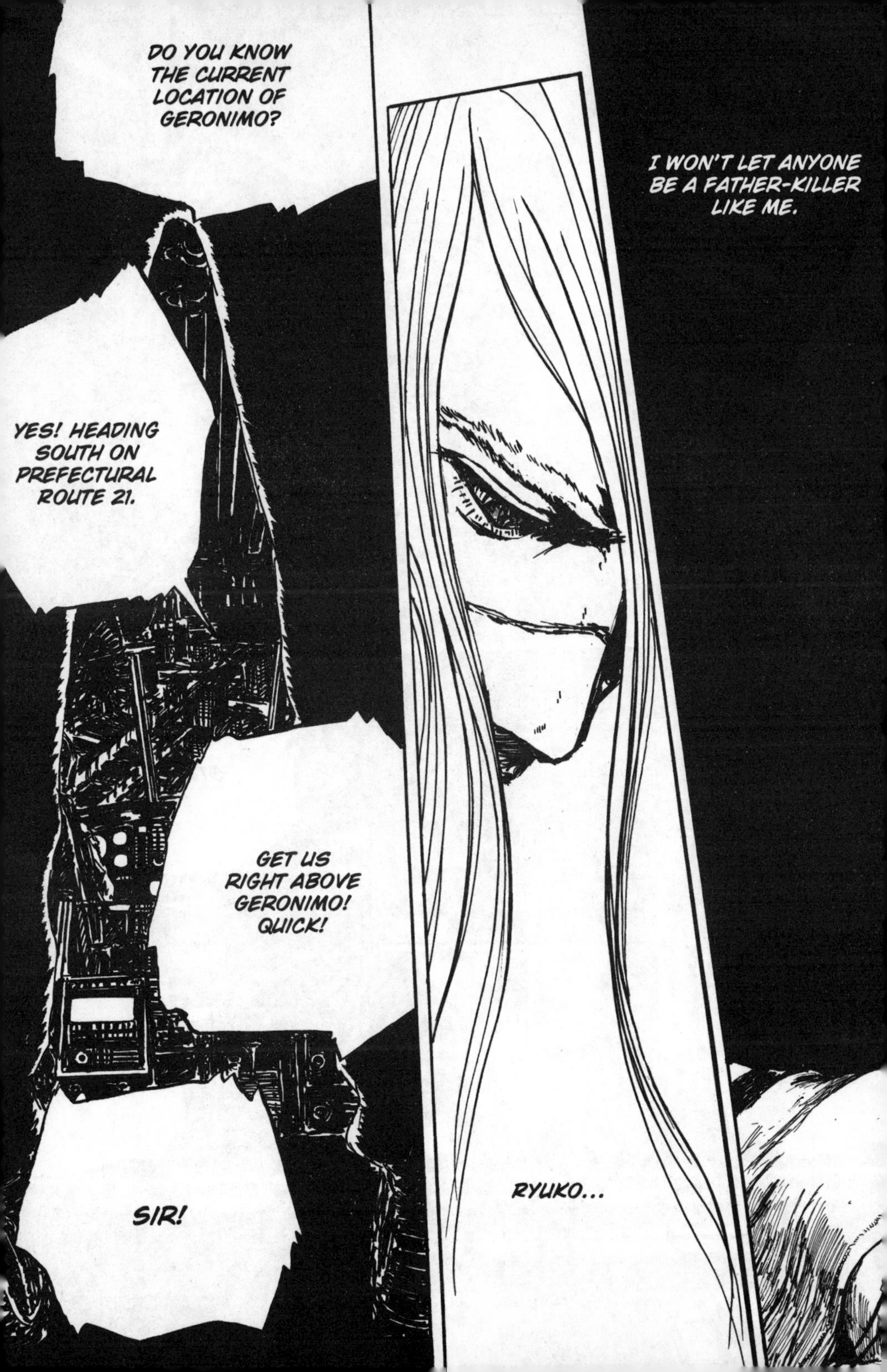
I WON'T LET ANYONE BE A FATHER-KILLER LIKE ME.
RYUKO...
DO YOU KNOW THE CURRENT LOCATION OF GERONIMO?
YES! HEADING SOUTH ON PREFECTURAL ROUTE 21.
GET US RIGHT ABOVE GERONIMO! QUICK!
SIR!

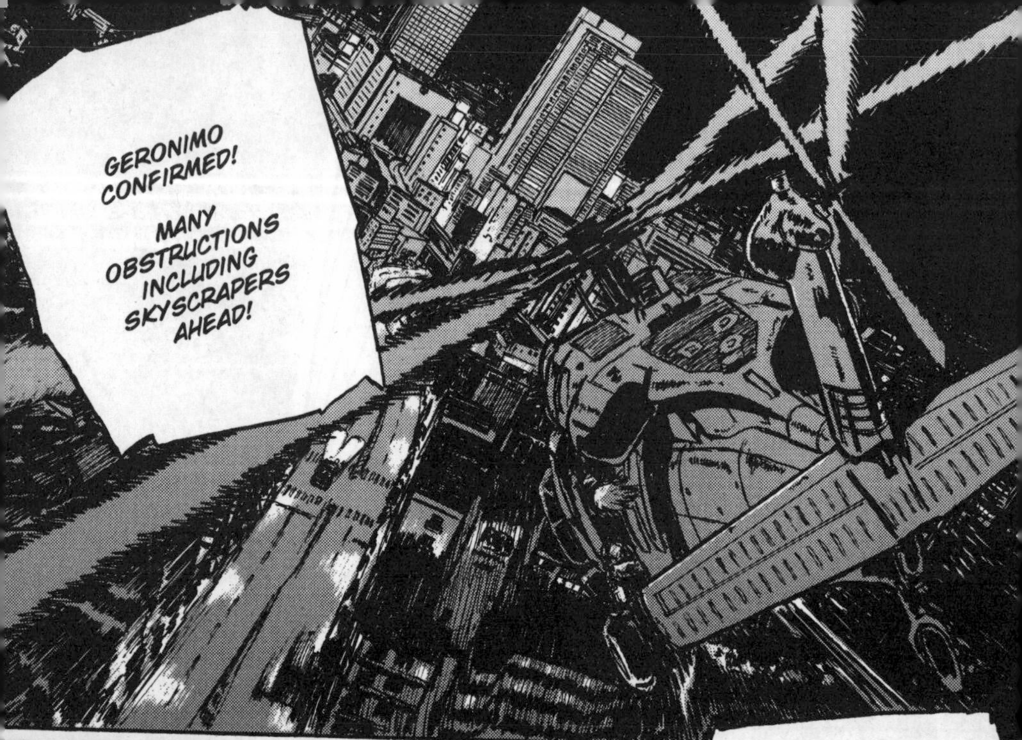
GERONIMO CONFIRMED!
MANY OBSTRUCTIONS INCLUDING SKYSCRAPERS AHEAD!
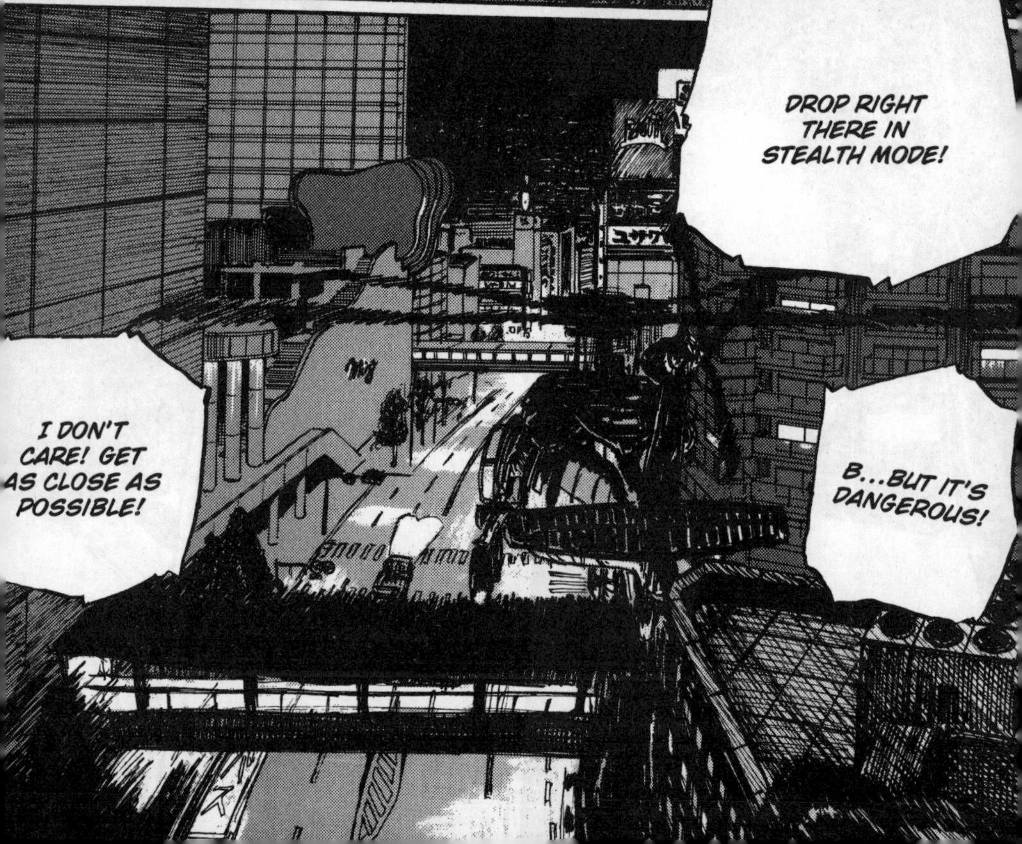
DROP RIGHT THERE IN STEALTH MODE!
B...BUT IT'S DANGEROUS!
I DON'T CARE! GET AS CLOSE AS POSSIBLE!

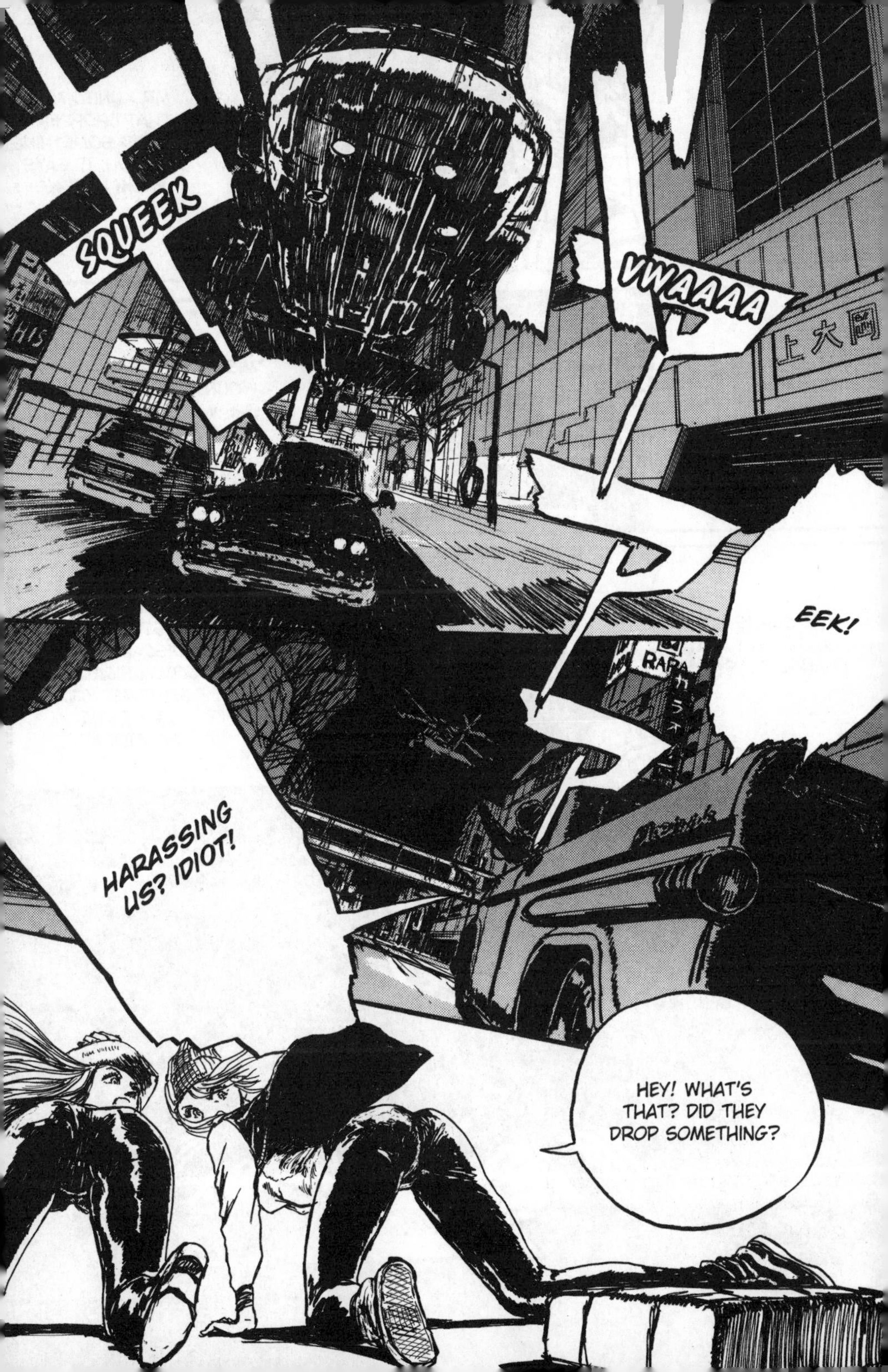
VWAAAA
SQUEEK
EEK!
HARASSING US? IDIOT!
HEY! WHAT'S THAT? DID THEY DROP SOMETHING?

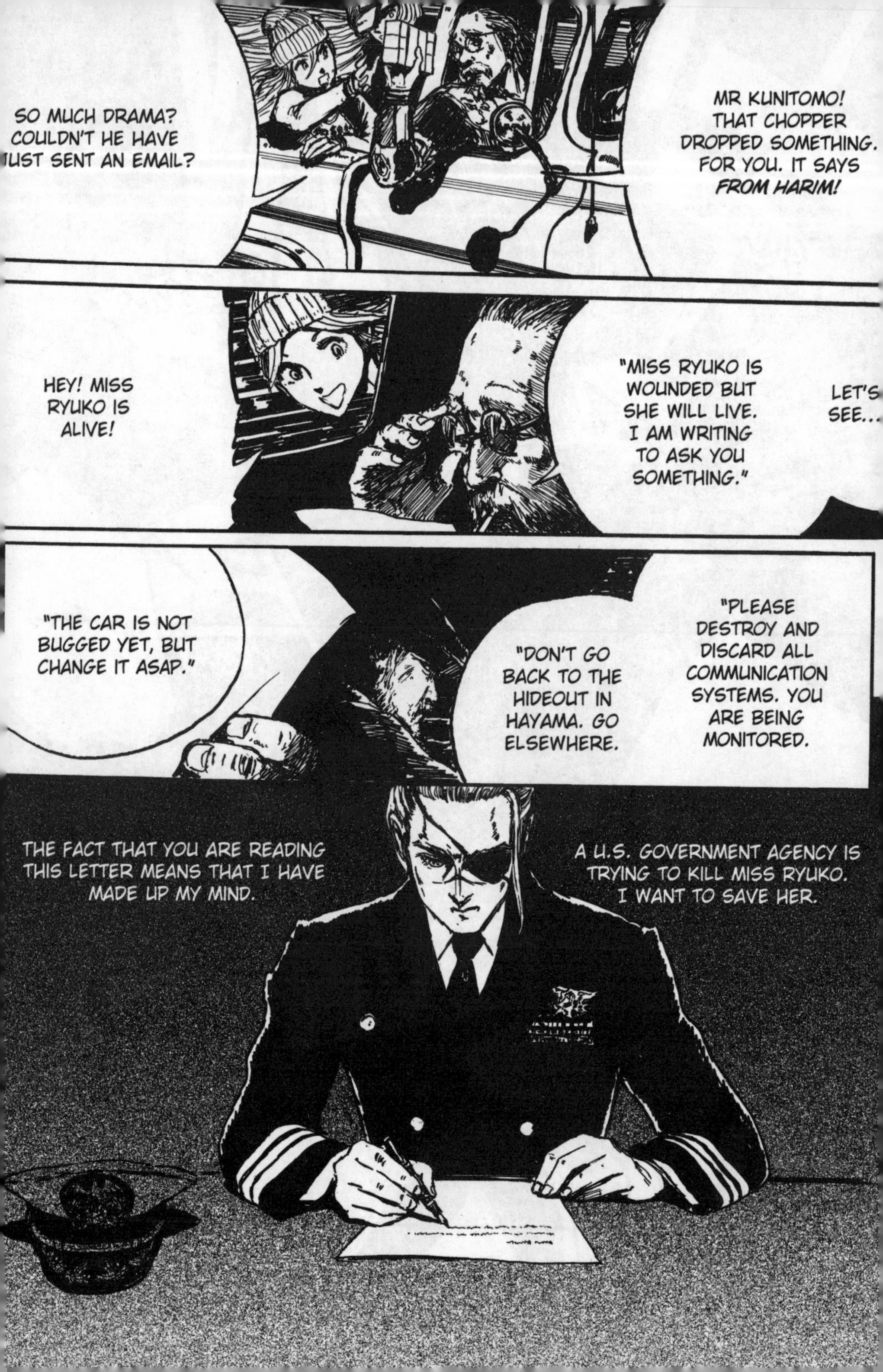
MR KUNITOMO! THAT CHOPPER DROPPED SOMETHING. FOR YOU. IT SAYS *FROM HARIM!*
SO MUCH DRAMA? COULDN'T HE HAVE JUST SENT AN EMAIL?
LET'S SEE...
"MISS RYUKO IS WOUNDED BUT SHE WILL LIVE. I AM WRITING TO ASK YOU SOMETHING."
HEY! MISS RYUKO IS ALIVE!
"PLEASE DESTROY AND DISCARD ALL COMMUNICATION SYSTEMS. YOU ARE BEING MONITORED.
"DON'T GO BACK TO THE HIDEOUT IN HAYAMA. GO ELSEWHERE.
"THE CAR IS NOT BUGGED YET, BUT CHANGE IT ASAP."
A U.S. GOVERNMENT AGENCY IS TRYING TO KILL MISS RYUKO. I WANT TO SAVE HER.
THE FACT THAT YOU ARE READING THIS LETTER MEANS THAT I HAVE MADE UP MY MIND.

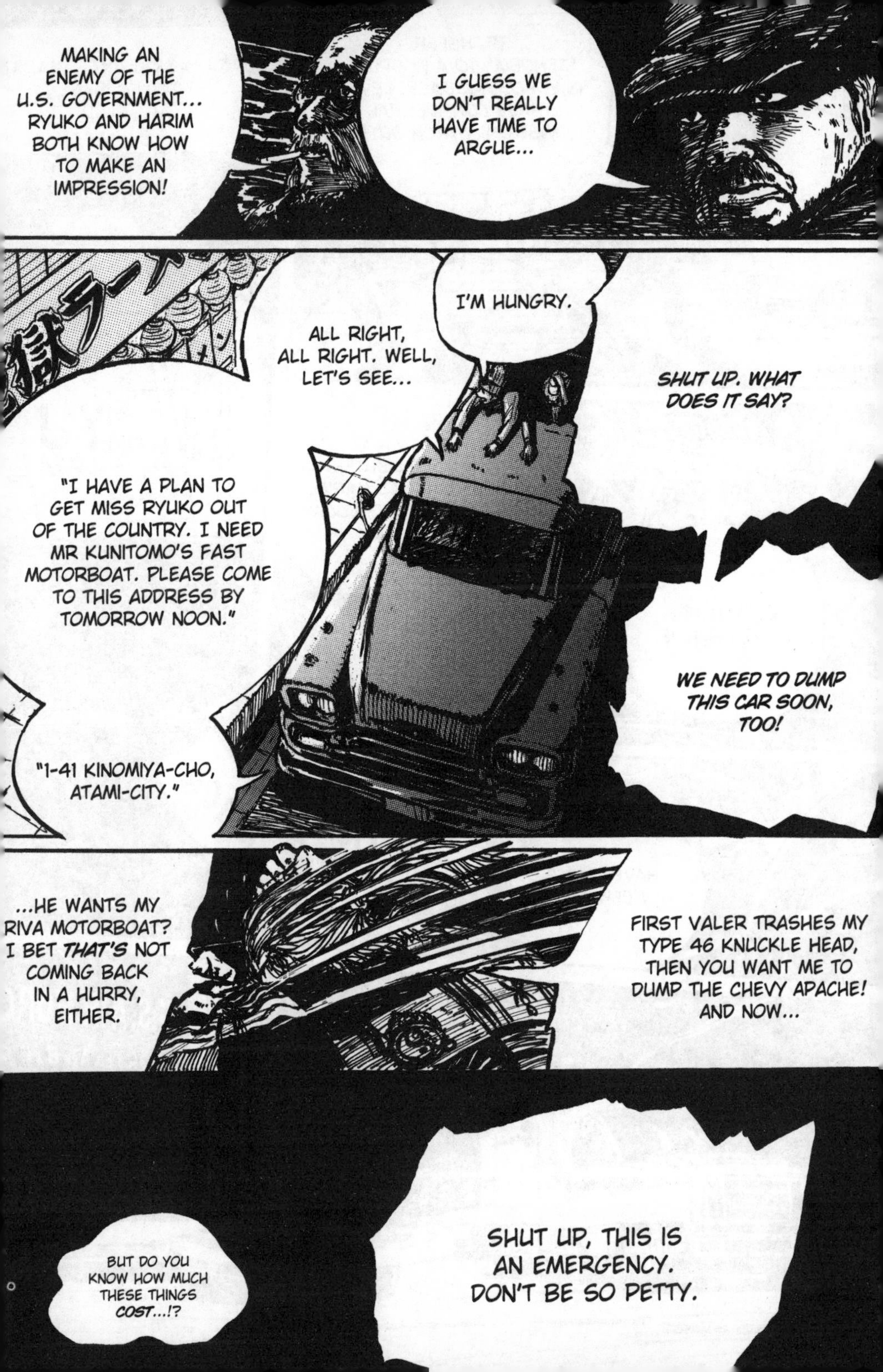
I GUESS WE DON'T REALLY HAVE TIME TO ARGUE...
MAKING AN ENEMY OF THE U.S. GOVERNMENT... RYUKO AND HARIM BOTH KNOW HOW TO MAKE AN IMPRESSION!
I'M HUNGRY.
SHUT UP. WHAT DOES IT SAY?
ALL RIGHT, ALL RIGHT. WELL, LET'S SEE...
"I HAVE A PLAN TO GET MISS RYUKO OUT OF THE COUNTRY. I NEED MR KUNITOMO'S FAST MOTORBOAT. PLEASE COME TO THIS ADDRESS BY TOMORROW NOON."
"1-41 KINOMIYA-CHO, ATAMI-CITY."
WE NEED TO DUMP THIS CAR SOON, TOO!
FIRST VALER TRASHES MY TYPE 46 KNUCKLE HEAD, THEN YOU WANT ME TO DUMP THE CHEVY APACHE! AND NOW...
...HE WANTS MY RIVA MOTORBOAT? I BET *THAT'S* NOT COMING BACK IN A HURRY, EITHER.
SHUT UP, THIS IS AN EMERGENCY. DON'T BE SO PETTY.
BUT DO YOU KNOW HOW MUCH THESE THINGS *COST*...!?

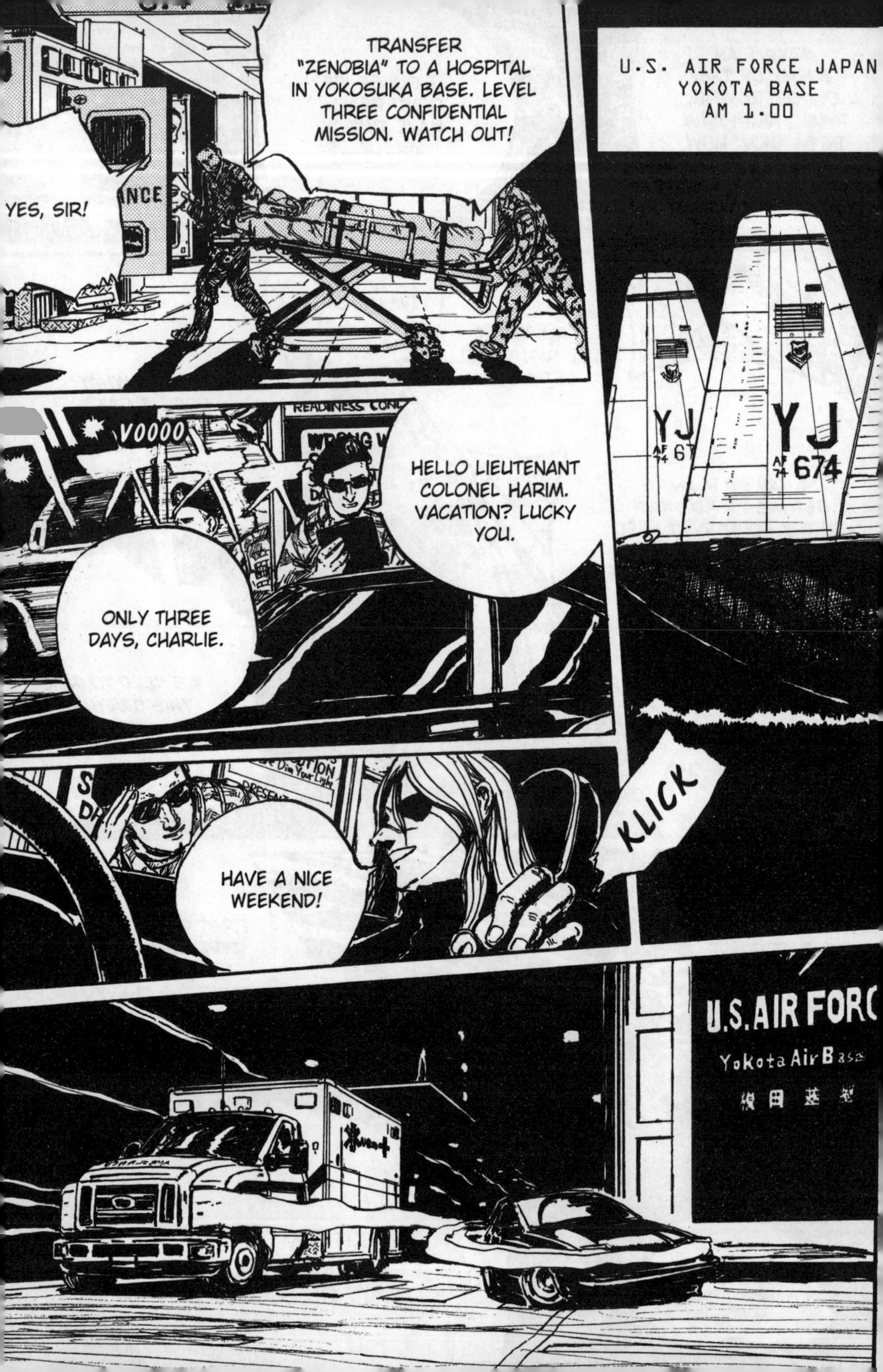
U.S. AIR FORCE JAPAN
YOKOTA BASE
AM 1.00
TRANSFER "ZENOBIA" TO A HOSPITAL IN YOKOSUKA BASE. LEVEL THREE CONFIDENTIAL MISSION. WATCH OUT!
YES, SIR!
HELLO LIEUTENANT COLONEL HARIM. VACATION? LUCKY YOU.
VOOOO
ONLY THREE DAYS, CHARLIE.
KLICK
HAVE A NICE WEEKEND!
U.S.AIR FORC
Yokota Air Base

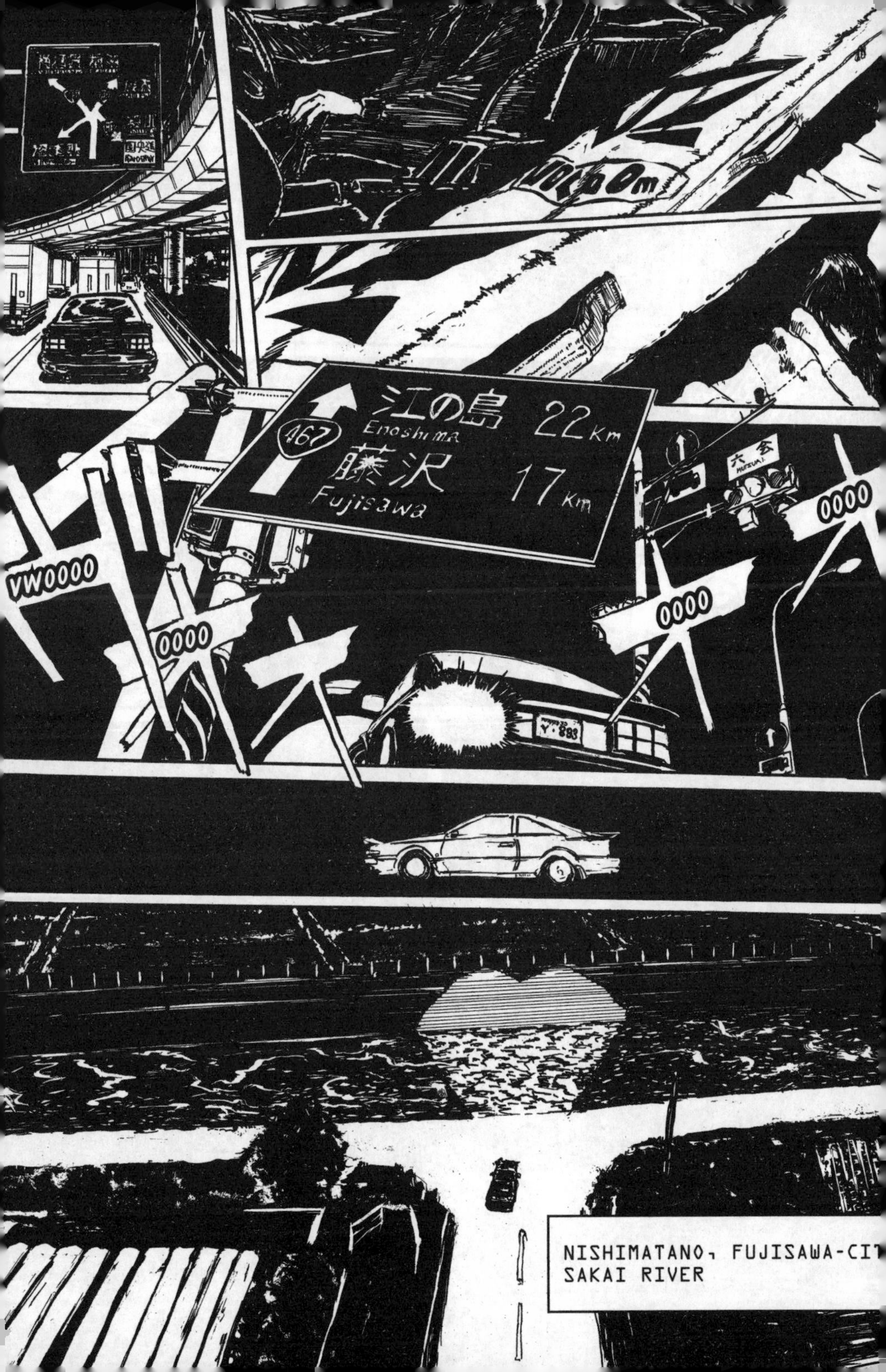

江の島 22km
Enoshima
467
藤沢 17km
Fujisawa
六会
MUTSUAI
VW0000
0000
0000
0000
NISHIMATANO, FUJISAWA-CIT
SAKAI RIVER

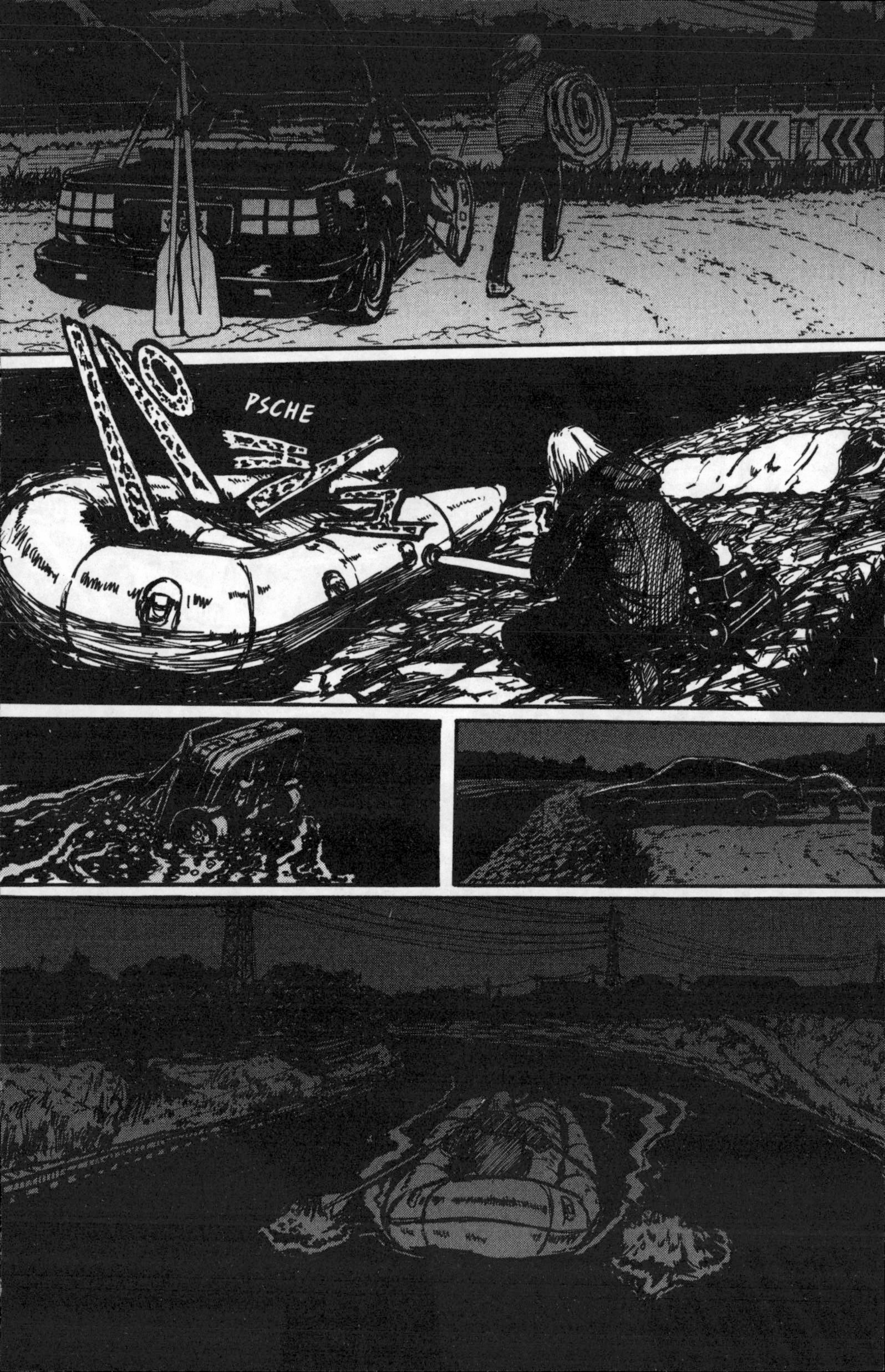
PSCHE

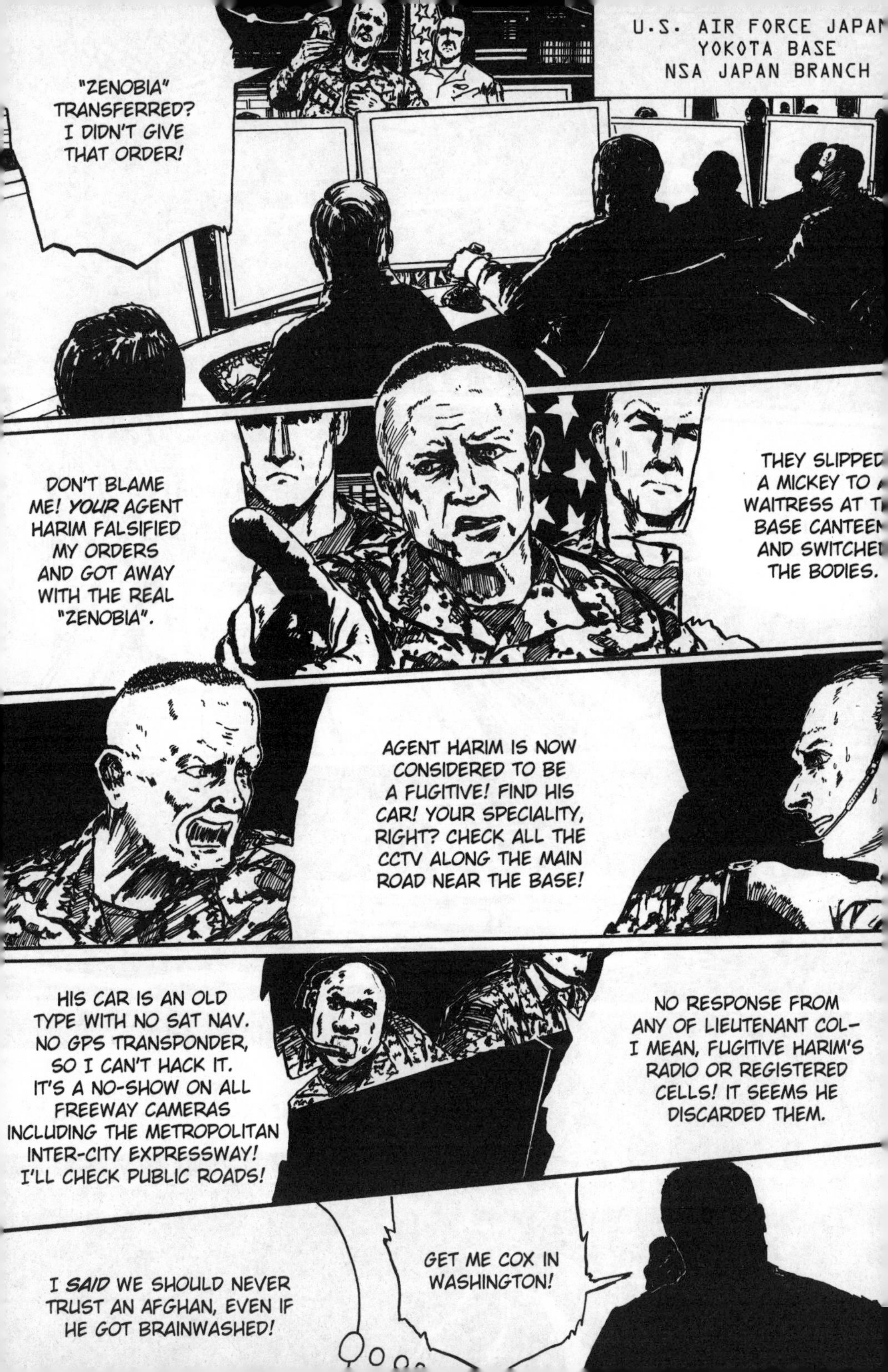
U.S. AIR FORCE JAPA
YOKOTA BASE
NSA JAPAN BRANCH
"ZENOBIA" TRANSFERRED? I DIDN'T GIVE THAT ORDER!
DON'T BLAME ME! *YOUR* AGENT HARIM FALSIFIED MY ORDERS AND GOT AWAY WITH THE REAL "ZENOBIA".
THEY SLIPPED A MICKEY TO WAITRESS AT T BASE CANTEE AND SWITCHE THE BODIES.
AGENT HARIM IS NOW CONSIDERED TO BE A FUGITIVE! FIND HIS CAR! YOUR SPECIALITY, RIGHT? CHECK ALL THE CCTV ALONG THE MAIN ROAD NEAR THE BASE!
HIS CAR IS AN OLD TYPE WITH NO SAT NAV. NO GPS TRANSPONDER, SO I CAN'T HACK IT. IT'S A NO-SHOW ON ALL FREEWAY CAMERAS INCLUDING THE METROPOLITAN INTER-CITY EXPRESSWAY! I'LL CHECK PUBLIC ROADS!
NO RESPONSE FROM ANY OF LIEUTENANT COL- I MEAN, FUGITIVE HARIM'S RADIO OR REGISTERED CELLS! IT SEEMS HE DISCARDED THEM.
I *SAID* WE SHOULD NEVER TRUST AN AFGHAN, EVEN IF HE GOT BRAINWASHED!
GET ME COX IN WASHINGTON!

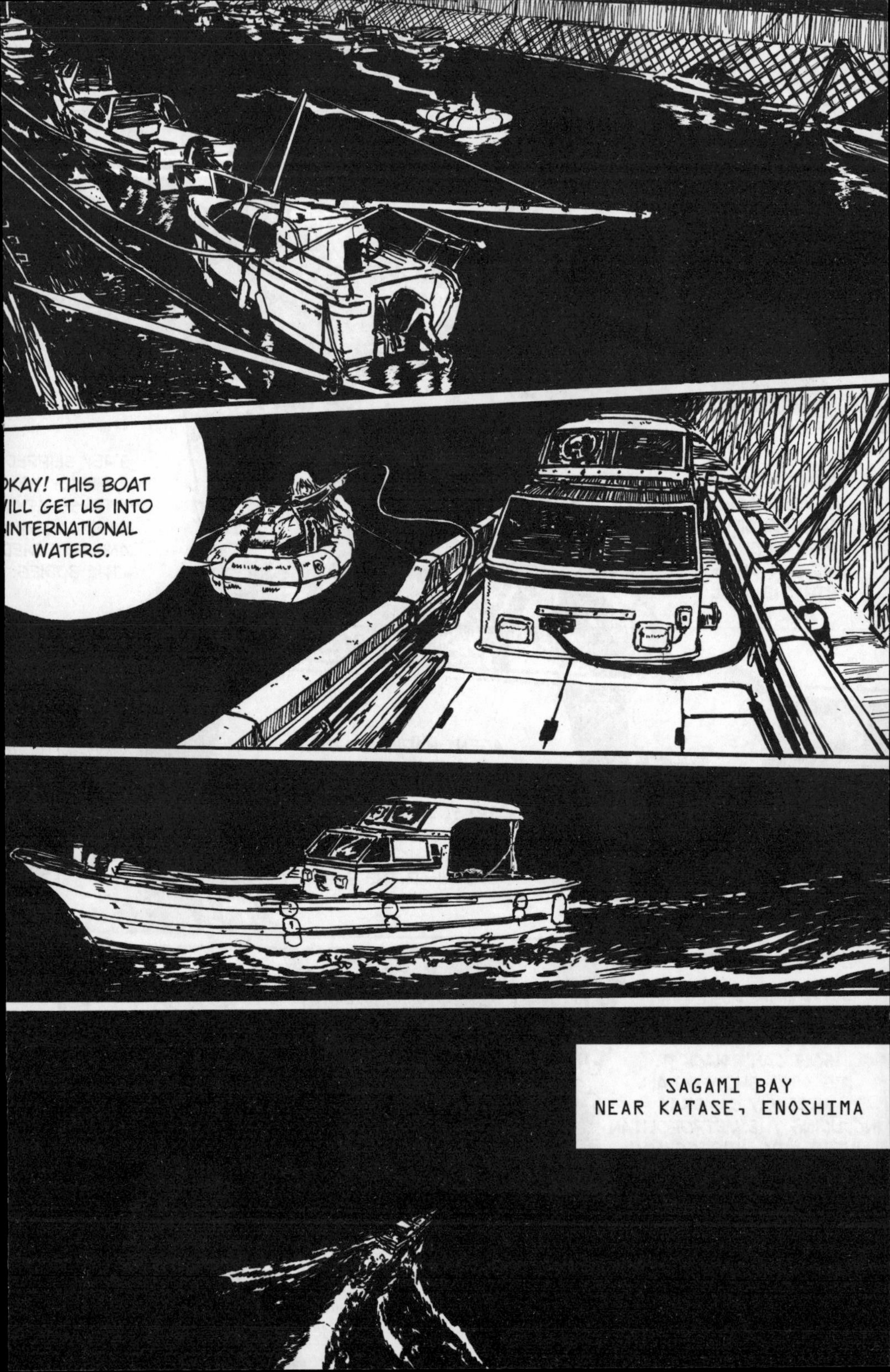

OKAY! THIS BOAT WILL GET US INTO INTERNATIONAL WATERS.
SAGAMI BAY
NEAR KATASE, ENOSHIMA

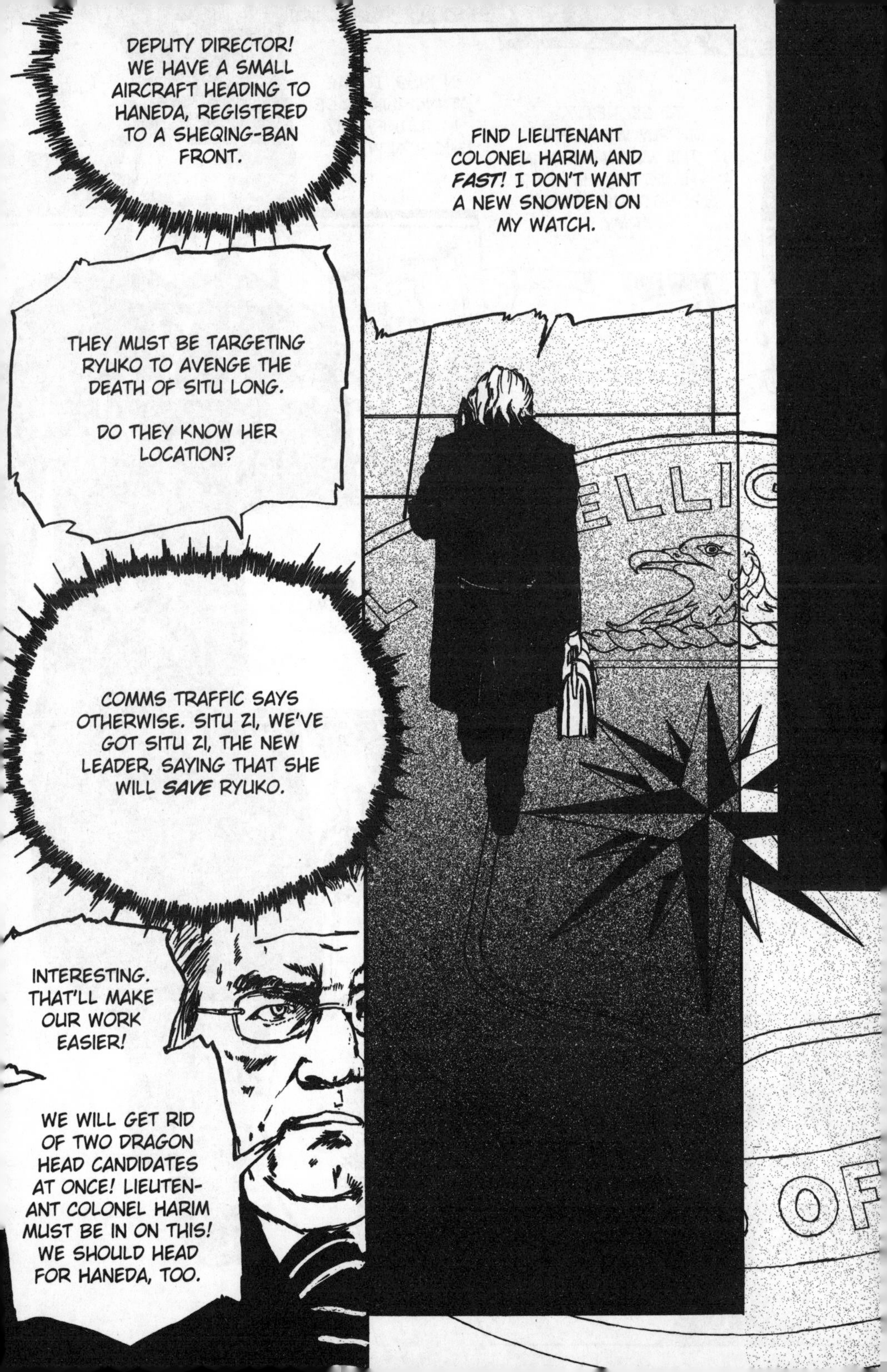
DEPUTY DIRECTOR! WE HAVE A SMALL AIRCRAFT HEADING TO HANEDA, REGISTERED TO A SHEQING-BAN FRONT.
THEY MUST BE TARGETING RYUKO TO AVENGE THE DEATH OF SITU LONG.
DO THEY KNOW HER LOCATION?
COMMS TRAFFIC SAYS OTHERWISE. SITU ZI, WE'VE GOT SITU ZI, THE NEW LEADER, SAYING THAT SHE WILL *SAVE* RYUKO.
INTERESTING. THAT'LL MAKE OUR WORK EASIER!
WE WILL GET RID OF TWO DRAGON HEAD CANDIDATES AT ONCE! LIEUTEN-ANT COLONEL HARIM MUST BE IN ON THIS! WE SHOULD HEAD FOR HANEDA, TOO.
FIND LIEUTENANT COLONEL HARIM, AND *FAST*! I DON'T WANT A NEW SNOWDEN ON MY WATCH.

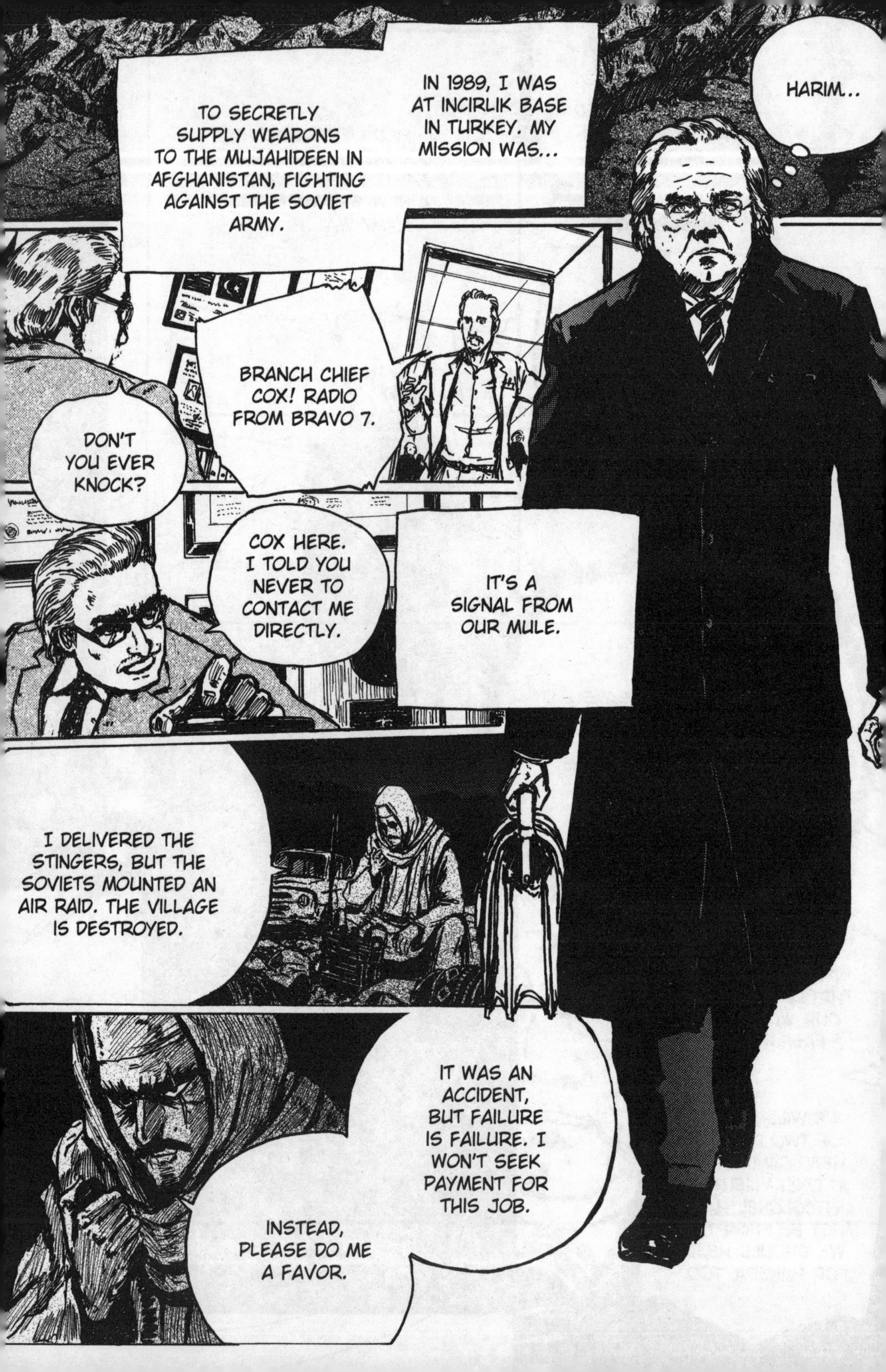
HARIM...
IN 1989, I WAS AT INCIRLIK BASE IN TURKEY. MY MISSION WAS...
TO SECRETLY SUPPLY WEAPONS TO THE MUJAHIDEEN IN AFGHANISTAN, FIGHTING AGAINST THE SOVIET ARMY.
BRANCH CHIEF COX! RADIO FROM BRAVO 7.
DON'T YOU EVER KNOCK?
IT'S A SIGNAL FROM OUR MULE.
COX HERE. I TOLD YOU NEVER TO CONTACT ME DIRECTLY.
I DELIVERED THE STINGERS, BUT THE SOVIETS MOUNTED AN AIR RAID. THE VILLAGE IS DESTROYED.
IT WAS AN ACCIDENT, BUT FAILURE IS FAILURE. I WON'T SEEK PAYMENT FOR THIS JOB.
INSTEAD, PLEASE DO ME A FAVOR.

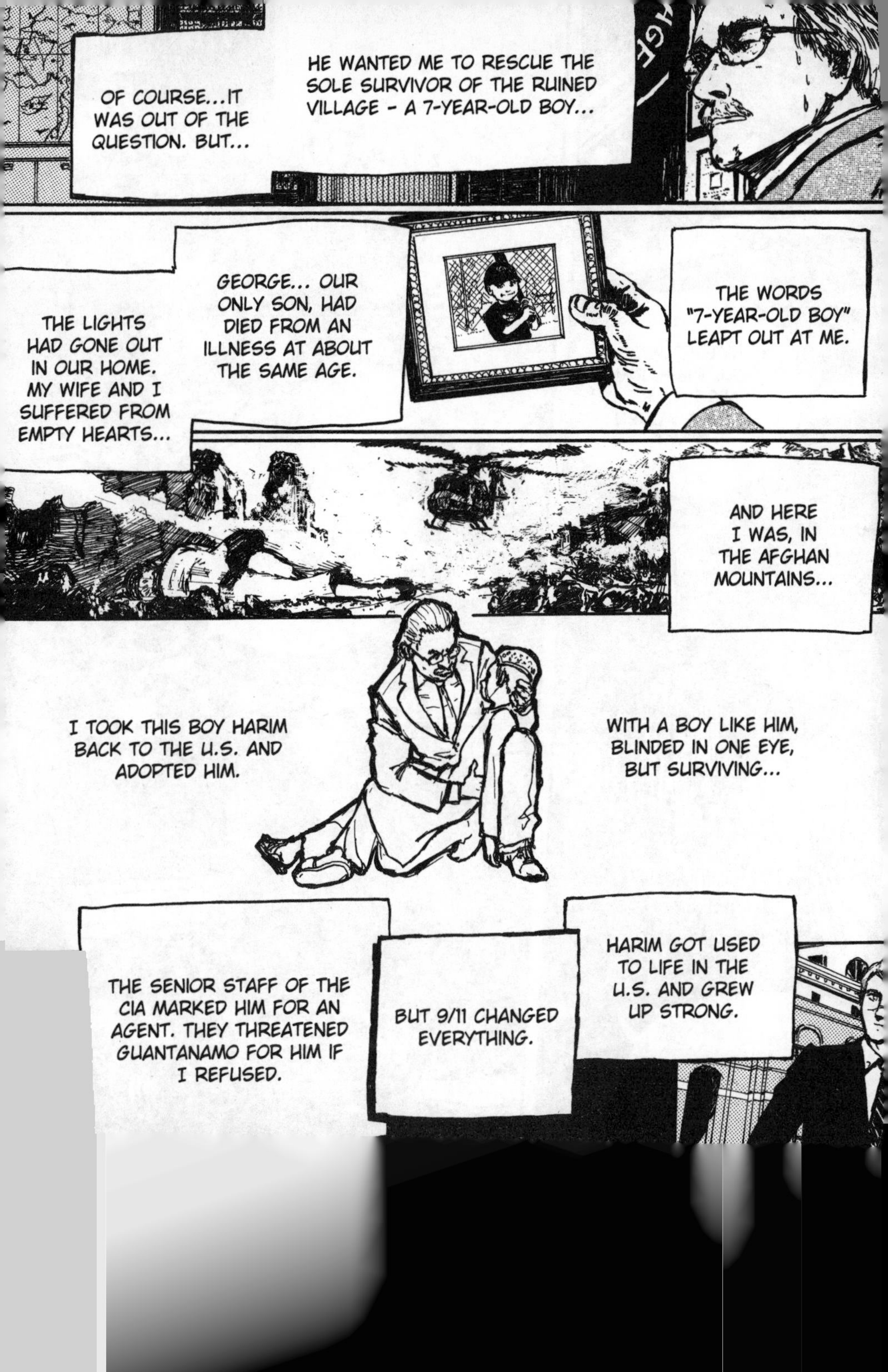
HE WANTED ME TO RESCUE THE SOLE SURVIVOR OF THE RUINED VILLAGE - A 7-YEAR-OLD BOY...
OF COURSE...IT WAS OUT OF THE QUESTION. BUT...
THE WORDS "7-YEAR-OLD BOY" LEAPT OUT AT ME.
GEORGE... OUR ONLY SON, HAD DIED FROM AN ILLNESS AT ABOUT THE SAME AGE.
THE LIGHTS HAD GONE OUT IN OUR HOME. MY WIFE AND I SUFFERED FROM EMPTY HEARTS...
AND HERE I WAS, IN THE AFGHAN MOUNTAINS...
WITH A BOY LIKE HIM, BLINDED IN ONE EYE, BUT SURVIVING...
I TOOK THIS BOY HARIM BACK TO THE U.S. AND ADOPTED HIM.
HARIM GOT USED TO LIFE IN THE U.S. AND GREW UP STRONG.
BUT 9/11 CHANGED EVERYTHING.
THE SENIOR STAFF OF THE CIA MARKED HIM FOR AN AGENT. THEY THREATENED GUANTANAMO FOR HIM IF I REFUSED.

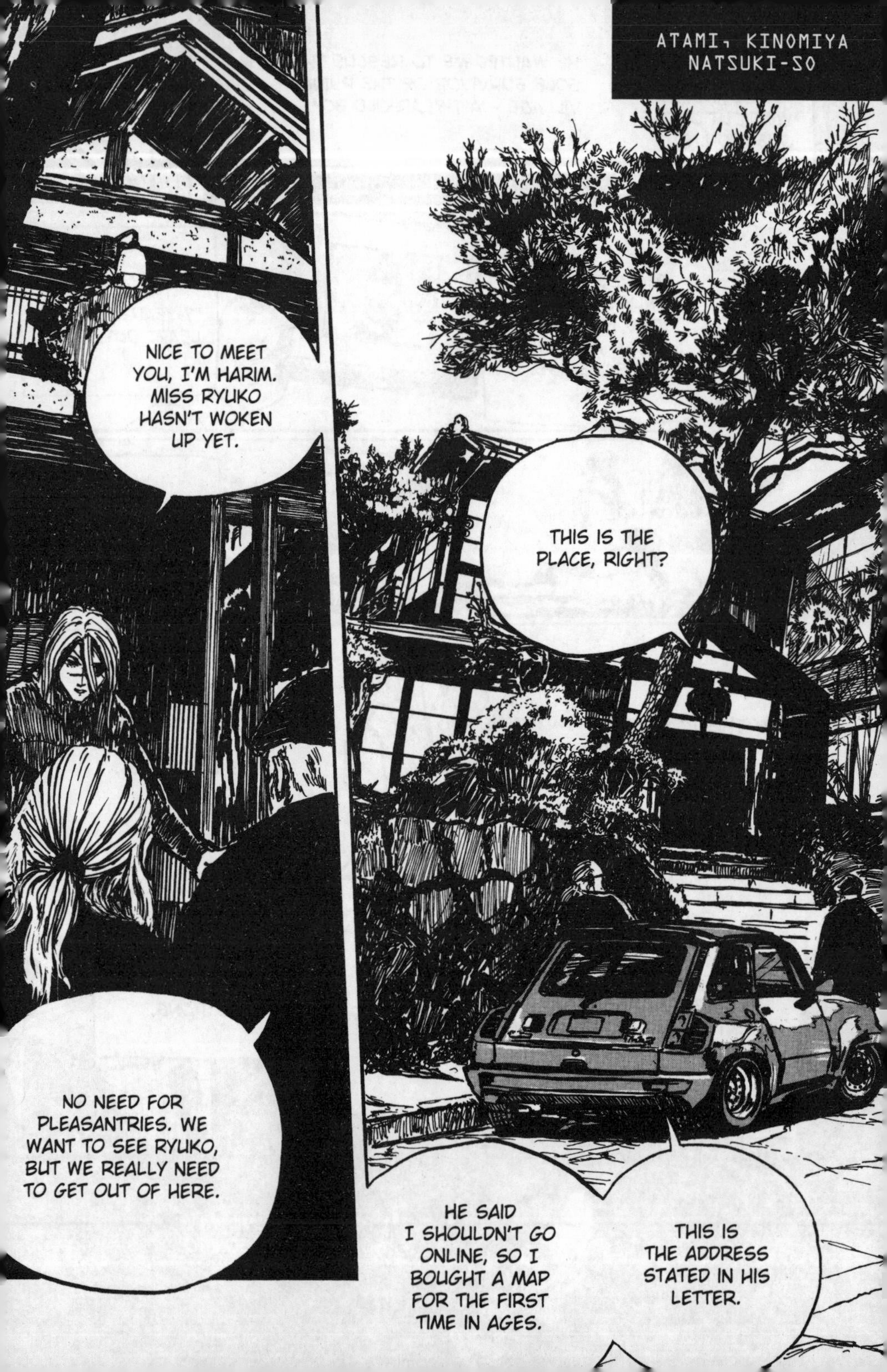
ATAMI, KINOMIYA NATSUKI-ZO
THIS IS THE PLACE, RIGHT?
THIS IS THE ADDRESS STATED IN HIS LETTER.
HE SAID I SHOULDN'T GO ONLINE, SO I BOUGHT A MAP FOR THE FIRST TIME IN AGES.
NICE TO MEET YOU, I'M HARIM. MISS RYUKO HASN'T WOKEN UP YET.
NO NEED FOR PLEASANTRIES. WE WANT TO SEE RYUKO, BUT WE REALLY NEED TO GET OUT OF HERE.

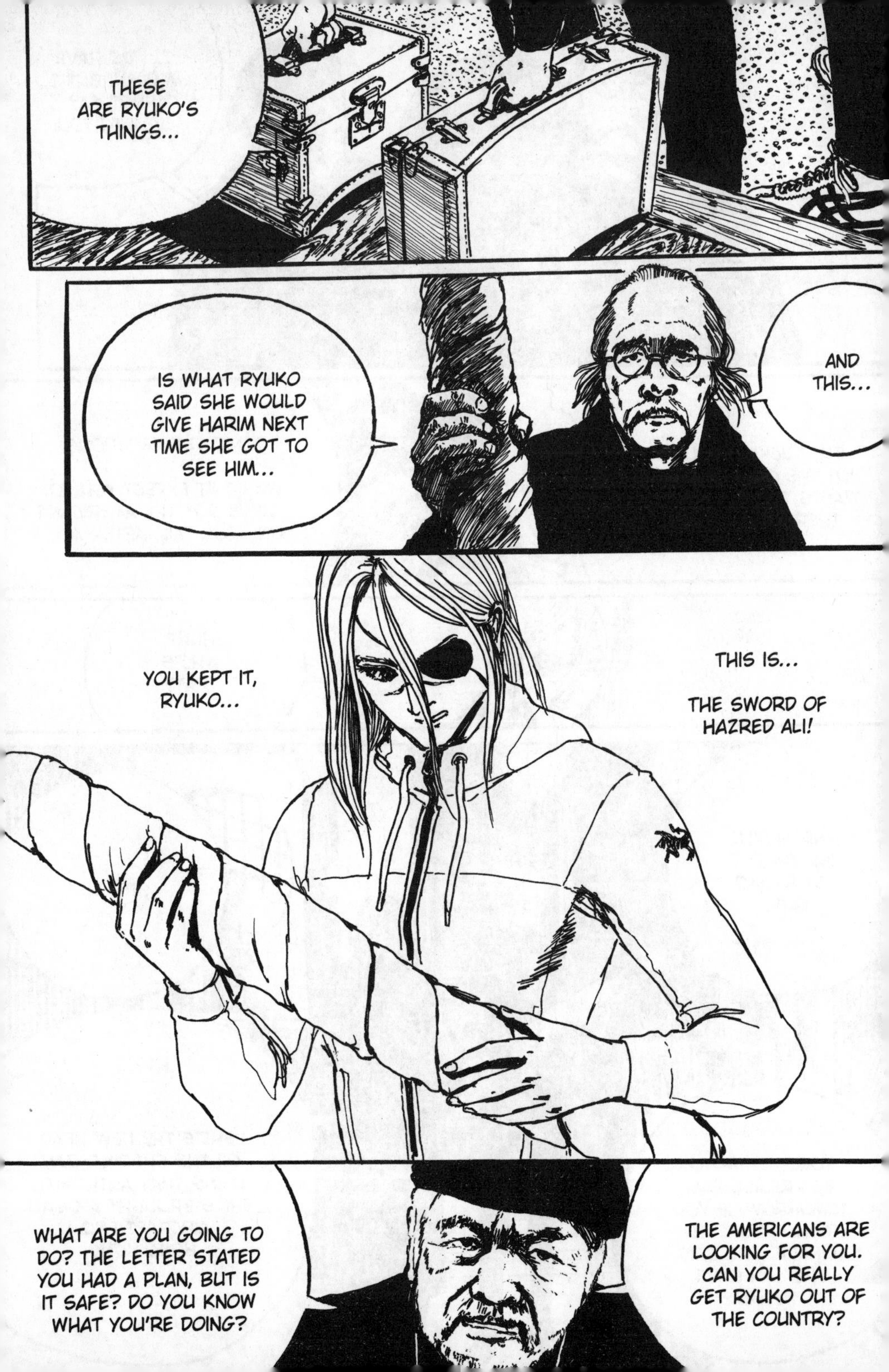
THESE ARE RYUKO'S THINGS...
AND THIS...
IS WHAT RYUKO SAID SHE WOULD GIVE HARIM NEXT TIME SHE GOT TO SEE HIM...
THIS IS...
THE SWORD OF HAZRED ALI!
YOU KEPT IT, RYUKO...
THE AMERICANS ARE LOOKING FOR YOU. CAN YOU REALLY GET RYUKO OUT OF THE COUNTRY?
WHAT ARE YOU GOING TO DO? THE LETTER STATED YOU HAD A PLAN, BUT IS IT SAFE? DO YOU KNOW WHAT YOU'RE DOING?

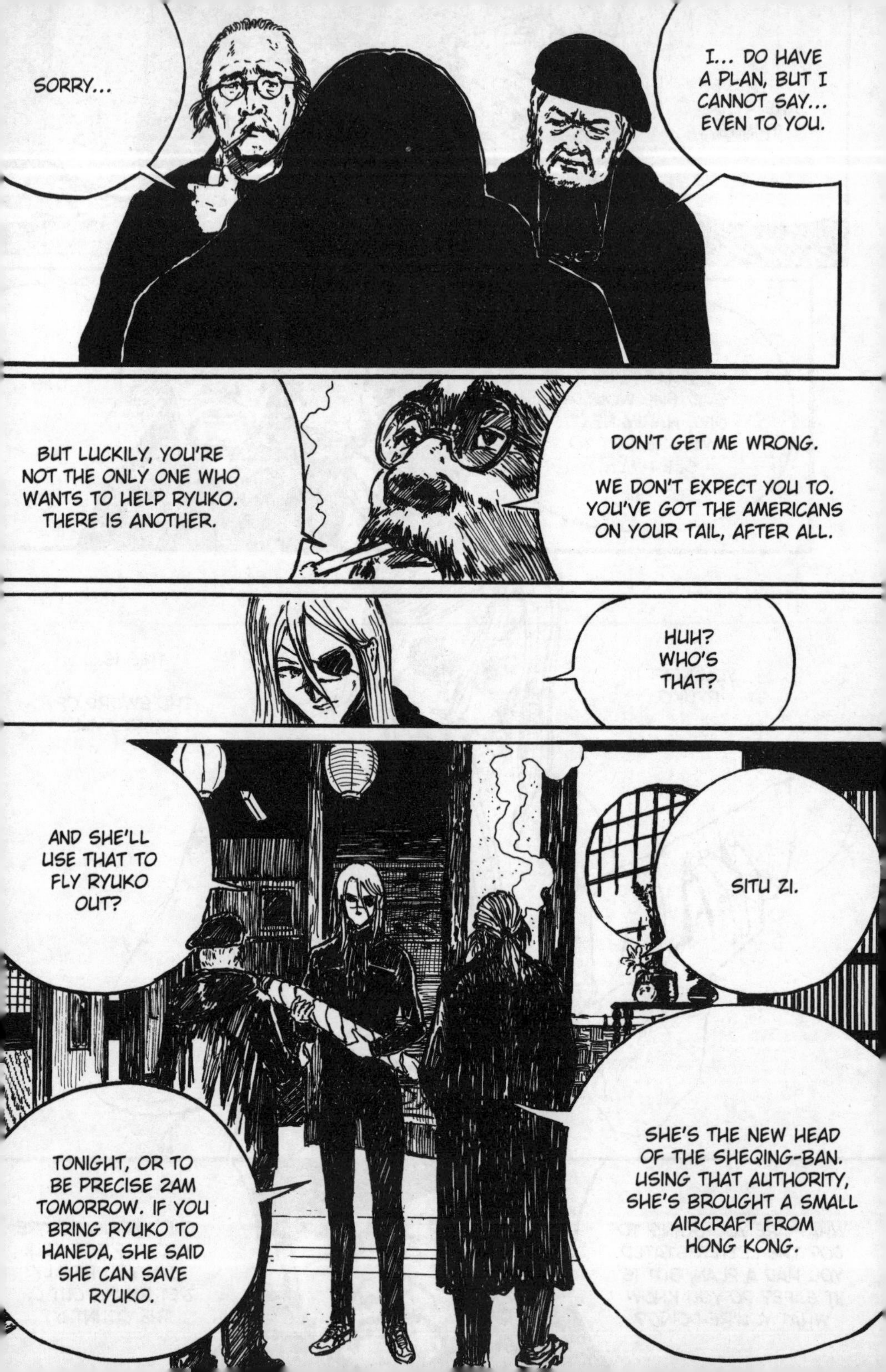
I... DO HAVE A PLAN, BUT I CANNOT SAY... EVEN TO YOU.
SORRY...
DON'T GET ME WRONG.
WE DON'T EXPECT YOU TO. YOU'VE GOT THE AMERICANS ON YOUR TAIL, AFTER ALL.
BUT LUCKILY, YOU'RE NOT THE ONLY ONE WHO WANTS TO HELP RYUKO. THERE IS ANOTHER.
HUH? WHO'S THAT?
SITU ZI.
SHE'S THE NEW HEAD OF THE SHEQING-BAN. USING THAT AUTHORITY, SHE'S BROUGHT A SMALL AIRCRAFT FROM HONG KONG.
AND SHE'LL USE THAT TO FLY RYUKO OUT?
TONIGHT, OR TO BE PRECISE 2AM TOMORROW. IF YOU BRING RYUKO TO HANEDA, SHE SAID SHE CAN SAVE RYUKO.

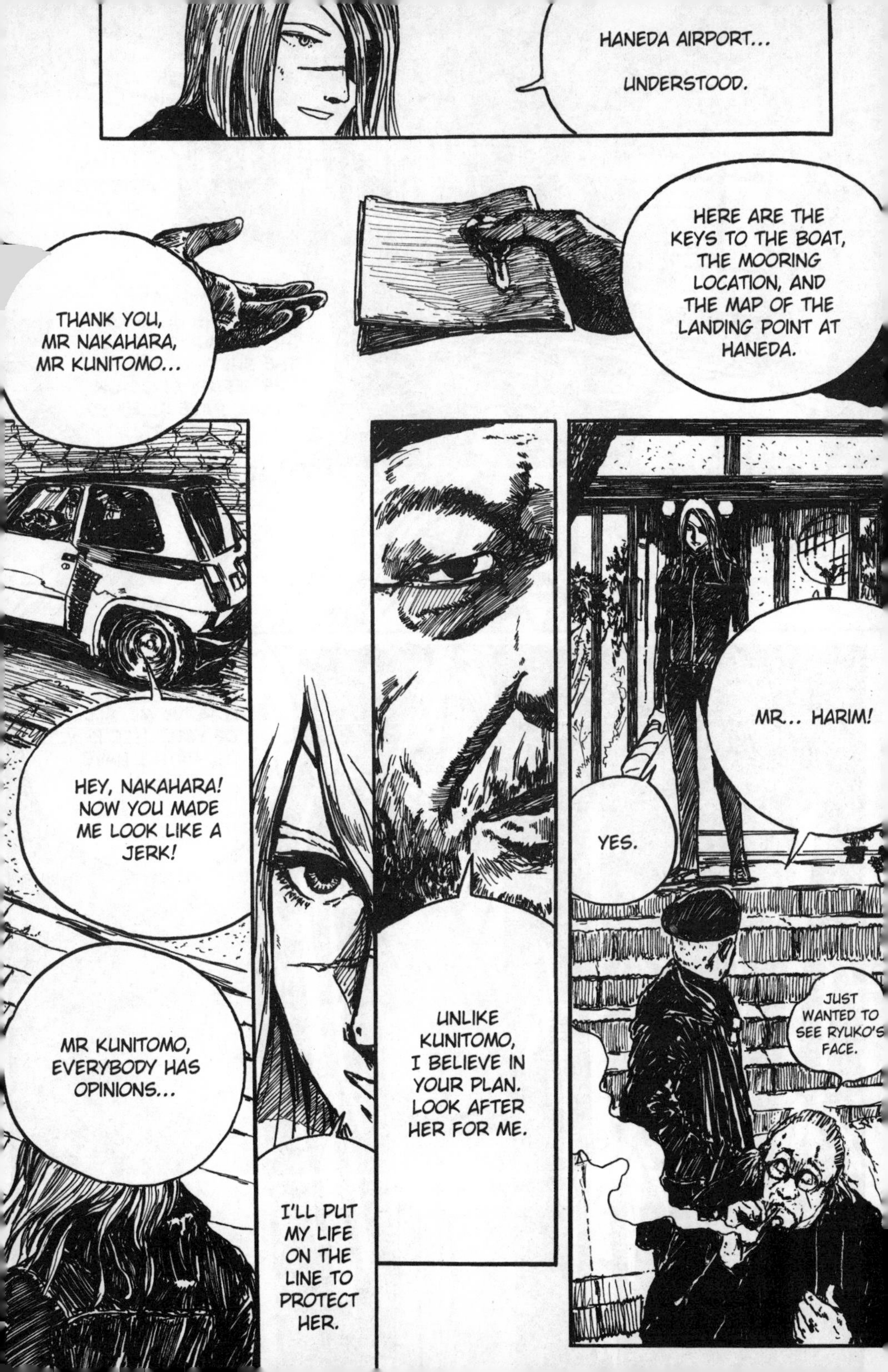
HANEDA AIRPORT... UNDERSTOOD.
HERE ARE THE KEYS TO THE BOAT, THE MOORING LOCATION, AND THE MAP OF THE LANDING POINT AT HANEDA.
THANK YOU, MR NAKAHARA, MR KUNITOMO...
MR... HARIM!
YES.
JUST WANTED TO SEE RYUKO'S FACE.
UNLIKE KUNITOMO, I BELIEVE IN YOUR PLAN. LOOK AFTER HER FOR ME.
I'LL PUT MY LIFE ON THE LINE TO PROTECT HER.
HEY, NAKAHARA! NOW YOU MADE ME LOOK LIKE A JERK!
MR KUNITOMO, EVERYBODY HAS OPINIONS...

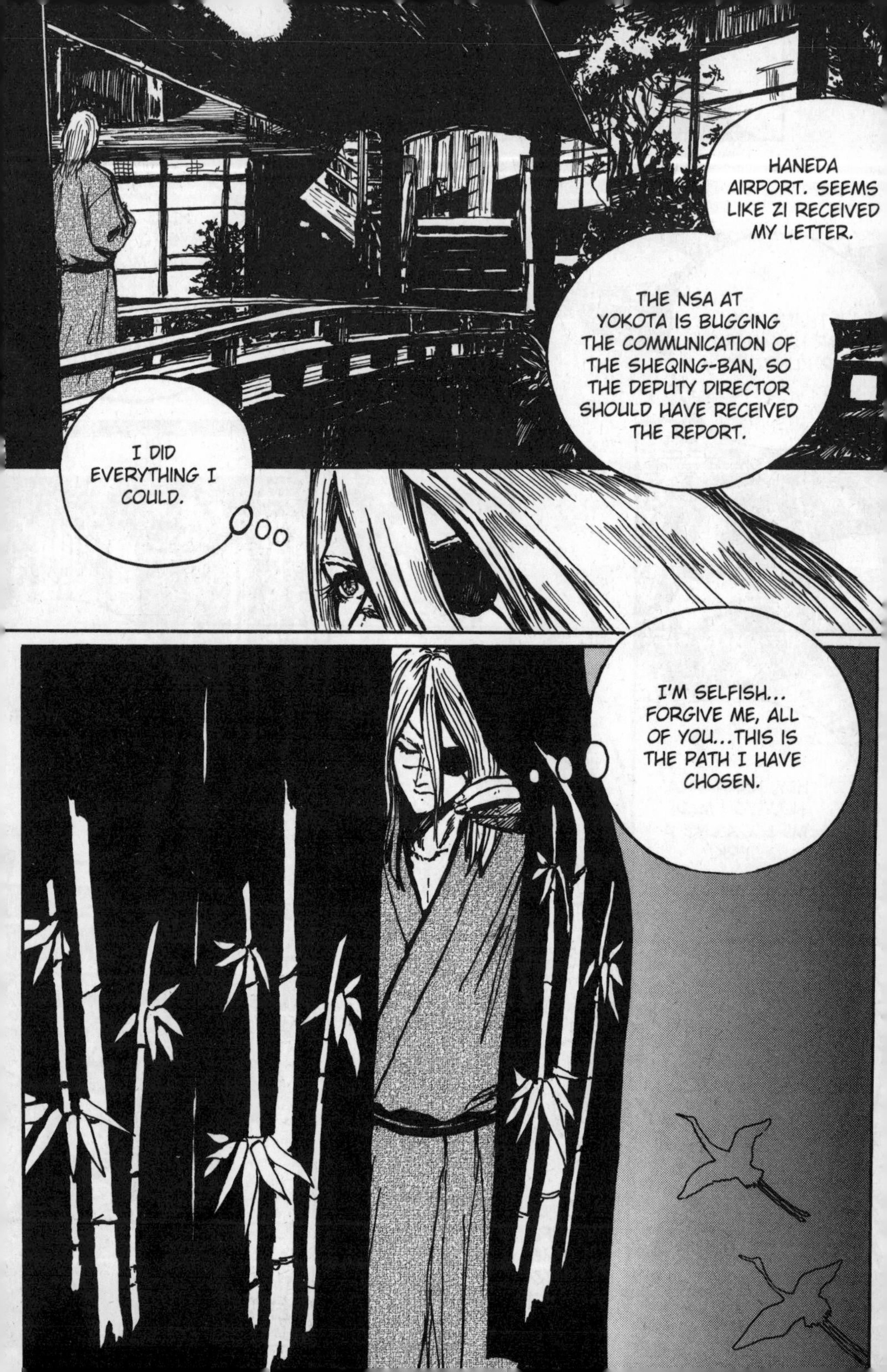
HANEDA AIRPORT. SEEMS LIKE ZI RECEIVED MY LETTER.
THE NSA AT YOKOTA IS BUGGING THE COMMUNICATION OF THE SHEQING-BAN, SO THE DEPUTY DIRECTOR SHOULD HAVE RECEIVED THE REPORT.
I DID EVERYTHING I COULD.
I'M SELFISH... FORGIVE ME, ALL OF YOU...THIS IS THE PATH I HAVE CHOSEN.

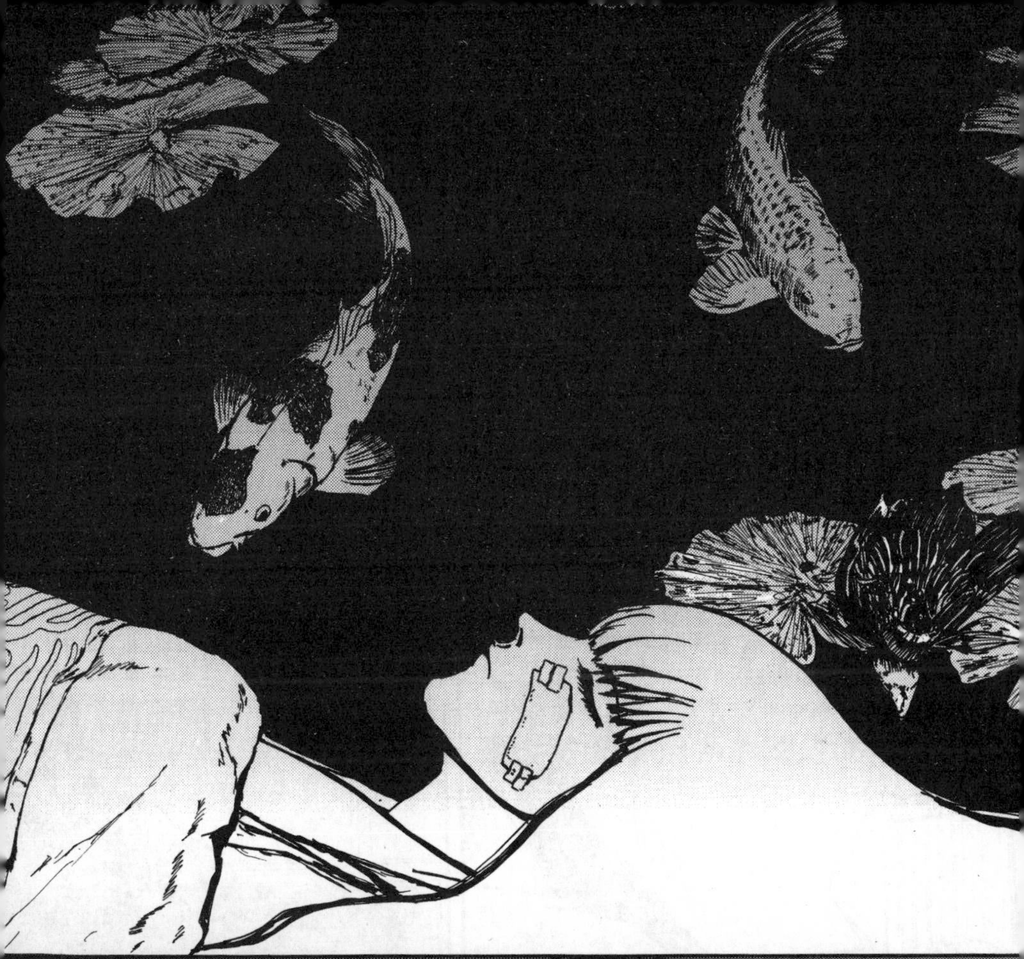
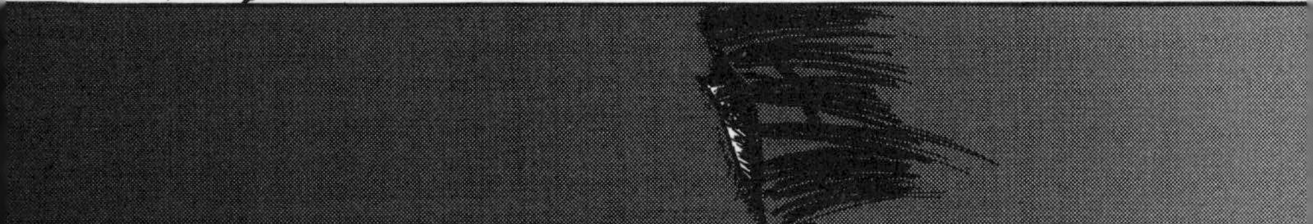
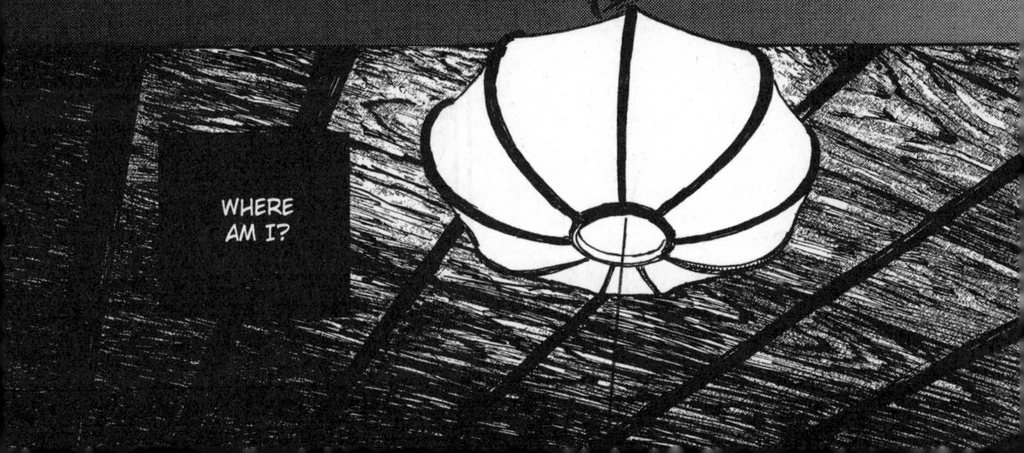
WHERE AM I?

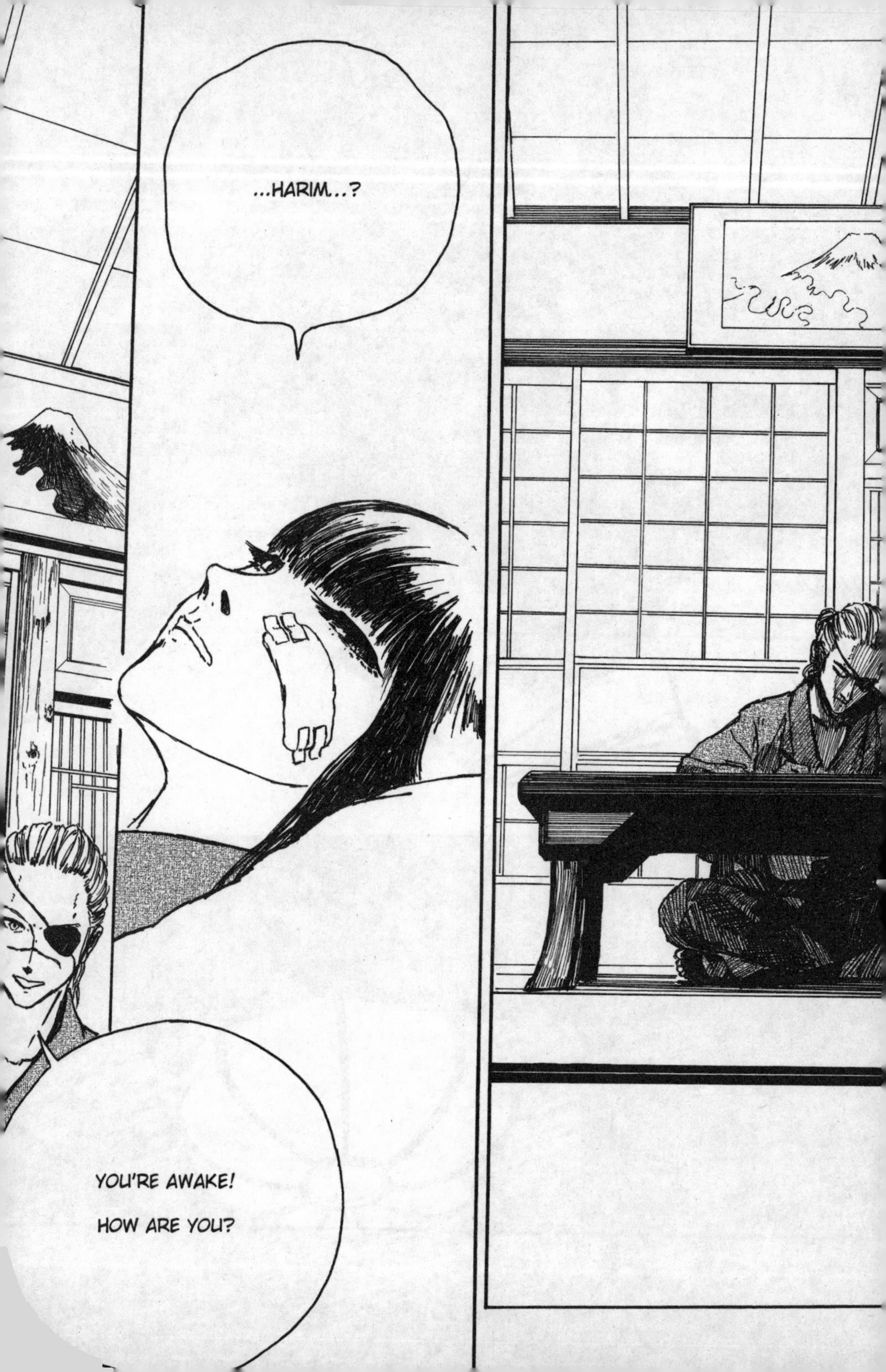
...HARIM...?
YOU'RE AWAKE! HOW ARE YOU?

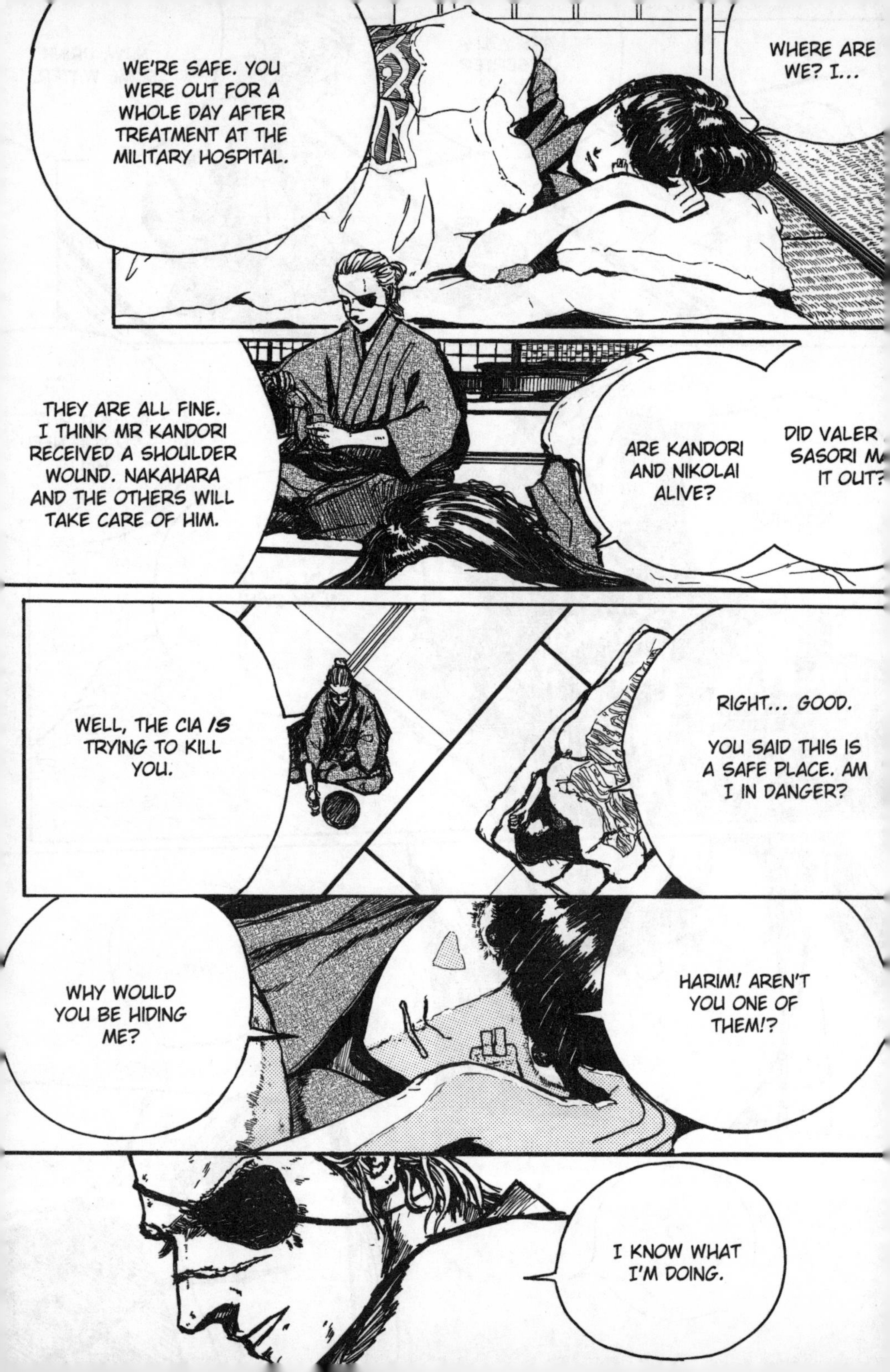
WHERE ARE WE? I...
WE'RE SAFE. YOU WERE OUT FOR A WHOLE DAY AFTER TREATMENT AT THE MILITARY HOSPITAL.
DID VALER SASORI MA IT OUT?
ARE KANDORI AND NIKOLAI ALIVE?
THEY ARE ALL FINE. I THINK MR KANDORI RECEIVED A SHOULDER WOUND. NAKAHARA AND THE OTHERS WILL TAKE CARE OF HIM.
RIGHT... GOOD.
YOU SAID THIS IS A SAFE PLACE. AM I IN DANGER?
WELL, THE CIA *IS* TRYING TO KILL YOU.
HARIM! AREN'T YOU ONE OF THEM!?
WHY WOULD YOU BE HIDING ME?
I KNOW WHAT I'M DOING.

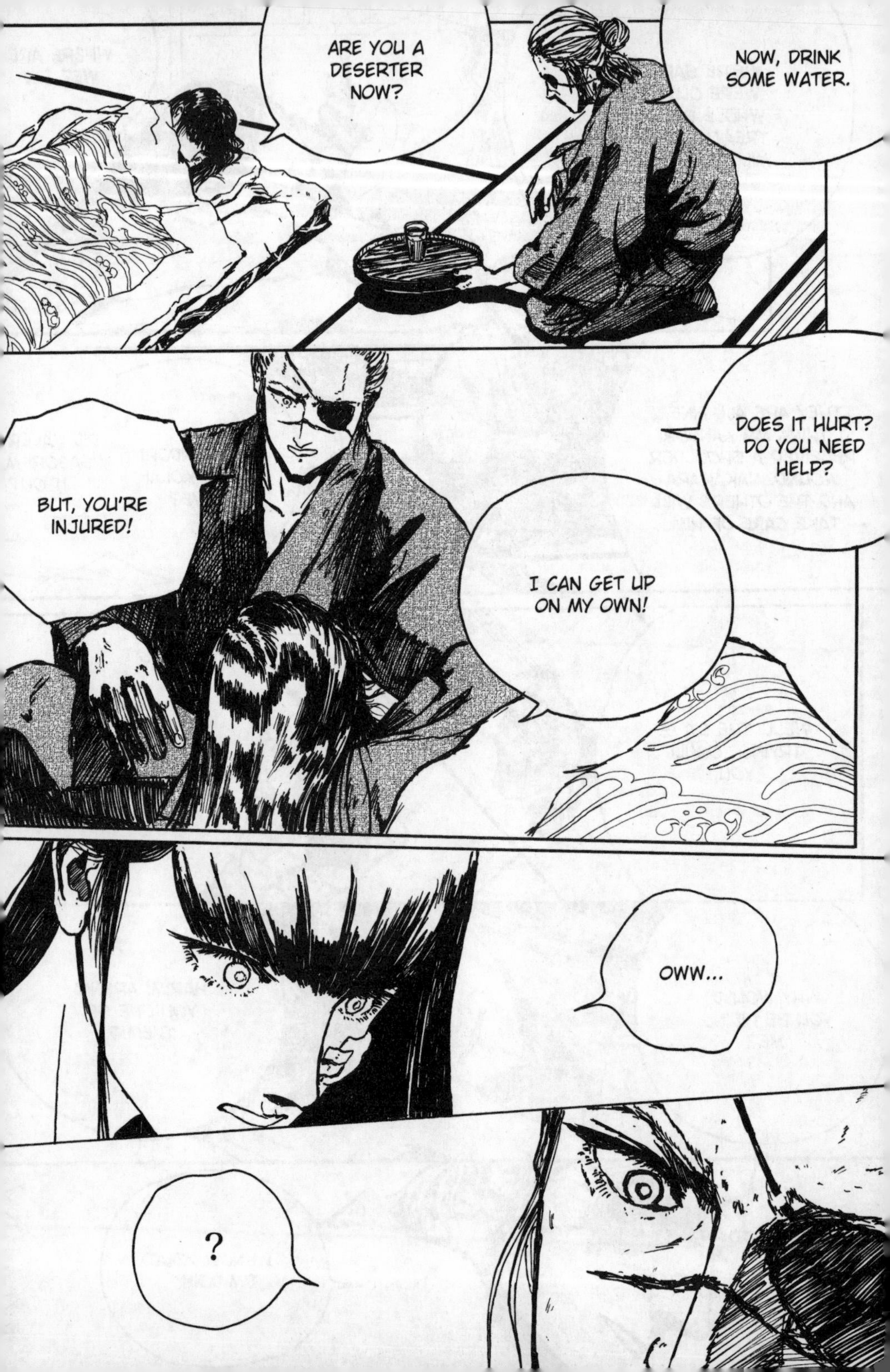
NOW, DRINK SOME WATER.
ARE YOU A DESERTER NOW?
DOES IT HURT? DO YOU NEED HELP?
I CAN GET UP ON MY OWN!
BUT, YOU'RE INJURED!
OWW...
?

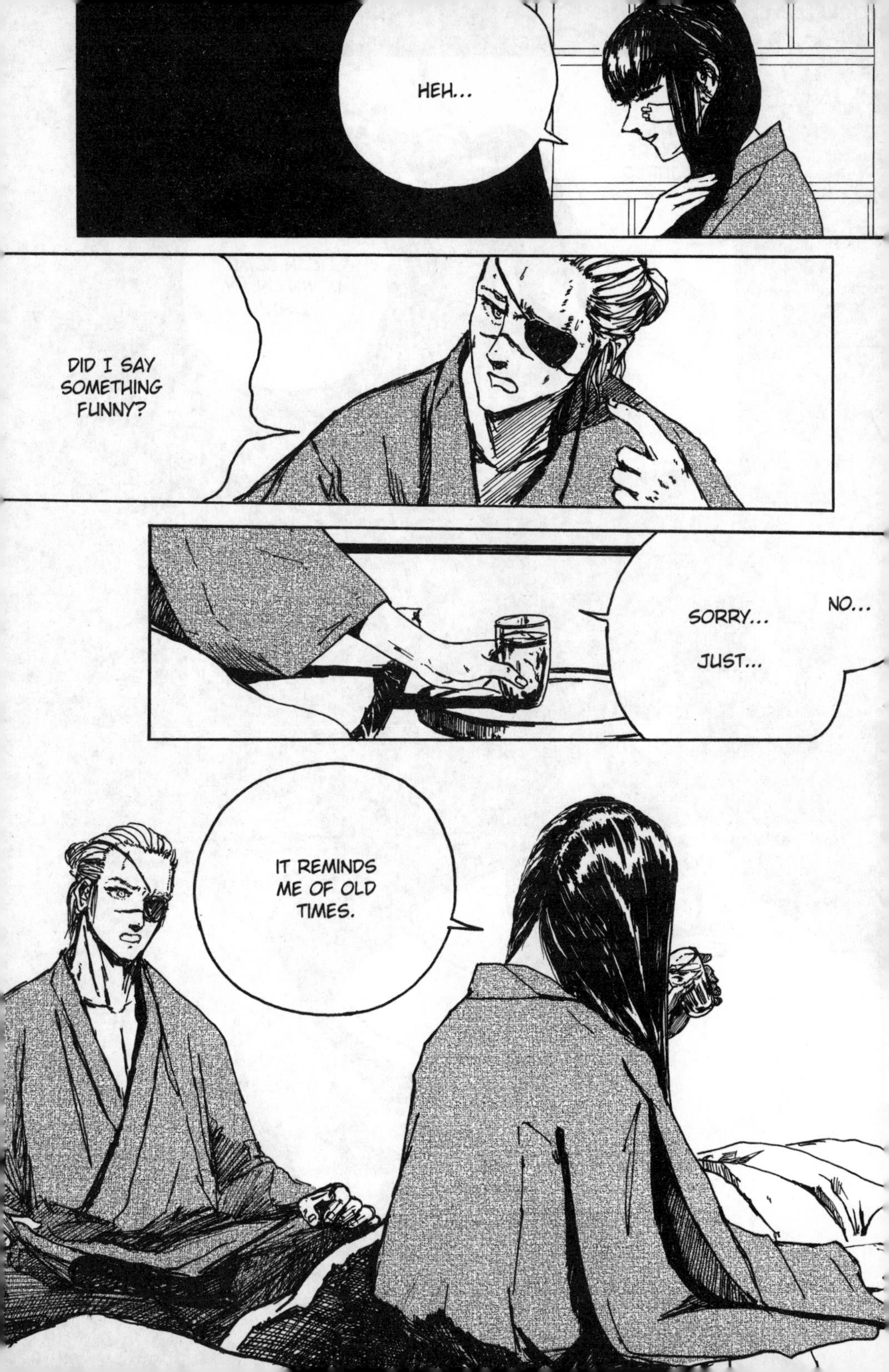
HEH...
DID I SAY SOMETHING FUNNY?
NO...
SORRY...
JUST...
IT REMINDS ME OF OLD TIMES.

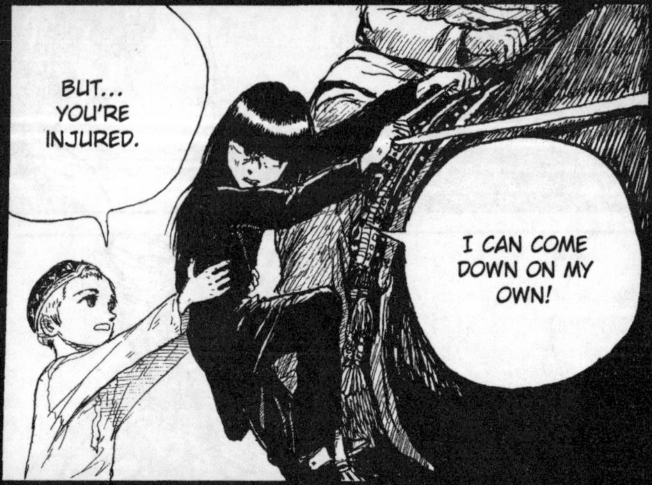
I CAN COME DOWN ON MY OWN!
BUT... YOU'RE INJURED.

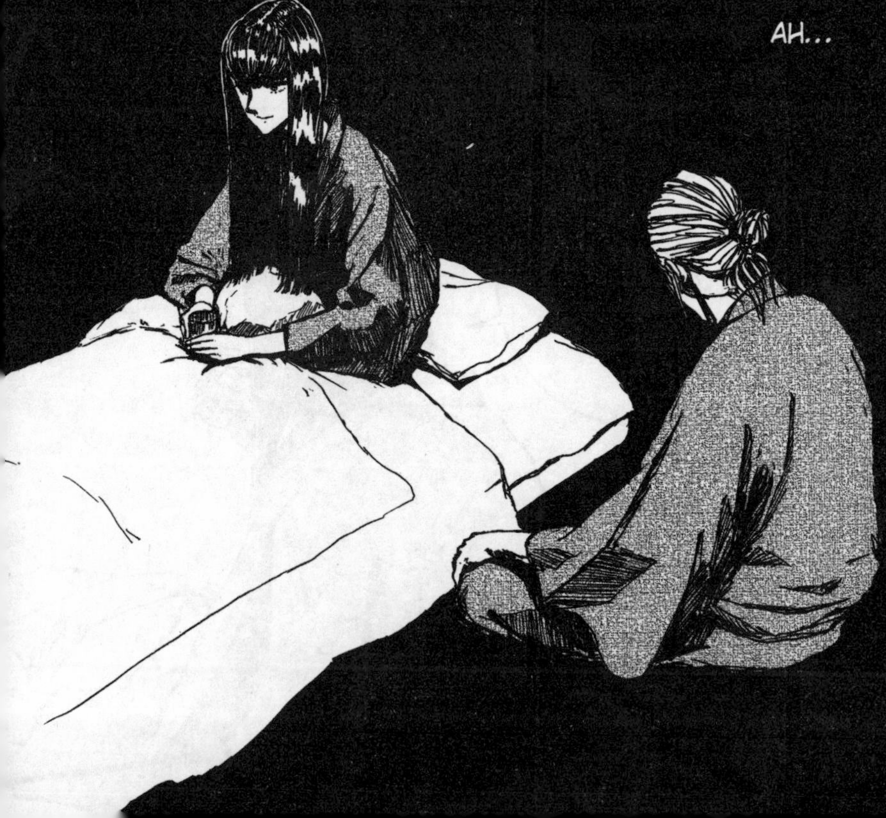
AH...

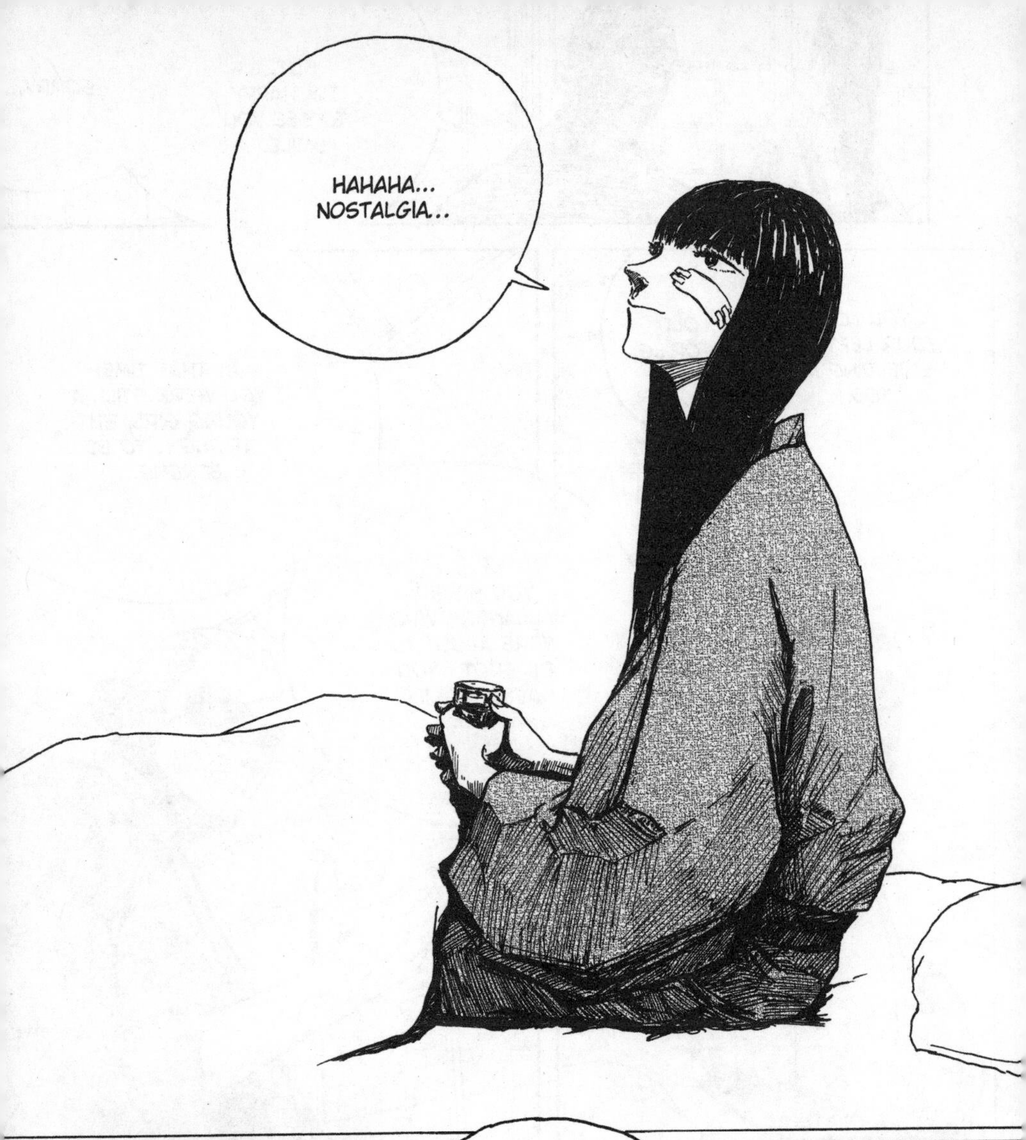
HAHAHA...
NOSTALGIA...
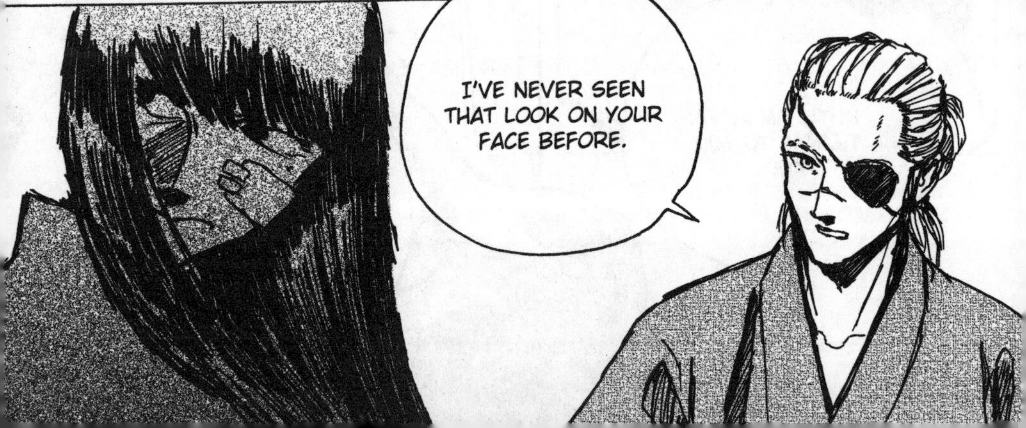
I'VE NEVER SEEN
THAT LOOK ON YOUR
FACE BEFORE.

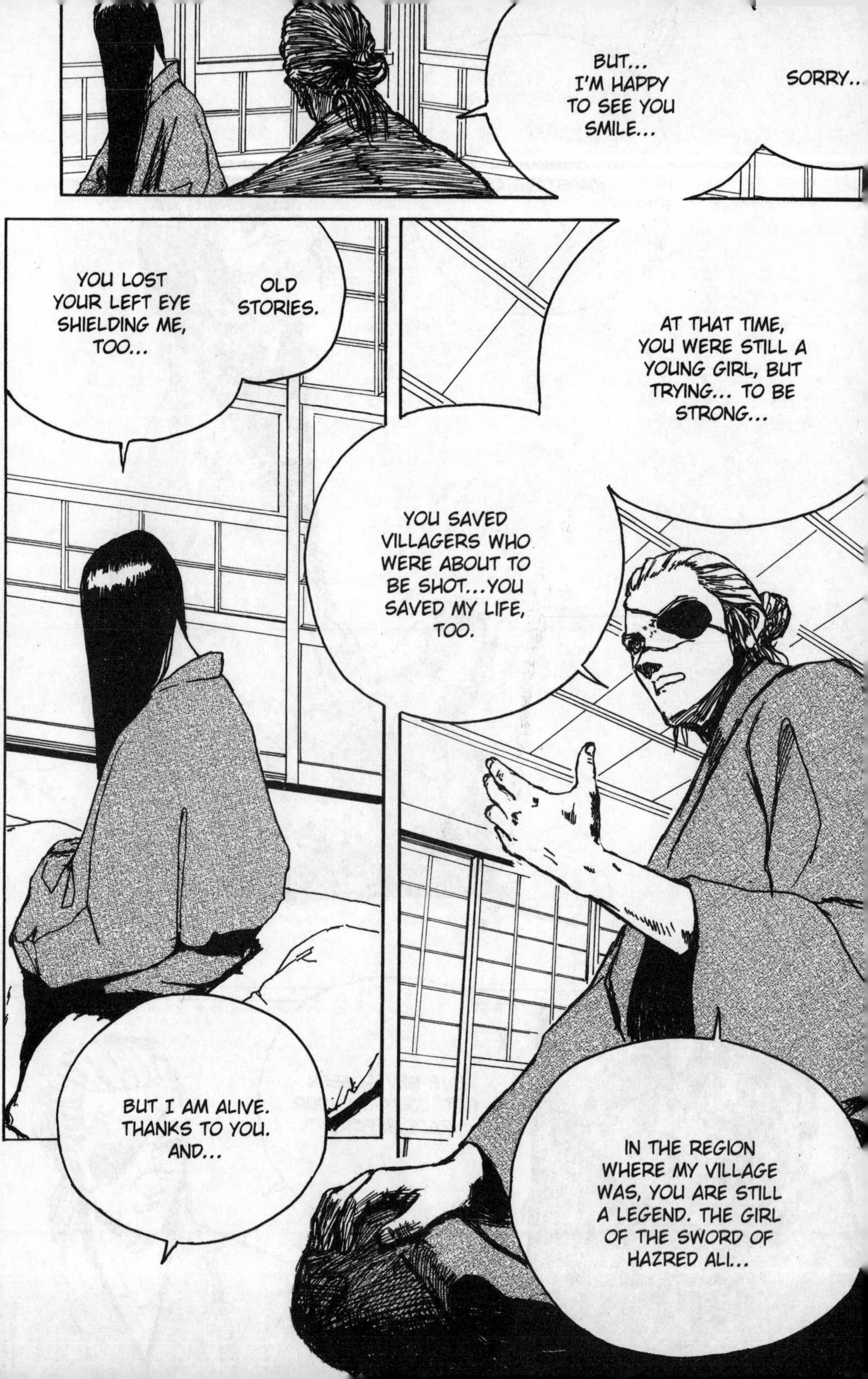
SORRY...
BUT... I'M HAPPY TO SEE YOU SMILE...
AT THAT TIME, YOU WERE STILL A YOUNG GIRL, BUT TRYING... TO BE STRONG...
YOU SAVED VILLAGERS WHO WERE ABOUT TO BE SHOT...YOU SAVED MY LIFE, TOO.
OLD STORIES.
YOU LOST YOUR LEFT EYE SHIELDING ME, TOO...
BUT I AM ALIVE. THANKS TO YOU. AND...
IN THE REGION WHERE MY VILLAGE WAS, YOU ARE STILL A LEGEND. THE GIRL OF THE SWORD OF HAZRED ALI...

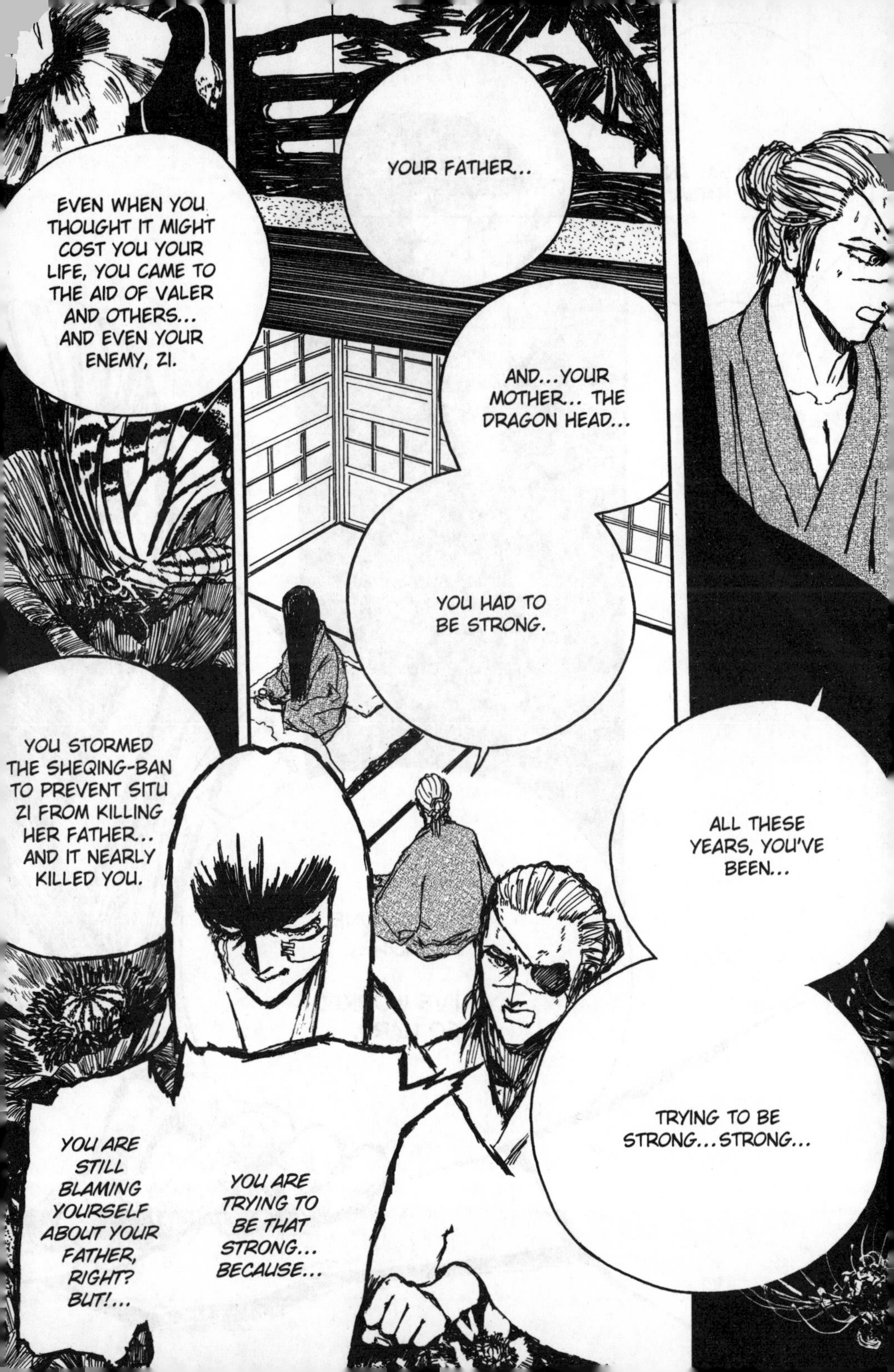
YOUR FATHER...
AND...YOUR MOTHER... THE DRAGON HEAD...
YOU HAD TO BE STRONG.
EVEN WHEN YOU THOUGHT IT MIGHT COST YOU YOUR LIFE, YOU CAME TO THE AID OF VALER AND OTHERS... AND EVEN YOUR ENEMY, ZI.
ALL THESE YEARS, YOU'VE BEEN...
TRYING TO BE STRONG...STRONG...
YOU STORMED THE SHEQING-BAN TO PREVENT SITU ZI FROM KILLING HER FATHER... AND IT NEARLY KILLED YOU.
YOU ARE TRYING TO BE THAT STRONG... BECAUSE...
YOU ARE STILL BLAMING YOURSELF ABOUT YOUR FATHER, RIGHT? BUT!...

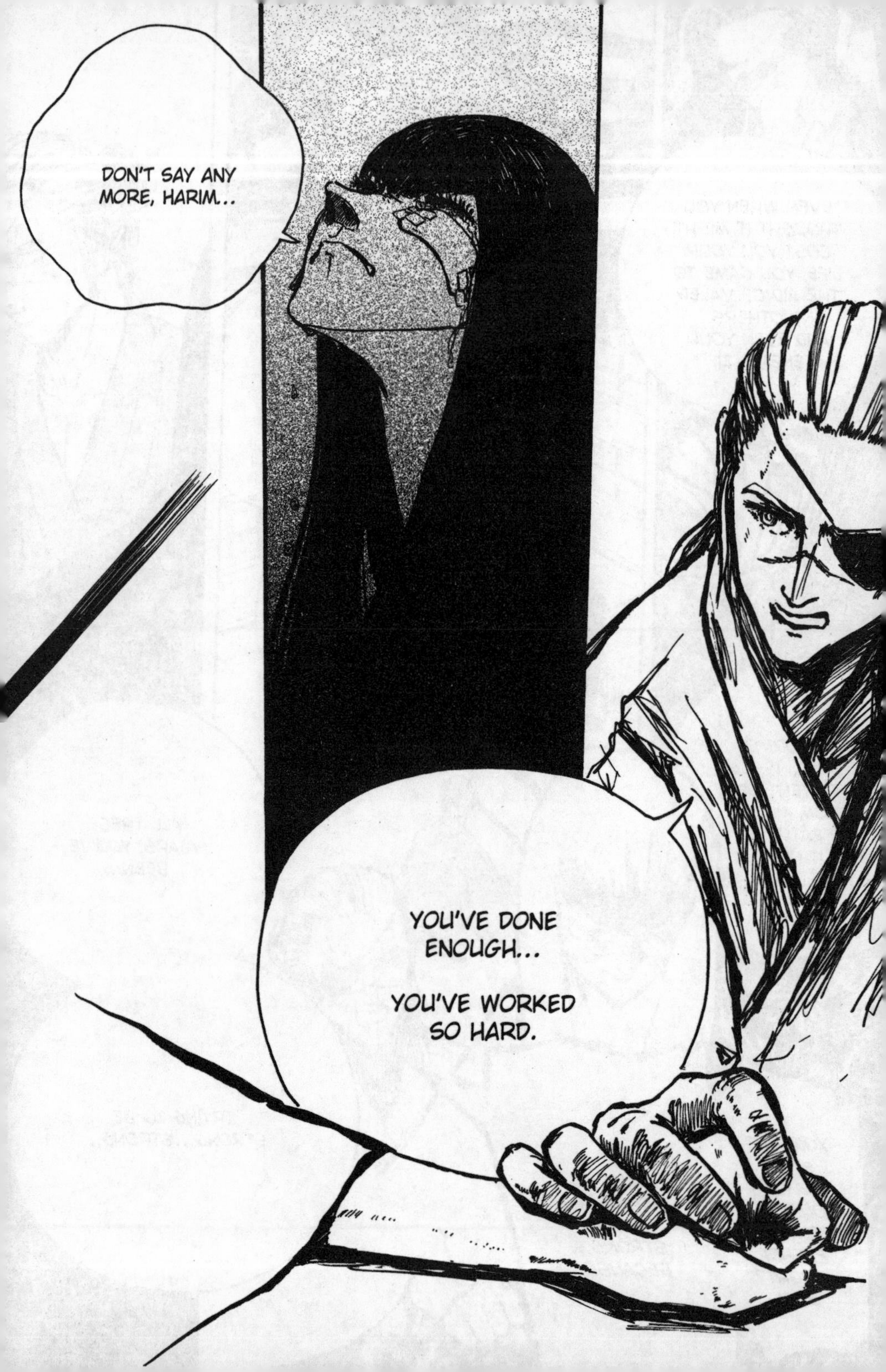
DON'T SAY ANY MORE, HARIM...
YOU'VE DONE ENOUGH...
YOU'VE WORKED SO HARD.

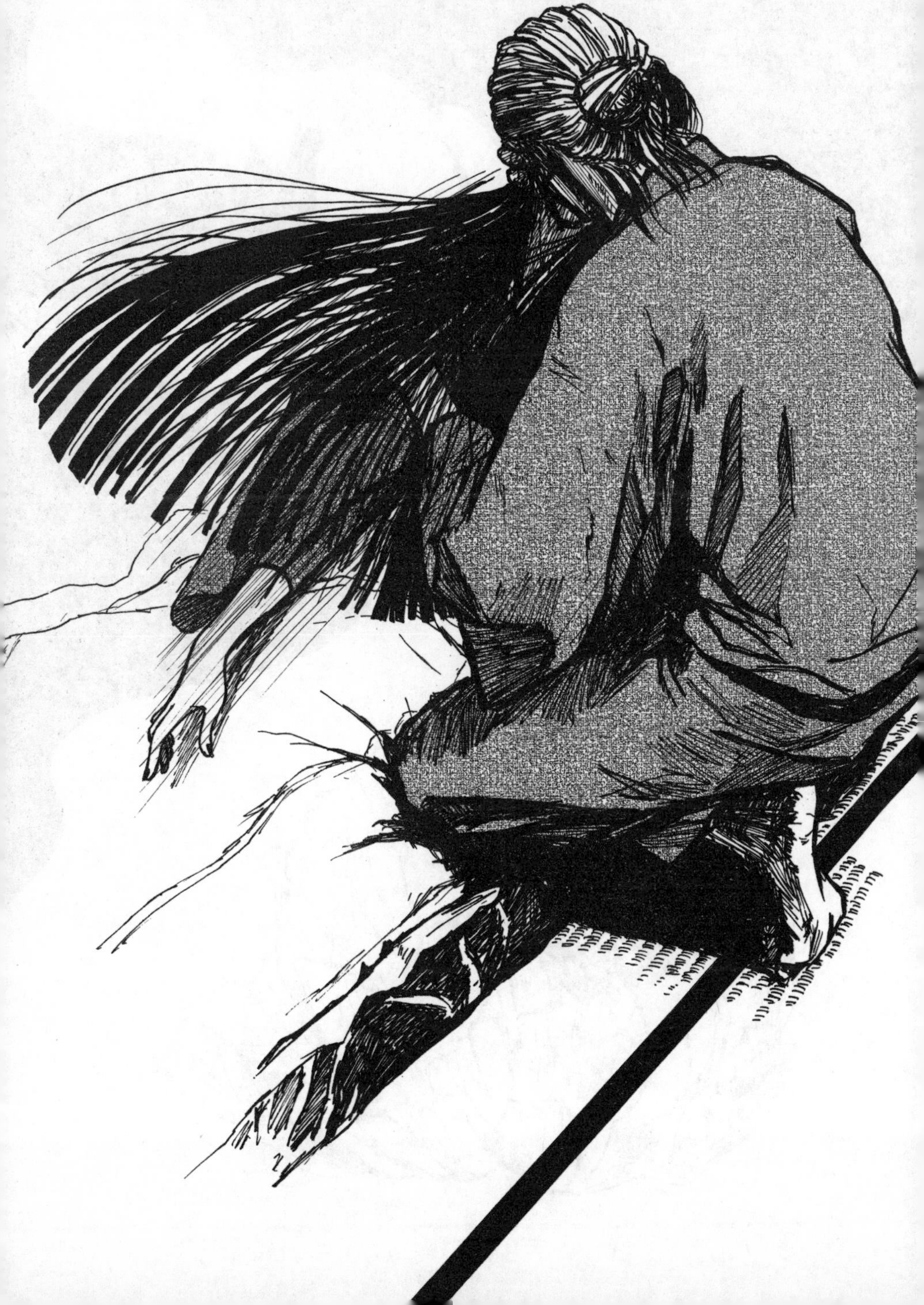

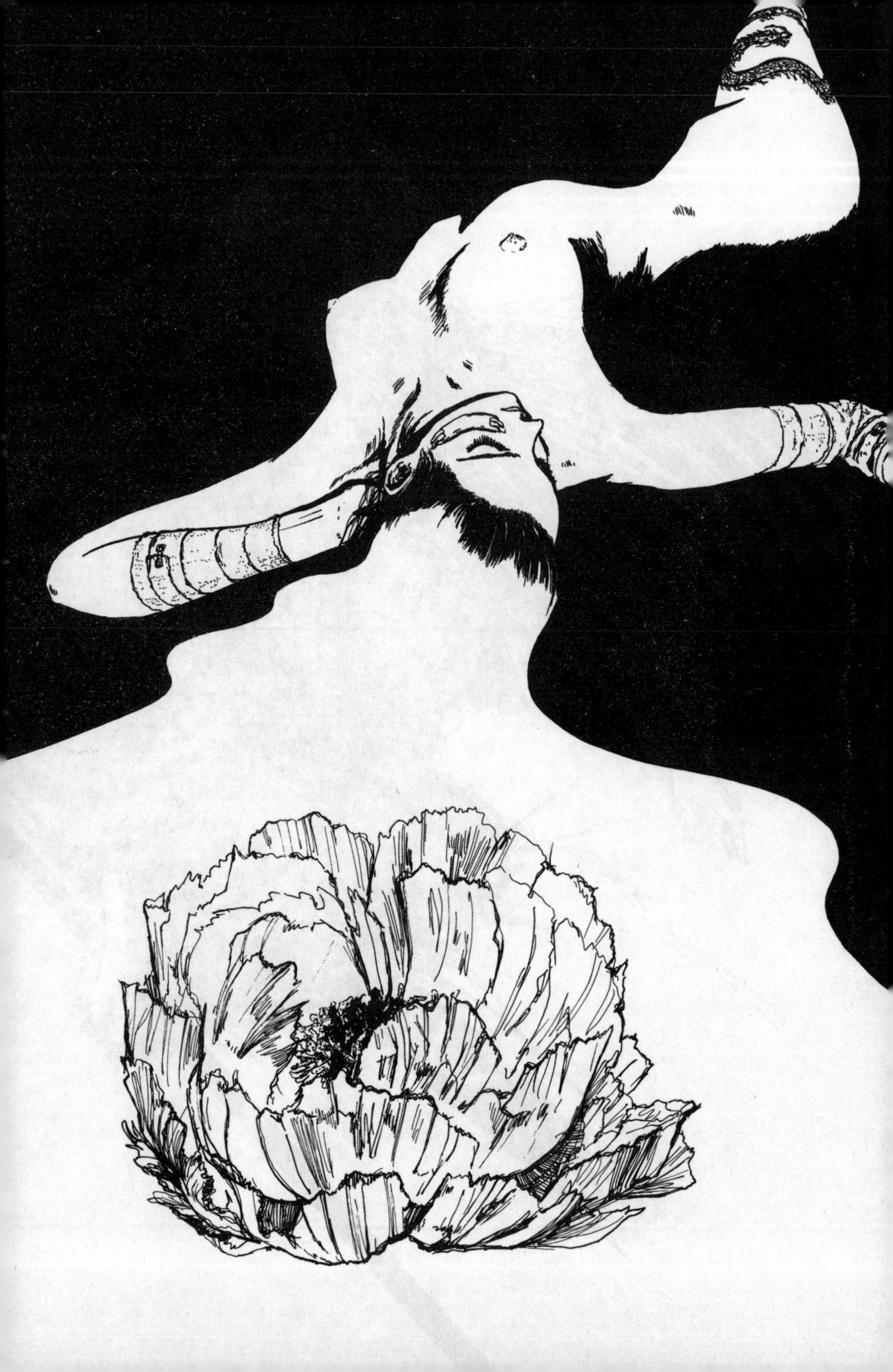

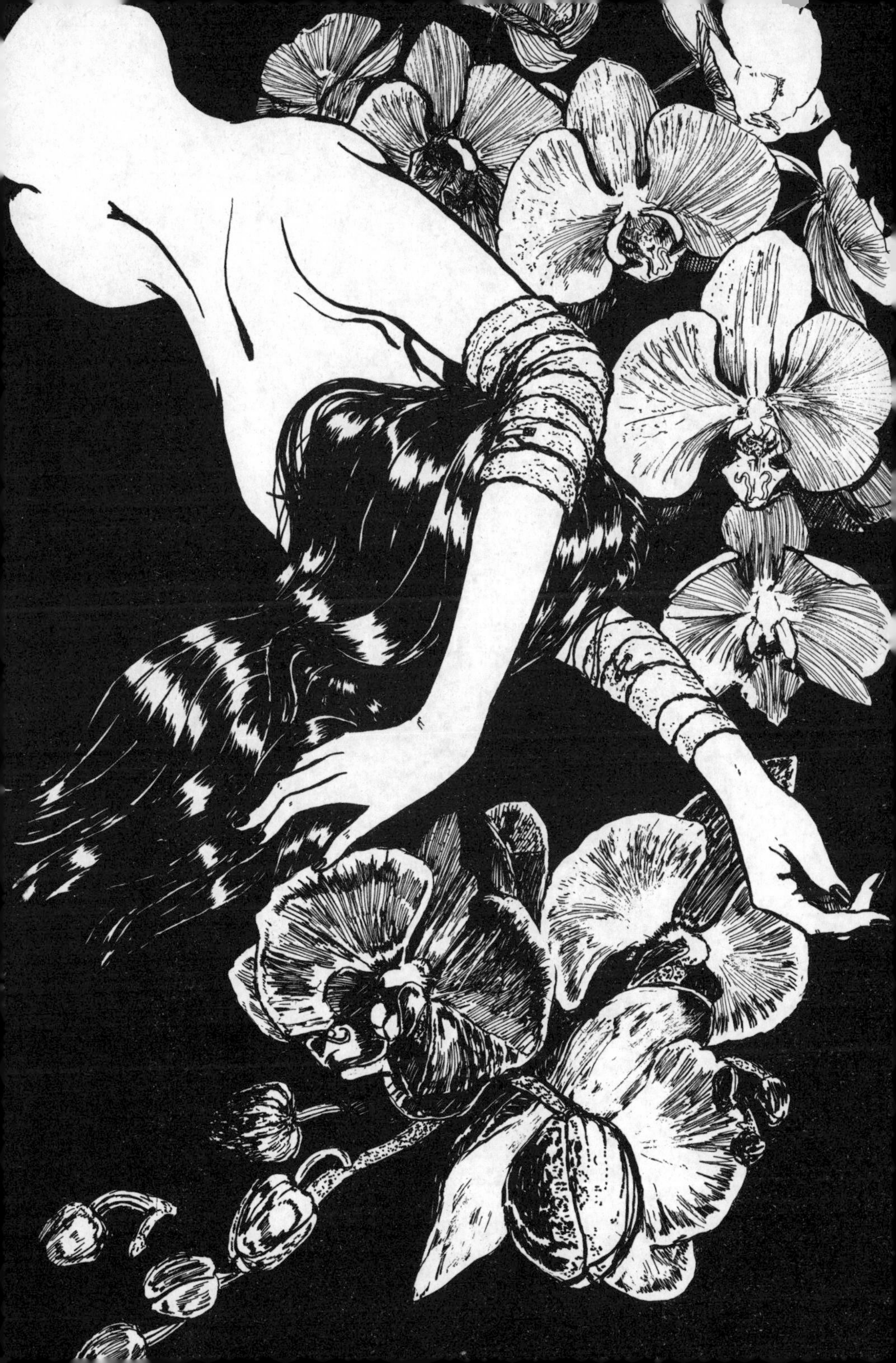

CHAPTER 11:
"ALL THINGS ARE EMPTY
AND SELFLESS"

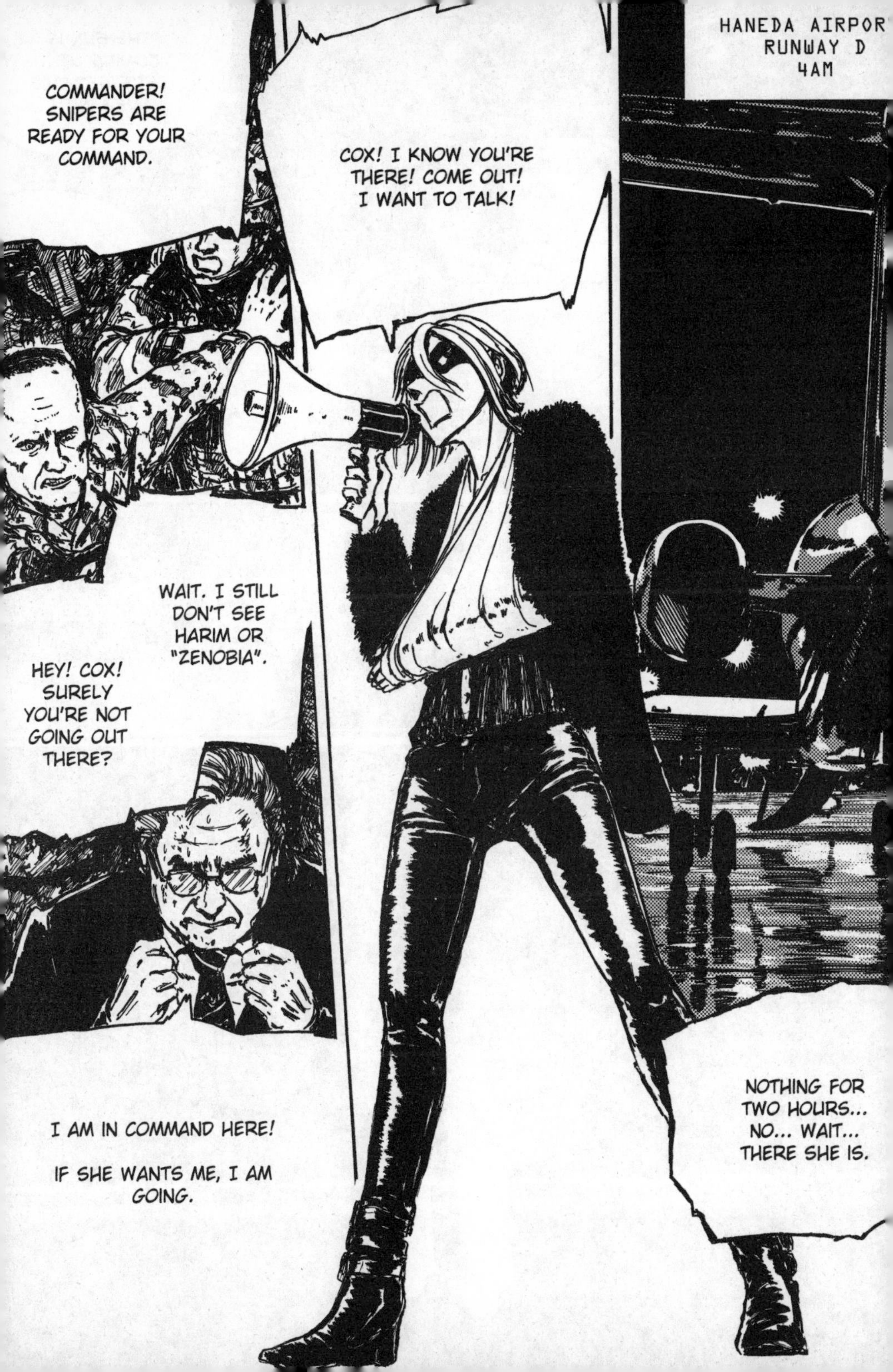
HANEDA AIRPOR
RUNWAY D
4AM
NOTHING FOR TWO HOURS... NO... WAIT... THERE SHE IS.
COX! I KNOW YOU'RE THERE! COME OUT! I WANT TO TALK!
COMMANDER! SNIPERS ARE READY FOR YOUR COMMAND.
WAIT. I STILL DON'T SEE HARIM OR "ZENOBIA".
HEY! COX! SURELY YOU'RE NOT GOING OUT THERE?
I AM IN COMMAND HERE!
IF SHE WANTS ME, I AM GOING.

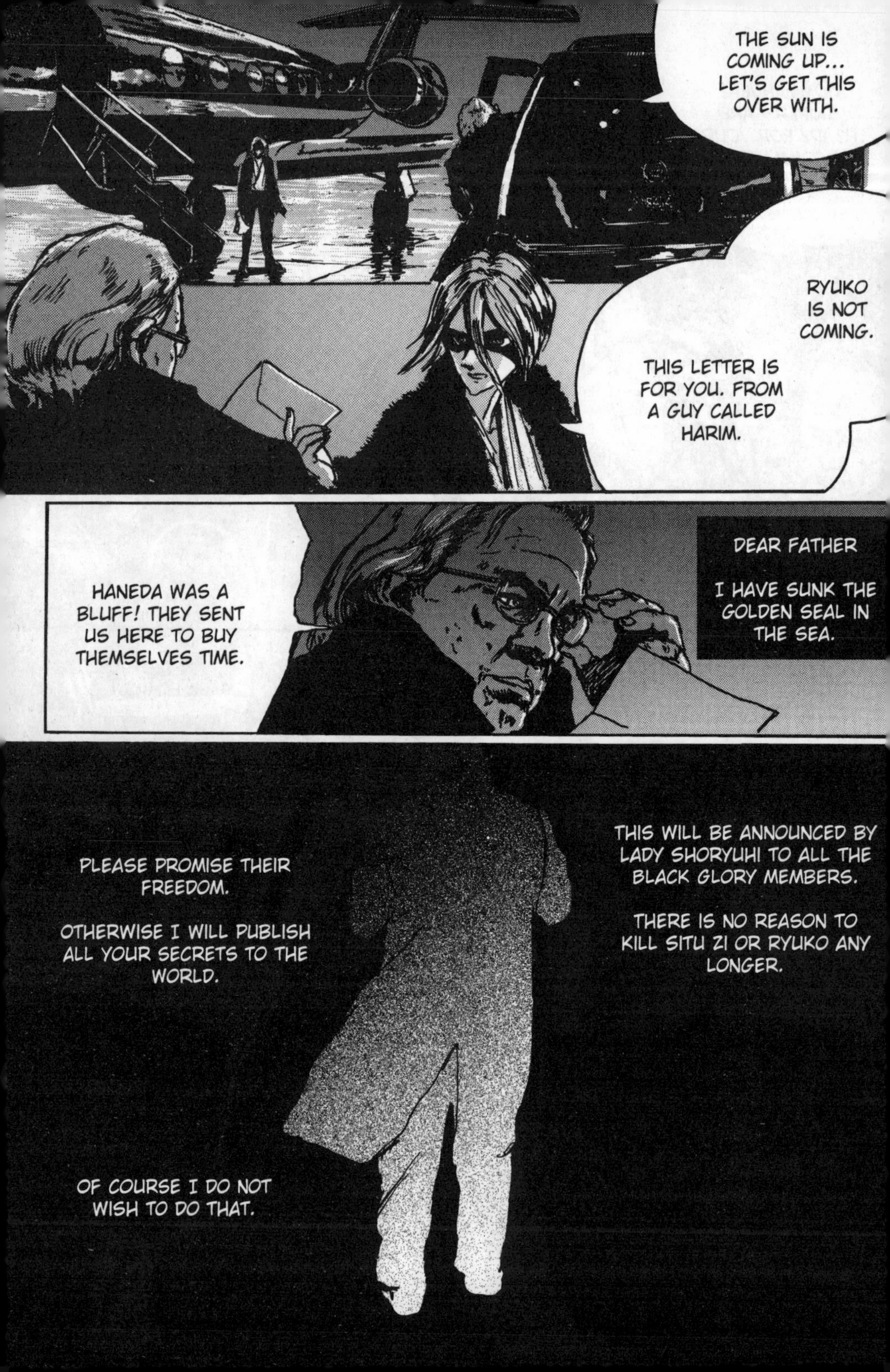
THE SUN IS COMING UP... LET'S GET THIS OVER WITH.
RYUKO IS NOT COMING.
THIS LETTER IS FOR YOU. FROM A GUY CALLED HARIM.
DEAR FATHER
I HAVE SUNK THE GOLDEN SEAL IN THE SEA.
HANEDA WAS A BLUFF! THEY SENT US HERE TO BUY THEMSELVES TIME.
THIS WILL BE ANNOUNCED BY LADY SHORYUHI TO ALL THE BLACK GLORY MEMBERS.
THERE IS NO REASON TO KILL SITU ZI OR RYUKO ANY LONGER.
PLEASE PROMISE THEIR FREEDOM.
OTHERWISE I WILL PUBLISH ALL YOUR SECRETS TO THE WORLD.
OF COURSE I DO NOT WISH TO DO THAT.

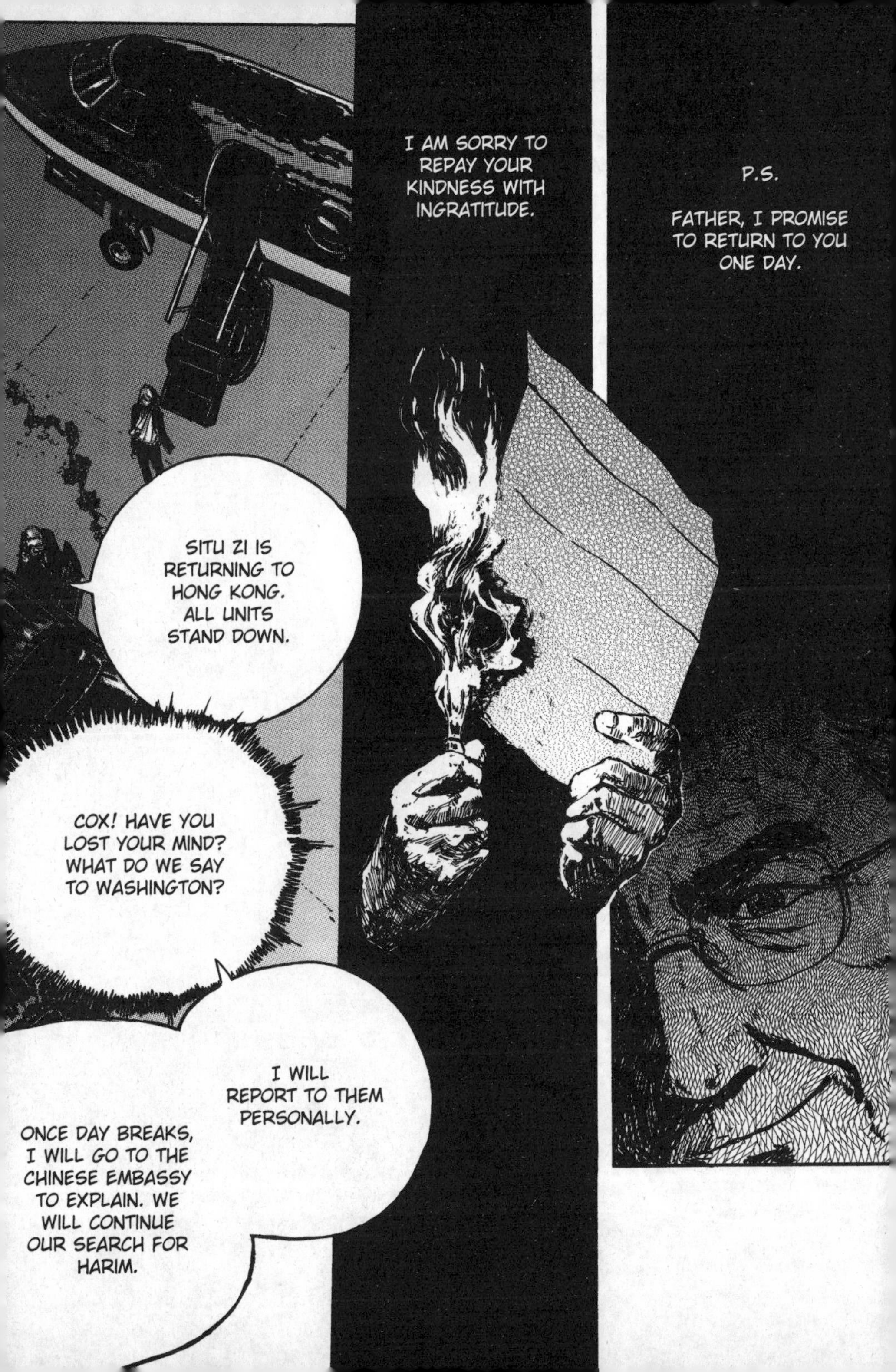
SITU ZI IS RETURNING TO HONG KONG. ALL UNITS STAND DOWN.
COX! HAVE YOU LOST YOUR MIND? WHAT DO WE SAY TO WASHINGTON?
I WILL REPORT TO THEM PERSONALLY.
ONCE DAY BREAKS, I WILL GO TO THE CHINESE EMBASSY TO EXPLAIN. WE WILL CONTINUE OUR SEARCH FOR HARIM.
I AM SORRY TO REPAY YOUR KINDNESS WITH INGRATITUDE.
P.S.
FATHER, I PROMISE TO RETURN TO YOU ONE DAY.

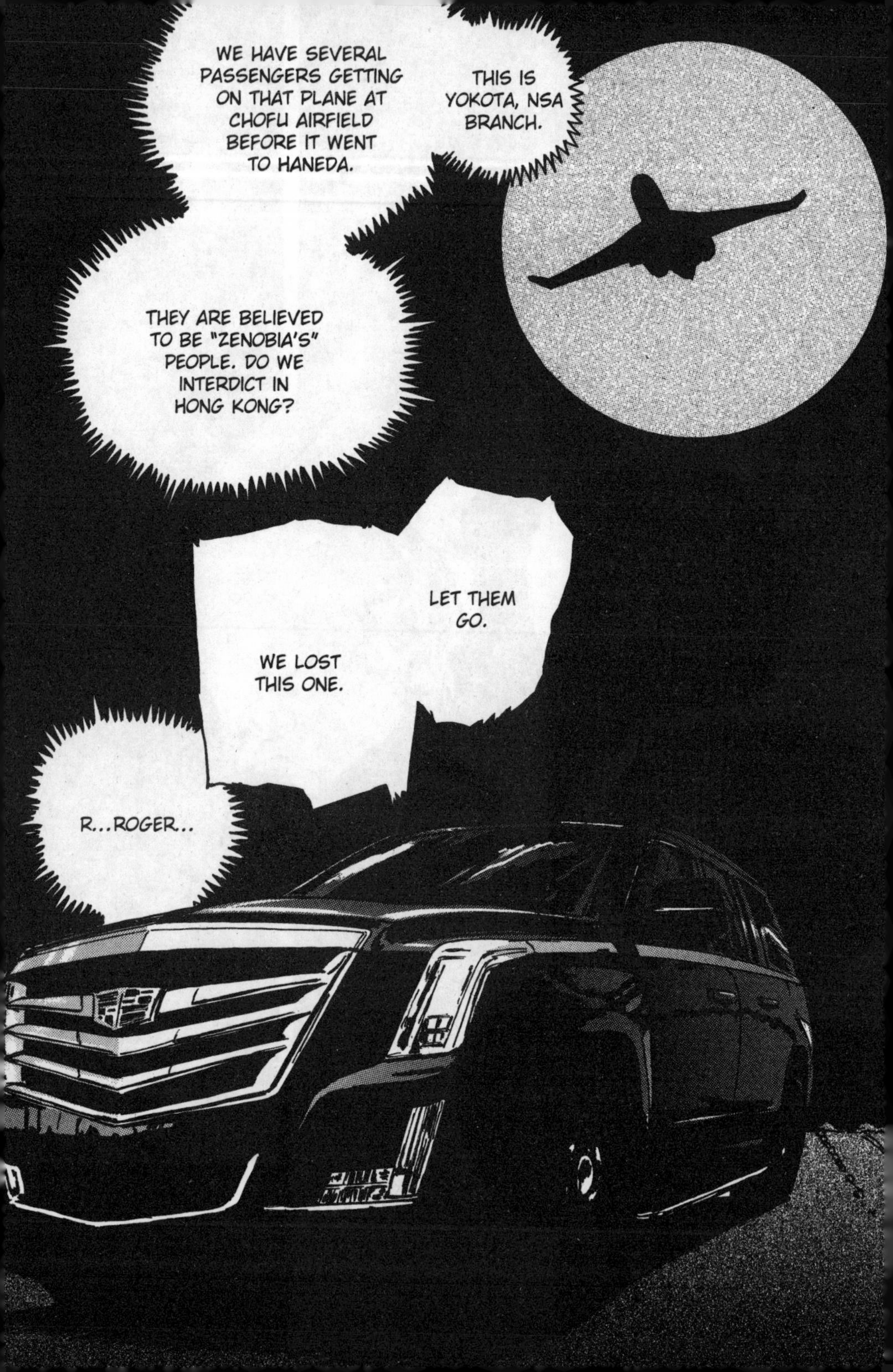
THIS IS YOKOTA, NSA BRANCH.
WE HAVE SEVERAL PASSENGERS GETTING ON THAT PLANE AT CHOFU AIRFIELD BEFORE IT WENT TO HANEDA.
THEY ARE BELIEVED TO BE "ZENOBIA'S" PEOPLE. DO WE INTERDICT IN HONG KONG?
LET THEM GO.
WE LOST THIS ONE.
R...ROGER...

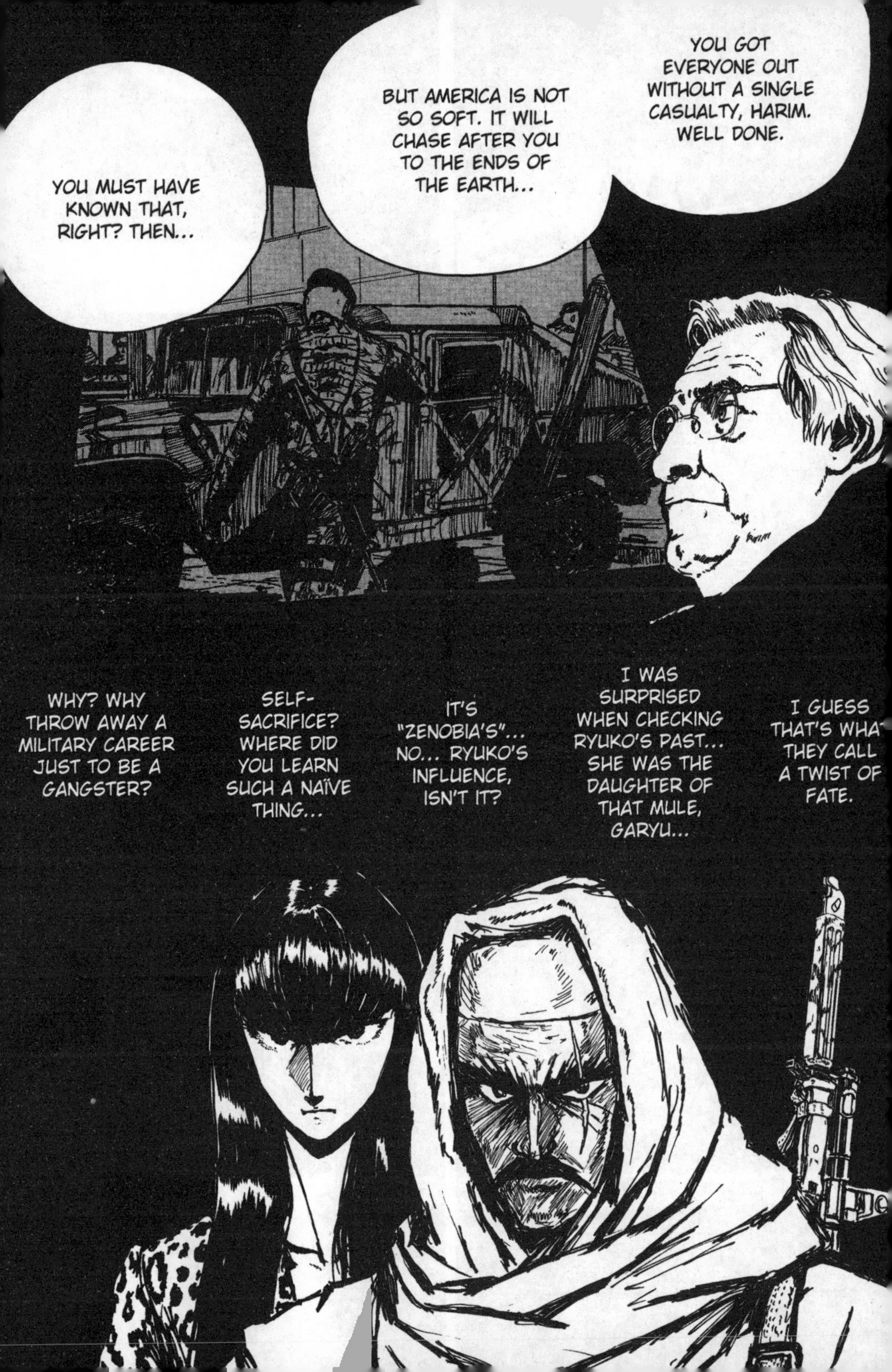
YOU GOT EVERYONE OUT WITHOUT A SINGLE CASUALTY, HARIM. WELL DONE.
BUT AMERICA IS NOT SO SOFT. IT WILL CHASE AFTER YOU TO THE ENDS OF THE EARTH...
YOU MUST HAVE KNOWN THAT, RIGHT? THEN...
WHY? WHY THROW AWAY A MILITARY CAREER JUST TO BE A GANGSTER?
SELF-SACRIFICE? WHERE DID YOU LEARN SUCH A NAÏVE THING...
IT'S "ZENOBIA'S"... NO... RYUKO'S INFLUENCE, ISN'T IT?
I WAS SURPRISED WHEN CHECKING RYUKO'S PAST... SHE WAS THE DAUGHTER OF THAT MULE, GARYU...
I GUESS THAT'S WHA THEY CALL A TWIST OF FATE.

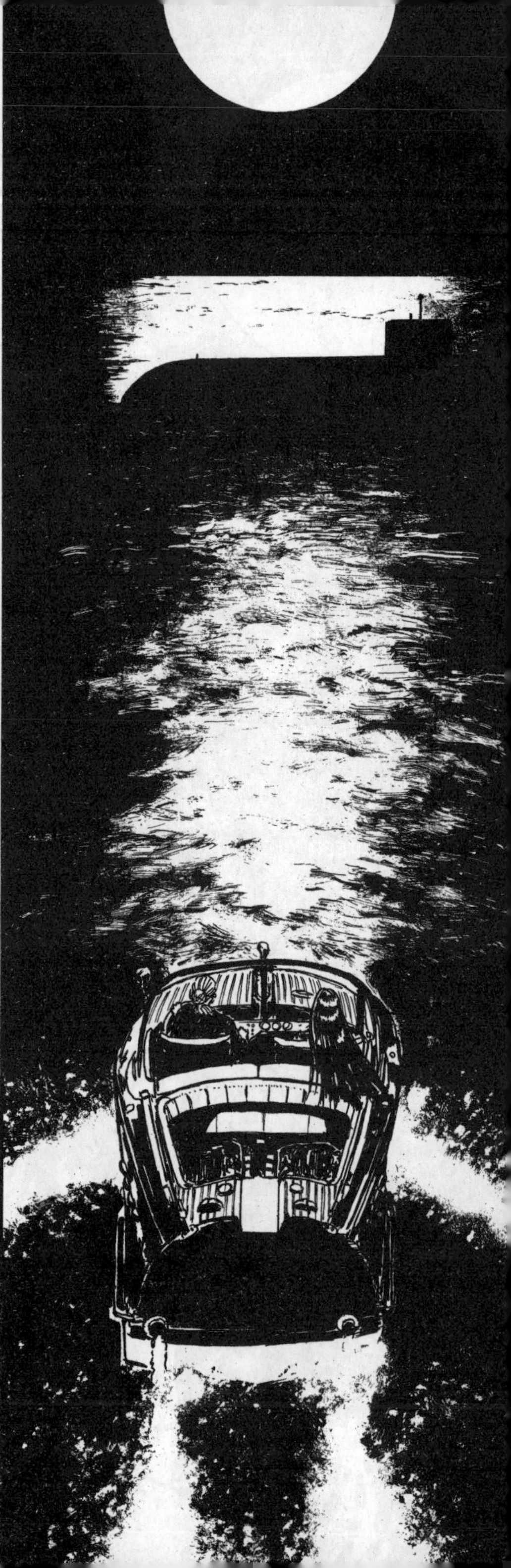
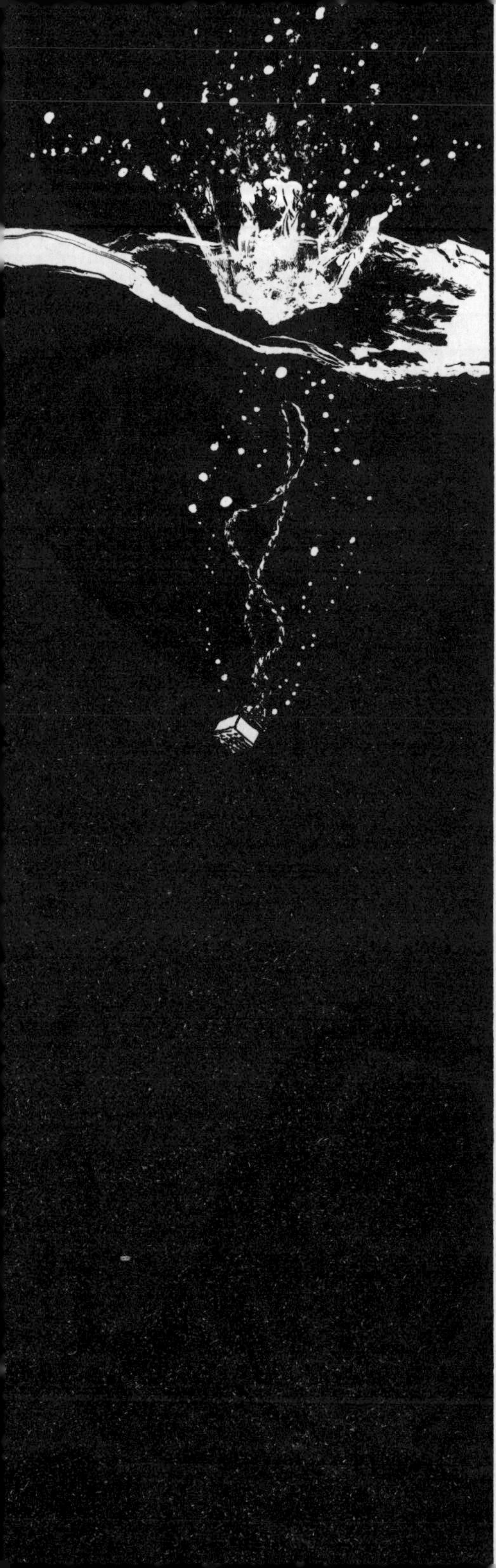

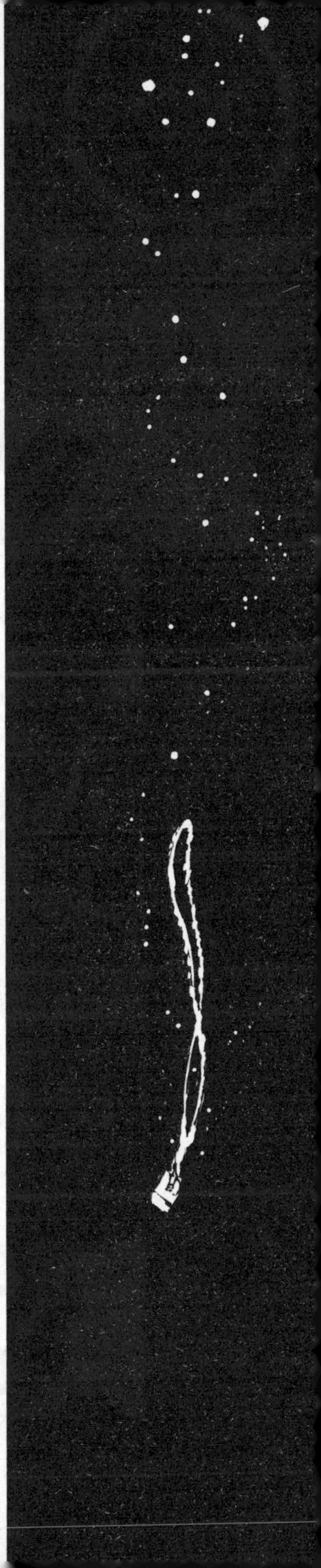

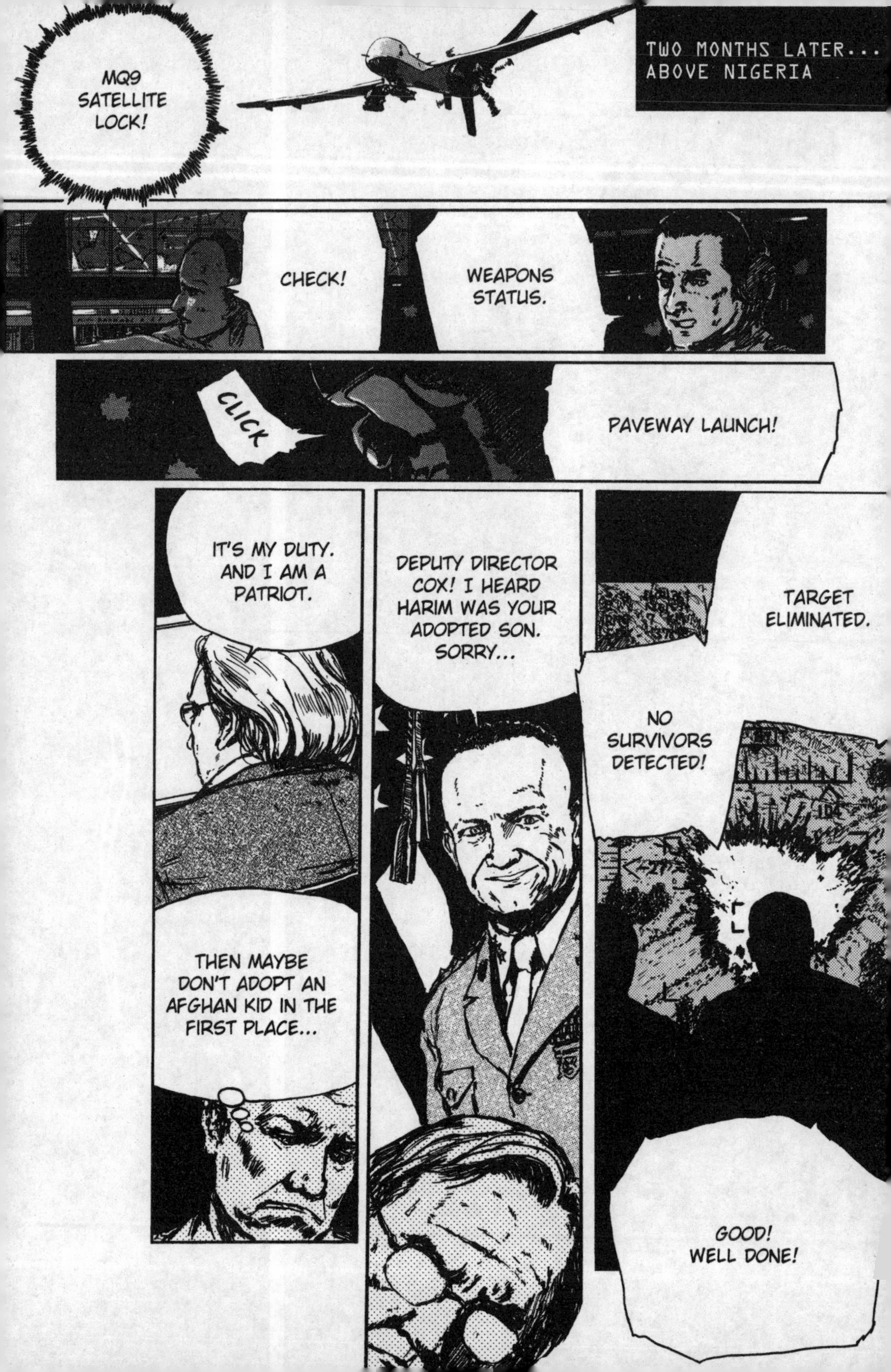
TWO MONTHS LATER...
ABOVE NIGERIA
MQ9 SATELLITE LOCK!
WEAPONS STATUS.
CHECK!
PAVEWAY LAUNCH!
CLICK
TARGET ELIMINATED.
NO SURVIVORS DETECTED!
GOOD! WELL DONE!
DEPUTY DIRECTOR COX! I HEARD HARIM WAS YOUR ADOPTED SON. SORRY...
IT'S MY DUTY. AND I AM A PATRIOT.
THEN MAYBE DON'T ADOPT AN AFGHAN KID IN THE FIRST PLACE...

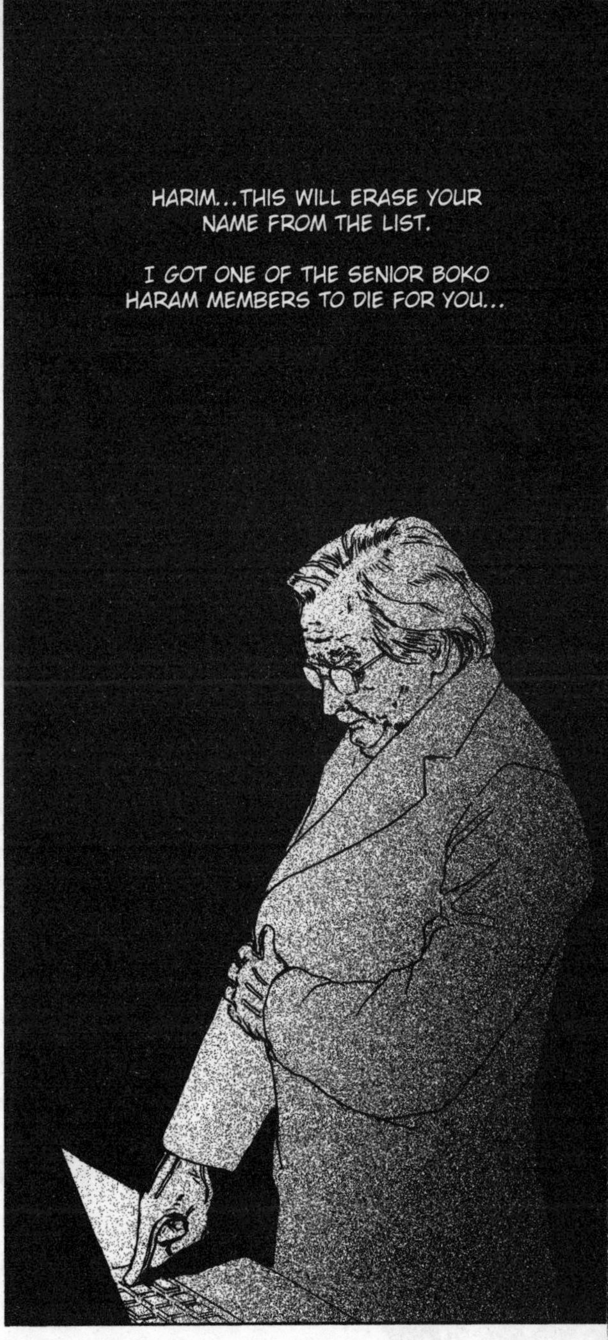
HARIM...THIS WILL ERASE YOUR NAME FROM THE LIST.
I GOT ONE OF THE SENIOR BOKO HARAM MEMBERS TO DIE FOR YOU...

I AM LOOKING FORWARD TO SEEING YOU ONE DAY. WHERE ARE YOU NOW?

MAYBE YOU ARE WITH RYUKO...?

THAT'S OKAY...

YOU ARE FREE NOW.

LIVE YOUR LIFE.

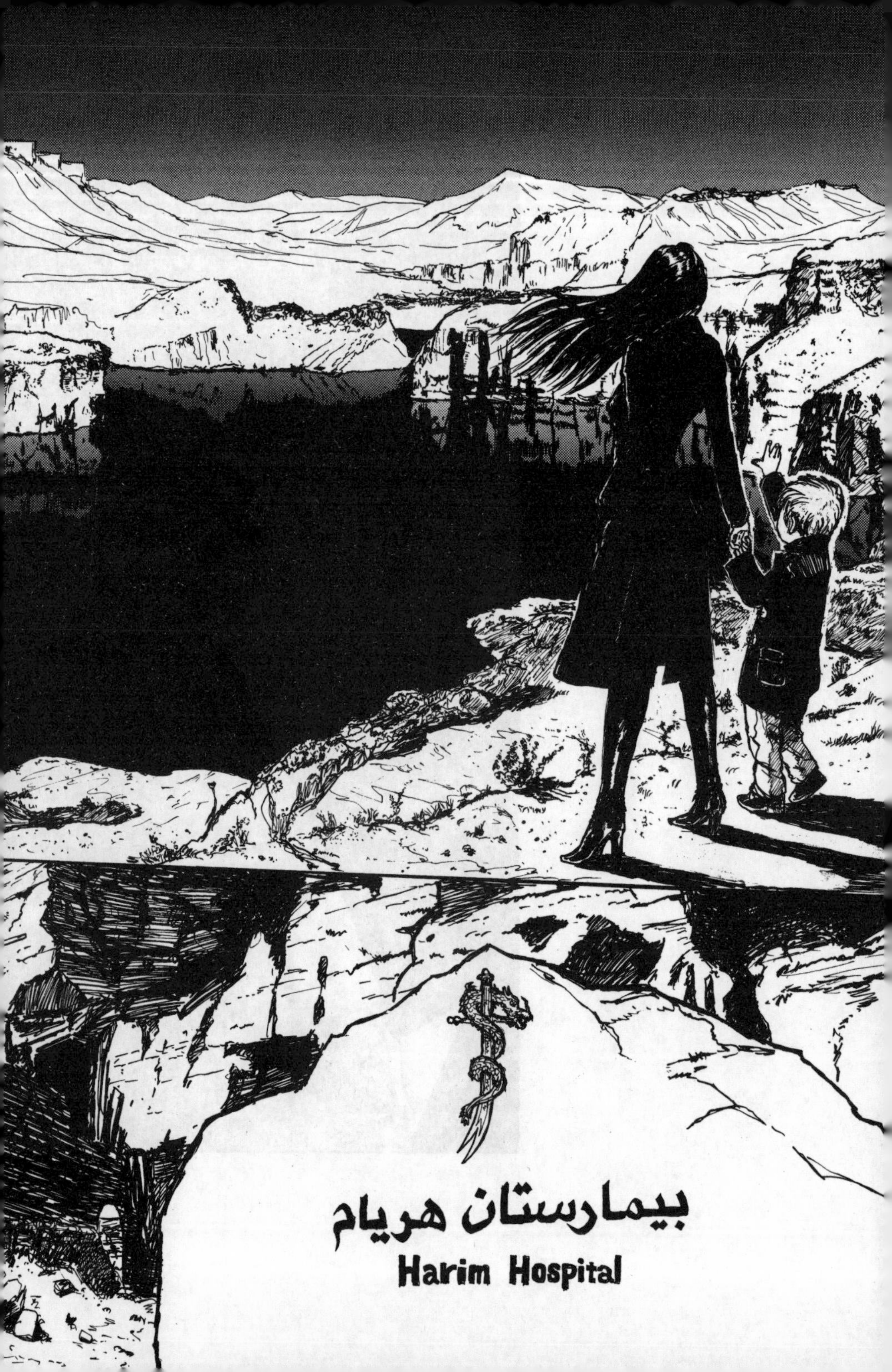
بيمارستان هريام
Harim Hospital

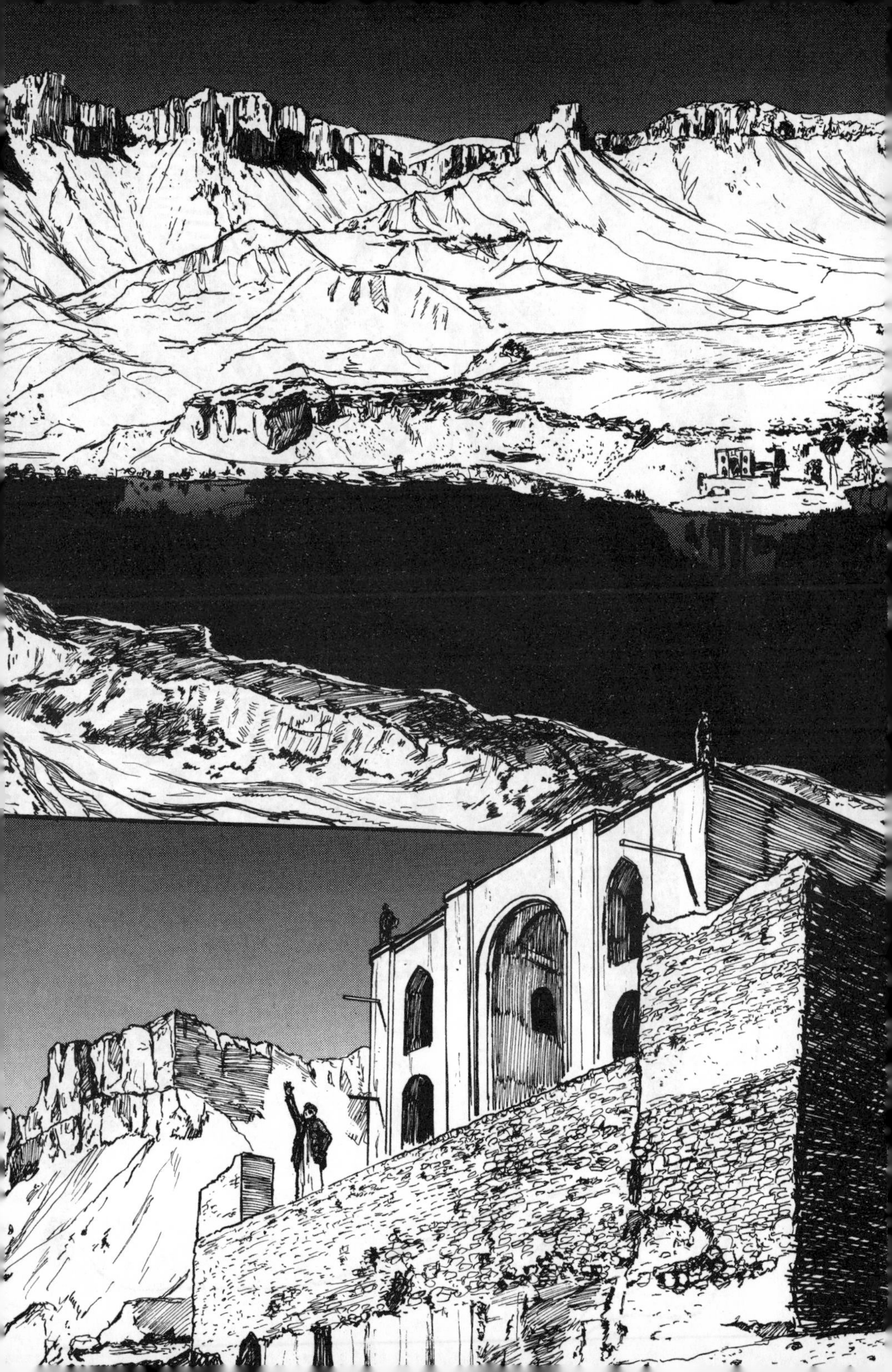

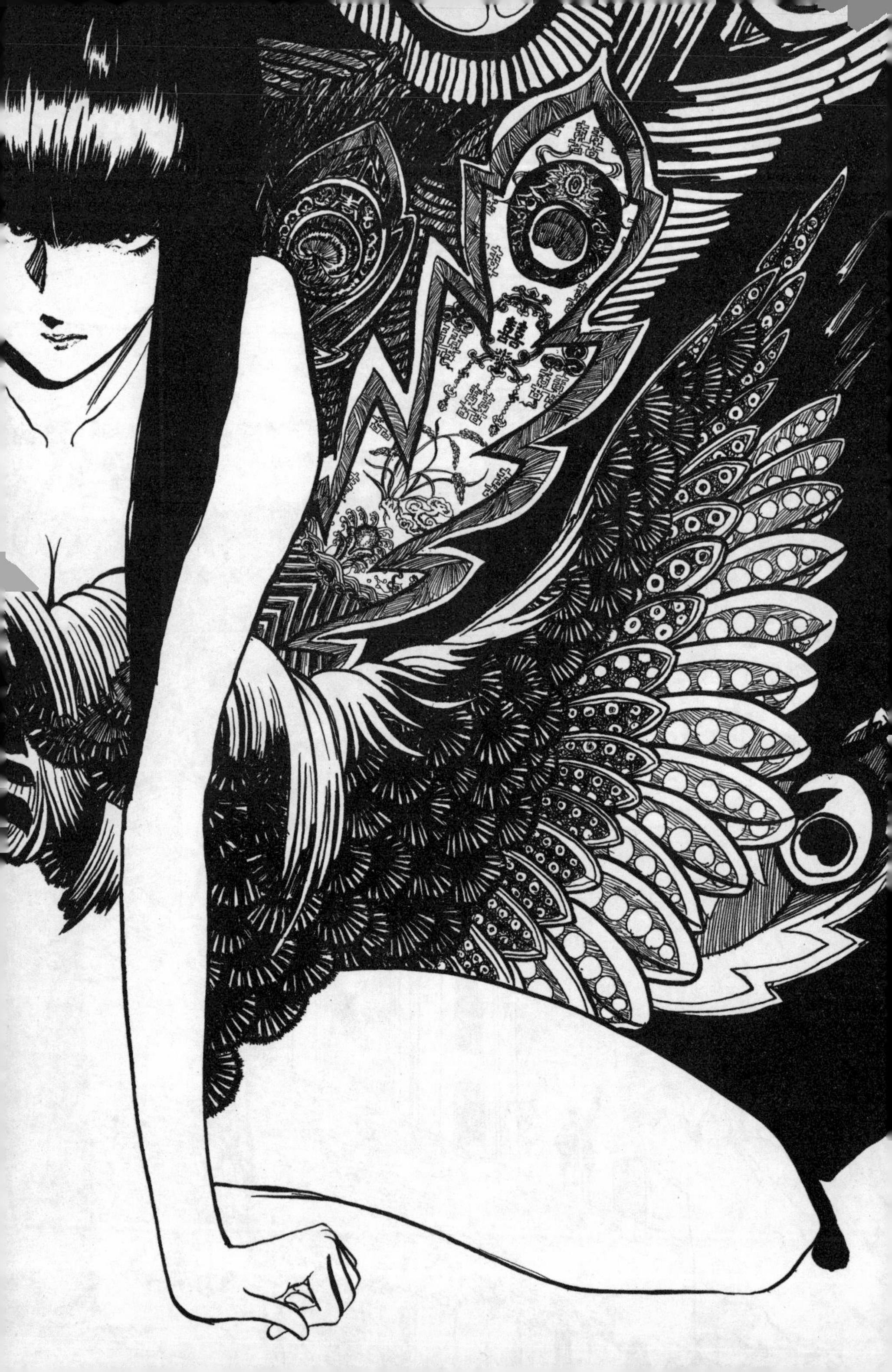

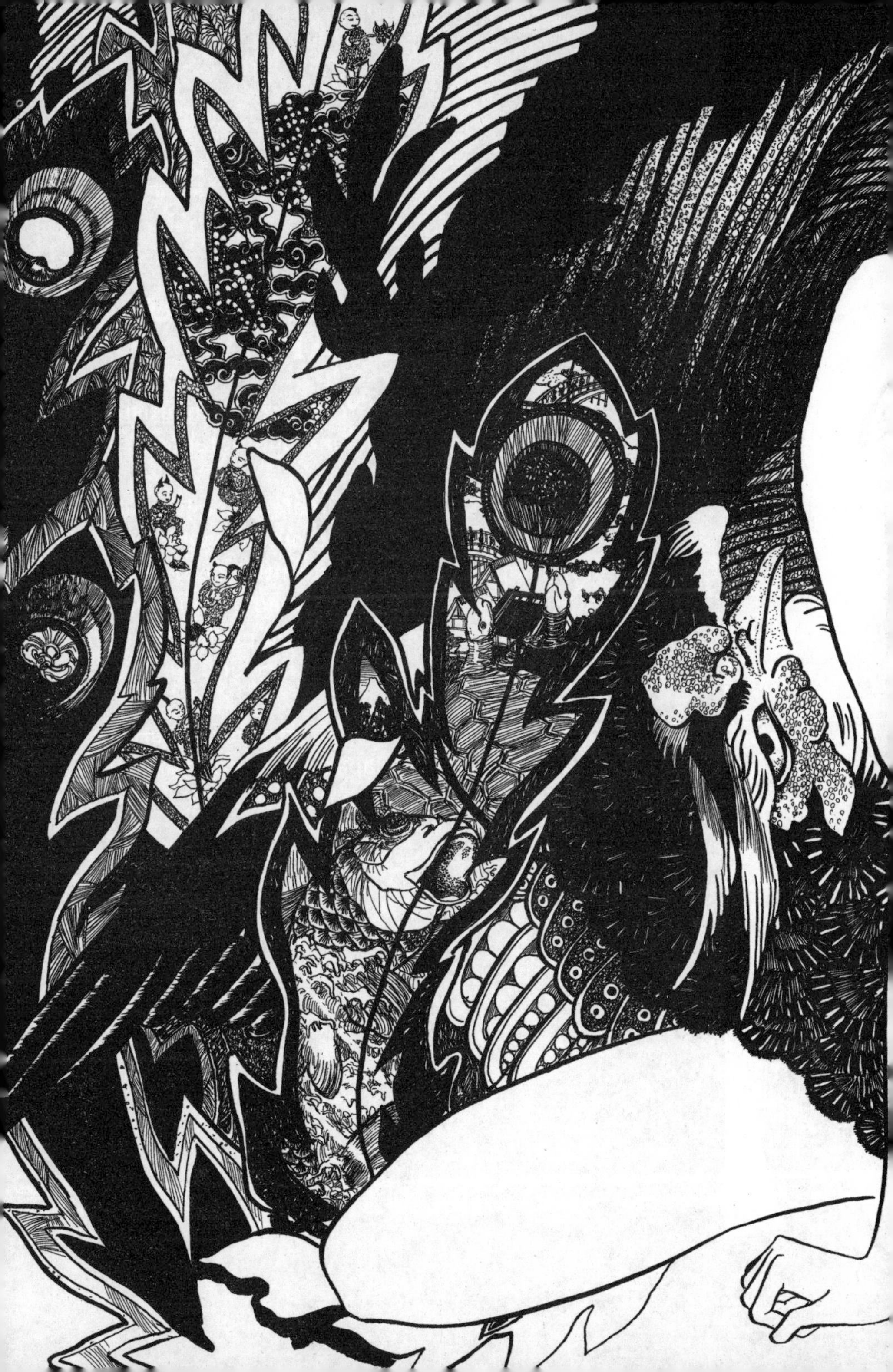

ELDO YOSHIMIZU BIOGRAPHY

Born in Tokyo, Eldo Yoshimizu is an artist, sculptor, musician, and photographer.

As a sculptor, Yoshimizu creates vast, jewel-like shapes and sinuous, vivid outlines which are among Japan's most significant pieces of public art. His work has been exhibited in galleries all over the world, and he has held positions as an artist in residence in Italy, France and New York.

Yoshimizu's character of Ryuko has appeared in art galleries around Japan and Europe and has now made her jump to manga.

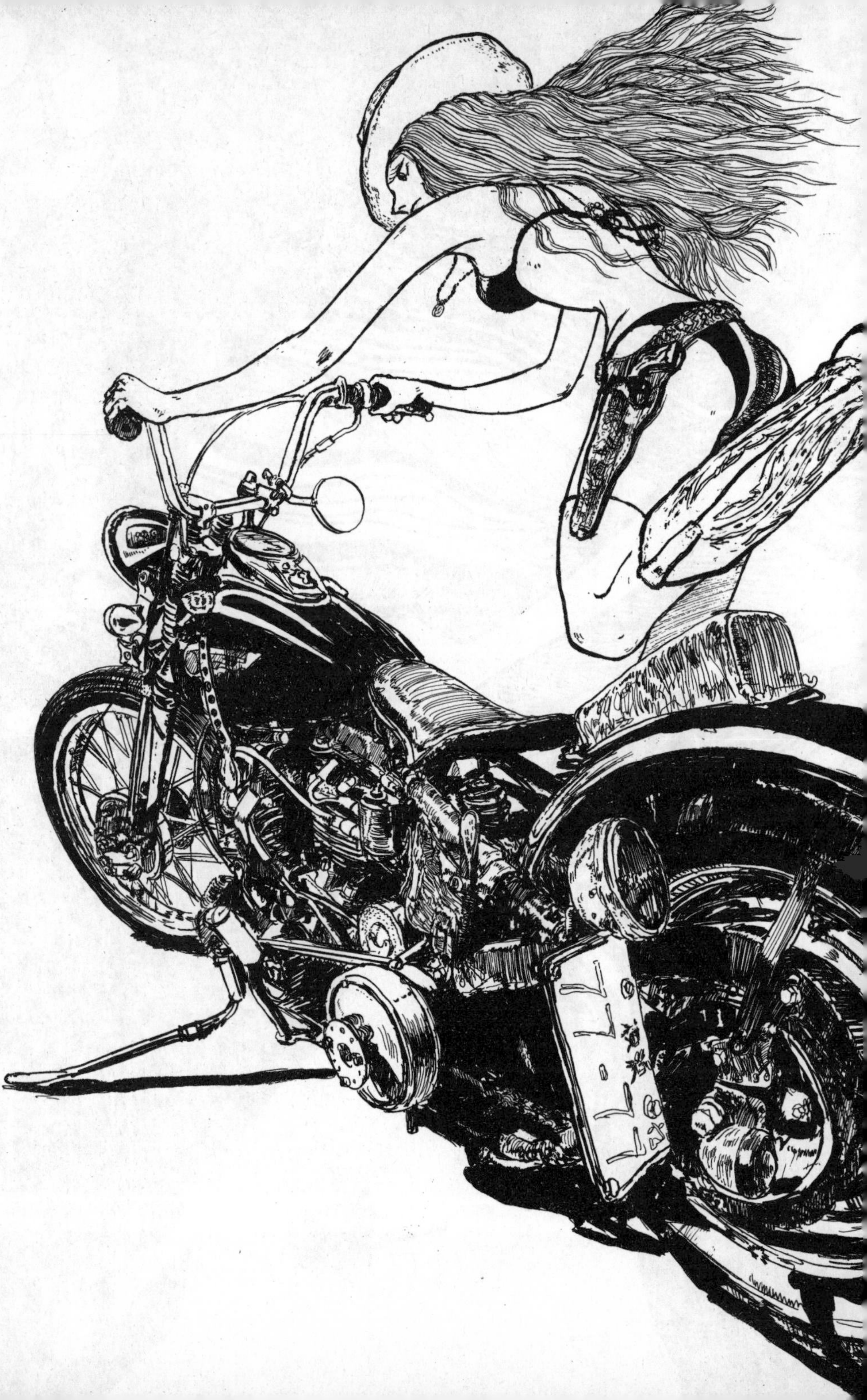

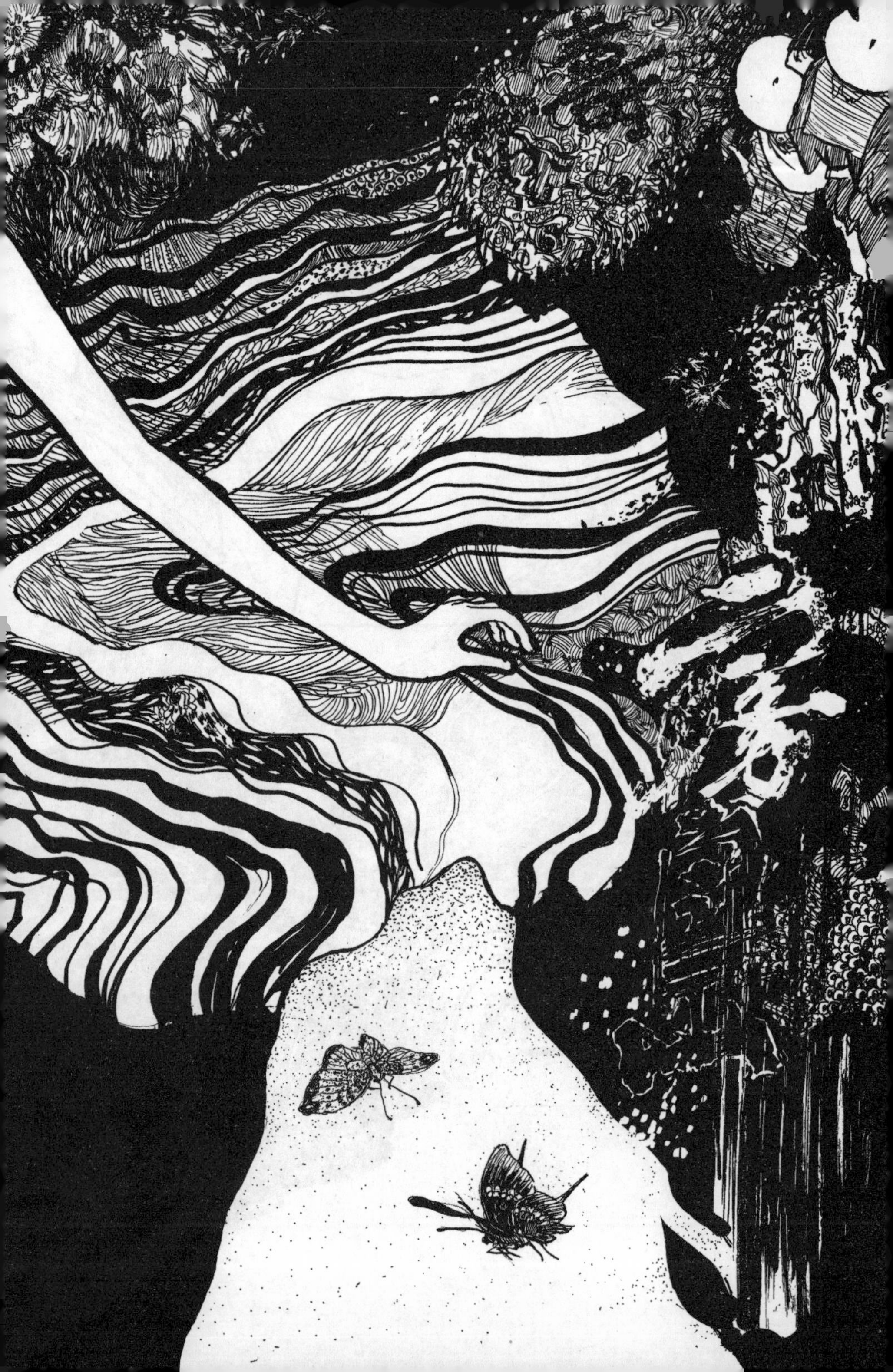

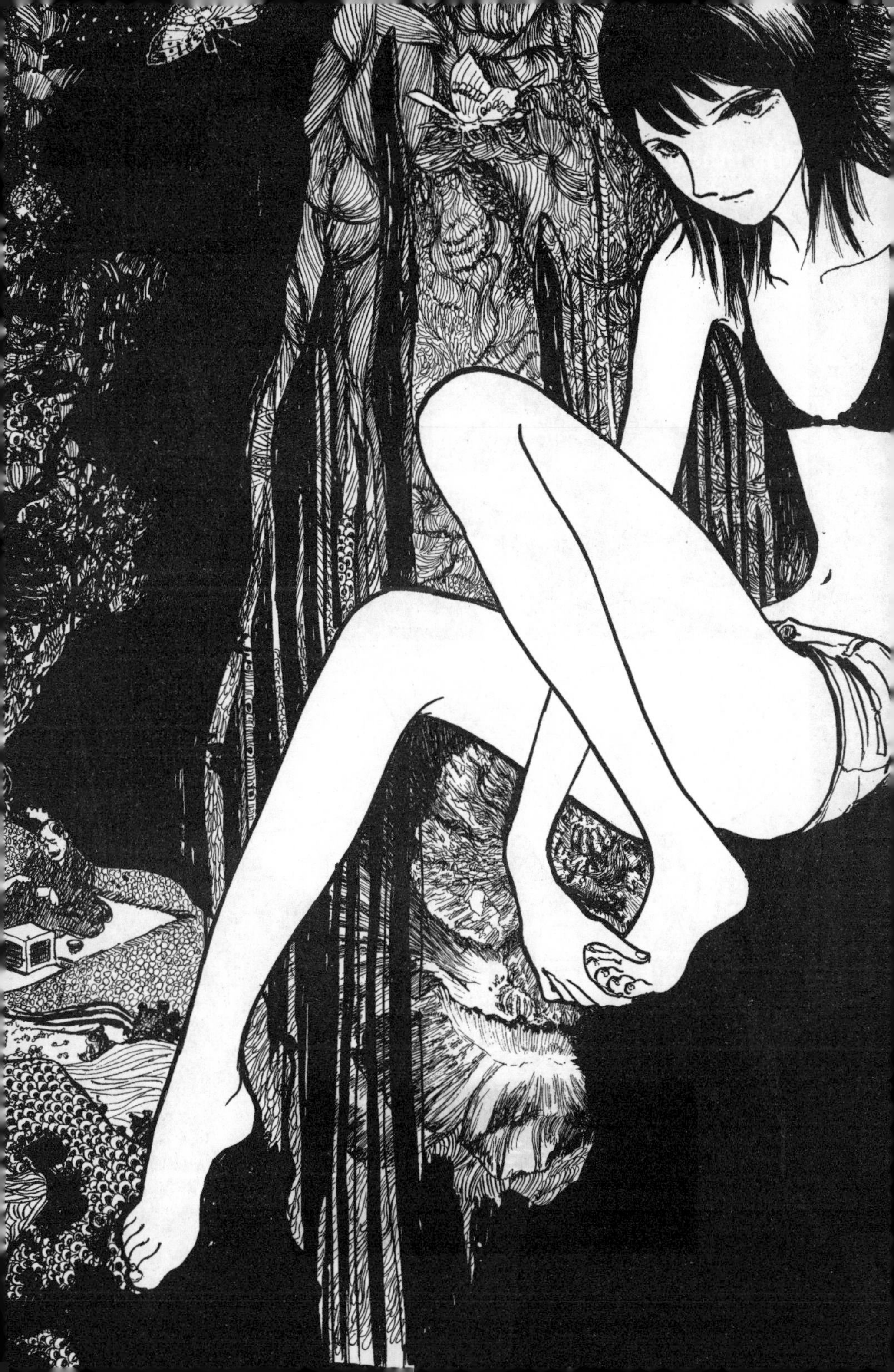

STOP!

R0201525508

09/

This manga is presented in its original right-to-left reading format. This is the back of the book!

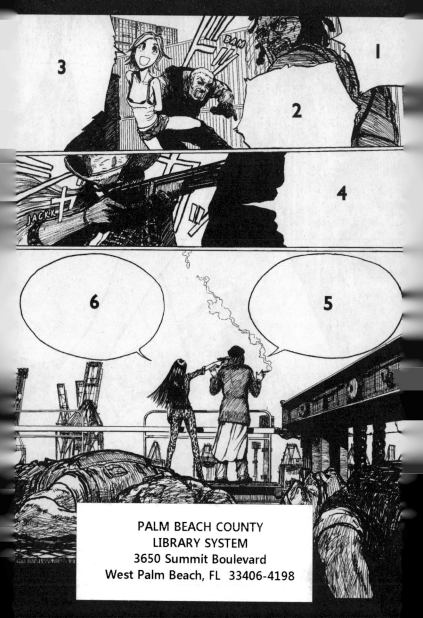

panels, and speech balloons read from top right to bottom left, a
above. Sound effects are translated in the panels